IN HOUSE

IN HOUSE

Covent Garden
50 Years of Opera and Ballet

JOHN TOOLEY

faber and faber

First published in 1999
by Faber and Faber Limited
3 Queen Square London WC1N 3AU

Photoset by RefineCatch Ltd, Bungay, Suffolk
Printed in England by Clays Ltd, St Ives Plc

© John Tooley, 1999
Line drawings © Julia Preston, 1999

Extract from letter on page 75
© The Trustees of the Britten-Pears Foundation; this
extract may not be further reproduced without the written
permission of the Trustees of the Britten-Pears Foundation.

John Tooley is hereby identified as author
of this work in accordance with Section 77
of the Copyright, Designs and Patents Act 1988

A CIP record for this book
is available from the British Library

ISBN 0–571–19415–X

2 4 6 8 10 9 7 5 3 1

Contents

v

List of Illustrations

16 Dame Margot Fonteyn and Rudolf Nureyev in *Marguerite and Armand*, 1963 (photo Cecil Beaton, courtesy of Sotheby's, London)
17 Norman Morrice, Director of the Royal Ballet 1977–83 (photo Alan Cunliffe)
18 Boris Christoff and Tito Gobbi, 1958 (photo Houston Rogers, courtesy of Theatre Museum, Victoria & Albert Museum)
19 Maria Callas and Tito Gobbi in *Tosca*, 1964 (photo Zoë Dominic)
20 Sir Geraint Evans in *Le Nozze di Figaro* (photo Houston Rogers, courtesy of Theatre Museum, Victoria & Albert Museum)
21 Plácido Domingo with Ande Anderson, Janice Green and Sir John Tooley, 1980 (photo Clive Boursnell)
22 Dame Joan Sutherland in *Lucia di Lammermoor*, 1959 (photo © British Travel and Holidays Association)
23 John Vickers as Peter Grimes, 1975 (photo Donald Southern)
24 Dame Kiri Te Kanawa in *Otello*, 1992 (photo Zoë Dominic)
25 Sir Thomas Allen as Don Giovanni, 1996 (photo Catherine Ashmore)

Vignettes on chapter opening pages drawn by Julia Preston.

Foreword

Who better than Sir John Tooley to write about the Royal Opera House, Covent Garden? It opened in 1732 and soon after was host to operas and oratorios by Handel, survived two fires, triumphed in the rivalries of competing theatres in the eighteenth and nineteenth centuries, and gradually became the centre for operatic life in England until it achieved its twentieth-century pre-eminence in opera and ballet under Sir David Webster and subsequently under Sir John.

I have always felt at home at Covent Garden because it has presented some magnificent productions under quite ideal circumstances and because it has an audience which is not only extremely knowledgeable but wonderfully generous in its appreciation of performers. In short, I have loved singing at Covent Garden ever since my début as Cavaradossi in *Tosca* in 1971, conducted by Edward Downes.

Some of the productions remain with special affection in my memory – such as *Les Contes d'Hoffmann*, conducted by Georges Prêtre and directed by John Schlesinger of cinematic fame. The result of this brilliant conception can still be seen on video. I also remember with special appreciation the new production of *Otello* conducted by Carlos Kleiber and later by Georg Solti, and directed by Elijah Moshinsky, or *La Fanciulla del West* which was conducted by Zubin Mehta and conceived by Piero Faggioni. I can mention countless other performances – all special because of high artistic standards, wonderful colleagues and a very special public. And among the memories of Covent Garden I will take with me to the end of my life there is Sir John, who was a brilliant general director, wise and kind at the same time, supported by all the people working in the house, orchestra and chorus, stage-hands, dressers and many others.

That Covent Garden has had a magnificent auditorium and quite inadequate backstage facilities is to state the obvious. The theatre is now being renovated, and as I write I am looking forward to participating in the reopening festivities in December of this year. Of course, I know that life backstage will be much more luxurious and efficient, let us say more twentieth or twenty-first century. All of us performers will appreciate it and will be grateful to those who made the renovation possible. But I know there will be a slight twinge of nostalgia for that musty old atmosphere which reminded you that Caruso also stood in the same wings waiting to make his entrance – a nostalgia for all those things that are celebrated in this book by my friend Sir John.

Plácido Domingo
19 June 1999

Preface

This is not a chronological history of the Royal Opera House since the war, but rather a series of comments and reflections on what has happened in those fifty years, the changes which have occurred, particularly in the last eleven years, and some of the personalities who have contributed to its success. The omissions are manifold and I seek the forgiveness of those not mentioned.

So many men and women made Covent Garden what it was, and what it will be again, that it would take a book three times the size of this to contain them and much longer than the eighteen months which I have had for writing this one. It is my first, and probably my last, book, one which I had a great urge to write but the difficulties of which I underestimated.

I have set out to be truthful and direct. I have written entirely from my own memory, with recourse to board minutes for the years after I had left, and to annual reports and the few available and relevant books for the checking of facts and dates. In the case of board minutes I am greatly indebted to Lord Chadlington, chairman at the time, for giving me permission to peruse the documents in the archives. Generally aware of what was happening through observation and what was being recounted to me, I was keen to be as accurate as possible with facts before committing anything to print.

Originally wanting to be a singer but then deciding that I had neither the talent nor the temperament to be much more than an indifferent session singer, I opted for a career in musical management. The army had taught me a little about management, but openings in the field I wanted to enter were not encouraging at the time, and I decided to improve my management knowledge by going into industry. I joined the Ford Motor

Company at Dagenham as one of their first graduate trainees, and became involved in a pay dispute in my first month. I and a handful of others had arrived in September 1948, and were being paid three shillings and ten pence per hour. In October another bunch of graduates were offered four shillings and sixpence an hour. We were furious, but our protests got us nowhere except for a dressing-down by the managing director, Sir Patrick Hennessy.

Throughout my life I have been fortunate in meeting men and women who would be helpful in one way or another. Dagenham was no exception. After only a few months on the shop floor I was summoned to the office of Horace Denne, the export sales manager, and very much the old-style Ford figure. This encounter was the making of my time there. He asked what I was doing at Dagenham and whom did I know. When I replied, nobody, he immediately warmed to me and said that we would get on well together. I explained that I had no intention of staying with Ford for long and that my ambitions lay with music. This made no difference to him, and I was taken under his wing. He taught me a great deal, not least how to handle those who say yes when they mean no.

After an instructive and profitable four years at Ford I was appointed Secretary of the Guildhall School of Music and Drama. Edric Cundell was the Principal, to whom a former singing teacher of mine, Robert Rowell, had sent a reference on the understanding that, if appointed, I would leave the Guildhall within three years. When I queried the reason for this time limit, I was told that I would soon be bored and would need another job. In fact I was never bored, and thoroughly enjoyed those years, as well as learning a great deal from Edric Cundell, a fine musician and conductor, who knew the music profession inside out. There were also many eminent musicians on the staff, Max Rostal and William Pleeth among the instrumentalists and Joseph Hislop and Megan Foster among the singers, to name but four, in whose company there was endless pleasure and knowledge to be gleaned.

I need not have worried about time, because as my third year at the Guildhall was beginning I was told by Edric Cundell, who was also on the Covent Garden board, that David Webster, the General Administrator of the Royal Opera House, was looking for an assistant and that he wanted to talk to me. A meeting was arranged, and so began the career for which I was longing, although it was to be many months before my engagement at Covent Garden was finally confirmed.

My first interview with David Webster was taken up with me recounting my career so far. After giving what I considered an exhaustive account of this, I heard Webster saying, 'Tell me more.' I went rambling on and was eventually told that he would be in touch. Nothing happened for months. Here I became aware of Webster's tendency to procrastinate. He wanted me, but Patrick Terry, the opera company manager, had applied for the vacancy and Webster was worried about the consequences of refusing it to him. After a nudging phone call to Webster, I was summoned to the office of Lord Moore, then Secretary to the Royal Opera House board, and later to be the Earl of Drogheda and its Chairman. We had an agreeable conversation. I was warned of the hazards of the career on which I was wanting to embark, and our discussion ended with the request that I should arrange to see Lord Waverley, the Chairman of Covent Garden and of the Port of London Authority.

My interview with him was a curious affair. It took place in his vast office at Trinity House and was largely occupied with questions about my age and whether I was younger or older than Lord Harewood, who was then working at Covent Garden as controller of opera planning. I said that I believed that I was younger. Not satisfied, Lord Waverley returned to this more than once. In the end I suggested that we should consult *Who's Who*, which proved that my hunch was correct. Having disposed of this, he then asked if there was anything else that I wanted to say or question him about. When I raised the matter of salary, the interview came to an abrupt end with the instruction that I should address this question to David Webster. I did, and there followed weeks of further delay before a letter of engagement arrived. This consisted of three or four sentences and was to suffice until the mid-1960s, when there was concern that I might be leaving Covent Garden. Then a more formal and comprehensive document, demanded by Lord Drogheda and mostly drafted by me at Webster's request, was produced.

This was typical of Covent Garden at that time. It was common for agreements to be by word of mouth and, if recorded, in the briefest of terms. There was a remarkable degree of trust, and often the recording of a deal was thought unnecessary. As the organisation grew in size and more employment legislation was introduced, more decisions had to be bound by contract or letters of agreement.

Arriving at Covent Garden in September 1955, I had the good fortune to be present at the beginning of a formative period of the Royal Opera House, and particularly of the Covent Garden opera. The first such period had been with Karl Rankl as music director until 1951, and the second with Erich Kleiber over the next three years. This time the music director was Rafael Kubelik, a great musician and the most remarkable of men, who through his musicianship and sense of humanity led the company to greater and greater achievements.

Unlike my successor, Jeremy Isaacs, I was caught up in the life and ways of an opera house from a relatively early age, and with men and women of the same sort of age, some older but mostly contemporaneous. This was a huge advantage for me. We grew up together and we knew each other's strengths and weaknesses. We were all ready to help and we had an ability to share, to rejoice in our successes and triumphs and to find ways out of our disasters. It was an extraordinary spirit which pervaded Covent Garden, partly related to professionalism but more profound even than that, a bond which reflected a family feeling and awareness and which held us tightly together as it drove us forward.

Formality and informality found their levels without a word uttered. Only at Covent Garden, I have sometimes thought, could the general director be followed down the street by the wigmaster (in this case Ron Freeman) calling after him, 'Come on, John, it's time you got your bloody hair cut.' Or, suffering from stiff shoulders, call on an orchestral musician to massage him. Jack Wakely, an athlete, a member of the percussion section until his tragically early death, and the husband of our much loved and revered opera stage manager Stella Chitty, did just that. An hour or so before the performance, he would come to my room, sweep all the papers off my desk, spread a towel on top and ask me to lie down. He would then work on my back until the half-hour call – an announcement regularly made thirty-five (not, despite its title, thirty) minutes before curtain up was due – came over the tannoy. This was the signal to stop and prepare for the show. Order was restored, Jack Wakely went to change and I would visit the dressing rooms, with my shoulders greatly eased.

Running an opera house was a huge challenge and demanding of time and energy. But it was also fun, and we went out of our way to make it so and to lighten the darker moments. It was our responsibility to provide the best possible conditions in which artists and staff could work and to enable performers to rehearse and prepare for performances in a relaxed but serious atmosphere. We needed to be around to calm anxiety and to encourage the insecure. All too few understand the agonies and excitements of performing, where sheer terror can take over and reduce a dancer's legs and feet to jelly or convince a singer that nothing of the evening's role can be remembered. More than once I have visited a dressing room and been greeted with 'I can't go on, John', or 'Don't expect too much of me tonight, I'm not well.' The latter was often the prelude to a marvellous performance, but the former required serious attention and persuasion. It was a matter of weighing up the true nature of the problem. Sometimes agreement to make an announcement was sufficient to relax a performer and get them over the hump of uncertainty about their ability to deliver a performance.

Opera houses are large communities in which each individual makes a particular contribution to the success of the whole. Binding everybody together, encouraging, recognizing and commenting on achievement, and reprimanding where appropriate, are all part of a day's work. Nobody can do this single-handed, and I was fortunate in having immediately around me a group of men and women who were immensely hard working and totally committed to Covent Garden. I had many long-suffering and efficient secretaries and PAs. These are too numerous to name in their entirety, and I mention only two: among the first, Patsy, who was to become my wife, and the last, Lottie Stevenson, who happily continued to work for me after Covent Garden.

Others who worked directly in my office included Paul Findlay. He was steeped in the ways of the Opera House, knew his way around and took over the planning of touring from me, as well as other things for which I no longer had time or which I thought should be delegated. He was a splendid assistant and later became Assistant Director. Anthony Russell-Roberts was my PA on Findlay's elevation and rapidly proved his value to me. Eventually he was persuaded by Bernard Lefort, the Director of the Paris Opera, to join his staff, which was an invaluable experience for him. There he remained until enticed to return to Covent Garden as administrative director of the Royal Ballet. Another constant source of encouragement, wisdom and common sense was Kensington Davison, the inspired Director of the Friends organisation from its foundation until his retirement.

As we entered a new era of financial reporting and control, and personnel management, Adrian Doran joined us as finance director and Guy

Bloomer in charge of personnel. Both were innovative, and were later succeeded by Philip Jones as finance director and Richard Wright as director of administration. What was pleasing was not only the manner in which they all discharged their responsibilities, but the way in which they fitted into the life of the community.

The technical departments and the orchestra both had senior managers in charge of them. For many years the technical director was William Bundy, an electrician by training, and endowed by nature with a fiery temperament, which could land him and me in trouble. Passionately committed, he sought the highest standards, but in pursuit of these his outbursts provoked strong reactions. When Bundy retired, he was succeeded by another man of the theatre and an assistant technical director at Covent Garden, Tom McArthur. In temperament he was the exact opposite of Bundy and often too relaxed.

For years the orchestra was managed by Morris Smith, a former trombone player, who was assisted by Honor Thackrah and Frank Stead. They were a formidable team until Smith's untimely death in 1967. Happily the other two continued with Smith's successors, the last of whom during my time was Bram Gay. He is a firebrand of a character and a trumpet player, who played with the Covent Garden orchestra after the Hallé and City of Birmingham Orchestras. A huge enthusiast for music and always in quest of higher playing standards, he was constantly in my room, discussing plans for the orchestra, seeking advice and talking about the well-being of the players. My office door was always open and Bram Gay was probably more in and out of it than anybody else in the organization.

Press relations are all important and can be difficult even when things are going smoothly, or so you think. I was helped here by Paul Findlay, who had previously worked in the press office with Sheila Porter and who assumed overall responsibility for press and public relations when working directly with me. There came a time when we needed more expert advice and help than we could provide from our own resources. With the assistance of a board member, Brian Nicholson, we persuaded Ewan Balfour to leave the security of the British Museum to join us. Suddenly we had in our midst the most likeable, loyal and well-connected PR person you could have wanted. He rapidly improved our relations with the press and began to make an impression on the world and the way in which it looked at us. There was a vast amount of work to be done, even within the Covent Garden area itself, as redevelopment plans began to emerge and public reaction to it was felt.

I have been fortunate in meeting so many performers, some of whom have become friends and with most of whom I have been on good terms. I admire their talents and their professionalism. In spite of my long exposure to this, I never cease to wonder at a singer coming at no notice to replace a sick artist, without knowledge of the production, and delivering a first-rate performance. I recall a *Rosenkavalier* performance. Our Baron Ochs was sick and Hans Sotin responded to a last-minute request to replace him. Flying to London in the afternoon, he talked to the conductor, Silvio Varviso, just before curtain up for a matter of seconds, to the effect that at bar so and so Varviso should watch him. Otherwise nothing else was said, and a faultless performance ensued. There have been instances when we have started performances with a singer still en route from the airport. Then there is no time for anything but to put the artist into a costume on arrival at the theatre, and to show them the way to the stage. On these occasions a producer and a répétiteur will usually have travelled from the airport with the singer. But then, emergencies apart, I am constantly amazed by the ability of singers and dancers to carry a large repertoire in their heads and deliver an opera or a ballet from it at a drop of a hat.

I am impressed by their discipline. For dancers it is relentless with daily classes, constant attention to physique and dancing through pain. Those who dance professionally are so committed that I regard their participation as more of a vocation than it is for a singer. For the latter life is still demanding but it is marginally easier. Neither really has the glamour which many associate with them. For the dancer, often on tour, and the successful international singer doing the rounds of opera houses and concert halls, any glamour soon wears off, as they face an endless succession of hotels and packing and unpacking of suitcases.

As I watch and listen with the utmost pleasure and anticipation to the plethora of talent by which we have the good fortune to be surrounded, the one thing which really troubles me is the rush in which many artists seem to be. Time for the acquiring of a secure technique and for serious preparation of roles is too often at a premium. Not only that, but time for actually living is jettisoned in favour of rapid progress and higher fees, with too little regard for the long-term view of a career and the development of a solid foundation of technique and artistry. The good manager will try to prevent this and will structure a sensible career pattern, but he may be overruled by an impatient singer. For the dancer it is another matter altogether, with a career which starts and ends much earlier than for a singer and which largely takes shape within the confines of a company.

If they are willing and able to do so, decisions can be taken by singers which determine the course of their careers and which provide them with a way of life conducive to great artistry and good living. Dame Janet Baker is a supreme example of this. How much both she and all of us have gained from her early decision that a constantly nomadic life was not, for her, the route to serious artistic achievement and her well-being. Of course not everybody is made in the same way, and I recognize that some flourish with a quite different way of leading a professional life.

This book, whatever its value may be, has only been made possible by the countless men and women who contributed to the success of Covent Garden. To all of them I say a huge thank you.

To my wife, Jenny, I am greatly indebted for many things, and in this instance for her unfailing support and encouragement in keeping the ink flowing, and for banishing me to Aldeburgh. As my greatest critic, with her sharp mind and her quest for perfection, she has let me get away with nothing.

Thank you to my four children, Sarah, Fiona, Rachel and Ben, for their constant loving support and for the joy which they bring me by just being themselves.

I am delighted that the chapter headings are illustrated with drawings by Julia Preston. They are apt and beautifully executed.

I owe a big debt to Francesca Franchi and Jane Jackson of the Covent Garden archives for their extraordinary willingness to help with access to documents and files and making research pleasurable. I am grateful to Amanda Jones and Rita Grudzian in the Covent Garden press office for assisting in sorting photographs, and to Janet Jempson for taking on the task of negotiating fees with photographers and their agents. In trying to reach Paul Findlay, I have usually talked to his wife, Françoise, who has kindly answered questions intended for Paul, and so many thanks to her as well as to him.

My thanks go to Sir George Christie for permission to quote from a letter of his father to Fritz Busch, to the Trustees of the Britten-Pears

Foundation for a letter from Benjamin Britten to Ralph Hawkes, and to all the others from whom I have quoted.

Claus Moser has refreshed my memory very effectively about selection procedures adopted in quest of candidates as my successor. To him and all board members who served with him, his predecessor, Lord Drogheda, and his successor, Lord Sainsbury, I owe a great debt of gratitude for their help to me in managing this great opera house. That we kept it going and passed to our successors a viable concern was important in itself, but it was more than that: the Royal Opera House was firmly established as one of the world's great opera houses.

I want to thank Belinda Matthews and Charles Boyle, my editors at Faber, for their help and encouragement of a novice author; Bob Davenport, the copy editor, for his corrections and guidance as well as encouragement to be more expansive on certain subjects; and finally Matthew Evans, the Chairman of Faber, for accepting the idea of the book in the first instance and for urging me to be more forthcoming in a few areas.

1 Beginnings

For reasons I have never understood, the theme of a sermon preached in Canterbury Cathedral many years ago by a friend of my family, Canon Aubrey Standen, has stayed in my memory. It was about the casual becoming the causal, and was illustrated by an account of Marie-Antoinette pulling aside the curtain in her coach out of curiosity to see what was happening outside, and so revealing herself to the crowds. They immediately seized her, and eventually led her to the guillotine. Her capture was a chance happening, like many other unexpected occurrences which have a direct or indirect influence on the course of events. So too did chance play a part in the rebirth of the Royal Opera House after the Second World War.

In 1944, over lunch, Philip Hill, chairman of Second Covent Garden Properties, the freeholders of the Royal Opera House, mentioned to Harold Holt, the distinguished artists' manager, that the lease of the Royal Opera House to Mecca Cafés, who had been running it as a dance hall since the beginning of the war, was about to expire. Hill asked if Holt would be interested in taking it over; he wanted the theatre restored to its proper function, and was willing to accept a lower rent than currently charged to achieve it. He needed to act quickly if he was to prevent the automatic renewal of the lease to Mecca in the absence of a successor.

Holt, aware of the huge task of restoration and assembling a company, declined, but immediately talked to Leslie Boosey, who was excited by the proposition and in turn won the support of Ralph Hawkes, his partner in the music-publishing and instrument-manufacturing firm of Boosey & Hawkes. Both were also directors of the Harold Holt agency.

They envisaged a rescue operation in the first instance, followed by an imaginative plan to restore opera and ballet to their rightful home. To this end Boosey and Hawkes were willing to spend significant sums of money. The war was still going on, and there was no way of presenting performances for the time being. Nevertheless, a new five-year lease was negotiated by the publishers, and they in turn, unable to use Covent Garden immediately, permitted Mecca to remain until September 1945.

There was an interesting intervention from John Christie, the founder of Glyndebourne Festival Opera, around this time. As early as April 1938, and in spite of his well-known views that the Royal Opera House was inefficient, he had written to Fritz Busch, Glyndebourne's principal conductor:

> I hope there may be a reasonable chance of managing Covent Garden as well as Glyndebourne, but I suppose it depends on whether [Sir Thomas] Beecham makes a muddle and a loss again this year [as he had in his previous season at Covent Garden]. This is in confidence, but I want Covent Garden to be combined with us. It is bound to be more efficient and more economical. It would mean I suppose thirty performances at Covent Garden followed by thirty performances at Glyndebourne – about twelve weeks . . .

The outbreak of war put an end to this idea – but only for the time being, since Christie was to return to it in the later stages of the war, only to have his proposals turned down by one of several consultative committees active at the time. He envisaged Rudolph Bing, general manager of Glyndebourne, as general manager of Covent Garden, and believed that Glyndebourne's methods and experience would be invaluable in re-creating the Royal Opera House. What he failed to realize, or over which he was perhaps unduly optimistic, was that a year-round operation could not be run on festival lines. He later sought meetings with Maynard Keynes, by then chairman of the trust overseeing Covent Garden, but Keynes wanted nothing to do with him and rebuffed him in what appears to have been an ill-mannered way.

In the meantime, Boosey and Hawkes issued an important statement of intent, which was to have a lasting effect on the development of opera and ballet at Covent Garden, and indeed up and down the country when in later years regional companies were formed. It read:

> We hope to re-establish Covent Garden as a centre of opera and ballet worthy of the highest musical traditions. The main purpose will be to

ensure for Covent Garden an independent position as an international opera house with sufficient funds at its disposal to enable it to devote itself to a long-term programme, giving to London throughout the year the best in English opera and ballet, together with the best from all over the world. If this ambition can be realized it is felt that it will prove to be a great incentive to artists and composers, since it will offer to them an opportunity for experience in the performing and writing of opera on a scale equal to that which has prevailed so long on the Continent but has been lacking so long in our musical life here in London.

This was visionary, and set the scene for the future in a way I suspect nobody had thought about until then. Boosey and Hawkes were willing to assume responsibility for much of the early cost of purchasing the lease and maintaining the building, and to sub-let the theatre to an independent company to manage it.

A general manager was required, and a cousin of Ralph Hawkes, Anthony Gishford, on hearing of the Covent Garden plan, led Hawkes to David Webster, whom Gishford had met previously in Liverpool and with whose record as chairman of the Liverpool Philharmonic Society he was familiar. Hawkes and Webster met for lunch at the Ritz in April 1944, and Webster left no doubt in Hawkes's mind that he was the person for whom they were looking. Webster had recently been offered an excellent contract by Metal Box, but was soon encouraged to drop this in favour of the Royal Opera House. Sir Robert Barlow, chairman of Metal Box, agreed to release him, and shortly afterwards Webster signed a contract for the Covent Garden appointment for sixteen months from August 1944, renewable at the end of December 1945 for a further twelve months.

The job he had taken on was daunting. The presentation of opera in the inter-war years, and earlier, had been based largely on importing singers from abroad, performing operas in their original language. Even a British chorus had not been engaged until 1919. In the absence of public arts funding, private syndicates had been formed to finance opera seasons. This system had been costly, haphazard and wasteful, and hardly a trace of it remained in 1945, except for a glorious nineteenth-century theatre, in which many great performances had been given, and a tradition which had grown up around them. The only survivors from the staff of this period were Frank Ballard, the chief machinist, Sid Cheyney, chief electrician, and Norman Feasey, a répétiteur, all of whom were to be invaluable in the huge task of reopening Covent Garden.

Initially a committee, the Covent Garden Committee, had been established to oversee the whole venture. In the autumn of 1945 this was replaced by the Covent Garden Opera Trust, whose membership was Lord Keynes as chairman, Leslie Boosey, Ralph Hawkes, Kenneth Clark, Samuel Courtauld, Professor Edward Dent, Sir Stanley Marchant, Sir William Walton and Sir Steuart Wilson. They were to take a number of far-reaching decisions which set the pattern of the future operation of the Royal Opera House.

In the first place, it was to be a national lyric theatre presenting both opera and ballet. Second, they conceived it as their duty to keep the theatre open all the year round, except for a few weeks in the summer for holidays and maintenance work. This implied the existence of full-time and permanent opera and ballet companies. They envisaged that each company would have the opportunity to perform at Covent Garden while the other was on tour, and that for certain periods both companies would share the stage, each performing three or four times a week. They also saw the possibility of occasional visits by foreign companies. This was in embryo the pattern of work which was to exist for some years, to change only when the opera company began to adopt the *stagione* principle (established and unchanging casts throughout rehearsals and performances) and when touring became more and more difficult, both financially and practically. What was not recognized in those early days was the extent to which opera and ballet companies can complement each other in an artistic and financial sense. The realization of that came later.

In search of a ballet and an opera company to take up residence at Covent Garden, eyes were naturally turned to Sadler's Wells. Its opera and ballet companies had survived the war, mostly on the road and with occasional seasons at the New Theatre. Both companies had a loyal following, and in those difficult days Tyrone Guthrie, then in charge of Sadler's Wells and the Old Vic, saw public support for them as bringing the possibility of their establishment as national companies.

There was a strong belief that Sadler's Wells Ballet was ready for the challenge of a larger theatre, but opinions about the opera company were less sure. In 1944 Tyrone Guthrie and Edward Dent had drawn up a Memorandum of Opera Policy, in which they expressed the view that opera in England was at a point in its development where emphasis should be laid on its literary and dramatic aspects. What they seemed to have in mind – especially for Sadler's Wells – because it appeared to them to be practical and suited to English talent and temperament, was an English version of the *opéra comique* tradition, with song and spoken dialogue. This was not envisaged for Covent Garden, and for this and other reasons related to Sadler's Wells's traditions the Covent Garden Opera Trust soon realized that a new company would have to be created.

Having reached this decision, the trustees were faced with a choice: either the old polyglot tradition could be followed, or a native company could be formed and trained, basing its work on a repertoire of foreign opera in translation in the hope that, if it succeeded in establishing a genuine national style of operatic representation, it would attract native composers and librettists to write for it. Thus there might slowly be built up a corpus of British works that would show that this country had an important contribution to make to the international repertory. This was the course adopted by the trustees. It was a bold move, which was not to achieve its objectives in full but which provided the foundation of a great international company.

It was a policy for the long term – and nobody could anticipate how long. However, the example of Sadler's Wells Ballet, established by Ninette de Valois in 1931, was a reminder that much progress could be made in developing a first-rate company from modest beginnings in as short a period as fourteen years.

Public funding of the arts was in its infancy at the time. When the trust was debating the future of Covent Garden, CEMA (the Council for the Encouragement of Music and the Arts), started in the early days of the war as an emergency mechanism to distribute funds for the regular provision of music, theatre, opera, ballet and literature to fortify national morale, had not yet been succeeded by the Arts Council; this was to happen in the following year, 1946. Nevertheless, the principle of using the public purse to fund the arts was well enough founded to leave few in doubt that it would continue after the cessation of hostilities. Without it, Covent Garden could not have been reborn in the manner intended by the trust.

A principle had been set, but money had not been committed fully to realize the aspirations of those arts institutions already in being or to be formed in the aftermath of the war. In his memoirs, *A Life in the Theatre*, Tyrone Guthrie wrote, 'I think it was a mistake, at the end of the war, that public money was used at Covent Garden to found another opera company, thus dividing in two the available funds, talent and support, which was barely sufficient for one.' He was not alone in this view.

Nevertheless, the trustees pressed on with their plans and backed their proposals with a huge act of faith. Discussions with the Sadler's Wells governors continued, and agreement was eventually reached with them and Ninette de Valois for the ballet company to be transferred. She was hesitant at first. She felt that the company was too small for Covent Garden, and that she needed time to build it up after the ravages of war and the loss of many male dancers to the services. At the same time she saw advantages in the company being attached to a prominent opera house and that the challenge of this might well be its making, in spite of the risk of its being subordinated to the needs of Covent Garden as a whole and used as a source of money for the opera. This was a fate which the ballet company was indeed to suffer at various times, but which did not hinder its development. Frederick Ashton, principal choreographer of Sadler's Wells Ballet, had no doubts about the wisdom of accepting the invitation, and was instrumental in persuading de Valois to delay her acceptance no longer.

The ballet company moved from Rosebery Avenue and reopened the Royal Opera House with a new production of *Sleeping Beauty* on 20 February 1946. With evocative and beautiful designs by Oliver Messel and the production in the hands of de Valois herself, it was a triumph and rapidly became a mainstay of the company. De Valois based her production on the version which she had created in 1939 at Sadler's Wells, with the aid of the choreographic notes and memory of Nicholas Sergueyev, a former répétiteur at the Mariinsky Theatre, St Petersburg, the experience of Ursula Moreton, who had appeared in the Diaghilev production of 1921, and her own memories of an abbreviated version, *Aurora's Wedding*, from the 1920s.

As for the opera, it was increasingly obvious that collaboration with Sadler's Wells would be impractical and undesirable. There was a strong wish on the part of the Sadler's Wells governors to manage Covent Garden, but with only a small representation of the Covent Garden Opera Trust involved. Furthermore, the trust's ambitions were different, its intended horizons wider. There was no alternative but to found a company from scratch.

This was a fearsome task – especially without anyone with experience and knowledge of an opera company and the functioning of an opera house. The most pressing need was to find a music director. At the beginning of 1945 David Webster had received a letter from Ralph Hawkes, who was now running the New York office of Boosey & Hawkes:

> There are, of course, numerous conductors here who are falling over themselves to get to London but I have seen all the top-notchers and, when the time is ripe, I think we shall be able to get what we want, but I must stress the fact that unless something is done by the end of March, we shall have a job to get [Georg] Szell for he is already a rising star at the Metropolitan and elsewhere and is very sensible of his success. Bruno Walter can be had in 1946 if we want him.

Hawkes went on to explain that Eugene Goossens might be available earlier, and would be helpful in putting the company together. This, incidentally, was a suggestion of Bruno Walter's, on the assumption that he himself was no longer in the running. Eugene Ormandy's name was to be added to the list, as was that of William Steinberg.

David Webster, whose dilatoriness had already become apparent, was not to be rushed into a decision. There was everything at stake, and a wrong move over such an important appointment could spell ruin. Most of those whose names had so far been suggested were discarded, on the grounds of their unsuitability for the immediate job in hand, their likely cost, or their inability to devote sufficient time to Covent Garden. The major exception was Goossens, to whom David Webster made an offer of a twelve months' engagement. This had been too long for Walter but was too short for Goossens. A counter-offer of two years was made, and Webster came under increasing pressure from Ralph Hawkes to persuade Goossens to sign. But, in spite of the House having opened and the first season of ballet having begun, Webster was reluctant to bring negotiations to a head, and in March 1946 Goossens broke off talks. In a letter to Ralph Hawkes, he wrote:

> Webster's own statement embodies my biggest misgiving when he says 'not that England is entirely devoid of good singers, but there are naturally few of them, and those few, for obvious reasons, are not well schooled in opera'. In other words, unless those few not well schooled in opera prove susceptible within a reasonable amount of time, either their places must be taken by the foreign artists (with imperfect diction) – thus defeating the main idea of the project – or else the whole idea of opera in English must be abandoned. It is the whole idea of making bricks without straw that alarms me a great deal . . .

7

I cannot safely undertake the responsibility for a project the artistic outcome of which I cannot foresee and consequently take full musical responsibility for. The real paucity of experienced operatic material (how could it be otherwise after what England has endured in the war?) plus my natural fear that after so much preliminary work the calibre of the artists themselves might prove an insuperable handicap to the success of the company, are the strongest reasons for my decision.

He went on to say that his decision could have been made earlier if a true statement of the situation had been forthcoming when he first requested it.

But delay on Webster's part paid off in this instance, and Covent Garden found itself with the kind of music director it most needed to found and launch an opera company. At the suggestion of Edward Dent, it was to be Karl Rankl, an Austrian musician and a refugee settled in England, with a wealth of operatic experience. This had been gained through membership of Felix Weingartner's music staff at the Vienna Volksoper, and later through appointments in Germany, including those of assistant to Otto Klemperer at the Kroll Theatre, Berlin, and music director of the State Theatre in Wiesbaden. Driven out by the Nazis, he conducted opera in Graz and then in Prague, until forced to flee in 1939. Webster had got to know him when he conducted in Liverpool.

After the stellar names so far discussed for the music directorship, his appointment must have seemed an anticlimax, but there was an awareness that the conductor most needed for this assignment would not necessarily be among the world famous – indeed, it was more than probable that the contrary would be the case.

An orchestra had been assembled by Joseph Shadwick, the former leader of the Sadler's Wells Orchestra, but there were no singers and no chorus. In the summer of 1946 Webster and Rankl went to America to listen to singers, and held auditions in London and other cities in search of soloists and choristers. In all they heard around two thousand singers, and engaged seventy for the chorus. It was while they were in Leeds that Webster met Douglas Robinson. He was invited to London to audition for the post of chorus master, and was appointed shortly afterwards, remaining at Covent Garden until the mid-1970s.

Rankl was proud of the quality of the singers whom he had selected, and when they assembled for their first rehearsal with Douglas Robinson, in the autumn of 1946, he asked each of them in turn to sing a scale. Content with what he heard, he handed them over to Robinson with the instruction to make them into a chorus.

With a chorus in place and an orchestra already at work, here was the beginning of the first ever permanent opera company at the Royal Opera House. Soloists presented much more of a problem. Opportunities for British singers to develop and make a career in opera in their own country were limited, and there was a serious paucity of singers with operatic experience. Most had made their careers in oratorio and on the concert platform; few had been given a chance to prove themselves on the stage. There had also been unjustified prejudice against native singers from a public brought up on foreign artists and unwilling to believe that British singers could ever be as good. Sir Thomas Beecham had championed them for many years, but for inexplicable reasons was to write disparagingly of them in his autobiography, *A Mingled Chime*, published in the final days of the war:

> English voices are unlike those of other nations; really robust tenors and true dramatic sopranos hardly exist amongst us, and high baritones are as rare as a perfect summer. The best among them are of comparatively moderate volume, pure and excellent in tone but lacking in power and brilliance in comparison with those of Italy, Germany and France.

Given his earlier support, this is a curious statement for him to have made. He also ignores the phases in which particular kinds of voices come and go in every country. For example, what would he have had to say about today's lack of Heldentenors and true Verdi baritones?

Against this background, Webster and Rankl staked their faith in the British singer. First-rate voices were to emerge from the chorus – Charles Craig, Michael Langdon, Josephine Veasey, Patricia Johnson and Kenneth Macdonald, to name but five. Geraint Evans, the first post-war British soloist to win international acclaim, who blazed the trail abroad for many other native artists, joined Covent Garden Opera direct from the Guildhall School of Music in 1948. It is greatly to the credit of the music and production staff of those first years that the list of such singers is long. What developed was a sensible mix of foreign and British singers working together – eventually to the point that the latter sometimes dominated the scene.

But the beginning was not easy, for singers needed to be convinced that there was a future for them in opera. There was uncertainty about the viability of a permanent opera company at Covent Garden, and some feared that the House might all too easily revert to international seasons. The oratorio tradition died hard in the British singer, and prompted Edward Dent, in a memorandum to the board, to write, 'If we are to make opera more important than oratorio in this country, it will inevitably take a good many years and we must be prepared to face a long and gradual transition period.'

Nevertheless, Webster pressed on, determined to promote a national lyric theatre, in which opera and ballet were of equal status and importance. For opera, he saw Covent Garden as a national opera house, attracting and inspiring composers to write for the company, with an ensemble of the best British and Commonwealth singers. He believed that this was the only way to build a repertoire of English operas. That this ideal was not fulfilled was hardly his fault. Some progress was made, but there were forces at work which made the concept of an all-British company untenable and which led the company on to the international scene more quickly than anyone could have imagined.

The Sadler's Wells Ballet was enjoying real success during this first season, and it would have been easy for Webster to have continued with ballet until ready to open with the opera in January 1947. He decided against this and, believing that audiences would respond well to visiting companies, invited American Ballet Theatre and the San Carlo Opera for guest seasons in the autumn of 1946. These were intended to whet the appetite of the public, and in that they were successful. Beniamino Gigli, Mario Del Monaco, Margherita Carosio, Carlo Tagliabue and Paolo Silveri, appearing with the Neapolitan company, were rapturously received, as were the dancers of the American company, led by Nora Kaye, Alicia Alonso and André Eglevsky.

With the opening of the first Covent Garden opera season drawing near, decisions on programming were pressing. Slender resources limited the choice of works. Anxious not to overexpose the opera company and wanting to give it as much support as possible on its first appearance, David Webster and the trust had been considering a variety of options, including Delius's *Hassan*, which Ralph Hawkes had earlier proposed. Eventually they settled on Purcell's *Fairy Queen*, in which the opera and ballet would both appear, in an edition prepared by Constant Lambert. Robert Helpmann played Oberon and Margaret Rawlings Titania.

Produced by Malcolm Baker-Smith and designed by Michael Ayrton, it ran for twenty-three performances and was a moderate success with both public and critics. It also effectively introduced an untried chorus and inexperienced soloists to the stage and stagecraft, and this in itself justified the venture.

Then came the major challenge for the opera company: its first production alone, on 14 January 1947. It was *Carmen*, a popular opera, but a strange and difficult choice because of its elusive quality, which few have been able to capture successfully. Also, with the best will in the world it was surely difficult to imagine Edith Coates – a wonderful trouper and an experienced singer, but devoid of Gallic spirit – delivering the kind of performance which would convince the public and critics that Covent Garden's course was set fair. The same was true of Karl Rankl conducting, and of Kenneth Neate, a former policeman from New South Wales and a fine but inexperienced tenor, as Don José. Hopes must have been pinned on Denis Noble, a well-established singer from pre-war days, as Escamillo, and on Beryl Grey as the solo dancer. It was the latter who stole the show – a sad commentary on the evening. In her inimitable manner, Edith Coates went all out and never spared herself, producing more and more raucous and unsteady tone. It was all done with the best of intentions and in the spirit which was to be the hallmark of Covent Garden – of a combined effort to achieve success for the company. On this occasion, however, energy was expended for little that was right.

In spite of the bad reviews the next day, there were expressions of goodwill and a true desire for Covent Garden Opera to succeed. But Webster did not help himself by selecting another French work for the second production, Massenet's *Manon*, with Reginald Goodall, not sympathetic to this repertoire, conducting. The only justification for this might have been the casting of Heddle Nash, a much loved and stylish singer, as Des Grieux, and the engagement of Frederick Ashton to direct and James Bailey to design. Unfortunately, amends for *Carmen* were not forthcoming.

It was an alarming situation for Webster: with two productions poorly received and further productions coming in at the rate of one a month, the chances of reversing a growing trend must have seemed slim. Nevertheless, hopes were pinned on *Der Rosenkavalier*, in a production by Joan Cross – one of the best sopranos this country has produced, yet not seriously courted by Covent Garden in those early days – and with designs by Robin Ironside. Karl Rankl was conducting an opera much more suited to his talents than *Carmen*, and the cast sang decently enough, but still success eluded them.

The decision to sing operas in English posed problems of casting. Virginia McWatters (Manon) and Doris Doree (the Marschallin) were two singers whom Webster and Rankl had auditioned in New York and on whom they were relying to bring lustre to Covent Garden and to complement the British company; but what had seemed one thing in New York turned out to be something else here. This was a blow, and the torrent of criticism directed at Webster and the Royal Opera House continued. Webster faced it stoically and in silence, aware that only achievement would eventually bring it to an end.

His faith in British singers remained unshaken, and he was convinced that the day would come when they were a powerful force on the world scene. But this did not happen quickly enough to turn the fortunes of Covent Garden at that difficult time. One of the few British singers who had won international stardom, however, was Eva Turner, who had scored a huge success as Turandot and in other roles in Italy in the 1920s and 1930s. She was the supreme Turandot, and I suspect that Webster wanted her in that role as much for making an impression on the company, by now dispirited and insecure, as for her certain triumph with the public. Her performances in 1948 fulfilled every expectation, and Constant Lambert, the Ballet's music director, who conducted them, proved himself a splendid conductor of Puccini.

With public subsidy covering a smaller proportion of total costs than now and clothes rationing still in force, it is amazing that so many new productions could be mounted at the beginning. In fact productions from pre-war years were brought back where they were available and usable. In 1948, for example, *La Bohème*, albeit directed by Peter Brook, was presented in sets from 1898 – copies of those designed by the famous artist F. A. von Hohenstein for Turin two years before – and continued to be so until 1974, when a new production by John Copley was mounted with designs by Julia Trevelyan Oman. Similarly, *Tosca* was played in sets from 1910, until these were replaced by Franco Zeffirelli's production with Maria Callas in 1964. Pre-war settings of the *Ring* wore less well, and were soon replaced by the designs of Leslie Hurry for a production by Rudolf Hartmann.

While the orchestra and chorus were progressing well, production standards left a good deal to be desired and were too often the butt of adverse comment. Opinions could be divided, as they were with *Die Zauberflöte* in 1947. Harold Rosenthal described this as 'execrable ... the beginning of a long chapter of misconceived productions', whereas Andrew Porter admits to 'very happy memories of Oliver Messel's magic world, created in the spirit of Schikaneder's stage-directions, with a lightness, elegance and decorative fancy too often missing in presentations more earnest than charming'.

Something had to be done, and David Webster concluded that the answer lay in the appointment of a director of productions – provided that he could persuade Karl Rankl to accept such an idea. Ideally he wanted an established theatre director like Michael Benthall or Tyrone Guthrie, but that was not to be, and in the end he took the astonishingly bold decision of inviting Peter Brook, the first of a new generation of theatre directors to make a mark. Brook, an iconoclast at heart, was entering a conservative world in which the stage director was a relatively new phenomenon; hitherto the singer, either personally or through a manager or maid, had generally told the stage manager where he or she would stand and at which moments he or she would turn to the left or right. Webster must have been aware of the risk he was taking in going for Brook, and must have concluded that it would probably pay off. In many ways it did – but it was an appointment ten or fifteen years ahead of its time.

Brook's first production, in May 1948, was *Boris Godunov*, with designs by Georges Wakhevitch, a Russian designer first brought to the West by the Théâtre des Champs-Élysées in Paris and later to be involved with other productions at Covent Garden. Paolo Silveri, then a bass, sang the title role in English, though later the arrival of the Bulgarian bass Boris Christoff, who would perform the role only in Russian and in the Rimsky-Korsakov version, would result in mixed-language performances – the first but by no means the last, as the problems of engaging foreign singers either unwilling or unable to learn their roles in English became apparent.

The *Boris* production was criticized for the scenery's domination of the characters and the action, but it did show a standard of theatrical achievement, which was important in itself in showing a way forward, and it did create excitement. *Bohème* was notable for its casting: Elisabeth Schwarzkopf as Mimi and Ljuba Welitsch as Musetta. The latter had pleaded with Webster to sing this secondary role, proclaiming that she wanted to be reunited with her old friend from Vienna. But there was another motive at work, which was shown on the first night, when she out-sang Mimi. Admirable though Schwarzkopf was, it was Weltisch's *Bohème*.

Le Nozze di Figaro, with designs by Rolf Gerard, was the next of the Brook productions. David Webster had wanted Elisabeth Schwarzkopf as the Countess, Irmgard Seefried as Susanna and Erich Kunz as Figaro, but this casting did not materialize. Schwarzkopf sang Susanna, followed by Seefried in later performances. The Countess was sung by the Australian soprano Sylvia Fisher, who was rapidly to become the company's prima donna, and Figaro by Geraint Evans, another singer on the brink of an international career. Fisher, the possessor of a warm and glorious voice, was helped dramatically by Peter Brook, who recognized that her special qualities needing sympathetic handling to enable her to fulfil her potential. She enjoyed a huge success – as did the rest of the cast.

What was important about this casting – and it was a practice to be followed in future years – was the placing of the inexperienced British singer alongside the established foreign artist. Schwarzkopf was perfect for this mentoring role. She understood Mozartian style and was an admirable colleague, helpful to the rest of the cast and wanting to be integrated into the production. Adèle Leigh, in the small role of Barbarina, absorbed everything she saw and heard, and showed the benefit of Schwarzkopf's example when she graduated to Susanna the following season. A year later Constance Shacklock was to enjoy the inestimable benefit of singing Brangäne in *Tristan und Isolde* with Kirsten Flagstad.

Adhering to the principle of opera in English did not make it easy to extend the repertoire. Reliance on English-speaking singers was restrictive, and in any event the public wanted to hear the great singers of the world, few of whom would or could perform in English. There were exceptions, as already described, and two unlikely ones in Kirsten Flagstad and Hans Hotter, who had agreed to perform *Die Walküre* in English. This was in March 1948, in a production by Frederick Schramm with pre-war designs for Acts 2 and 3, and by Reece Pemberton for Act 1. It was to be the only attempt to perform any part of the *Ring* in English in post-war Covent Garden; after experiencing the difficulties that the guest singers had with their words, David Webster was clear that the language rule had to be applied flexibly if singers essential for the satisfactory performance of certain operas were to be readily engaged. He formulated a compromise which enabled him to strike a sensible balance between operas in English and those in their original language, even to the undesirable point of mixed-language performances – a practice which fortunately did not last long but which saw the company through many a crisis in its first years. For example, Set Svanholm appeared as Walther in *Die Meistersinger von Nürnberg*, singing in German while the remainder of the cast sang in English. That would be an unacceptable state of affairs today, but it was worth it then to have as distinguished an artist as Svanholm in that hard-to-cast role.

In November 1947 Benjamin Britten's *Peter Grimes* was successfully presented at Covent Garden, following its triumphant debut at Sadler's Wells two years earlier. The next British work to appear, in September 1949, was Arthur Bliss's *The Olympians*, with a libretto by J. B. Priestley. Webster was right in thinking that the public was not ready for another contemporary British opera, but he was committed and relied on Peter Brook to bring about a miracle. It did not happen. The opera had a mixed reception and disappeared from the repertoire after ten performances. It deserved a better fate, and it would have been prudent to postpone it until the public and the company were better able to deal with it.

The huge demands which *The Olympians* made on the company were reflected in the poorly rehearsed programme which followed, though *Salomé* – another Brook production, with Ljuba Welitsch in the title role and Salvador Dali as designer – was seen as a possible saviour of the season.

Understandably David Webster was keen to widen the list of conductors, but he found Karl Rankl unwilling to entertain the idea of guests and insistent on working with the director of productions, even though their relationship was fraying at the edges and during rehearsals for *The Olympians* they had been barely on speaking terms. This was particularly unfortunate as Webster had just heard from Ralph Hawkes in New York that Fritz Reiner was free and willing to conduct both *Salomé* and *Götterdämmerung*. His engagement would have been a real coup, but it was not to be.

Rankl disapproved of Dali's designs, and sent a telegram to Webster in New York explaining that the sets were absolutely impossible for the requirements of the music and singers. Even then there was the complaint (to become very familiar over the years) that the singers would not be heard because of their positioning too far upstage. Other features were also likely to cause dissent: a stationary moon, which failed to turn red, and John the Baptist's head lowered on a silver salver from the flies. It was all too much for Rankl, and he stormed out of the theatre before the first night, vowing never to return. In fact he did, persuaded by Webster.

Welitsch gave performances of great distinction, but the production inevitably roused the wrath of many critics. However, public interest was stimulated, and business at the box office was lively the morning after opening. None of this was enough to save this production. It was, it is true, way ahead of its time, but many wished for its continuation in the repertoire. Instead, a production by Christopher West, with designs by Clement Glock, was substituted in later seasons.

Exasperated by public and critical response to his productions and by the difficulties of working in the opera house, Peter Brook left Covent Garden by mutual consent at the end of 1949. He was replaced by his assistant from Stratford, Christopher West, as resident producer – a downgrading of his role. Brook was never to return to an opera house. I suspect that the compromise involved in the presentation of opera was more than he could tolerate.

The opera company continued to grow in stature as it gained greater confidence and became a more and more cohesive whole, with a mixture of British and foreign singers working well together. A pattern for the future was being set, and practices harmful to artistic progress were being eradicated. One of these was the use of deputies in the orchestra – a long-established tradition in the music profession, whereby a player offered a better or more lucrative job elsewhere would accept it and send another player to take his place in the orchestra for which he was originally engaged. This happened regardless of whether the substitute player would have rehearsal time or whether he even knew the opera or ballet. This was where British musicians' skill at sight-reading was an asset, even though in these circumstances it was abused. Henry Wood had fought against this practice for many years and had made employment in his Queen's Hall Orchestra conditional upon players attending all rehearsals and performances.

The arrival of Morris Smith as orchestra manager in 1948 brought about a similar change at Covent Garden. Smith was a trombone player, who had been encouraged by Malcolm Sargent to transfer from the tenor to the bass instrument because of the shortage of players of the latter. It was sound advice, from which Smith and Covent Garden were to benefit. His progress in the profession was rapid, and he soon became a professor at two London conservatoires, where he was in a good position to discover talented players while they were still young and unknown. Smith was a skilful operator in the minefields of orchestral management, and there were to be few of the country's most outstanding players who had not appeared with the orchestra at one time or another. His enthusiasm and love for the orchestra were infectious, and contributed hugely to its growth and acceptance as one of the truly great opera orchestras of the world. At a much later date Carlos Kleiber was to describe it to me as the finest in Europe.

With the aid of Honor Thackrah and Frank Stead, another trombone player, who had made his debut at Covent Garden in a stage band in 1928, Morris Smith ran a benign but firm regime in which the deputy played no part, except by agreement. Between them they took wonderful care of conductors, who responded warmly and sometimes took refuge in their office in search of calm and tranquillity. The orchestra is the bedrock of an opera house, and Smith and his team made doubly sure that this was the case at Covent Garden and that everyone knew it.

As the Sadler's Wells Ballet scored a major triumph in New York at the Metropolitan Opera House in October 1949, and Margot Fonteyn and the company were thrust on to the world scene with the success of *Sleeping Beauty*, David Webster was aware that at home there was a real need for fresh musical leadership if the opera company was to fulfil its potential and achieve similar world renown. Rankl's refusal to countenance the engagement of guest conductors was a thorn in Webster's side, and was impeding the company's growth. Furthermore, Webster must by then have realized that the company would outgrow Rankl before long.

The trustees were keen that other conductors should be brought in. Vittorio Gui was one suggestion, but he was unwilling to consider an engagement unless he could conduct Wagner and Mozart in addition to Italian operas. Such trespassing on the music director's repertoire would have made it even more impossible to have persuaded Rankl to accept Gui. Guido Cantelli, a protégé of Toscanini, was also proposed, but unsurprisingly declined to consider an invitation because of his symphonic commitments.

Webster then made an unexpected but inspired move: he approached Erich Kleiber, whom he met in Switzerland and who was enthusiastic about coming to London. The big question then facing Webster was how to persuade Rankl to accept him. He tried every ruse in the book, including the acceptance of Sir Steuart Wilson as deputy general administrator (not a precise parallel to the Kleiber/Rankl situation, but an appointment made for the good of the House). All were to no avail. Finally, determined to have Kleiber, Webster simply engaged him in the face of Rankl's opposition and anger. The company was ready for him, and responded strongly to this next influence for good.

2 Music Directors

It is ironic that the man to whom the Royal Opera owes so much for the laying of its foundations and its early development should have been outgrown by the company which he worked so hard to establish. Without training in the routine which Karl Rankl had learned from working in opera houses in Germany before the war, the company could never have started its climb to world standing.

Karl Rankl was a kapellmeister in the German tradition rather than a star conductor. But he was exactly the kind of musician whom Covent Garden needed at the time, and through his knowledge and experience he was successful in launching the opera company. Though he did not altogether fulfil the management's aspirations in those first five years, it is doubtful if others would have fared any better, and they might well have not laid the foundations as securely as Rankl did, enabling the company to move on to the next stage of its development and to take such advantage of the opportunities afforded by the engagement of Erich Kleiber and others after him.

Rankl's departure from Covent Garden in 1951 was a sorry affair, which some remembered with distaste for a long time. David Webster faced an impossible situation: Rankl strenuously opposed the engagement of Kleiber, but Webster clearly understood the necessity of bringing him to Covent Garden if progress was to be made. In addition to the news of Kleiber, Rankl was to learn that Sir Thomas Beecham, who had conducted at the Royal Opera House before the war, was returning to conduct *Die Meistersinger* and Balfe's *Bohemian Girl*. Insult was then added to injury for Rankl, as Clemens Krauss was invited to conduct *Tristan und Isolde* in the summer of 1951. Understandably, this was resented by Rankl, who by now really had no alternative but to resign. This he did with effect from the end of the 1950/51 season.

It was a strange decision of Webster's to have deprived his music director of performances, let alone of a work as important as this and one so close to his heart. It was, after all, in this repertoire that Rankl had made the greatest impression in performance. However, Krauss was a catch, and it would have been foolish of Webster to have lost him. And Rankl's obduracy over guest conductors has to be recognized. Rankl was an obstacle to progress in terms of what he could now offer the company himself and his resentment at the introduction of conductors more talented than he, from working with whom the company was more than ready to benefit. Nevertheless, Webster's humiliation of his music director, to whom he was indebted for building the company from nothing, was shabby, and damaged his reputation. It was also untypical of him, and to my knowledge was never to be repeated.

In negotiation with Krauss, and probably conscience-stricken, David Webster did keep the fifth and final performance of *Tristan* for Rankl. It was an ungenerous way of saying thank you and goodbye to a conductor to whom so much was owed. The only real consolation for Rankl was that he was conducting the last performance which Kirsten Flagstad was to sing at Covent Garden.

Looking back over those first five years, there seems to have been an unrealistic expectation of standards of performance and achievement. This arose, I believe, from a failure to recognize the newness of the enterprise, the limitation of its resources – often extemporized – and the problems inherent in developing a new tradition of a year-round operation. Critics could helpfully have taken a longer view, without forfeiting their right to make fair comment on the deficiencies of what they were seeing and hearing.

Webster and Rankl had to endure a constant barrage of criticism from every quarter, unrelieved by much favourable comment. It must have hit Rankl particularly hard. He was often in the pit and experienced the public reaction first hand. He was also a refugee and, arriving in England in middle age, found himself having to adjust to different attitudes and a different lifestyle. His resignation, unhappy as were the circumstances in which it came about, was surely a release for him from the burdens and responsibilities which he had been carrying at Covent Garden, with little praise or appreciation to lighten the load. Interestingly enough, after the announcement of his resignation, an improvement in the quality of his performances was remarked upon, and he even won praise from Ernest Newman, previously among the fiercest of his critics.

Rankl's final performance with the company was on 31 July 1951. He returned to the House only once: to a performance of *Moses und Aron*, by his old teacher, Schoenberg, in 1965. It was a sad ending to a long career in opera, and his bitterness was exacerbated by the omission of his name from the Coronation programme of 1953. Dismayed and angry, he wrote to Kenneth Clark, one of the first trustees of Covent Garden, 'I suggest that this amounts to almost a falsification of historical facts. Apparently Mr Webster has seen fit to omit any reference to the man who, unaided by anybody and hampered by antagonism from all sides, nevertheless succeeded in building up from scratch an opera company that still exists.' By now he was with the Scottish National Orchestra, and it was to Glasgow that David Webster sent a letter of the kind he was so skilful in writing, defusing the grievance with an explanation of the purpose of the brochure in question.

A successor to Rankl was not to be appointed immediately. Nobody had been identified as a possible music director, and, after his experience with Rankl, Webster was in no hurry to find one. He believed that there could be an advantage in dispensing with the appointment, relying on a few first-rate conductors to give regular performances and on Lord Harewood, who had joined the staff as controller of opera planning, to provide artistic advice and continuity. There were to be two such inter-regnums during Webster's time: 1951–5 and 1958–61.

By now Covent Garden was a close-knit community, with a family solidarity which held together those working permanently for it and made it an opera house to which artists wanted to come. With Erich Kleiber, Clemens Krauss, John Barbirolli, Rudolf Kempe, John Pritchard, Fritz Stiedry and Franco Capuana appearing at regular intervals, Webster felt secure, but he hoped that he could persuade Kleiber to accept a regular appointment of principal conductor, if not of music director. However, Kleiber was not to be enticed, and after the 1952/53 season he was not to return.

His departure reopened the issue of a music director. The board felt that too much was resting on Webster's shoulders and that the House would benefit from the presence and influence of an eminent musician in that position. John Barbirolli was one possibility and was already work-ing closely with the company, but it was an association which was to end after three years. Webster had been toying with the idea of Pritchard, a first-rate musician, working very successfully at Glyndebourne. Rudolf Kempe, who had already made a deep and what was to be a lasting impression at Covent Garden, was another possibility, although he was tied to Munich and not immediately free. Webster also considered Benjamin Britten, although he never mentioned the subject when he spent a weekend with the Harewoods at the same time as Britten. We will never know whether this was because of shyness, of which there was a streak in Webster, or because of a conviction that Britten's appointment could be a wrong and embarrassing move.

Among board members, Leslie Boosey was particularly active in proposing potential music directors. Early in the search he had suggested Eugene Goossens and John Barbirolli, and by July 1954 he was advocating Otto Ackermann and Hans Schmidt-Isserstedt in preference to Kempe. Surprisingly, he went on to suggest that Rafael Kubelik's attitude to opera was more broad than that of Kempe.

As it turned out, Kubelik was to be appointed music director from the beginning of the 1955/56 season. It was at Lord Harewood's suggestion that Webster went to hear him conduct Janáček's *Jenůfa* at Sadler's Wells in the spring of 1954. He was impressed and, despite Kubelik's limited operatic experience – largely concentrated in the two years he was in charge of the opera in Brno, from 1939 to 1941 – keen to pursue him. Kubelik was subsequently engaged, and conducted Smetana's *The Bartered Bride* in a new production, in English, at Covent Garden in the spring of 1955, as a prelude to his arrival in the autumn. The overture, with its rhythms incisively and buoyantly stated and yet infused with warmth and joy, still rings in my ears. It was a demonstration of music-making of a rare kind, to be followed by many others, all leaving a lasting impression on the company. It was Kubelik who really taught the orchestra to play with love and humanity.

From the beginning he was insistent on developing an ensemble, and went out of his way to ensure that every opera for which he was responsible was cast as far as possible from company members. He respected loyalties, and he set a standard of artistic and personal integrity which was as important for the House as a whole as for the company itself. His approach to every aspect of the company was straightforward, and there can be no doubt about the contribution he made to its growth – both as a musician and as a human being. When he arrived, nearly a decade after the founding of the company, there were still many who were ready to write off the whole enterprise. Kubelik proved them wrong, and by giving confidence to the orchestra, singers and staff he took them forward by leaps and bounds in the all too short period he was at Covent Garden and in spite of vicious attacks upon him, as a foreign music director, and on the company's spending of public money.

Kubelik's first opera at Covent Garden as music director was Verdi's *Otello*, with a magnificent cast including Ramón Vinay, Gré Brouwenstijn and Tito Gobbi, and with Peter Potter as producer and designs by Georges Wakhevitch. It was a huge success and a real demonstration of what the company could do.

On the first day of rehearsals Kubelik was quickly to show his mettle when Gobbi failed to appear. He would not accept any absenteeism without good reason, and told Webster that he would not work with Gobbi and that a replacement must be found. I remember the incident well. I had just arrived at Covent Garden as David Webster's assistant, and was mostly working in the boardroom adjoining his office while a window was being put into the only vacant space which could be found as an office for me. Webster outlined the situation and invited me to attend the meeting at which Kubelik would state his case. This was very simple: Gobbi was not there, so a substitute had to be engaged. Without the entire cast present at all sessions, the opera could not be satisfactorily prepared. Otakar Kraus, a compatriot of Kubelik's and a member of the company, was scheduled to take over the final performances from Gobbi, and it was decided that he should now sing them all. The news of Gobbi's sacking hit the newspaper headlines and was soon heard around the world. The effect was salutary, although Gobbi continued to protest that he had been unfairly treated – and by a conductor relatively inexperienced in opera. The performances vindicated Kubelik's action, however, and peace was eventually to be made with Gobbi.

Kubelik's unwillingness to compromise unreasonably was to be demonstrated time and time again, in relation to casting, rehearsal time or language. An example of the last occurred in the 1958/59 season, when Boris Christoff was cast for the title role in *Boris Godunov*, an opera so far sung in English by the entire cast except for Christoff, who performed in Russian, unable to learn and sing it in English. Mixed-language performances had been quite common but were on the wane and were finally banished by Kubelik. An opera now had to be presented in one language, and if *Boris* could not be performed in English then the entire cast would learn it in Russian. It was a mammoth undertaking, particularly at a time when singers were still coming to terms with learning roles in any language other than English, let alone one so remote from their experience as Russian.

When Kubelik was appointed, there was some fear that Rudolf Kempe might not return. This proved to be groundless: Kempe wanted to keep his Covent Garden connection and was encouraged to do so by Kubelik, who was not jealous of other conductors and welcomed all who would contribute to the well-being and advancement of the company. Another guest conductor was to be Carlo Maria Giulini, who first came to conduct memorable performances of *Don Carlos* in a glorious production by Luchino Visconti in 1958.

The major triumph of Kubelik's regime, and the one which epitomizes it most fully, was the 1957 production of Berlioz's *Les Troyens*. Following the staging of more or less the complete opera in Germany at the end of the last century and of a shortened version in Paris in 1921, there had been a lull in performances until 1935, when Erik Chisholm and the Glasgow Grand Opera Society performed the complete work. It was generally regarded as an unwieldy epic and too long to be presented in one evening. Kubelik and his cast – drawn entirely from the company, with the exception of Blanche Thebom as Dido – proved that belief wrong. With a straightforward and economical production by Sir John Gielgud, in designs by Mariano Andreu, Rafael Kubelik and his singers, performing in English, swept all before them. They demonstrated that the whole opera could be comfortably contained in an evening, and that its length, difficulties of casting and cost were not obstacles to its place in the repertoire. All of this was being shown by a company barely ten years old. In addition to the collective success, the production brought Jon Vickers convincingly to the attention of the world, within a year or two of his discovery by Webster in Canada and a successful debut in *Un Ballo in Maschera*. The eyes of the world were from now on increasingly turning to Covent Garden.

But Rafael Kubelik, the most human and sensitive of musicians, was not destined to be a music director for long. The rough and tumble of opera-house life were not for him, and the extent to which he gave himself to the company and his colleagues was tiring him. He had been shaken by a letter from Beecham, published in *The Times*, attacking the engagement of a foreigner as music director, in response to a letter from Kubelik himself in defence of English singers. Neither the hurt of this nor that of the failure of *Die Meistersinger* in 1957 was totally salved by the success of *Les Troyens*. His three-year contract was due to end in the summer of 1958, and he decided not to renew it.

So Covent Garden lost a truly remarkable musician and a very special man, who was not to conduct at the Royal Opera House again as often as we wanted. In later years overtures were made to him, but other commitments and ill health did not permit his return. It would have been wonderful if he could have conducted other Czech operas and for Covent Garden to have gained still more from his inspired music-making. His three years in London brought untold benefits to the company, and his contribution to its growth and development must never be forgotten or underrated. His approach to music was imbued with a deep spiritual quality, and his integrity and humanity were unmistakably clear in his performances. How I wish that we could have had more of him! We might not have had the excitement of what was to follow, but we would have had something more profound and lasting.

Another interregnum followed, during which the chairman, Viscount Waverley, died and was succeeded by the Earl of Drogheda. Here was a quite different person in charge, passionate about the Royal Opera House and intensely interested in all its detail. Nothing escaped his notice, and he could leave nothing alone. His interference could be infuriating, but there was no doubting that we shared a common aim: the success of the Royal Opera House.

To secure a place for Covent Garden on the world opera map, he argued the case for all operas to be performed in their original language. Increasingly this was already happening, and was wanted by British singers who were beginning to receive more and more invitations to sing in overseas theatres. It suited everybody to make the change – but not to the total exclusion of performances in English where works and circumstances demanded it, as was the case when Shostakovich's *Katerina Ismailova* was performed in English in the 1963/64 season, to facilitate understanding of a complex plot.

The need to find a successor to Kubelik remained. The names of Giulini and Kempe came up, and Benjamin Britten was proposed as a musical consultant, a role which he was willing to fulfil in giving informal advice. Other names which had been mentioned earlier were those of Georg Solti, Jaroslav Krombholc and Nello Santi.

An introduction to Solti was arranged by the Hungarian pianist Ilona Kabos in 1959, and over lunch an invitation to be Covent Garden's next music director was extended to him by Lord Drogheda. Solti was pleased to be asked, but after fifteen years as music director of Munich and Frankfurt he was not sure that he wanted to continue in an opera house. Moreover, he was not free, since he had recently signed a contract with the Los Angeles Philharmonic. This was to change. On his return to Los Angeles he discovered that, without consultation with him and contrary to his contract, Zubin Mehta had been engaged as assistant conductor. A row ensued and Solti resigned. He was now free to accept Covent Garden, which he did after seeking the advice of Bruno Walter.

It was agreed that he would begin as music director in the autumn of 1961. Before that he was to conduct *Der Rosenkavalier* in December 1959, with a magnificent cast including Elisabeth Schwarzkopf, Sena Jurinac and Kurt Böhme. Thus Covent Garden had its first taste of this dynamic musician, brimming with energy and imparting an excitement and rhythmic incisiveness in a manner to which orchestral players did not immediately warm. The musicians and staff did not quite know what to make of him, nor he of them. English ways were a mystery to him, and he could not understand how anything was ever achieved in what he clearly perceived as such a relaxed, even amateurish, manner. There appeared to him to be no formal hierarchy; most people called each other by their Christian names, yet respected those in authority and got on with their jobs.

After a successful *Rosenkavalier* he agreed to return early in 1961 to conduct a new production of Britten's *Midsummer Night's Dream*, which was followed by Gluck's *Iphigénie en Tauride* at the Edinburgh Festival. Webster was apprehensive about reaction to the engagement of another foreigner as music director and was determined to introduce him quietly to the House and the public. This paid off, and there was no adverse response until later – and that did not concern his origins.

In the summer of 1960 I was in Vienna and was invited to lunch by the Soltis at the Imperial Hotel, where they were staying. It was an agreeable occasion, with Solti insisting that I ate Tafelspitz – a Viennese boiled-beef dish. But I sensed an air of suspicion: I think he could not make head nor tail of this Englishman sitting opposite him. His wife, Heidi, on the other hand, was quite different and rapidly saw me as an ally. They would increasingly come to rely on me in London, and we all became good friends. I even found myself acting as intermediary when their marriage broke up. This was not an agreeable task, but Solti was showing as much trust in me as he ever could in anybody, and I wanted to help.

On looking back over the last fifty years, it is interesting to see how, more often than not, the right person has been in place at Covent Garden at just the right moment. This was true of Solti, whose arrival was opportune both for him and for Covent Garden. His international career was starting to flourish, and he needed a great opera house or orchestra from which to launch its next stage. Covent Garden gave him that platform. The opera company, having benefited greatly from working with Rafael Kubelik and other distinguished conductors and stage directors, was more than ready for – in fact needed – another boost of artistic leadership and inspiration.

At the beginning, Solti declared it his intention to make Covent Garden Opera the finest opera company in the world – a laudable ambition, which suited everybody. At the same time, this statement was marred for many by his view that there was precious little good about the existing Covent Garden, which needed all the overhaul and reviving which he could provide. Of course, there were improvements to be made – there always are. More rehearsal time was necessary, the orchestra had to be enlarged, and technical standards required attention. He believed that the chorus would gain from another chorus master, or at least from importing a European chorus master from time to time to supplement the work of Douglas Robinson by coaching in certain works. This made sense and has been a practice adopted over the years. But overall the company was not in the poor shape that Solti implied.

Solti, publicity-conscious, did not feel that he was being handled well by the press department. In those early days – and indeed in the years that followed – he craved recognition and encouragement. However, the press was often hostile to him. *Iphigénie* had not been well received in Edinburgh, and there continued to be an underlying current of adverse comment on his conducting, which some found episodic, superficial ('Solti skating over the score' was one *Times* headline) and inflexible. This was obviously disturbing and disagreeable, and, when sections of the audience expressed their views through booing, the whole London scene became increasingly difficult for him.

He was not helped initially by the productions for which he was conducting. After *Iphigénie* had been brought to London, a new production of the *Ring* was started, with Hans Hotter both singing and directing, and with designs by Herbert Kern in the place of Henry Moore, whom David Webster had hoped to entice into designing for the stage but who had declined the invitation. *Die Walküre*, the first part of this new *Ring* cycle to be performed, was badly received. The rest of the cycle with this team was abandoned and a fresh start was made with Günther Schneider-Siemssen replacing Kern and with Hotter as before.

An audience used to Rudolf Kempe's lyrical, restrained and subtly wrought approach to the *Ring* found themselves listening to something quite different with Solti – more dramatic and theatrical, and with climaxes built to fever pitch. In pursuit of this welter of excitement, the overall shape of an act, or indeed of the whole opera, could suffer – a point on to which critics would repeatedly latch.

Solti was nothing but adventurous, and agreed to the engagement of theatre directors for some of the operas for which he was responsible. The first was Peter Ustinov, to direct a triple bill of Ravel's *L'Heure Espagnole*, Schoenberg's *Erwartung* and Puccini's *Gianni Schicchi*. Unused to opera production, Ustinov sometimes failed to leave time for the music, and an outburst from the pit would ensue. This led him to give Solti the nickname of Soltissimo, and to lean over the orchestra rail and say, 'Now, Maestro, we must be cool and calm.' The results of these endeavours were mixed, with the Puccini inevitably receiving the most attention from Ustinov and *Erwartung* the least. I don't think he understood this piece, and poor Amy Shuard was left wandering aimlessly through the woods.

Solti's next encounter was with Sam Wanamaker, in Verdi's *La Forza del Destino*, and this was also to be unhappy in its outcome. The celebrated Italian painter and designer Renato Guttoso had been engaged for the decor. Unfortunately, he and Wanamaker fell out, and it was eventually decided that Wanamaker should finish the designs. These were sparse and innovative for a nineteenth-century opera, and were many years ahead of their time.

Casting had also been problematic, with Leontyne Price and Jon Vickers not available as had been hoped. Carlo Bergonzi, the greatest of tenors but a poor actor, had been pushed into acting by Wanamaker, with inevitable results, and Floriana Cavalli, recommended by Carlo Maria Giulini following her success in the Verdi Requiem in Leeds the previous year, sang Leonora. Sadly, she was not in good form when she arrived for rehearsals, but Solti decided to persevere with her, only to have her sing disastrously on the first night. She was heavily booed, as was John Shaw, an Australian baritone brought into the company to replace a favourite with the audience, the French Canadian Louis Quilico. It was a disastrous evening, which hit Solti badly. I often wonder if the outcome might have been different had the soprano been good: public response can so easily be influenced by the success or failure of the leading lady.

Solti was not faring well critically with Mozart. In his first season, *Don Giovanni* had been mounted with a wonderful cast in a production by Franco Zeffirelli. Unfortunately, Zeffirelli's strongly romantic conception resulted in gigantic sets which dwarfed the singers and the action, and scene changes seriously impeded the dramatic flow of the opera. Musically, Solti won few plaudits, and among the cast Cesare Siepi was critical of Solti's approach to Mozart. With a cast to dream about for a new production of *Le Nozze di Figaro* a year later – including Ilva Ligabue, Mirella Freni, Teresa Berganza, Tito Gobbi and Geraint Evans – public and critical response to his Mozart conducting was little better, with complaints about the orchestra being too loud and the music too hard-driven. Again he was not helped by an uninspired production, by Otto Fritz Schuh.

This was a worrying and disagreeable time for Solti, who was on the point of quitting, unable to tolerate any more adverse criticism and booing. It was also uncomfortable for Covent Garden, as it faced the premature departure of its music director, and under the unhappiest of circumstances.

On returning home one night from Covent Garden, I was telephoned by Solti to be told that he could not remain in London. He asked me to see him immediately at his house, because he had something that he needed to show me. When I arrived, he took me to his white Mercedes, over which had been written with a black felt-tip pen, 'Go home Solti.' This was shattering for him, as was my discovery the next day that posters on Charing Cross station had been similarly defaced. There was a serious anti-Solti campaign afoot which had to be defused. The fact that he and Jon Vickers had fallen out, with Vickers vowing never to sing with him again, was not helping.

In his memoirs, Solti regrets this incident with Vickers but professes ignorance of the reason. However, it was clear. It was a matter of two immensely strong characters confronting each other. The tenor felt himself in a straitjacket as Solti tried to impose his interpretation of Siegmund, and also found the orchestra intolerably loud. Properly protective of his voice, he decided to have no more of Solti for fear that damage would be done. It was interesting, if disturbing, to discover how widespread this anti-Solti mood was around town. For example, an assistant in a record shop – a Covent Garden regular – one day told me that she and a good many others supported Vickers and were worried about the loudness of the orchestra under Solti in relation to all singers.

The booing continued, and a way of stopping it still had to be found. It came through a chance phone call from a doctor friend to tell me of her disquiet over what was going on. She was a regular in the gallery and, knowing most of those around her, said that she could identify the boo-ers. There were only a small number, all frequenting the upper parts of the House. I suggested that I should talk to them and explain the damage they would do to Covent Garden if they persisted. Fifteen or sixteen agreed to meet over supper in Hampstead. As you would expect, they were committed and intelligent opera lovers but genuinely dismayed by Solti's musical approach. I explained the psychological harm that can be inflicted on performers by booing and asked that, instead of booing, they should simply not applaud if they were discontented with a performance. They felt this was an ineffective way of showing their disapproval, but, having told me what was troubling them, they agreed not to indulge in further booing at least for the time being. They were true to their word.

Solti had suffered grievously during his first two years in London, and the renewal of his contract was in doubt, despite the support of the board and management and our insistence, at times of greatest stress, that the future was unimaginable without him. Facing booing is a hor-rible and destructive experience, and it becomes even worse when its occurrence is expected every time a curtain call is taken. There were occasions when I had physically to push Solti to take calls because of this. Failure to appear increases the indignation of the discontented in an audience; defiance by performers has to be shown by continuing to take calls. At Bayreuth, Wolfgang Wagner, keen on controversy, delights in pushing artists through the metal door in the iron curtain to face the audience reaction, whether good or bad.

The extent to which Solti's first years might have been made easier by the appointment of a director of productions or by different producers from those engaged is hard to answer, since the reasons expressed to me for the hostility were usually related more to the pit than to the stage. But what might have emerged from the start was a consistent style of musical and dramatic approach to opera, which would have created a lasting legacy.

September 1964 saw the first complete *Ring* with Georg Solti. Happily it was a success and demonstrated the strength of Solti's musical author-ity and his increasing acceptance by public and critics, although the latter were never to be really comfortable with him, nor he with them. The same season was also the occasion of two of Solti's major triumphs and contributions to Covent Garden: a production of Schoenberg's *Moses und Aron*, with Peter Hall as director and John Bury as designer, and *Arabella*, directed by Rudolf Hartmann and designed by Peter Rice.

The Strauss found Solti in his element. The sounds from the pit were sumptuous, and Hartmann – a lifetime of Strauss opera productions behind him – ensured that the stage action was in accord with the score. The glorious cast included Lisa della Casa and Dietrich Fischer-Dieskau, in his Covent Garden debut. But just as important were the rest of the cast, which consisted entirely of British singers – mostly from within the company. Solti was quick to see the benefit for the company in developing its own talent, and never missed an opportunity to do so. Indigenous artists mattered to him, and many benefited from working with him.

Solti had accepted that some operas would be performed in English. One was the Schoenberg. The total resources of Covent Garden were concentrated on this production, which proved to be disruptive to the maintenance of the repertory around it but at the same time gave Solti and Hall the space and time for preparation which a work of this complexity requires. It was a *succès d'estime* – one of the company's greatest post-war triumphs, attracting enthusiastic audiences and wide critical attention and acclaim.

Covent Garden's world standing was now established on the foundations firmly laid by Rankl and Kubelik. *Les Troyens* had shown how a young team could rise to the heights, and as the years went by it was clear to all that such successes were not one-off chance happenings but the product of a talented and increasingly confident company. Solti was enhancing this growth through his ability to energize rehearsals and performances. It was an extraordinary gift of his to attend a rehearsal which was slow, perhaps even dull and boring, and suddenly bring the whole scene to life in a way which fired singers and orchestral musicians to give more than they thought they could.

Moses und Aron was also important because it fulfilled an earlier wish of Solti's, for a regular working relationship with Peter Hall. They went on together to productions of *Die Zauberflöte*, *Eugene Onegin* and *Tristan und Isolde*.

Another theatre producer, Clifford Williams, from Stratford, was introduced to Covent Garden by Joan Ingpen, a former agent but by then occupying Lord Harewood's position. In January 1966 Williams directed

Der Fliegende Holländer in designs by Sean Kenny. It was not a success – largely, I believe, because the unusual concept, dependent on a moving platform, was ahead of its time and because the Dutchman's ship could not be seen by those in the gallery. Here Solti suffered for reasons other than musical.

Another Strauss opera was introduced to Covent Garden by Solti in the summer of 1967. *Die Frau ohne Schatten* was musically magnificent but let down by the staging. This was again in the hands of Rudolf Hartmann, who, with the support of Solti, opted for Josef Svoboda as designer. Hartmann's traditional direction and Svoboda's unconventional designs resulted in a complete mismatch of styles, to the detriment of the production.

Solti's international career had really taken off. His recording of the complete *Ring*, which he had made for Decca with the Vienna Philharmonic, had stunned and delighted record buyers and many critics. Chicago and Paris were beckoning, and his desire to lead a great symphony orchestra was strong. Nevertheless, he wanted to complete ten years at Covent Garden, so that he had a stay in round figures in London and could claim twenty-five consecutive years as a music director of opera companies in Europe. His wish was granted, which also enabled us to achieve something which we all wanted: a visit by the Royal Opera – as, from 1969, it now was – to Munich and Berlin, under his direction.

This took place in April and May 1970, with a repertoire of *Don Carlos*, *Falstaff* and a new opera by Richard Rodney Bennett, *Victory*. Solti and Edward Downes were the conductors, and the casts were largely British. The visit was hugely successful, and showed European audiences how far opera in England had advanced. The boost to the morale and spirit of the company was immeasurable.

Solti was bent on success and went out of his way to bring it about. Maximum impact and excitement were the order of the day. In Berlin, for example, he had the pit floor raised to its highest convenient level so that the introduction to the auto-da-fé scene in *Don Carlos* could be as forceful as possible. In Berlin there was one lapse in his judgement of singers' attitudes and feelings when before *Don Carlos* he urged the cast to remember company interests rather than their own. Naturally they wanted personal success, but that of the company came first, as it had always had done. They were so aware of this that they needed no prompting, and resented the implication that it might have been otherwise.

Georg Solti certainly enabled the Royal Opera to secure a place on the world cultural map, and in so doing he encouraged many British singers and helped to develop their careers. The downside was his inability to trust and his wish to impose his interpretation too inflexibly upon singers and musicians. Some could accept this, others could not. His quest for precision in orchestral playing meant that he left nothing to chance or to the responsibility of the individual player. Every chord had to be balanced, often with an assistant conducting while Solti listened from outside the pit. It was a slow process, and could result in a loss of spontaneity as well as being irritating to the players.

This gave rise to ribbing by musicians impatient of his methods and of his technique, which was not the soundest (as has also been true of some other great conductors). There might be a flick of the wrist at an unexpected and inappropriate moment, or a sudden shake of the head. An example of this occurred in a performance of *Rosenkavalier* when the E flat clarinet player was counting endless bars' rest, caught Solti's eye and saw a flick of the head. He believed that he still had ten bars to go but, assuming that the maestro must be right, came in. He was several bars early! Accidents happen, but players do look for security.

At the end of one tiring rehearsal, a player raised his hand to ask a question. Solti, also tired, was requested to look at bar so and so, and, after frantic page turning and bar counting, his attention was drawn to the second-horn part. Solti was mystified. 'What is it?' he asked impatiently. 'Very beautiful, Maestro, isn't it?' replied the player. A silly story, but it illustrates a point, which British players more than any others are capable of making when they reckon enough is enough.

During his Covent Garden days, Solti's recording career prospered. He was winning many prizes, and Decca employed him to the full. The orchestra and chorus, believing that there could also be opportunities for them to make discs, looked to him as music director to ensure that they were included in some of these recording projects. Sadly, he appeared not to recognize a need or obligation to do this. *Don Carlos* was the only complete opera recording made by Covent Garden forces under his direction in those ten years; another recording, that of *Eugene Onegin*, was to follow some years later. It seemed to most people that he was so intent on his own career and pursued it so ruthlessly that he did not want to hinder its progress by arguing about the use of Royal Opera House resources when the Vienna Philharmonic was on offer. There can be no doubt that Decca preferred that orchestra to Covent Garden's, but by then Solti was surely in a strong enough position to have struck a deal which would have given a reasonable proportion of his recording work to his own orchestra and chorus. This would have endeared him much more to the House.

He was a man of extremes: autocratic and ruthless in his work, but full of warmth and charm when the occasion demanded, in both personal and professional life. He was concerned and compassionate to anyone in need, and performed many acts of generosity. His family brought him huge pleasure and contentment. Even so, he was forever studying new scores and restudying familiar ones, all with an eye on the future and engagements well into the next century. A restless energy was at work and could never be really stilled.

Whatever the downsides – and in his early lack of success and his failure to use the Royal Opera House orchestra and chorus extensively for recordings, there were some both for him and for Covent Garden – the Solti years will go down in the annals as a hugely important and memorable period in the Royal Opera House's post-war development. His arrival was timely, and he made the company identify its weaknesses and find remedies and greater strengths to take it on to higher standards of performance.

As the fame of Covent Garden Opera grew, there was an increasing feeling that its progress and its world standing should be recognized by the addition of 'Royal' to its title. The Queen was petitioned through the Home Secretary for the granting of this accolade, and on 22 October 1968 the Home Secretary informed Lord Drogheda that Her Majesty had approved the recommendation that the Covent Garden Opera Company should in future be known as the Royal Opera. This was a fitting tribute to a company which from modest beginnings in 1947 had in the course of two decades achieved international status and acclaim.

Solti continued to conduct at Covent Garden regularly except for one unfortunate interlude which occurred after his unhappy experiences at Bayreuth with a controversial Peter Hall production of the *Ring* in the summer of 1983. At the end of the cycle he told me that he never wanted to conduct opera again. I protested at the time, and suggested that he would eventually change his mind after further reflection. I heard no more on the subject, and after this I was not to be so much in touch with him for reasons attributable to him. Eventually he told me of his hurt and disappointment that he had received no invitation to conduct at Covent Garden for a long time. I reminded him of what he had told me, to which he replied that he had not intended to include the Royal Opera

House in this ban. How we all wished that he had been explicit at the beginning and that we had not taken him at his word!

As Solti's regime was coming to an end, there was much discussion about a successor. We did not want there to be a gap, and so an early decision was important. There was general agreement that the next music director should be an Englishman, which limited the field but still left a difficult choice. Four conductors emerged as candidates: Colin Davis, Charles Mackerras, John Pritchard and Edward Downes. In the end Colin Davis was approached and came to Covent Garden in September 1971.

Although he was a well-established conductor, having been music director of Sadler's Wells Opera from 1961 to 1965 and chief conductor of the BBC Symphony Orchestra from 1967 to 1971, and had conducted at Covent Garden on a number of occasions, including a memorable production and recording of *Les Troyens* in 1969, the aura which had surrounded Solti on his departure did not make Davis's arrival comfortable or easy. The House had become used to Solti and his ways, and suddenly there had to be a fresh start and adjustment to different habits and demands. There was an air of uncertainty. Questions were also being asked about the reality of Solti's legacy, the condition in which he left the company, the extent to which he had developed his career at its expense, and so on. Then attention would turn to Colin Davis. Was he going to leave musicians in their posts or was he going to seek early replacements? These and many associated topics occupied break times in the canteen and the pubs. But soon unease disappeared and the House settled down to another fruitful period with Colin Davis continuing as music director for fifteen years.

From the beginning Davis was convinced that a director of productions would be an asset, helping to raise production and technical standards and providing greater consistency and cohesion in production style. Peter Hall was the obvious choice, and he agreed to accept the post. Having worked at the Royal Opera House on a number of productions, he knew the weaknesses, the inconsistency of the technical operation, and the dangers of a creeping generalization and approximation in technical areas – especially lighting. These were not the product of incompetence or indifference – far from it – but the result of time pressures and cramped and outmoded facilities. Nevertheless, we believed that we could achieve more, even with our relatively primitive equipment, with Hall in place.

A pattern of work for the three of us quickly evolved. Regular planning meetings were essential, and in the absence of one of us measures were to be taken to ensure that the missing person was kept informed of decisions and problems. It was also proposed that, if there was failure to agree, I would be the arbiter and my judgement would be accepted.

This planning for the future took place in the year before Colin Davis and Peter Hall were due to take up their appointments – a year during which Hall produced three operas: Michael Tippett's *The Knot Garden* with Colin Davis, and *Eugene Onegin* and *Tristan und Isolde* with Georg Solti. Hall's presence in the House over a longish period showed how we would benefit from him being regularly with us. Alas, that was not to be, for by the end of the *Tristan* performances in the summer of 1971 he had asked to be released from his contract, which was to begin a few months later. It was a great blow.

I believe that, as the result of his recent experiences at Covent Garden, Hall doubted that the organization could deliver performances at a consistently high technical standard. I also sensed that he wanted to be seen to be free in the event of the National Theatre considering him to be its director. This was always denied, but it would have been understandable, since it was common knowledge that Laurence Olivier would soon be stepping down, and nobody would want to miss the chance of succeeding him. If the technical factors at Covent Garden had been more satisfactory the outcome might have been different, even though I suspect that Hall's heart really lies in the straight theatre, albeit with regular excursions into opera. Nevertheless, I lament our failure to stay together.

The first production for Colin Davis was *Le Nozze di Figaro* – or *The Marriage of Figaro*, as we wanted it. We had been debating the language issue for some time, and were generally agreed that most operas should be sung in their original language but that there were exceptions which dictated a flexible language policy. With the interchange between characters in *Figaro*, particularly in the recitatives, we believed that there would be real advantage in the understanding of the audience if this opera was performed in the vernacular. We knew there would be opposition from the board, who were wedded to a policy of original language only, forgetting that even with Rafael Kubelik some works had been given in translation, and their first reaction was indeed predictable and unyielding. We continued to argue the case for exceptions to the rule, however, and eventually we won them over – but only after dinner for the entire board at my home in Earls Court Gardens and on the understanding that future performances of *Figaro* would not always be in English.

We had no doubts that the cast would be happy with the outcome, but we had overlooked one factor: the intransigence of Reri Grist, who refused to perform in English. Her contract, signed long before this debate, indicated Italian. She outmanoeuvred us, and we had no option but to revert to the original language. It was a huge disappointment, but we had established a new principle which would make future discussions on the subject easier.

Another memorable event occurred with this production: the discovery of Kiri Te Kanawa. We already knew about her from the Opera Centre, where she was studying, but none of us was quite prepared for what we heard when she auditioned. It was an exciting moment, even if the decision to put such an inexperienced singer into the major role of the Countess was a gamble. But somehow there was no doubt in our minds that she would succeed, and we all felt compelled to go ahead with her. She proved an outstanding success, and so began her extraordinary career.

Colin Davis, already a well-established conductor of Mozart (as of Berlioz and Tippett), was in his element as he conducted his first production at Covent Garden as music director. Always willing to seek and take advice from well-informed musicians and linguists, he demonstrated the benefits of working with Ubaldo Gardini as the coach for opera in Italian and Italian opera, and he was increasingly to rely on Gardini (the husband of Sylvia Fisher) as he moved into that repertoire. With a production by John Copley, and a strong cast, *Figaro* was an auspicious opening for Davis, although his success was to wane for a while as he moved into territory less familiar to him.

From the beginning of the Davis regime we had determined to present contemporary opera as frequently as possible, and later we embarked on a programme of one newly commissioned work each year. This was ambitious and likely to run into trouble, but we believed we had a responsibility to encourage the writing of new opera and pressed on accordingly. The commissioning fell into place without difficulty, but its fulfilment in performance was another matter. Here we were often hampered by lack of money, which resulted in postponement or, in the case of Thea Musgrave's *Harriet*, inability to produce the delivered work at all. This was acutely embarrassing and a hard decision for the composer to accept.

The first modern opera to be presented in this period was not a commissioned work, but one on which its composer, Peter Maxwell Davies, had been working for a long time, with little expectation of having it performed. We knew about *Taverner*, and approached Maxwell Davies about presenting it at Covent Garden. The work perhaps suffered from too long a gestation period and its structure could have been tighter with some dramatic advice during its writing. Nevertheless, the production and performances made for compelling music theatre and created a marked impact.

In presenting contemporary opera, it is too often the case that financial considerations prevent revival after the first performances, with the result that there is not the opportunity to establish works securely with the public and to consolidate their place in the company's repertoire. We experimented with *Taverner* by repeating it at the end of the 1972/73 season with two other operas – Richard Rodney Bennett's *Victory* and Michael Tippett's *The Knot Garden* – in a series of performances at reduced prices. This experiment won modest public support and ideally should have been repeated, but unfortunately our limited resources made that impossible.

Achieving a balance between the classical, the romantic and the contemporary in the repertoire was too often frustrated by financial considerations: the need for high box-office returns and to use resources prudently. The outcome was usually not in favour of the contemporary work, much as we wanted to expand that territory. In the mid-1980s I was keen to present an opera by John Eaton, an American composer who had written a work based on *The Tempest* and who was interested in writing more. Many regard him as the most interesting and original of American opera composers. True, the forces which he requires are large and his language is far from straightforward, but he writes superbly for the voice. Unfortunately the financial risks were too great for us and his work remains unknown in the UK. It was a huge pity that we could not sensibly pursue this and similar ideas because of our slender funds. There was a steady flow of suggestions from composers, with works either already written, such as Robin Holloway's *Clarissa* and William Alwyn's *Miss Julie*, or projected, like Peter Maxwell Davies's *Resurrection*. Sadly, none saw the light of day at Covent Garden.

Colin Davis strongly supported the company ideal, with the integration of guest and company singers when operas demanded casting beyond our own resources. This became increasingly the case as the company's permanent strength declined because of financial stringency and the desire of many singers to freelance, while keeping Covent Garden as their home base. Ease of travel was making this common practice in European companies, and the long-held concept of the ensemble from which most operas would be cast was on the wane. At Covent Garden it had always been the custom to invite the greatest singers of the world to appear there, and the public expected that this would be so. Happily, there has for many years been a strong desire among conductors, singers and directors to come to London, and often for fees lower than they have enjoyed elsewhere.

Davis recognized the desirability and necessity of continuing to invite guest singers, but found himself frustrated by the late arrival of some who considered rehearsal periods too long or whose contracts had to recognize that they would be unavailable at the beginning of rehearsals. At such moments a decision whether to continue with them has to be made, and if their presence is considered vital a compromise has to be accepted. We struggled to avoid this and, aware of the Gobbi incident with Kubelik, insisted on stringent adherence to the contract. Sometimes accused of presenting instant opera, we could convincingly reject this charge, even though we may not have always won the battle over lateness. What late arrivers forget is that the rest of the cast has assembled on time and that the other singers may not know their roles as well as they themselves do (or think they do) and want the rehearsal time, which will be really profitable only if the cast is complete and as scheduled for performance. Resentment and discontent are easily provoked in these situations.

His first years at Covent Garden were not easy for Colin Davis. Public response was hesitant and on occasions hostile to his initial stylistic uncertainty in Italian opera and Wagner. However, his performances were well prepared, and his strong instinctive musicianship, coupled with his friendly personality, was winning him support in the House, in spite of moments of unease, particularly in relation to the board. Part of this difficulty arose, I think, from a constant ill-defined search for something beyond himself, which, coupled with a sense of insecurity and a tendency towards self-deprecation, made him feel ill at ease in the presence of board members and quite a few others. Ways around these difficulties were found, and as he gained confidence many things fell naturally into place. For me, life with him was stimulating and adventurous.

We were both concerned about access, aware not only that seat prices could be a deterrent, but that the red-plush atmosphere of the Royal Opera House itself could be intimidating to some. In our minds the solution was simple: take out the seats in the stalls for a week or so and introduce opera and ballet proms. This we did and, in association with the BBC, the first prom performance was given in 1971, with Boris Christoff as Boris in *Boris Godunov*, to be followed by an annual series, generously supported by the Midland Bank from 1972 until closure in 1997. These performances not only brought new audiences but enabled many regulars to move down from the amphitheatre and enjoy the close proximity of the stage. It was mainly this informed body which created a stimulating audience–performer relationship. At the end of every prom performance, singers, dancers and conductors invariably commented that performing to this audience was a rare and treasured experience. Boris Christoff, who was initially reluctant to participate in a prom performance, was moved to tears by the audience's response.

Another innovation was opera matinees, to enable those who lived out of London, or did not want to travel at night, to come to opera as well as ballet on a Saturday afternoon. Arrangements were made with British Rail and regional arts boards to facilitate travel and theatre-ticket purchase. Unfortunately the response was not as good as we had hoped and, financial considerations apart, pressure on the stage for rehearsals made Saturday afternoons less and less available for performances. A modernized stage will solve this problem.

Davis was also open to a fresh and less expensive production style. An early example of this was Britten's *Peter Grimes*. This was due for revival in the 1974/75 season. Elijah Moshinsky was to re-produce it, with Tim O'Brien and Tazeena Firth overhauling the Tanya Moiseiwitch sets and costumes. The estimated cost of this was £15,000, which seemed to me a ludicrously large sum of money to spend on an existing production. So I asked the team if they could make a new production for this amount. They returned with a model which would have cost £45,000. I rejected it, and urged them to think again. This resulted in the production which is still in use and which cost £21,000 to make. This production has always been well received by audiences and critics, but was not so enthusiastically received by the composer, who objected to the absence of curtains between scenes – a requirement stated in the score but impossible within the context of this design concept.

Soon after Davis's arrival, thought had to be given to the *Ring* and its centenary in 1976. If Peter Hall had still been with us, we would have looked no further. But by then he was director of the National Theatre, and we were more inclined to look to a German-speaking producer who was immersed in Wagner but who had not yet directed the *Ring*. Having seen one production by Götz Friedrich, I suggested that he might be the person for whom we were looking. We decided to explore this possibility, and I met Friedrich at Amsterdam Airport. The discussion was good, and he was engaged, with Josef Svoboda later appointed as the set designer. *Das Rheingold* and *Die Walküre* were to be produced in the 1973/74 season, followed by *Siegfried* in the next year and *Götterdämmerung* and the complete cycle in 1976. The collaboration between Davis and Friedrich was highly successful. Some found fault with Davis's early conducting of Wagner, but generally the performances were well received.

The year of the *Ring* centenary, 1976, was also important for the Royal Opera for another reason: an exchange with La Scala, Milan. When the United Kingdom joined the Common Market in 1973, a fund was established to finance cultural exchanges. Since it had been set up by Geoffrey Rippon, who as Chancellor of the Duchy of Lancaster had negotiated Britain's entry into the European Community, it was known as Rippon money. Through the British Council, I bid for £250,000 of this to finance an exchange between London and Milan. The bid was successful, and negotiations with La Scala began. In the midst of these, John Henniker Major, with whom I had arranged these funds, had been compelled to leave the British Council, but as he did so he assured me that our money would be secure with his successor. It was.

We proposed to take to Milan Berlioz's *Benvenuto Cellini*, Britten's *Peter Grimes* and Mozart's *La Clemenza di Tito*, which had been newly introduced to Covent Garden by Colin Davis in the 1973/74 season. All of these operas were new to La Scala. The Italians were to bring their outstanding and incomparable Giorgio Strehler production of Verdi's *Simone Boccanegra*, Rossini's *La Cenerentola* and the Verdi Requiem, all conducted by Claudio Abbado. For us this was a huge undertaking. Here was a company barely thirty years old challenging one of the oldest and most distinguished opera houses in the world – an operatic shrine.

Preparations were going well until during a visit to Milan some months before our exchange I discovered from a conversation with Paolo Grassi, the soprintendente of La Scala, that he had no money for his part of the deal. This was an extraordinary state of affairs. Usually it is the other way round, with the foreign company in funds and Covent Garden not. Grassi said he had no way of finding the money, and the situation looked bleak until a few weeks later when he was in London. One evening he was with me at a performance which also happened to be attended by Denis Healey, the Chancellor of the Exchequer. Knowing of Healey's interest in music, in Italy, in things Italian and in opportunities to speak Italian, I introduced Grassi to him and explained the dilemma. Without hesitation he asked Grassi if he could discuss the problem with Signor Colombo, the Italian Finance Minister, whom he was shortly to meet at a conference. Naturally the offer was accepted enthusiastically, and within days the money was in place for La Scala's visit. As a token of their gratitude, La Scala presented the Chancellor with a facsimile of the autograph of Verdi's *Falstaff* after their first London performance.

Touring is a wonderful way of pulling companies together and strengthening company spirit – especially when a challenge like that of playing at La Scala is involved. Successful foreign visits also stimulate home-audience interest and appreciation. Our season in Milan was an unqualified success – triumphant even – which brought great dividends in its wake, not least in firmly establishing Colin Davis as music director. It was also intensely gratifying that he had been engaged to conduct *Tannhäuser* at Bayreuth, the first British conductor to be invited there. Many things were falling into place for him.

An embarrassing episode preceded our opening in Milan. At a press conference, attended by La Scala's management and ourselves, there was much delving into the relative costs of running the two companies, the size of subsidies and the financing of this exchange. The Italian press was amazed at the differences, and pressed Grassi hard for a justification of La Scala's much higher level of expenditure and subvention. He, a shrewd and political creature, ducked the questions with remarkable skill, but the comparisons reported in the newspapers did not help his cause.

For years Covent Garden was managed by a small but efficient and dedicated team. After Georg Solti's departure, it was not long before Joan Ingpen left her position as director of opera planning to take up a similar appointment in Paris at the invitation of Rolf Liebermann and at Solti's suggestion. This is a key appointment in any opera house, and there are few men and women well-enough qualified – with the necessary musical and operatic knowledge and judgement of singers – to fill these posts around the world. There was one person, Helga Schmidt, whom I wanted to join us. Following a period at the Vienna State Opera, she had been working for the impresario Sandor Gorlinsky in London and was on the way to New York, at the invitation of Schuyler Chapin, the then general manager of the Metropolitan Opera House, to occupy the same position at the Met as I wanted her to fill in London. I phoned her immediately, and almost as she was boarding the plane I persuaded her to drop the Met and come to us. It was an unfriendly act for the Met to swallow, but her arrival at Covent Garden added greatly to our strength and prestige. The daughter of a distinguished Viennese musician, and a reliable judge of singers and conductors, there are few people in the operatic and musical world whom she does not know. She is also a person with whom it is a joy to work, and, together with her able assistant, Jenny Selby, she was soon immersed in planning and casting with Colin Davis and myself.

By the beginning of the 1980s Helga Schmidt's health was troubling her and I sensed that she needed respite from a demanding job and would benefit from more time at home in Italy. In the end she decided to leave us, and we were faced with finding a replacement. She had set a standard which it was hard to follow, but there was another person whose work I had greatly admired: Peter Mario Katona, at the time head of the artistic administration in Hamburg and working with Christoph von Dohnanyi as intendant. Before this he had been in Frankfurt, again with Dohnanyi as intendant, and with Gerard Mortier, the director of the Salzburg Festival. His credentials were impeccable, and there was no doubt that we needed him above anyone else. When I first approached him, he said that he very much wanted to be at Covent Garden, but that loyalty to Dohnanyi made it impossible for him to leave Hamburg. I was disappointed, but could only admire his strong sense of commitment. We looked around for other candidates, but could find none of the stature of Schmidt or Katona. Then came the news that Dohnanyi was going to Cleveland. I phoned Katona to say that the situation was now surely different and that he could be free to come to Covent Garden. He agreed, and has been artistic administrator ever since and a vital source of continuity – particularly through the troubled times of the last few years, when his sense of loyalty has stood Covent Garden in good stead.

Collaboration on the *Ring* brought Colin Davis and Götz Friedrich closely together, and we began to consider a formal appointment for

Friedrich at Covent Garden, ideally as director of productions. He was pleased to be asked, but declined because of his post as chief régisseur at Hamburg, believing that he had not time to fulfil both functions adequately. Instead he became principal producer. Unfortunately this became little more than a title, and he made no input to our deliberations on planning and casting. This was disappointing but probably inevitable given his other commitments and a later deteriorating relationship between him and Colin Davis following an unsuccessful production of *Idomeneo* with unconvincing designs by Stefan Lazidiris which led to frustration on the part of both the conductor and the singers – although Friedrich was to return to work with Davis on *Lulu*. In any event, Friedrich was to become intendant of the Deutsche Oper in Berlin and would have been compelled to give up ties with us.

Davis went from strength to strength as music director and principal conductor, interested and concerned about the programme as a whole, and attending performances other than his own. He realized that it was important to have the great conductors of the world at Covent Garden if standards were to be maintained and improved, and, unlike his predecessor, he was not jealous but gave us a free rein to engage whoever we thought was best suited to particular operas. Thus we were able to bring to London an array of conductors who contributed significantly to the development of the Royal Opera.

Another important aspect of Davis's work at Covent Garden was his desire to conduct ballet. The response from the Royal Ballet was lukewarm, because of their fear that he would not understand dancers' needs and might adopt uncomfortable tempi. Davis was determined to prove them wrong. Michael Somes, the guardian of the Royal Ballet's heritage and the dictator of musical standards, presented the biggest challenge to Davis. For a time they worked together constructively, but disagreements between them meant that the partnership was destined not to last. Nevertheless, fine performances were given and there is no doubt that the Royal Ballet gained from this collaboration.

For Davis there was no question of the Royal Opera House being a museum: rather, it was a vital and vibrant institution where the art of music drama was presented freshly and continually renewed. In all aspects of life Colin Davis is in quest of the truth. This enables him to make music speak with the most telling effect – vividly and meaningfully. With all composers, but particularly with Mozart, he has the ability to penetrate the surface and reveal what is beneath, directly and truthfully.

There are few, if any, who can rival his understanding of the genius of Mozart and convey so tellingly its many facets, its laughter and its pain and suffering. Davis gave of himself generously at Covent Garden. He was demanding – and rightly so – but he infused everybody with his enthusiasm for music and the theatre. For all of us, work was serious but also fun.

As he progressed through the repertoire, he began to conduct operas with which he was less familiar, but to all of them he brought the same flair and intuition. *Werther* and *Samson et Dalila*, for example, he swept along with a deeply felt ardour and made us listen to them with fresh ears. In addition to conducting the operas of Michael Tippett, with whose works he has always been closely associated, and those of Britten, he introduced other twentieth-century operas to the repertoire, including the three-act version of *Lulu* and Zemlinsky's *Eine Florentinische Tragödie*, both of which were receiving their first British performances. The company was increasingly inspired and driven to higher achievements by him.

His commitment to the company was shown in all sorts of ways, and not least in ensuring that Covent Garden forces were engaged for his opera recordings. He was also loyal to soloists, and gave as many opportunities as possible to that large group of singers who regarded Covent Garden as home. He was protective of singers and was careful not to expose them in roles for which they were not ready or for which they were unsuitable. He was well aware that a career could be ruined by wrongful exposure, especially in Covent Garden's unhelpful acoustic. Those who enjoyed success at the Coliseum or Bayreuth – both theatres with good and flattering acoustics – could suffer a different fate at Covent Garden, with its short reverberation time. If a role could not be well cast, the opera was abandoned until a suitable singer appeared. This caused us to offend Michael Tippett when we said that we could not find all the right singers for a new production of *The Midsummer Marriage* which we had planned for his eightieth birthday.

In the autumn of 1979 the Royal Opera visited Korea and Japan for the first time and performed *Tosca*, *Peter Grimes* and *Die Zauberflöte*, all conducted by Colin Davis, except for two performances of *Tosca* which were conducted by Robin Stapleton. It was an immensely enjoyable as well as successful tour, and again showed the strength of the company and its sense of common purpose. Not surprisingly, *Peter Grimes* was the least well booked of the three operas in both countries.

After its first performance in Seoul, however, it became the talk of the town and tickets for the second performance were in great demand. In Japan the work was well received but no more interest was aroused. The difference in audience response was revealing.

Another major overseas event took place in the summer of 1984: the first visit of the Royal Opera to America, to give eleven performances at the Olympic Arts Festival in Los Angeles. Once again the programme included *Peter Grimes* and *Zauberflöte*, but with the addition of a new production of *Turandot* by Andrei Serban in designs by Sally Jacobs, receiving its first performance at the Dorothy Chandler Pavilion. All the performances were conducted by Colin Davis – a marathon for him, but all-important for the company. Mounting a new production of an opera is difficult and demanding even in your own theatre, and away from home it is still more fraught. The way in which the technicians, the staff and the company rallied and responded to every situation was heart-warming and showed once again how powerful the family spirit was.

Turandot was rapturously received, as were the other two operas. The season caused the Los Angeles critic Martin Bernheimer to write:

> The Royal Opera deserved the euphoria it created here. Our British visitors set standards ... This was grandiose opera produced by a major company. Los Angeles hadn't seen anything like it for a long, long time ... Most important, perhaps, this company commands the services of a great conductor, a great chorus and a great orchestra. That claim cannot be made for many companies here or abroad.

Our visit aroused the interest of a number of people wanting to re-establish regular opera performances in Los Angeles, and brought about the creation of the Music Center Opera Company a year or two later. Peter Hemmings became its director and Placido Domingo its artistic adviser, shortly to be its director.

Colin Davis, confident and totally immersed in the Royal Opera, wanted to renew his contract beyond the 1985/86 season, at which point he would have completed fifteen years. The board recognized his success and his huge contribution to the growth of the company, but neverthe-less believed that it was time to bring in another music director. Sad as I was to see him go, I believe that the decision was right – partly because fifteen years is a long time, and partly because of the immediate future: the redevelopment of the Opera House, its necessary closure and reopening, all of which demanded continuity in management and artistic direction. In that regard my own contract was due to expire three years later, and that had to be taken into account at the same time.

There had been much discussion about a successor to Davis, focusing initially on Zubin Mehta. I had talked to Mehta a number of times about coming to London, but he had doubts and eventually told me that he thought he was the wrong person for Covent Garden in the light of his poor standing with the London critics. Claudio Abbado was approached, but declined on the grounds that he did not want the administrative chores of an opera house – his La Scala experience had been enough. Riccardo Muti, unsure about where he wanted to go, except that he had his eyes on La Scala and that Philadelphia was seeking an extension of his contract, also said no. Another consideration with him was that his children were being educated in Ravenna and when his American contract finished he wanted ideally to be based in Italy. Daniel Barenboim was also suggested by the board, but for both professional and personal reasons he was unwilling to commit himself to London.

As these discussions were continuing and bringing no positive results, it seemed to me that one distinguished musician, already working on our doorstep for part of each year, was the ideal candidate for us. This was Bernard Haitink. Having spent most of his career on the concert plat-form, he lacked long theatrical experience, but he had conducted at Covent Garden and had been music director at Glyndebourne for some years. In my judgement everything pointed to him – not least his standing in the world, his fine musicianship and his skill as an orchestra trainer. The board agreed, and Haitink was persuaded to join us from the beginning of the 1987/88 season.

At the same time we appointed Jeffrey Tate as principal conductor, with the object of involving him in programme planning – an area in which Haitink welcomed help and guidance – as well as ensuring his regular appearance at Covent Garden. The news of this appointment aroused concern that the repertoires of the two conductors overlapped and that it would have been better to have had a principal conductor who was stronger in the Italian repertoire. There was some truth in that, but I believed that Tate and Haitink could complement each other through careful and sensible planning. Sadly, this plan scarcely worked at all, as Tate was rarely available for meetings and gave little advice. What turned out to be a better and more practical solution was the later appointment of Sir Edward Downes to be associate music director and principal conductor.

Bernard Haitink had first come to Covent Garden in the 1976/77 season, to conduct *Don Giovanni*. With a problematic production and an imperfect cast, this was not the happiest of debuts for him, and later experiences can have done nothing to convince him that opera is the easiest of art forms with which to be involved. Later, in the 1982/83 season, came *Don Carlos* in French. The language limited the choice of singers for the role of Don Carlos in particular, with most candidates being unwilling to relearn it. While the remainder of the cast was excellent – with Thomas Allen, Robert Lloyd and John Tomlinson enjoying success as they made their debuts in their respective roles – the tenor left much to be desired.

Another problem revival was *Un Ballo in Maschera*, with Montserrat Caballé and Luciano Pavarotti. Some days before the opening, Pavarotti had telephoned to tell me that his father had to undergo surgery in New York and that he needed to be at his bedside. This meant that he would not be available for the first night. Would I release him? If I didn't agree I reckoned that he would go anyway, and I decided to authorize his absence. I immediately informed Haitink, who was understandably not at all happy about this. He agreed that there was nothing else to be done but find a replacement. He would leave the whole matter to me. Serious trouble ensued because we could not find a suitable tenor who was available for the last rehearsals and the opening. Eventually we discovered a Spanish tenor who was free, and he was immediately booked. He gave an acceptable performance, and the next day asked if he could return to Madrid. Having conceded that Pavarotti could miss just one performance, I agreed – only to receive a call from New York an hour or two later to be asked if he could be away for a second performance, because his father still needed him. I refused: I said I could support his absence for one performance on grounds of filial duty, but not two. Pavarotti agreed to return, but to safeguard the performance I asked Helga Schmidt to recall the Spaniard. Her telephone call to Madrid was not well received, because our tenor had discovered from a *Sunday Times* article about the search for a replacement that he was the twenty-third tenor whom we had approached. There was no way that he would come back. Fortunately, Pavarotti returned on time.

If this was not enough for Bernard Haitink, he had to face another incident when Caballé walked off the stage during the love duet in Act 2. The curtain was lowered and I went in search of her, to find her protesting that the duet was so adrift that the only thing to do was to stop and start again. There was some truth in that, but I wished she had left it to Haitink to sort out and that she had not taken such precipitous action. I could not imagine what I could say to the public. Ever resourceful, she suggested that I should tell the audience that she was unwell but that she would be all right in a short while. That is what I did, and we started again – this time successfully.

Haitink was rapidly discovering that conducting opera with certain singers was like negotiating a minefield. He was to endure other such experiences, but his skills as a conductor and his increasing confidence in opera saw him through many a difficulty.

One of the qualities which I knew Haitink would bring to music-making at Covent Garden was a meticulous attention to detail and the application of discipline to maintain it. One of the fastest routes to declining standards is the cutting of corners. Time in an opera house is often against you, and the urge to let something go is hard to resist, but resist it you must. I well remember Haitink's first orchestral rehearsal of *Arabella*. The opening bars are full of notes, and more often than not there is a scramble to get through them. Haitink, however, went carefully through those bars, ensuring that every note was properly played. In the break I happened to encounter some of the players, who said they could not understand why so much attention was being paid to the opening passage. It had never been done before, and they thought it a waste of time. I made a point of talking to the same players at the end of the rehearsal and was given a different story. They now saw the point and found the opening convincing. For them it was a transformation.

I recall another encounter on the same subject when Colin Davis was rehearsing *Die Walküre* and I happened to be talking to Frank Stead, the orchestra steward and formerly Sir Thomas Beecham's principal trombone in the London Philharmonic Orchestra in the 1930s. He too expressed surprise that so much time was being spent on certain passages: Bruno Walter, with whom he had played, had never done so, he said, and appeared to be unconcerned that not all the notes were in place. I suspect that rehearsal time in those days was at even more of a premium than now, techniques were less secure, and expectations were lower.

Like Colin Davis, Bernard Haitink also wished to conduct ballet, and in this he has benefited from changing attitudes of dancers and the absence of the inflexible regime of Michael Somes. For the conductor to be so warmly greeted by the dancers on the stage, and before the public, is testimony to his musicianship, the quality of the orchestral playing and the achievement of high musical standards without compromise but with understanding of dancers' expectations and needs.

In our one year together, Bernard Haitink and I were at odds over a production of *Parsifal*. His chosen director was Bill Bryden, a distinguished theatre director, whose production of the mystery plays Haitink had much admired. He was right in that, but wrong in believing that the naivety which Bryden had presented in these plays stood him in good stead for *Parsifal*. Following early discussions with Bryden, Haitink asked me to listen to the director's ideas. We met one Sunday evening. I did not warm to what Bryden told me and was generally unhappy with his concept, which seemed to me inappropriate and in danger of losing the heart of the work in a cliché-ridden plan to mount it in the ruins of a bombed Dresden. I phoned Haitink and told him of my reaction. He insisted on Bryden, nevertheless.

As music director, and for a production which he was conducting, he was absolutely right to stand by his choice, even though I disagreed with it. Moreover, I seemed to be a lone voice, and when discussion of the production came to the board – which by then was looking at its financial implications and the likely year-end out-turn – my reservations won no support. By then Haitink was talking about resignation if he was denied *Parsifal*. Obviously this was to be avoided, but equally I did not want failure for him or for the House. Unfortunately the production turned out poorly.

Many years ago we recognized the need for the orchestra to give concerts at regular intervals if it was to reach higher levels of achievement and to attract, and keep, the best players. These cost money to promote, and when financial difficulties emerge there is a temptation to abandon them in favour of something else in the theatre which seems more pressing. As the Royal Opera House reopens, it is to be hoped that concerts and their funding will feature prominently and permanently in the plans.

I am convinced that an orchestra normally playing in the pit should be of sufficient size both to meet theatre needs and to give regular concerts. It should not be an exact replica of the Vienna Philharmonic/Vienna State Opera Orchestra arrangement. Not all players in the latter are members of the Philharmonic, and I believe that all players should be of equal status. There can also be no doubt that the orchestra must be managed by the management and not by the players. Among the reasons for Covent Garden's success have been the control of the orchestra and ensuring that the same players attend all rehearsals and all performances

– a policy not maintained in recent years. There are few opera houses in Europe where such a practice prevails: most are at the mercy of external managements or the players.

The London orchestral scene is showing few signs of greater financial stability, and some relief of the pressure on the limited funds available might be found through joining a London orchestra with that of the Royal Opera House. I explored this in the past and made some progress, but circumstances were never quite right to win agreement in the face of opposition from players wanting to keep their independence. The situation today is different, however.

Bernard Haitink's decision to stay at Covent Garden until 2002 is important and encouraging. It is through his loyalty to the orchestra, the chorus and many soloists that there is a company in place at all. It might well have been a matter of starting from scratch when the theatre reopens. Already the achievements and practices created by the talents and commitment of hundreds of men and women have been damaged. But this is not irreparable, and under his artistic leadership the rebuilding process can begin in a modernized and fully equipped theatre. The Royal Opera is fortunate to have such a fine conductor and musician at its head.

Indeed, the opera company has been fortunate in all its music directors, all of whom have brought individual and valuable qualities to it. Each has taken the company on to another stage of its development, building on its strengths and correcting its weaknesses. Five music directors in the space of fifty years is about the right number, but what is much more significant is the contribution that each of them has made to the growth of the company, given the timing of their arrival and the needs of that particular moment in the company's history. It is a wonderful record.

3 Conductors

The list of conductors who have appeared at Covent Garden in the past fifty years makes impressive reading and illustrates the policy of maintaining the predominance of music and the seeking of drama through it.

After a period of initiation under the guidance of Karl Rankl, by the beginning of the 1950s the opera company was ready for new and greater challenges. Sir Thomas Beecham, that quixotic genius among British conductors, had spent more of his time engaging in wars of words with the new regime about the supposed inadequacy of English singers and the engagement of foreign conductors than in conducting at Covent Garden, although he did conduct a handful of performances of *Die Meistersinger* and a new production of Balfe's *Bohemian Girl* for the Festival of Britain in 1951. Some years later it was hoped that he would conduct *Les Troyens*, but this came to nothing. Shortly after deciding against it, he died. If only he had been less bitter about the direction in which Covent Garden was going after the war and could have accepted a role which was there for him to play, the company would have greatly benefited from the conducting of this remarkable musician, to whom so much is owed for his championing of opera and higher standards of performance and his promotion of opera both at Covent Garden and elsewhere earlier in the century.

David Webster, well attuned to the world of conductors, knew that Erich Kleiber was the conductor above all others whom he had to persuade to come to Covent Garden. Ideally he wanted him as music director, but he had to settle for less, and then for only three years. What matters is that Kleiber was there at a crucial moment, and moved the company forward dramatically – first with *Der Rosenkavalier*. This was given a tumultuous ovation by the audience. Everybody – audience and performers alike – knew they were in the presence of a great musician who was enabling the company to find new depths of meaning in the music and the text and to give performances of a stature and expressiveness beyond anything of which the orchestra and singers had thought they were capable.

Kleiber had warmed to the British singers, who included Sylvia Fisher as the Marschallin and Constance Shacklock as Octavian, and was to embrace and promote others in the future. His impact on the company was significant in many respects – for the overall standard of orchestral playing, of singing and of production – and with *Rosenkavalier* he laid the foundations for all future Strauss performances at the Royal Opera House.

Tchaikovsky's *The Queen of Spades* was to follow soon after, and again Kleiber was to create miracles with both singers and orchestra. There was a late change of cast: Raoul Jobin was replaced by Edgar Evans as Herman a month before the opening. Evans, a relatively new member of the company, did not know the role, but Kleiber, having heard him read through some of the part, sent him off to work with Peter Gellhorn, a member of the Covent Garden music staff, and, delighted with his rapid progress, took him into the cast. This was the beginning of another career thanks to a perceptive and trusting conductor.

Kleiber had a vivid and engaging personality, but was a tyrant when the moment demanded. On first arriving at Covent Garden he was met by Michael Wood, the press officer, who greeted him with the hope that there would be no difficulties or trouble. To this Kleiber replied, 'If there is no trouble, I will make it!' He was demanding, and applied a rigorous musical discipline, but he had the ability to fire the imagination of players and make even the least talented members of an orchestra sit up and play well. There was also a streak of kindness in him, and he never humiliated players, knowing when to stop if they were unable to give him what he wanted at the time.

A Covent Garden percussion player, Jack Wilson, told me of an occasion when he made a wrong side-drum entry in a *Rosenkavalier* performance. He was mortified, and insisted on apologizing to Kleiber at the end. As he explained why he had come, Kleiber turned and said, 'Mr Wilson, I should be apologizing to you, not you to me. We all make mistakes, and I should not have looked at you in the way that I did.'

Kleiber conducted a wide range of operas during his three years at

Covent Garden, and finished with new productions of *Wozzeck* and *Elektra*, the former in English and the latter in German. Alban Berg's opera is a work of huge complexity, presenting orchestra and singers with untold difficulties, but the way through them was eased by this inspired musician, with whom this work had become synonymous. For example, he subdivided the very long bars in the orchestral parts, which made it easier for the players to assimilate the notes and rhythms. Interestingly, Maurits Sillem suggested this again for a revival of *Wozzeck* in 1975, but by then the players were happier to play from the parts as originally written and considered the subdivision a complication.

Kleiber could not be persuaded to return after *Elektra*. There were fee problems, but I suspect that there were other reasons, too, upon which John Russell touched in his life of the conductor. 'He was by nature an absolutist, and in a world like that of the English stage, where compromise is universal and a creeping gentility saps all that should be direct and unfearing, he could never have survived.' At this point in its post-war history Covent Garden was still finding its way, money was short, and there was an endless need to economize. A Kleiber was needed to counter the resulting compromises, but it was not a climate in which he would continue for long.

The Kleiber period was of the utmost importance in showing the company the way forward, in demonstrating what they could do, and in instilling confidence. His son, Carlos, whom he was to discourage from becoming a conductor, was to perform similar miracles thirty years later.

Another vital influence around this time was Rudolf Kempe. Formerly principal oboe with the Leipzig Gewandhaus orchestra, he understood from first-hand experience the problems confronting musicians in an orchestra and helped players to build their self-confidence. He rapidly became popular with the orchestra, singers and audience, and his regular visits to Covent Garden were eagerly awaited. Soon after I arrived at Covent Garden, Morris Smith, the orchestra director, in recounting Kempe's popularity, urged me to be in the auditorium when he came into the pit for the first day of rehearsals. I witnessed Kempe being met by the noisiest and most friendly greeting that any conductor is likely to receive.

As the relationship between him and the orchestra developed, the playing took on a distinctive style – broad and warm – for performances of the German romantic repertoire which he was mostly conducting. Dynamics and texture were important to him. Pianissimos had to be exactly that. Haydn Trotman, the bass and contrabass trombone player, used to tell me that Kempe's demand for quiet playing was such that often he could barely get his instrument to speak. It was at this point that the conductor would be satisfied. He had a sensitive ear for balance and was always considerate of singers, winning their lasting respect and affection.

Karl Rankl had mounted the *Ring* remarkably early in the life of post-war Covent Garden and had had considerable success with it. However, it was Rudolf Kempe who gave the most memorable performances of this epic, his warm and relaxed approach unfolding the story within huge, overarching spans of music.

It was also Kempe who showed how successful and how valid a north-European view of *Madame Butterfly* could be. It was in the 1957/58 season that he agreed to conduct this, with Victoria de los Angeles in the title role. First, he decided to play the second act without the usual interval, which makes the task of the soprano even more taxing, but which de los Angeles was willing to accept. He then brought to rehearsal and performance all his familiar qualities of music-making. The results were amazing and won the instant approval of audience and critics. He was to repeat *Butterfly* with Sena Jurinac two seasons later, but opportunities to move with him further into the Italian repertoire never came.

He continued to conduct at Covent Garden until the 1965/66 season. By then Solti was conducting the *Ring* and Otto Klemperer had arrived. This meant fewer openings for Kempe, irrespective of his own schedule. Also, he was not enamoured of Solti's approach to music, and declined later invitations, telling me he would return only when Solti was no longer music director. True to his word, he came to conduct *Elektra* in the 1973/74 season, and was amazed, he said, to find that the orchestra could still play so well. Tragically, we were not to see him at Covent Garden again.

In 1951 Sir John Barbirolli returned to Covent Garden after an absence of fourteen years, and during the next three he conducted many memorable performances of operas by Puccini and Verdi. In this repertoire he was superb, and instilled a sense of correct performing style as well as demonstrating his skills as an orchestra trainer. He brought passion to his music-making, and helped players and singers to be more expressive and free. Sadly, he was not to return after the 1952/53 season, during which he conducted *Tristan und Isolde* and Gluck's *Orfeo ed Euridice*. The latter was to be Kathleen Ferrier's final appearance on the stage.

In December 1954 another British musician, Sir Malcolm Sargent, conducted the world première of William Walton's *Troilus and Cressida*. The preparation for this was inauspicious, with the composer accusing Sargent of not knowing the score, and later Walton was firmly of the view that the opera's lack of success was due to the conductor's incompetence. Sargent was not an obvious choice for this work, and I have always thought that it was David Webster's earlier association with him at the Liverpool Philharmonic which led to his engagement. Sargent was persuasive and persistent, as I was to discover several years later when Webster let it drop that he had agreed to him reorchestrating *Les Sylphides*. Sargent had set his heart on doing this, and had put Webster in a corner from which he could not escape. We did not need a new version – the Roy Douglas orchestration was more than acceptable – and, to make the situation worse, Webster failed to discuss this with Dame Ninette de Valois and it was only a few days before the orchestral rehearsal that the company learned of its existence. I realized what had happened and felt deeply for Webster, calming his uneasy relationship with de Valois as best I could.

It was at the end of this rehearsal that I met Jack Wilson, the percussion player of the Kleiber incident, on the Covent Garden Underground platform. Wilson started to discuss Malcolm Sargent's relationship with orchestral players and said that he did not understand why players disliked Sargent, except that he had been brought up in the profession to believe that this was what you did. It was part of orchestral folklore, dating from a skirmish between the conductor and some players in the mid-1930s. He considered it unfair and enjoyed the security of Sargent's technique – 'After all there are not many conductors at whose stick you can look after two hundred and fifty bars' rest and find it in exactly the same position as it was at bar one.'

In the spring of 1958 there arrived at Covent Garden another great conductor who was to leave a lasting impression: Carlo Maria Giulini. By now matters of style and convention in the performance of the German romantic repertoire had been well learned, and it was the Italian repertoire which was in need of the influence of the great practitioners. Giulini was to show the orchestra how to play Verdi and how to play with nobility. In the next season Tullio Serafin was to build on this with Donizetti's *Lucia di Lammermoor* in memorable performances by Joan Sutherland, and later with Bellini's *La Sonnambula*.

Giulini, a man deeply fired by his Christian faith and of great moral and artistic integrity, was aware of the degree of compromise inherent in opera, but went out of his way to minimize it. When preparing Verdi's *Don Carlos*, he insisted that all rehearsals be attended both by him and by Luchino Visconti, the producer and designer of the opera. This meant that each knew exactly how work was progressing and could comment and contribute accordingly. It was rare for a producer and conductor to collaborate so closely, and it is seldom that a producer sits throughout orchestral rehearsals, but the benefits were there for all to see and hear in thoroughly prepared performances of a cohesively wrought production which was to become a classic. New standards had been set.

In the following years Giulini returned to conduct *Il Barbiere di Siviglia*, *Falstaff*, *Il Trovatore* and *La Traviata* – the last two operas with Visconti as producer. By 1967, however, he had decided that opera involved him in more compromise than he could accept, and *Traviata* was to be his final production. (By chance, it was also the first complete opera to be transmitted live on television, which was in itself a momentous event.) Performances of *Le Nozze di Figaro* by the Rome Opera in New York the next year were to be his last in the pit for a long time.

Guilini's integrity was to be admired, but his decision deprived opera of a serious and inspiring musical influence. It was therefore with excitement that, some thirteen years later, I responded to a telephone call from Ernest Fleischman in Los Angeles telling me that Giulini – then principal conductor of the Los Angeles Philharmonic – was interested in conducting *Falstaff*, subject to certain conditions, some of which were to be met by sharing a production between Los Angeles, Florence and Covent Garden. The most important stipulation was that the same cast, with the possible exception of Dr Caius, would be engaged for all the venues. At the time, Giulini wanted Franco Zeffirelli to direct. A meeting with him, Giulini, Fleischman and myself was arranged in Los Angeles, but when the appointed day arrived there was no sign of Zeffirelli. Giulini was furious, more on my behalf than his, and asked that we find another producer. This was not an easy task. It was important that the producer should be able to listen to Giulini but be equally capable of standing on his own feet. Nobody came readily to mind, until one day I remembered Ronald Eyre, recalling vividly his wonderful production of Berlioz's *Béatrice et Bénédict* at the Buxton Festival. I also thought that he would get on well with Giulini personally. Happily, they did warm to each other on first meeting.

The theory of shared productions tends to be more beautiful than the practice, unless you happen to be the venue in control and have responsibility for the making. In this instance, Los Angeles had the first performances and Florence the last, with Covent Garden in the middle, in the 1981/82 season, and with the responsibility of building the scenery and making the costumes. It was exactly what we wanted – and, more importantly, it ensured the return of Giulini to the Royal Opera House.

Ronald Eyre was later not to find life so easy with Giulini, who was unsmiling and insisted that *Falstaff* was not a comedy. Humour and wit were consequently in short supply, and usually cut out by Giulini altogether. It was a pity that he took this view, because the production was excellent, lacking only that essential dimension of laughter, which was inherent in it but not obviously on show.

Throughout the London rehearsals Giulini was in solemn mood, and during one rehearsal he took me aside and said, 'John, if you and I were really true to ourselves, we would never be involved with opera. The compromise is too great.'

There is a deeply serious trait in Guilini's make-up which led him to believe that he was not ready to conduct various works until he had reached a certain age and degree of experience. For example, he conducted Mozart's last three symphonies only when he was past forty. I invited him to conduct *Aida*, but he declined because he said that he had nothing to add to what anyone else had achieved with this opera.

Two other Italian conductors, Claudio Abbado and Riccardo Muti, were later also to bring to Covent Garden the best of Italian traditions of music-making. In the 1967/68 season Abbado had conducted a revival of *Don Carlos*, but it was to be several years before he returned to conduct again – in the 1974/75 season, for a new production by Otto Schenk of *Un Ballo in Maschera*. Verdian style was by now second nature to the orchestra, but Abbado found emotion in the playing too submerged at the beginning and had to work hard to bring it to the surface. He was so used to being with the La Scala orchestra, which gave this to him so spontaneously, that he was surprised by its initial absence.

Another long gap ensued before he was with us again, in the 1983/84 season for Andrei Tarkovsky's production of *Boris Godunov*. Abbado had conducted this opera at La Scala, using the original Mussorgsky orchestration but with some of the inner parts filled out with clarinets and horns. This experience indicated that, to make a real impact, large string forces were also required. I promised that he would have them.

The first rehearsal came, and during the interval Abbado expressed contentment except for there being one fewer desk of violas than he and I had agreed. I sent for the orchestra director, Bram Gay, who explained that he had omitted one desk because it could not be fitted into the pit and it was a waste of money to call the players for rehearsal. There was sense in that, but Abbado thought otherwise and insisted on having the missing violas. At the first rehearsal in the pit, Abbado, well aware that there would be pandemonium, took his place on the podium and stood for twenty minutes with his arms folded and looking down, while the players, muttering and cursing, sorted themselves out in a space too small for such a large orchestra. He then began, without a word from the players. It was a masterly display of orchestra psychology.

Riccardo Muti, another fine musician and disciplinarian, displayed his mettle during a revival of *Aida* in the 1976/77 season. He has always maintained that players are not being serious unless they are in the pit throughout a rehearsal or performance. This was contrary to the habit at Covent Garden, where players – particularly the percussion section – do leave the pit during long gaps in their playing, provided that they can come and go without disturbance. (From time to time I protested about the amount of movement when I found it distracting.) Having been abroad during rehearsals and the first performance of *Aida*, I was surprised to find at the second performance that the trombones were seated at the beginning of Act 3 when it had been customary for them to remain out of the pit during fifteen minutes' tacet. At the end of the act Muti explained that if they had not been in the pit he would not have continued.

Riccardo Muti brings remarkable musicianship and an identifiable style to his performances. The discipline – often rigid and unyielding – is very much in the tradition of Toscanini, but within this there are a passion and expressiveness which leave audiences cheering. However, the martinet streak in him is allied to a strong belief that what the composer originally wrote is what should be performed. This has led him to reject many established conventions and practices, which has brought disappointment to both performers and audiences, particularly where high notes are concerned, depriving the latter of excitement and the former of applause.

Muti was to return for a new production of *Macbeth* in March 1981. First, he demanded a chorus of 140, which was about twice its normal size. Only with this number of singers could the full impact of the Act 2 finale really be made, he argued. I conceded his point, and the results were marvellous. What I was less happy about was the extent to which he dictated to Elijah Moshinsky, the producer, exactly where he considered everyone should be on the stage. The end result was musically splendid but dramatically feeble, because he wanted singers to be so static that the outcome was not much more than a concert performance, except for the scenery and costumes. The same was the case with his other Covent Garden production, Bellini's *I Capuleti e i Montecchi*, although it was then less obviously harmful because of the nature of the work and the smaller number of singers involved. It also fitted more happily with Luigi Pizzi's conception of the work.

The German repertoire was to be given another huge boost by Otto Klemperer, a giant of a man and musician, who was enjoying vast acclaim in Great Britain through Walter Legge's decision to bring him to London to conduct the Philharmonia Orchestra in concerts and an extensive recording programme. Covent Garden was able to take advantage of his presence, and the opera company benefited hugely from both his conducting and his stage direction. He had strong and clear views about the visual and dramatic content of staging, and oversaw this with the assistance of Christopher West, for many years resident producer at the Royal Opera House.

The weight of Klemperer's authority was awesome, and it was certainly felt in *Fidelio*, the first of his Covent Garden engagements. He seemed happy to be directing this opera again, and was extraordinarily active as he showed singers what he wanted on the stage. He was also accommodating with some changes of tempi, which won him favour with the cast. On the first night, 24 February 1961, he was nervous, not having conducted a staged performance for more than ten years. However, it was a triumph, ending with a jubilant ovation for Klemperer from the audience. Critical response was warm, though some were disapproving of the playing of the Leonore No. 3 overture after the dungeon scene. It was a strange decision of his to perform this, since he had been adamantly opposed to it on earlier occasions. A streak of perversity had got the better of him, but it was worth the dramatic sacrifice to hear such thrilling performances.

In January of the following year he conducted and directed a new production of *Die Zauberflöte*. With sets by Georg Eisler which Walter Legge likened to 'a provincial monumental mason's junk yard', it was not the triumph of *Fidelio* and demonstrated the danger of becoming too beholden to a conductor only able and willing to work within a very circumscribed set of options. Some in the audience were left disappointed – bored even – except during the Papageno scenes, which seemed to bring Klemperer to life and arouse his humour. By now the physical direction of singers and orchestra was at a minimum, and the movement of the right hand almost invisible. At one performance, during Pamina's G minor aria, the orchestra noticed that Klemperer was not conducting at all and appeared to be asleep. Charles Taylor, the leader, was about to prod him when Joan Carlyle skipped a beat. Klemperer immediately came to and started to conduct. In the meantime, the players, obviously aware of what had happened, had caught up with Carlyle. In Klemperer's view he had saved the day!

In April 1963 came the last opera which Klemperer was to conduct: *Lohengrin*. In spite of its length, and the physical and mental strain involved, he delivered performances of incredible intensity, with a dramatic sweep and glorious sound. The production itself was barely adequate, but the musical splendour more than compensated for its failings. Many regarded this as one of the greatest Wagnerian evenings of post-war Covent Garden.

Klemperer's appearances at Covent Garden left their mark on all associated with them. This was particularly so with *Fidelio*, where musical and dramatic truth was evident in every note and every phrase, wrought with the authority of a musician imbued with all the traditions of working in Germany in the inter-war years. It was a memorable experience.

One of those who assisted Klemperer on *Lohengrin* was Reginald Goodall – a Wagnerian if there ever was one, but whose immense talents were never really displayed to the public for far too many years. He had conducted the first performances of *Peter Grimes*, at Sadler's Wells in 1945, but at Covent Garden, or with the opera company on tour, he often found himself conducting works with which he had little sympathy. With the arrival of Rudolf Kempe, who effectively took over the Wagner repertoire, and later of Solti, with whom he had no rapport, conducting opportunities dwindled, and he spent his time coaching singers in Wagnerian roles in the amphitheatre bar (inevitably nicknamed Valhalla). He was a superb coach, but his talents demanded more of him.

It was Sadler's Wells Opera, encouraged by Edmund Tracy, which gave Goodall the real opportunities to show his true value as a

Wagnerian conductor, in *Die Meistersinger* in 1968, although there had been glimpses of this in the same opera at Covent Garden in the 1958/59 and 1959/60 seasons and in a memorable *Walküre* on tour in 1954. Orchestral musicians were devoted to Goodall, and admired his musicianship and profound knowledge of Wagner. A disciple of Hans Knappertsbusch, he lacked a good technique and was not easy to follow, but players went with him. There was a strong pulse always to be felt, even if it was sometimes not visible through the hand.

One example of the affection in which musicians held Goodall occurred early in my time at Covent Garden. There was a rehearsal of *Turandot* in the crush bar, but the conductor taking it was unwell. Morris Smith suggested that I ask Goodall to take his place. This was a most unlikely work for him, but he did know it and, much to my surprise, he agreed to come. As he raised his hand to begin *Turandot*, the orchestra broke into the *Meistersinger* prelude. Later in the same rehearsal, Goodall's right hand was going lower and lower, to a point where it was scarcely visible above the stand. Suddenly a voice from the back of the orchestra – that of the principal double bass, Fred Wigston – was heard: 'Lift it up a bit, Reggie, so that we can see it!'

Time and space were of the essence with Goodall, which is why his engagements with Welsh National Opera worked so well. The WNO plays in seasons, with gaps between. During these periods, singers and orchestra can concentrate on rehearsal and preparation, without the pressure of performance. Covent Garden could never provide such conditions, and there was insufficient time for Goodall and performers to settle down comfortably with each other. The *Parsifal* of 1971 was an example of this, with a reasonable amount of rehearsal time, but with the chorus and orchestra also rehearsing and performing other works during this period and Franz Crass, engaged as Gurnemanz, becoming ill. We were fortunate in finding Gottlob Frick free for the first night. He was so elated by his success that he said that he would sing the remaining performances. This was a rash undertaking for a singer of his age; nevertheless, we were delighted – until the next morning, when Frick telephoned to say he had thought more about staying and felt it unwise. He was right, but it left us in search of another Gurnemanz and we ended up with a different singer for each performance. It was an incredibly unhappy outcome for Goodall.

He and I used to talk with each other a lot. I found his comments about singers and conductors illuminating, and he had a lot to say about opera and music in general as well as Wagner. I wanted him to conduct *Tristan und Isolde* at Covent Garden. Sadly, various pressures – including difficulties in finding suitable performance slots with the rehearsal time which he needed, and the unwillingness of some singers to perform with him, because they sought greater security in performance than he gave – prevented this from being realized. The influence which he brought to bear on standards in his quiet, unassuming way is inestimable.

Covent Garden has been fortunate in the large number of distinguished conductors who have performed with the opera company. One who appeared all too infrequently was Jascha Horenstein, who came for *Fidelio* in the 1961/62 season and returned only once, for some remarkable performances of *Parsifal* in 1973. He was far from well at the time, and died shortly after the last performance. In spite of being weak and near collapse, he conducted performances of extraordinary luminosity, imbued with a deep spiritual quality.

A Viennese conductor who had made a strong impact on the public when conducting the Vienna State Opera during their 1947 visit to London was Josef Krips. Naturally immersed in the Viennese traditions of Mozart and Strauss, he was an excellent musician, but renowned for his bad temper. He first came to conduct *Don Giovanni* in the 1963/64 season, and did not return until the 1970/71 season, for *Meistersinger*, followed by *Rosenkavalier* and *Fidelio* in the two succeeding years.

By then he had mellowed, although we were to witness an outburst of his old temper during a Saturday performance of *Meistersinger*. Notices had been displayed around the House and announcements had been regularly made that this performance would begin at the earlier time of 5 p.m. I had gone to the theatre to see the performance started and was met by Stella Chitty, the stage manager, to be told that the singer performing Fritz Kothner had not arrived. Kothner is not on for the first twenty-five minutes of the opera, and, since the singer concerned was very reliable, I said that we should begin on time even though he was not in the House. The overture was played and we were into the church scene when Stella Chitty informed me that the singer was still not there. Kothner's entrance was fast approaching and something had to be done. I remembered that a chorister, Glynne Thomas, had once studied it as a cover. We sent for him and I told him that he was now Kothner until the other arrived. Understandably, he protested that he could not remember the part. I told him to go on with a score – it seemed reasonable for Kothner to have a book in his hands. We sent a message to the prompter,

63

but could not send one to the conductor. All went well until Thomas started to thumb through the pages to find his next entry. Having discovered that, he regained confidence, and when we tried to call him off the stage on the arrival of the real Kothner he was reluctant to leave.

I went to the pit to greet Krips at the end of the act. He was furious. He never wanted to work with the late singer again, and demanded that I should send him away. I let Krips go to his room and went to see him towards the end of the interval. He was still very angry, as I knew he would be, but he gradually calmed down. I then pointed out that there was much of the opera left and that it would be intolerable for him as well as for the singer, who was mortified by his mistake, to continue in this state of tension. Krips agreed. He came on to the stage and shook the singer by the hand. Life returned to normal and the show went on, the audience seemingly oblivious of having heard two Kothners.

Other guest conductors have come much more often, and some – including John Pritchard, Charles Mackerras and Silvio Varviso, to name but three – have made special contributions to the growth of the company. Mackerras first became known as the arranger of one of the best ballet scores ever produced – *Pineapple Poll*, a mélange of Arthur Sullivan's music – and later of the music of Verdi for another ballet by John Cranko, *The Lady and the Fool*. He is a remarkable, all-round musician, who straddles musicology and practical music-making with consummate skill and ease. The works he has conducted at Covent Garden cover a wide spectrum, and to each he has brought distinctive and special qualities. His approach to Mozart stood in strong contrast to that of Georg Solti, as was shown in *Così fan tutte* at the end of the 1960s. He adopted an authentic style, with some decoration – a style which he has developed over the years. In Handel he has shown how an orchestra with modern instruments can play effectively in a baroque style.

Silvio Varviso, a shy and nervous man, is another all-round musician who establishes a relationship with orchestras and singers in a way which ensures that all will give of their utmost to him. He is unassuming and unshowy, but a fine artist who has helped the Royal Opera on its way.

John Pritchard was one of the most gifted conductors to emerge in post-war Britain. His credentials were excellent, having worked with Fritz Busch at Glyndebourne, where he enjoyed a superb grounding in Mozart. As Glyndebourne's chorus master, he found himself conducting *Don Giovanni* there in 1951, following the sudden illness of Busch.

His Covent Garden debut came the next year, and he continued to visit throughout most of his life. He was responsible for a number of first performances – Britten's *Gloriana* in 1952, and Tippett's *The Midsummer Marriage* in 1955 and *King Priam* in 1962 – and was an immensely popular conductor. He was often too undemanding of players, but because of his innate musicianship, which they respected, and because of his obvious trust of them, orchestras would play superbly for him. Singers loved him and found security with him in spite of his laid-back approach.

A conductor who arrived at Covent Garden very late in life was Karl Böhm. He was one of several conductors of his generation, and younger, whom I suspect David Webster did not approach partly for fear of upsetting Solti, who had some reason to be wary of a group of conductors (including Herbert von Karajan) who dominated the Salzburg scene. Böhm had only been in England once before to conduct, and that was with the Dresden State Opera in 1936. I had the impression that he was aware of anti-German feeling at the time and was not eager to return to London. However, I thought it worth trying to persuade him, and I attended a performance of his at the Paris Opéra. He was surprisingly interested in my proposition of *Le Nozze di Figaro* in the 1977/78 season, and we continued discussion over a dinner given by Deutsche Grammophon. This was at a faraway restaurant, and the drive there seemed endless. Böhm thought the same, and shortly I was to hear him singing from the front seat, 'It's a long way to Tipperary.'

We had assembled a strong cast for him. He was content with this, but was critical of the production in that there was an interval between Acts 3 and 4. We managed to reduce this to a long pause, which made him happier. Rehearsals went well, with relatively little direction from him. His beat was not always clear and it took time for the cast and orchestra to settle down with him. The performances were a success, although one nearly ended in disaster, with the finale of Act 4 in danger of disintegrating. Böhm did not respond quickly enough, and the performance was saved by Janet Craxton, the principal oboe, who managed to give a lead and pull it together.

During the second interval of one performance Teresa Stratas, who was singing Susanna, said that she felt unwell and needed some help with tempi from Böhm to see her through the rest of the evening. I suggested that we went to see Böhm together, since I was going to his room anyway – I spent a lot of intervals with him. When Stratas had explained her problem, he responded sympathetically and, promising his support, recommended her to take a pill which he removed from an array of bottles in a case. She feigned swallowing it, but as we left she threw it away, convinced that it would be unwise to take anything of the kind from him and safer just to take an aspirin.

Böhm returned in the autumn of 1979 for *Così fan tutte*. He had a wonderful cast – including Brigitte Fassbaender, Herman Prey and Geraint Evans – with whom he was happy to work. It all went well, but in many ways it was too late for Böhm. He was often tired, which exacerbated an underlying irritability in his make-up. Interval chats remained entertaining, however, and as I announced myself on entering his room he would invariably call out, 'La voce di padrone!' One evening I raised the question of artists' fees with him, and asked why he created such havoc with me in arguing over his. He paused and replied, 'I just want you to show that you still love me.'

We had one catastrophe with him. I wanted to take him to dinner, and he was keen that we should go to an Italian restaurant. I chose La Famiglia in Langton Street, where we ate well and had a good time together. However, the occasion was spoiled by the loss of that famous beret of his, which had been carefully hung up as we entered but was missing as we left. He was devastated, and there seemed to be nothing that we could do to console him or make amends.

Late in his life though Böhm's arrival at Covent Garden was, we were able to savour and benefit from contact with a great musician immersed in the Viennese tradition of Mozart playing.

A conductor whom we failed to bring to Covent Garden was Leonard Bernstein. He and I had talked about possibilities, usually focusing on *Fidelio*. Then one day in the early 1970s Schuyler Chapin, who was his manager at the time, telephoned to say that Bernstein would like to conduct a new production of *Madame Butterfly* at the Royal Opera House, with Franco Zeffirelli directing, and hoped that we would be interested. I replied that we wanted Bernstein but not *Butterfly*, of which we already had a splendid production which we had no plans to replace. Chapin was silent, amazed that I could be rejecting such an offer and probably thinking that I was out of my mind. I then suggested an alternative: a new production of *La Bohème*, which we did need to replace our existing one in sets and costumes dating from 1898. Chapin was relieved to have something to take to Bernstein, and agreement was reached for him to conduct *Bohème* in the 1973/74 season. The production went ahead, but regrettably without Bernstein, who had decided to take the year off for composition.

There is a small band of conductors who are head and shoulders above their peers and who possess a special, yet indefinable, quality which enables them to make music to a standard and of a luminosity unattainable by most others. One is Carlos Kleiber, who was persuaded by Helga Schmidt to come to Covent Garden to conduct *Der Rosenkavalier* in place of an ailing James Levine in the summer of 1974. This was the only occasion on which we had managed to pin Levine down to dates, mostly because of his Metropolitan Opera commitments, which occupied the greater part of the year. Illness prevented him from coming that summer, and other opportunities have never been found. Covent Garden has been deprived of the experience of working with an immensely gifted musician.

I had heard Kleiber conduct *Rosenkavalier* in Munich and had talked to him after the performance. (On this night, untypically, he had conducted from a score, which prompted his mother to go to his dressing room to exclaim, 'Carlos, darling, I thought you knew this opera by now!') He was non-committal, but I sensed that he was persuadable, though not without difficulty. In fact securing Kleiber was nothing short of a miracle. He dislikes working, is very choosy about where he conducts, and ideally prefers not to conduct anywhere. But after a shaky start he warmed to Covent Garden, and to all of us, returning several times.

His first rehearsal with the orchestra was difficult. He was well aware of his father's standing and popularity with the musicians, which made him ultra-sensitive to players' reaction on his first appearance. At the end he said that the players spent most of the rehearsal staring at him and wondering if he was the son of his father. Subsequent rehearsals were easier and productive, although it soon became apparent that he lacked his father's understanding of when to stop. In the last act of *Rosenkavalier* there is a triplet figure for trombones, which the section could not play in the way he wanted. He went on remorselessly, humiliating them and causing them to say that they wanted never to play for him again. They did play, but it took time to get over this episode.

He was not happy with the cast, and after a week of rehearsal he would have liked to replace most of them. When he told me this, I reminded him that he had been contracted to conduct this group of singers, and said there was no question of any being replaced. 'Funny you should say that to me this morning,' he replied. 'My wife has just told me to be more Christian, and now you're telling me to behave. So, let's have an alfresco *Rosenkavalier.*' We then moved into serious rehearsal, culminating in a series of glorious performances, and with the orchestra clamouring for his return.

Three years later, return he did – for *Elektra*, insisting on Birgit Nilsson in the title role. She was not eager to sing with Kleiber, whom she did not know, and it took a visit to Paris and a lot of talking on my part to persuade her. To my horror, within forty-eight hours of rehearsals beginning, Kleiber was asking why he had Miss Nilsson in the cast. I reminded him of his demand, which he then recalled. He went back to work a little sheepishly, and conducted a series of magnificent performances.

Before he went into the pit each night, he invariably asked me if he should conduct the work differently, to which I replied in the affirmative. There were subtle changes, which kept singers and orchestra alert and took them on to higher and higher achievements. Such an approach depended for its success on a close rapport with the orchestra – which he certainly had at Covent Garden, declaring it to be the best opera orchestra in Europe – and on the musicality of the singers. Where this was not in evidence, and with a chorus, things could end in tears, and at one stage he told me he would only conduct operas with truly musical soloists and not requiring a chorus.

In the autumn of 1979 we experimented with the idea of taking an existing production of a well-worn opera and engaging a distinguished conductor to take it to pieces and reassemble it. This would mean extended rehearsal time and high expenditure. The opera was *La Bohème*, and the conductor Carlos Kleiber. It paid off, and we went into performance with a restudied and revivified production of a staple repertory work. I wish that we could have done more of this, but time and money were against it.

We had planned a production of Giordano's *Andrea Chénier* for February 1980, but abandoned it in an attempt to balance the budget. This left a hole in the programme which we were considering how to fill when Franco Zeffirelli proposed a new production of Verdi's *La Traviata* for performance at Covent Garden in February 1980 which was to be the basis of a film to be made in studios at Teddington shortly afterwards. It was an exciting project, in which we wanted to be involved. We had Kleiber and Placido Domingo in place, but Kleiber and I could not agree with Zeffirelli about the casting of Violetta. He was set upon Teresa Stratas, but, as much as we both admired her as a great actress-singer, we did not believe that she could manage the vocal difficulties of the first scene. Zeffirelli persisted, saying she reminded him of Maria Callas and there could be no other choice. We still disagreed, and so lost Zeffirelli and the film, which was later made with Metropolitan Opera forces and at Cinecittà in Rome.

This loss was also our good fortune. We substituted *Otello*, and at next to no notice found Margaret Price and Silvano Carroli free for Desdemona and Iago. With them, and with Domingo and Kleiber, we achieved performances of *Otello* of such stature that there seemed nowhere else to go next.

Kleiber was at his best, firing the imagination of players as few others can do, and encouraging singers and players to take risks. In one rehearsal I remember him going through the passage before Desdemona's entry in 'Salce! Salce! Salce!'. He stopped after a few bars and complimented the players, going on to ask, 'Have you ever thought what Desdemona was doing at this moment? She was casting a petal here and a petal there. Let's play it again.' It brought a transformation from decent playing to inspired playing. Later, he and Margaret Price were at odds over a certain phrase. When she would not, or could not, sing it in the way he wanted, he threw down his baton and walked out of the pit. Everyone was aghast. I knew where he had gone, and I decided to give him ten minutes or so to cool down. I went into his room and found him roaring with laughter and asking if I thought he had been out long enough. I replied, 'No, give them another five minutes.' He did, and the rehearsal resumed with everything falling readily into place.

The opening performance was rapturously received, and I had no doubt that one of these performances had to be broadcast. The BBC Opera Department had run out of money, however, and could see no way of relaying a performance. I appealed to Aubrey Singer, managing director of BBC Radio, who was enthusiastic but who confirmed that there were no available funds. I was unwilling to let these miraculous performances go by without giving more people the opportunity of hearing one. I thought about commercial radio, and telephoned John Whitney, the managing director of Capital Radio, to ask if there was the remotest chance of him relaying a performance. He asked for twenty-four hours to think about it, and next day said he would go ahead. This was the beginning of an association with Capital Radio which enabled us to reach a wider audience with a number of opera broadcasts. It was not, however, a popular move with the BBC, some of whose staff were outraged by our action.

Contrary to popular perception, Kleiber's repertoire is much larger than one might think, largely because of his time in Stuttgart, where he would conduct with little or no rehearsal. This is why he once told me that he wanted either a lot of rehearsal time or none. If we were suddenly without a conductor, we were not to hesitate to phone and put a proposition to him. We did, but the opera or the circumstances were never right. If they had been, he would have come.

Kleiber was to return for a new production of *Otello* and, much later, for a revival, but the magic of those 1980 performances was not recaptured, nor the gaiety and laughter of previous meetings and phone calls. Few encounters with him failed to produce new thoughts about music or other matters, and he was keen that you should be aware of things. For example, he telephoned one day to ask if I had seen a TV transmission of *Turandot* from La Scala. I told him I had watched the first twenty minutes. 'That was all that was necessary,' he said. 'You saw from Lorin Maazel the best example of conducting technique ever. I wanted to be sure that you had seen it.' On another occasion, in Munich, he asked if I had heard Dimitri Mitropoulos conducting Verdi. I said I had not, and so after lunch I was taken to a shop to find discs. None was available, but by the time I had returned to the hotel there was a set of *Un Ballo in Maschera* in my room, with instructions to listen to it and tell him what I thought.

The practical joker was also in evidence. When meeting at the Vierjahreseiten Hotel in Munich, we found a message from Leonard Bernstein to visit him in his room, where he was rehearsing *Tristan und Isolde*. We went, and were invited to attend the orchestral rehearsal in the afternoon. Over lunch, Kleiber asked the time of my plane to London. We decided that we had time to go to part of the rehearsal. We entered the hall by the wrong door and found ourselves on the platform. Making our way to the seats, Kleiber asked, 'How do we get out?' I indicated the exit, which prompted the question, 'How will you know when to leave for the airport?' I told him that I had a watch, to which he replied that I would be so absorbed in Lennie's conducting of *Tristan* that I would not notice time passing. He paused and then said that he would set the alarm on his watch. I begged him not to, which prompted the reply, 'I'll tell you what. You stay where you are and I'll move to the other end of the row. My alarm will go off, you stand up to go, and Lennie will think that it's your watch.' Happily, the alarm was turned off!

One other production which we had hoped he would conduct was the highly successful *Les Contes d'Hoffmann* in 1981. However, he was unsure about the version to be performed, and, in spite of research, he could not come to definite conclusions. He was also uncomfortable with John Schlesinger, who had been engaged to direct it. None of us could persuade him to take a positive view, and we knew that we had lost him after he had seen and detested Schlesinger's film *Sunday, Bloody Sunday*. How much was due to this and how much to musical doubts I do not know.

Throughout these years runs the name of one conductor whose loyalty to the company and whose participation in its growth and development are beyond measure: Sir Edward Downes. From the beginning as a horn player, and then as a member of the music staff before becoming an established conductor, he has been actively concerned with the growing processes of the Royal Opera and contributing hugely to them. Musicians like him are the backbone of opera companies, and without them progress would be minimal. He once said to me, 'I may not be Toscanini, but I'm a damn sight better than many of the foreigners who come here.' Echoes of Beecham!

However distinguished the conductor, without a first-rate music staff preparing singers and assisting at rehearsals his success would not be realized. The building and maintaining of such a staff has always had priority at Covent Garden. Some staff members have left to become conductors and some to do other work, but wherever they are they carry with them the benefits of having often worked with some of the world's greatest conductors. There is good reason for the Covent Garden music staff to be sought after by singers for coaching and for their services to be valued by recording companies and by festivals such as Bayreuth and Salzburg.

4 Composers

It was fitting that the first work in which the opera company was involved at the Royal Opera House after the war was by Henry Purcell, England's greatest composer, with whom two other English composers, Benjamin Britten and Michael Tippett, had a particular affinity. For it was Britten and Tippett, above all others, who led the way in establishing an indigenous operatic tradition in keeping with the aims and aspirations of our founding trustees.

The creation of a national style of operatic presentation which would attract composers and librettists to write for it, envisaged as stemming from the performance of operas in English, was a utopian dream – the product of serious thought, no doubt, but unrealistic in that there were factors at work in the operatic world which would inevitably take Covent Garden down other paths if it was to achieve another aim, not stated in those early days: of becoming a great international opera house. Britten and Tippett, too, were clear about the direction in which they were going, and I am sure would have been unaffected by the language in which other operas were sung. Nevertheless, their operas were a huge boost to this first ideal, and became important components of the company's repertoire.

New works and new productions are the lifeblood of any performing company. Performers need the stimulus of fresh ideas about standard repertoire works and the musical and dramatic challenges of newly composed operas. Stagnation can all too easily set in if the means of extending artistic and musical horizons are absent for too long. While the number of operas written for performance at Covent Garden in the last fifty years is smaller than we wanted, the need to challenge audiences and performers has been well met by those which we were able to present.

Peter Grimes found its way to Covent Garden two years after its successful opening at Sadler's Wells in June 1945, and was conducted by Karl Rankl. It was right that he should have been the conductor, given the importance of this work and his position as music director, although some would have argued the case for Reginald Goodall, who had conducted the work's first performances and to whom it appears that Britten may have promised exclusivity of conducting for two years. *Grimes* was slow to gain ground with audiences, however, and even the 1959 recording with the composer conducting did little to rouse more interest. It was only later that it could be featured in programmes with assurance of a good box office.

By now Benjamin Britten was writing small-scale operas for the English Opera Group, a company which he had formed in 1947 with Peter Pears, John Piper and Eric Crozier, and with more or less the same objectives as the Covent Garden trustees – namely, the creation and performance of new operas and the encouragement of poets and playwrights to tackle the writing of librettos in collaboration with composers. In addition, economy of means was to be explored. Britten used to tell me that he had found musical economy, but complained that this was not matched by visual economy. This was valid comment, but the stage picture is an essential part of opera, however strongly you reject visual elaboration.

Composing for the English Opera Group did not distract Britten from writing for larger theatres. In December 1951 *Billy Budd*, commissioned by the Arts Council for the Festival of Britain, was first performed at Covent Garden, with the composer conducting. Originally it was to have been conducted by Josef Krips, but he withdrew because of difficulties in reading the manuscript score. Perhaps because of its all-male cast, it has not won wide public support, but with its large number of singers and widely differing characters it presents many possibilities for the creation of individual vignettes. It is an ideal company work.

For the Queen's coronation in 1953 the Royal Opera House had commissioned another opera from Benjamin Britten. Entitled *Gloriana*, it was set in the later years of the reign of Elizabeth I, and the portrayal of an ageing monarch was seen by some as inappropriate to the celebration of a young queen's coronation. Conducted by John Pritchard, and with Joan Cross in the title role and Peter Pears as Essex, it was played to a largely uncomprehending and unsympathetic audience. Its poor reception was a blow to Britten. It is a wonderfully written work, vividly contrasting the private and public worlds, with Tudor allusions ingeniously interwoven with music in the composer's own style. Revived once in the following season, with Reginald Goodall conducting, it has not re-entered the Covent Garden repertoire – a mistake – and interest in it flagged until a new production by English National Opera in 1984.

Two operas followed which have been performed on large stages but are essentially chamber works, with small orchestral forces. First came *A Midsummer Night's Dream*, originally composed for the Jubilee Hall at Aldeburgh but quickly finding its way to Covent Garden, where it has held a regular place in the repertoire. The other was *Owen Wingrave*, an opera commissioned by the BBC for television but composed by Britten with the stage in mind and performed at Covent Garden in 1973. It did not capture the public imagination, however, and performances have been infrequent, although increasing interest in it is being shown elsewhere.

It is hard to know whether the *Gloriana* experience discouraged Britten from writing more large-scale stage works. Certainly King Lear and Anna Karenina were subjects going through his mind, and at least one misconceived endeavour to persuade him to adopt the Karenina story was tried. Shortly after I had been appointed to succeed David Webster, in autumn 1969, I was staying at the Red House in Aldeburgh and during the course of a walk by the sea Britten stopped and said, 'John, it's all different now, and I'm going to write a big work for you and Covent Garden.' He did not talk any more about it. A year later he and Peter Pears travelled to Australia to explore the Bush with Sidney Nolan. Britten became fascinated with Aboriginal culture and every aspect of human endurance, and on his return he told me that he and Nolan wanted to write a ballet based on this Australian experience. Would I mind, he asked, if he composed the music for the ballet before he embarked on the opera? Naturally I told him that we would be thrilled to have both, in whatever order. Sadly, we were to have neither, because ill health was beginning to dog him and he was intent on writing what became a valedictory work, *Death in Venice*, with which we were glad to be associated through our then management of the English Opera Group.

It has always been my belief that Britten's earlier attitude to David Webster and Covent Garden was coloured by the failure to follow up an invitation to be involved with the *Fairy Queen*. He was upset by the choice of Constant Lambert as editor of the performing edition and wrote to his publisher, Ralph Hawkes, on 30 June 1946, saying amongst other things: 'The other matter is Covent Garden. As you know I am keen to write an opera for it. But when we will discuss agreements and terms (will we?), it must be clear that I have the veto on performers & producer & conductor. I have no faith in an organisation which has Lambert as assistant conductor, & on the committee behind it – Walton & [E. J.] Dent. After all remember what happened about the *Fairy Queen*, which after all I was invited to be concerned in as clearly as I am now invited to write an opera. If you want to tell the committee this do – I am not frightened of them. I have now other stages to take my works if they don't like my conditions.'

Michael Tippett's personality was very different from Britten's. When you were talking to Britten after a performance of one of his works, invariably he would say, 'Funny old piece, isn't it?' With Tippett, after a performance of something of his, there would be exuberant cries of delight at what we had just heard. Tippett possessed a joyous vitality, which was infectious and exhilarating for all who came in contact with him. His presence at rehearsals and performances was a source of inspiration and encouragement.

Forever adventurous, inquiring and in search of new ideas, Tippett progressively broadened the basis of his approach to operatic composition. His first four operas, all performed at Covent Garden, cover a wide spectrum of styles and presented the company with greater and greater challenges. From the lyricism of *The Midsummer Marriage* there was a move to the sparseness and angularity of *King Priam*, underlining the brutality of the world of Homer's epic. This had its première in Coventry, during a festival to celebrate the building of the new cathedral. In 1970 came *The Knot Garden* – different again, with a score influenced by jazz and blues idioms. Ideas from this were expanded in his next opera, *The Ice Break*, commissioned by Covent Garden for performance in 1977. This was his most concentrated work, and one which he described to me as his most succinct. It was also Tippett at his most experimental. The acts were so full of ideas that their brevity sometimes seemed a mistake.

Michael Tippett was eighty in 1985, and for this birthday we had planned a new production of *The Midsummer Marriage*. However, we encountered casting difficulties and, rather than present an inadequately sung production, decided against going ahead with it. Tippett was upset by the decision and by the delay in reaching it, which led to *The*

Midsummer Marriage being mounted by English National Opera and his next opera, *New Year*, going to Houston and Glyndebourne. Age was probably going to dictate a decline, if not an end, to operatic composition, but Colin Davis and I were saddened by the outcome of a decision we believed we had made in his best interests.

William Walton had long been seized by the idea of writing a truly lyrical opera, and embarked on *Troilus and Cressida*, with a libretto by Christopher Hassall based on Chaucer. It was, he used to say, to be an English bel canto opera. The gestation and writing were slow, composition beginning in 1948 and finishing in time for a première at the Royal Opera House in December 1954. It had a cool reception, and fared no better when repeated in Milan and San Francisco. The music is magnificent, but the work is let down by the language of the libretto, the weakness of some of the characterization, and the looseness of the dramatic structure. Walter Legge's advice was sought by Walton, or perhaps thrust upon him, at one stage in the work's composition. According to Legge's account, his recommendations for tightening the structure were rejected by Walton out of his loyalty to his librettist.

The failure of this opera haunted Walton for the rest of his life, and the reception of the operas of Britten and Tippett brought no comfort to him. In 1976, following the success of the low-budget *Peter Grimes*, we decided to re-present *Troilus* on a similar basis, but with Cressida sung by a mezzo-soprano, Janet Baker, for whom Walton had rearranged the part. (Interestingly enough, this did not involve a huge amount of transposition from the previous soprano part.) The outcome was no better than before, and left Walton, already a sick man, depressed by being deprived of the accolades which he believed were his due. A later production by Opera North (also recorded, as the 1976 production had been) was more warmly received and owed much to its production by Michael Warhus and to the conducting of Richard Hickox, which somehow made the work's weaknesses less obvious.

Walton did write one other opera: a one-act extravaganza for the English Opera Group, based, at the suggestion of Peter Pears, on Chekhov's vaudeville *The Bear*. First performed at Aldeburgh in 1967, it has proved popular and has enjoyed many performances. At a press conference in Covent Garden's crush bar to announce this work, the sound of music came through the curtains from the auditorium during a short lull in the proceedings. Walton, not recognizing it, asked what it was. I told him the orchestra was rehearsing Mátyás Seiber's score for Kenneth

MacMillan's ballet *The Invitation*. 'Ought to be ashamed of himself,' came the reply.

More of Walton's acerbic wit and comment was to be heard later in the year, when the English Opera Group was performing at Expo '67 in Montreal. Benjamin Britten was there with the company, and so was William Walton for other reasons. One day Britten telephoned to suggest that he take Walton to dinner. I agreed, thinking that it would be the two of them. Not at all, and when I revealed that I was not free on the proposed date I was told that I must either cancel what I was doing (attending *Elektra* by the Vienna State Opera at the Place des Arts) or change the dinner date. There was no way that Britten would dine with Walton alone: I had to be there. *Elektra* was cancelled and the day arrived for dinner. Britten called to recheck the time, and urged me to go to his hotel in plenty of time for several Martinis before crossing the street to Walton's hotel, where we were to dine. As we were about to enter the hotel, Britten felt in his pocket and exclaimed that he had left his wallet behind. I told him that it didn't matter and that I would pay. It was an odd moment, because he was clearly looking for excuses to delay meeting Walton, and I wondered why this should be so. The reverse might have been more understandable. After ordering drinks, there was an awkwardness lasting twenty minutes or so. Then suddenly the ice was broken and Walton and Britten were away, discussing everyone and everything, with nobody escaping Walton's barbed remarks. It was a conversation which should have been recorded.

Between *Peter Grimes* and *Billy Budd*, two other English operas were performed: *The Olympians*, by Arthur Bliss, with a text by J. B. Priestley, in 1949, and *The Pilgrim's Progress*, by Ralph Vaughan Williams, in 1951. The former was dogged by adverse conditions at Covent Garden at the time of its production, with neither the audience nor the company ready for such a piece, but even so it is doubtful that it would ever have found a regular place in the repertoire.

Described by the composer as 'A Morality', the Vaughan Williams work is not an opera in the conventional sense but more like a pageant with beautiful, meditative music, and it failed to elicit a strong audience response when first produced professionally. However, performances by students of the Royal Northern College of Music, and a recent concert performance with Richard Hickox conducting, have revealed a stronger structure than was apparent in those early performances and suggest that this work could produce a satisfying theatrical experience if attempted again. It contains a strong emotional and spiritual force which cannot be ignored.

When Peter Hall was still with us and we were discussing a commissioning programme, we decided to invite John Tavener to compose an opera. He settled on the subject of St Thérèse of Lisieux, with Rimbaud acting as her guide through purgatory and hell. The librettist was Gerard McLarnon, and the producer David William.

The problem which this work posed – the portrayal of the inward life against an uneventful outward life – was not solved in this production, and probably never can be. For the work to be effective the listener needs to be free to allow the imagination to roam, and probably this can happen only in a concert performance. The production was a worthwhile attempt, but demonstrated how difficult some human experiences can be to convey on the stage.

The title role had been written for the American soprano Elise Ross, the then wife of Simon Rattle, but when we came to rehearsals Tavener was unhappy with her and asked that she be replaced. I explained the humiliation of this and urged perseverance with her. Tavener was adamant, however, and in the end I agreed to a replacement, Vivien Townley. It was a hard decision, which provoked the wrath of Simon Rattle, who very properly had risen to the defence of his wife.

We were concerned that no opera by Hans Werner Henze had been produced at Covent Garden. Here was a leading composer, with a considerable operatic output, totally unrepresented on the London stage. There had been talk about presenting *The Bassarids* at Covent Garden, but this came to nought after David Webster had seen it in Salzburg and commented unenthusiastically. It was later to be performed by ENO at the Coliseum.

My own opinion was that we had missed the boat with Henze's existing operas and that we should commission a new work from him. This we did, and over lunch one day Henze outlined what he had in mind. At this juncture he knew that he wanted Edward Bond to write the text and that he envisaged the action taking place in various parts of the stage and of the auditorium itself, each segment of action being accompanied by a separate orchestra with its own individual and identifiable sonority. Each character was to be allotted his or her melodic shapes and chord groupings.

Eventually called *We Come to the River*, it was an immensely complex project, with eighty singing parts to be cast, but it had the potential to revolutionize opera production. I was keen that we should experiment with ways of moving beyond conventional stage situations to embrace the audience and auditorium in the action. It did not work out as I had hoped, however, because the original ideas were modified and the action was confined to the stage and the pit. The aural differentiation between the locations was insufficiently defined to lead the listener from one position to another as I had imagined would be the case.

The previous year, 1975, I had persuaded Christopher Hunt to join the artistic administration, and I was to be thankful that I had, because the Henze project was so complicated and time-consuming to organize that without one person working full-time on it we would not have been able to put it together. It was also imperative that this person was musical and familiar with contemporary music. Hunt met all those requirements. Henze directed the work and David Atherton conducted it, revelling in its complexities and bringing his musical and organizational talents to bear on a venture which all too easily could have collapsed without firm control.

It was in the mid-1960s that Edward Downes, who had been conducting a work by Harrison Birtwistle, told me of a conversation with the composer about writing an opera. I jumped at this and telephoned Birtwistle to find out more about his ideas. He described what he and Stephen Pruslin, his intended librettist, were planning. The outcome was an immediate commission to compose an opera to be called *Punch and Judy*, for the English Opera Group. It would be performed in the Jubilee Hall during an Aldeburgh Festival. I telephoned Benjamin Britten and, with some trepidation, told him what I had done. He responded enthusiastically. Plans were laid for the work's first performance at the Jubilee Hall in June 1968, with David Atherton as conductor and Anthony Besch directing. The first night was a critical success, but some of the audience were bewildered by the work and overwhelmed by the sheer volume of sound in the small space of the hall. Benjamin Britten and Peter Pears left hurriedly at the end, apparently appalled by what they had heard. As far as I know, Britten never spoke to Birtwistle.

Whatever the immediate reaction to this work, I had no doubt that Birtwistle was a creative and imaginative composer whom we should encourage to compose more opera. I talked to him again and commissioned another work, this time for Covent Garden. Although the subject was agreed – the Orpheus myth – getting started proved difficult. We met several times, and later were joined by Peter Zinovieff, whom Birtwistle wanted as librettist. Our discussions were frequently hilarious, but progress towards a way forward was slow. In the midst of this Birtwistle had been at Glyndebourne and was increasingly fascinated by Monteverdi and the possibility of making a performing edition of one of his operas. This, in turn, was persuading him to conceive his opera about Orpheus on a smaller scale than we had envisaged and to look to Glyndebourne for a commission. I realized that we had lost Orpheus but might gain a Monteverdi opera – a hope not fulfilled.

Glyndebourne were keen on the Birtwistle project, but, instead of telephoning me to say so, they went ahead with negotiations and called much later to tell me what they had done. I was angry about how they had handled this, but agreed that the commission could be taken over on condition that Covent Garden was reimbursed with the proportion of the composer's fee already paid.

Birtwistle began work in 1973 and was making good progress when in 1976 it became apparent that the scale of the work had grown to such an extent that performances at Glyndebourne would not be possible. The commission lapsed and was revived by ENO in 1981, resulting in performances there in 1986. *The Mask of Orpheus* was a huge critical success, and audience response was encouragingly positive – a reflection of Birtwistle's growing standing and an indication of a developing public interest in contemporary music.

Undeterred by his experiences with *The Mask of Orpheus* and its slow progress to birth and realization on the stage, Harrison Birtwistle came to see me some time after the ENO performances. Not much was said for a while. I felt that he wanted to ask for another commission but could not bring himself to do so. I was right, as I was to discover on pressing him. Thus *Gawain* was born, and was to be a feather in the cap of the next Covent Garden regime.

Two other important European composers were missing from the Royal Opera House: Karlheinz Stockhausen and György Ligeti. The latter welcomed our invitation, but health and other commitments made him wary of accepting another commission. The former, on the other hand, leaped at the opportunity.

I knew of Stockhausen's plan to devote twenty-five years to the writing of an opera for each day of the week, under the collective title of *Licht*. The first, *Donnerstag aus Licht*, had been finished and had already been performed in Milan. *Samstag aus Licht* was under way but not ready. In

1982 I went to Amsterdam to hear part of *Donnerstag* and to discuss plans for London performances with the composer. Of great musical complexity and requiring the integration of electronic music with singers and instrumentalists, it would be an immensely complicated and expensive work to produce, and I was concerned about finding adequate rehearsal time and the means of funding it. The period we initially chose was in mid-season, because that suited Stockhausen and his family, who were essential members of the cast. However, performing a work of such complexity in the midst of other operas and ballets adds to its cost, and I was keen to move it to the beginning of a season. Meanwhile, I was in regular contact with Stockhausen, who one day said that he realized that the second act was the most difficult and expensive for the orchestra. This being so, he had decided to rescore it for a quintet, for which he would find players in Germany and bring them to London rehearsed. I expressed surprise that a score for a large orchestra could effectively be reduced to a quintet. He agreed that the sound would be different, but said he could still achieve what he wanted.

I was still uncomfortable about the placing of this production, and told him that it was in all our interests to postpone it to the following September, 1985. Stockhausen was furious, and wrote the rudest letter I have ever received. There were no grounds for this. It was a matter of postponement, not of cancellation, but he was angry that his plans were being thwarted. When we came to rehearsal he saw the advantages of postponement – of working in an otherwise empty theatre. From then on he was happy, and declared that his interests had never before been so thoughtfully considered.

The introduction of equipment for electronically produced sound was not easy in the old theatre, and it is to be hoped that proper consideration has been given to this in the modernized Covent Garden. Electronics are an expanding ingredient of contemporary music, and ease of access for the necessary equipment must be part of a modern opera house's facilities.

Having visited the Savonlinna Festival, which has been responsible for stimulating serious interest in opera in Finland and beyond since its founding in 1970, and having heard some of the distinctive and individual but accessible music which was coming out of that country, I decided to investigate the Finnish scene more closely. Joonas Kokkonen's *The Last Temptations* had already made its mark and found a place in the Finnish repertoire. Two other composers of note had also appeared –

Aulis Sallinen and Einojuhani Rautavaara – and it was to the former I turned for a work for Covent Garden.

Sallinen had demonstrated in his first opera, *The Horseman*, that he was a musical dramatist. He followed this successful work with another, *The Red Line*, which was to occupy a regular place in the repertoire of Finnish National Opera. For the Covent Garden opera – *The King Goes Forth to France*, a joint commission by the Savonlinna Festival, the BBC and the Royal Opera – he turned to Paavo Haavikko for a libretto. Produced by Nicholas Hytner in 1987, this work was attended by high hopes, but, inventive and individually voiced though Sallinen's music is, the symbolism and obscurity of the text were an impediment to its success and the response from critics and audience was mixed.

In the fifty years since reopening after the war, less opera has been composed for Covent Garden than was originally hoped for. A school of native composers and writers has not materialized in quite the manner envisaged. Nevertheless, the record is quite good – particularly when seen in the context of a number of economic factors affecting theatres, composers and audiences.

Given the perpetual underfunding of the performing arts, box-office considerations have been critical for managements in programme building – not leading to the exclusion of twentieth-century work, or of classical opera with small audience appeal, but requiring a balance tilted more towards the popular and crowd-pulling repertoire.

For the composer, three factors are important: money to live on while composing, a publisher's ability to produce scores and orchestral parts, and some guarantee of performance. The general scene has not been encouraging for the young composer – nor, indeed, for the more established musician. Too often money set aside for a contemporary work has been swallowed up in the mêlée of budget balancing – a situation which Covent Garden has not escaped.

In a way, commissioning an opera is the easy part. It is what comes later that gives rise to many of the difficulties. Publishers face the prospect of a large investment in the preparation of scores and orchestral material with the likelihood of a relatively small financial return from hire fees and their share of the composer's royalties arising from what could well be a mere handful of performances. It is great credit to publishers that they have found their way through the financial thickets and have stood by their composers and by us. It is more important than ever that at least part of the cost of material publication is covered in grants for commissions negotiated with the Arts Council and other funders.

For those unfamiliar with opera, and even for those who are knowledgeable but are unsure about a work, contemporary or classical, there is an element of risk in spending money on tickets. Only the most inquiring and adventurous will go ahead with ticket purchase. This is where European opera houses gain so much from the *abonnement* subscription system, which guarantees the management income whatever the programme and whether or not subscribers attend. There are no refunds. Rolf Liebermann, when intendant at Hamburg, used to tell me that his progressive programming would have been impossible without this system.

Such considerations had no part in Mrs Thatcher's market-forces policy, which largely negated the fundamental principles of public funding of the performing arts as first conceived. The arts need financial support not for purposes of feather-bedding but to enable them to provide access to all and to enable all art forms to find new and stimulating ways of communication. If new routes are closed, staleness will set in and all sense of adventure will be lost. It is not yet clear to what extent this is recognized by the government and the Arts Council today, but I wish that the omens were better.

5 Producers and Designers

Guest producers come and go, but, if successful, their work continues to be seen season after season. Continuity is provided by a team of resident producers and stage managers, working closely with the original producer on preparation for the first performance, and reconstructing the production as faithfully as possible on its return to the repertoire. This is a difficult task. A production built around one group of singers does not necessarily sit comfortably on others with differing personalities, differing performing skills and probably established, if not rigid, views of the way roles should be played. A revived production also has to be energized: vivid explanations of what the original producer had created are needed to convince singers of its validity.

Covent Garden's first resident producer was Peter Brook – on the face of it, an unlikely choice, being young and inexperienced and having progressive attitudes to production. At that moment, however, what was needed was new creation rather than re-creation, there being nothing from the past to revive. Productions were either completely new, as they were for Brook with *Boris Godunov*, *The Olympians*, *Le Nozze di Figaro* and *Salomé*, or were produced within pre-war sets, as was the case with *La Bohème*.

The conditions were not right for Brook, as I have already described, and after two years he left, being succeeded by Christopher West, who was in turn followed by Ande Anderson and later by John Copley. In 1974 the latter was to produce the first new post-war *Bohème*, with sets and costumes designed by Julia Trevelyan Oman. It was a huge success, and demonstrated Copley's strong theatrical sense and ability to capture and portray the spirit of a work. Both Anderson and Copley knew how to put a production together again by the quickest means without sacrificing quality. What they and those working with them have achieved in reviving opera after opera is remarkable. There have been lapses, but perhaps this is inevitable given the nature of what they do. John Copley, frustrated by the lack of opportunities at Covent Garden, has successfully forged a career of his own beyond Covent Garden; others have remained with the Royal Opera and continued in this essential work.

Although Peter Brook was years ahead of his time – and particularly so in relation to a fledgling opera company – his imaginative ideas and his theatrical sense were a source of inspiration to the singers, if not to Karl Rankl, who clung to a conventional view of stage production. Brook was not to return to opera in a proscenium theatre. I tried on several occasions to persuade him to direct at Covent Garden, and we once nearly succeeded when he agreed that *Don Giovanni* was the opera he would like to produce and said that he would do this with Colin Davis conducting. Over lunch one Saturday with Brook, Davis and myself, agreement was reached – or so we believed. But by the following Monday it was off. Brook had thought more about it and, concluding that he was still far away from being able to work in a proscenium opera house, asked to be released from our verbal understanding. It was a huge disappointment. Curiously enough, some fifteen years later, in 1998, he was to direct *Don Giovanni* at the Aix-en-Provence Festival. Successful though that was, it was not in a conventional theatre and I doubt that it signals any second thoughts about opera production.

Apart from the pleasure of being with him and listening to the ideas which flowed from his fertile mind, one of the good things which came from those Peter Brook encounters was the reminder that Sally Jacobs, who had designed his famous production of *A Midsummer Night's Dream*, had returned to London. The timing of his letter telling me this was opportune. We had planned a new production of *Turandot*, which was to be a central feature of our season at the Olympic Arts Festival in Los Angeles in the summer of 1984, and we were having immense difficulty in arriving at an imaginative production and design solution. John Copley, by then a freelance producer, put forward a proposal with designs by Robin Don. They did not strike us as being right, and we moved on to others.

For many years we had been under attack from the art community, and particularly from David Sylvester, for not engaging painters and sculptors as designers for opera and ballet. For dance, a number of artists had in fact already successfully designed sets and costumes. However, the two-dimensional aspect of painting lends itself more readily to ballet than to opera, where the three-dimensional is often essential. Nevertheless, we took the comments of Sylvester and others seriously and had for a long time been of the opinion that our design standards needed to be improved – and consistently so. A design committee of the board, under the chairmanship of Sir Colin Anderson, with Colette Clark as secretary, had undertaken excellent pioneering work, but with not too much evidence of this on the stage. More progress was to be made with the appointment of Bryan Robertson, the critic and former director of the Whitechapel Gallery, as design consultant. He was a joy to work with. He has a real understanding of the theatre, and proposed a number of painters who had an obvious flair for stage design – as evidenced by their spatial sense and feeling for colour – or whose enthusiasm for it might be aroused.

The relationship of colour and music is a fascinating subject which exercises the minds of a number of artists. David Hockney is a wonderful example. I had talked to him about designing *Turandot*, but his other commitments – including his absorption with photography at the time – made this impossible. Happily, we were able to bring two parts of the triple bill which he had designed for the Metropolitan Opera to London: Stravinsky's *Le Rossignol* and Ravel's *L'Enfant et les Sortilèges*. I happened to be with him in his studio in Los Angeles when he was determining the shade of blue appropriate to a particular passage of Stravinsky. The differences were hard to detect, but to his sensitive eye and ear – later to be damaged by growing deafness – they were significant.

In the course of discussions about *Turandot*, Bryan Robertson mentioned Patrick Procktor as a potential designer. I knew something of Procktor's work, and decided to follow up Robertson's suggestion. Procktor and I met, and I believed that *Turandot* and he could be a good match. The problem was finding a stage director who would be able to accommodate Procktor's ideas, or at least give him free enough rein to stimulate his creative imagination. Several suggestions were made, but none seemed appropriate. Then Giancarlo Del Monaco was proposed. I was unsure about him, but asked him to come to London in the hope that I might be wrong and that he would be the person for whom we were searching.

Patrick Procktor went out of his way to find a modus vivendi with him, but to no avail: Del Monaco had fixed ideas about *Turandot*, and it became increasingly obvious that he and Procktor could not work together. I wanted to keep Procktor, but it was difficult to see how to do this. Few stage directors want a designer imposed on them, and we had not found one willing to accept either such an imposition or Procktor's ideas. It was becoming clear that I would have to abandon Procktor, though I was loath to do so for many reasons – not least because I still believed that, if only the right director could be found, he would deliver magnificent designs. But the search was fruitless.

Then a chance conversation with Robert Slotover, an artists' manager, brought up the name of Andrei Serban, a Romanian producer, of whose theatre work I had heard a great deal – particularly a much acclaimed *Cherry Orchard* in New York – and whose productions for Welsh National Opera I had seen. He seemed to be the person for this project – sadly, to work not with Patrick Procktor but with an experienced stage designer. Beni Montresor, who had designed *L'Elisir d'Amore* and *Benvenuto Cellini* for the Royal Opera in 1976, was very keen to be involved; indeed, because of earlier discussions, he believed that we were under an obligation to engage him. I did not share that view and knew that we needed a quite different kind of designer to enable Serban to work to best effect. Serban is prolific with ideas and is not always able to distil them to the point of discarding the less good and embracing the best. We needed an intellectual designer with well-developed views of how *Turandot* might look and how it might be produced. Sally Jacobs was surely the person.

She quickly assessed the situation and created designs which were wonderful to look at, practical and confining in their operation, and suited to the action. What emerged in the collaboration between Serban, Jacobs and the choreographer, Kate Flatt, was a successful amalgam of the techniques of Chinese theatre and grand opera. Later Jacobs was to work with Andrei Serban on *Fidelio*, producing designs after William Blake which were imaginative and symbolic but lacked the means of containing and focusing movement.

Turandot was universally admired, but *Fidelio* was disliked by the majority and praised only by a perceptive few. What went wrong was that Serban came up with half a dozen versions of the last scene. At the penultimate stage rehearsal I told him that he must revise it. He agreed, but said that he had neither the time nor the means to return to the first version, which he knew to be the best. An otherwise illuminating production was therefore spoiled by a final scene running out of control. Then, when this production returned, Serban heeded the critics too literally and revised it so drastically that everything good about it was rejected along with the obviously wrong. We thus lost the makings of an important and illuminating production.

There was a period of nearly ten years, beginning with the 1958/59 season, when the Covent Garden scene was dominated by two Italian producers-cum-designers: Luchino Visconti and Franco Zeffirelli. The style which they brought from Italy was essentially a return to nineteenth-century stage pictures – not, however, through painted canvases and flats, but through three-dimensional built scenery. This was magnificent to behold but difficult and time-consuming to handle – particularly in the cramped backstage areas of the Royal Opera House. Intervals had to be prolonged, and seemed interminable to a restless public. In the case of *Rigoletto*, designed for Zeffirelli by Lila di Nobili, the first scene was followed by an interval lasting twice as long as the scene itself. I protested to Zeffirelli about this, to which came the reply 'The first scene is a ravishing feast for the eye, and an audience needs twenty-five minutes to savour it.'

Productions from these two came thick and fast, beginning in 1958 with Visconti's production of *Don Carlos* – which rapidly became a classic – followed in 1959 by Zeffirelli's *Lucia di Lammermoor*, in which Joan Sutherland triumphed. *Cavalleria Rusticana* and *Pagliacci* were presented with extraordinary and detailed realism: it was quite common for Zeffirelli to send postcards depicting a Sicilian wagon or a costume, explaining that these were what he wanted and would we please copy. Some of these productions may seem old-fashioned, but many have stood the test of time superbly. Zeffirelli's *Tosca*, created for Maria Callas and Tito Gobbi in 1964, remains unsurpassed, and so, in my judgement, does *Don Carlos*, presenting a perfect environment for the action to unfold in and containing some of the best perspective painting to be seen anywhere. Its only weakness lies in the auto-da-fé scene. Visconti came to this scene last – partly, I think, because he did not know what to do with it and partly because money was running out – and coloured banners stretched from side to side were an inexpensive way of filling an empty-looking stage.

Two of Zeffirelli's productions we borrowed – *Alcina* from Venice and *I Puritani* from Palermo, both operas being vehicles for Joan Sutherland. The Handel was presented in an elaborate eighteenth-century pastiche, and the Bellini in a copy of nineteenth-century sets – simple but effective. We had chartered space on a steamer to bring the *Puritani* sets and costumes from Palermo. Unfortunately, the boat ran into atrocious weather while making its way down the west coast of Italy to Sicily, and was so delayed that there was no chance of the scenery being in London in time for our performances. Air freight was the only solution, and two planes of suitable size were hired. When loading began, most of the scenery was found to be too large for the hold doors, in spite of earlier careful measurement checks. I was telephoned by our carpenter supervising the loading and, having spoken to the soprintendente of Palermo, I was clear that the scenery had to be sawn into smaller sections. Such was the enthusiasm of the Italian carpenter instructed to do this that we were left with hundreds of small pieces like a jigsaw puzzle. By some miracle, and with the help of Palermo's master carpenter, we were able to reassemble them in London. The sets were returned to Palermo by boat – and not as the puzzle we had received.

Visconti and Zeffirelli worked within a style which they consistently sustained, although for Visconti there came a moment when a search for novelty took over and ended in two less convincing productions: *Der Rosenkavalier* (art nouveau) and *La Traviata* (Beardsley black and white). After *La Traviata* with Visconti in 1967 and *Tosca* with Zeffirelli in 1964, however, we were not to see this pair of eminent Italians at the Covent Garden again. The style and insight which they brought to their work was of huge importance to the Royal Opera House and was warmly welcomed by the public, but what they represented had to give way to other influences. Self-indulgence was always lurking in the background, with both of them, and was to erupt on a large scale in productions which Zeffirelli was later to make for La Scala and New York. It is true that audiences in both these cities like spectacle, but Zeffirelli has fulfilled their desires at gigantic cost to the companies. Even if the money can be found, there is a limit to what should be spent on a production, not only from an artistic standpoint but also from that of public perception. The spending of ludicrous sums of money brings disrepute in its wake, playing into the hands of those hostile to opera and, where public funding is concerned, bringing discredit to its management.

In spite of the financial risk, I did ask Zeffirelli to direct a new production of *Carmen* which we were planning for the 1972/73 season, with Sir Georg Solti conducting. Two years previously I had talked to Giorgio Strehler about this opera and had reached an agreement with him – much to my surprise. A change of mind was expected, and it came shortly afterwards. I was on holiday on Elba a few weeks after the

Strehler meeting and I came across a friend of his who told me that Strehler was having doubts about the standard of his English and was wary of directing through an interpreter. As it turned out, there was another problem, which I suspected was at the heart of his objections, and that was the opera itself. As I had arranged with him, he eventually met Solti and confronted the maestro with the statement that he was not interested in directing *Carmen* unless he could rewrite the text.

That being the end of that, I suggested Zeffirelli to Solti, who was keen that I should talk to him. Zeffirelli jumped at the chance of returning to Covent Garden and regarded *Carmen* as the perfect vehicle. From the beginning he wanted to play Acts 3 and 4 together, which I welcomed since it makes dramatic sense to do so. However, there was a snag. Zeffirelli believed that he needed to move the beautiful Act 4 entr'acte to a later point in the act. This was unlikely to be acceptable to Solti or to any of us. The entr'acte had its rightful position – after all, Bizet did know what he was doing.

There was also to be another problem, which came as a bolt out of the blue in a telephone conversation. Zeffirelli had concluded that he did not know how to produce the Habanera satisfactorily and told me that he wanted to cut it. Naturally I replied that this was out of the question. Undeterred, when we came to meet Solti, Zeffirelli repeated quite seriously what he had said to me. Solti was flabbergasted by both requests. We parted, and it was to be some time before Zeffirelli and I met to talk about another project – the production of *La Traviata* at the Royal Opera House as a prelude to a film.

Having lost Strehler and Zeffirelli, we turned to Michael Geliot to direct *Carmen*. It was designed by Jenny Beavan and David Fielding, and kept its place in the repertoire for some years. Some fourteen or fifteen years later, when considering a new production, our thoughts turned to the film director Louis Malle, whom I had heard might be interested in producing an opera. He agreed to meet, but with little hesitation rejected *Carmen*. While he accepted that the opera was a Frenchman's observation of Spanish life, he felt that for a Frenchman it was nothing more than a cliché. The opera which really interested him was *Così fan tutte*, for which I would have engaged him if my time at Covent Garden had not been coming to an end.

Another Italian producer who was to make an early impression but was then to lose his way is Piero Faggioni. With designs by Ken Adam, he created a stupendous production of Puccini's *La Fanciulla del West* in which he showed extraordinary attention to detail and used the chorus brilliantly by creating vignettes around each of them. Naturally he quickly won their respect and affection as well as producing a wholly convincing gold-mining community.

The board had been discouraging of spending money on a production of *La Fanciulla del West*, some directors considering it a poor work unworthy of a place in Covent Garden's repertoire. Some of us thought otherwise. Fortunately we created a very successful production, which led Sir Isaiah Berlin after the first performance to say to me, 'Many congratulations, John, on making the third rate into the second rate.'

There was no doubt that we wanted Faggioni to return, which he agreed to do for a production of Puccini's *Manon Lescaut*. By now he was becoming increasingly absorbed with creating his own designs, which he believed offered the best chance of arriving at a design solution which would accommodate his production ideas and plans. Having seen some of his sketches, I thought that he was right and awaited the drawings for *Manon Lescaut*. They were marvellous – quite the best that I had seen for this opera – but I was concerned about the depth of stage the set would require for its full effectiveness and the difficulties that would be created in the handling of other scenery. Faggioni was asked if he could limit the setting depth, but he believed that this would destroy the visual impact and understandably he refused. After much thought the project was abandoned, and we lost what I think could have been a well-integrated production of an opera which all too readily falls into the episodic form in which it was composed, thus detracting from its dramatic success. A modernized Covent Garden can now easily accept a production such as Faggioni proposed.

A glance at Royal Opera productions over the years reveals cycles in which various producers have dominated the scene. Following Visconti and Zeffirelli came Peter Hall, and then Götz Friedrich.

Hall's first production was the justly acclaimed *Moses und Aron*, with Sir Georg Solti and Hall's regular collaborator as designer, John Bury. Hall was anxious to fill the stage with animals at the appropriate moments, and was particularly keen to have a camel. Inquiries about sources of supply eventually took us to Colchester Zoo. We were apprehensive about having so many animals in the theatre, but Hall swept aside all objections – in spite of the zoo director warning me that if a camel came near a donkey it would rapidly become uncontrollable. In order to lessen possible damage and not to put any of the cast at risk, I suggested that we should rehearse the animals separately after a Sunday technical rehearsal. The animals were led on stage, and within moments the camel saw and smelled the donkey and went berserk. It was chaos for a time, with the camel kicking the raised stage floor so hard that one of its hooves went through it. Peter Hall was then convinced, and we did not see the camel again.

Moses und Aron presented many musical difficulties and was a huge challenge for the company, but surely and inspiringly led by Solti and Hall, and with Forbes Robinson and Richard Lewis in the title roles, they gave momentous performances of this opera, one of the great master-pieces of the twentieth century and the work which best encapsulates Schoenberg's musical ideals and his feelings about his Jewish faith. Inevitably the orgy scene attracted much attention from press and pub-lic. The composer's widow attended rehearsals and the first night. When I asked for her reaction to the production, she replied that her husband would have been content with it apart from the orgy – which he would have regarded as not nearly wild enough.

Covent Garden seems to have had something of an obsession with *Die Zauberflöte*, because five productions have been made since the war. The first, in 1947, was by Malcolm Baker-Smith, with designs by Oliver Messel. The second, in 1956, was by Christopher West, with designs by John Piper and Alix Stone. The third, in 1962, was by Otto Klemperer, with designs by Georg Eisler. The fourth, in June 1966, was by Peter Hall, who, in collaboration with his designer, John Bury, returned to the original requirements of Mozart's librettist, Emanuel Schikaneder (the first Papageno), and illuminated the action with flying machines, trap-doors and transformations where these are demanded in the stage direc-tions. If less elegant than the 1947 production, the sublime music and the magic prevailed. These qualities were present in the next production by August Everding and Jurgen Rose.

The 1970/71 season was an all-Hall production year, with *The Knot Garden*, *Eugene Onegin* and *Tristan und Isolde*, giving a taste of what might have been achieved if he had been able to stay as joint director of the Royal Opera. He worked with three different designers in these, and in each opera there was the indelible mark of a creative imagination at work. The abstract sets of Tim O'Brien provided what he needed for the Tippett opera, and Julia Trevelyan Oman's detailed and authentic scen-ery and costumes for *Onegin* were right in every respect – the production smelled of Russia, and caught vividly the contrast between the scene in which Onegin and Lensky clash at a ball in the bourgeois household of Mme Larina and the grand ballroom scene in St Petersburg. In *Tristan*, Hall and John Bury wanted to make a visual differentiation between the moments of darkness and light by having sections of the scenery move apart during the action. For example, the ship divided when Tristan and Isolde were together, and similarly in Act 2 the tower from which Brangäne sings her warning was moved upstage while the lovers remained in the foreground. It was an inventive plan, but it could be seen from the model that the amount of movement possible would be too limited to achieve what Hall and Bury wanted; nevertheless, they wished to proceed with it. I agreed, and their plan was tried in the first run of performances, although lack of space did mean that it was subsequently abandoned.

Peter Hall brought to opera a very real theatrical sense, coupled with deep musical awareness and reverence. For Covent Garden, he was also able to impose a discipline on the technical operation of performances. With daily changes of sets between rehearsals and performances, and in the cramped and unmechanized stage conditions then prevailing, the exacting standards which we sought were hard to maintain, but his influence was all-important.

In the 1987/88 season he returned to Covent Garden with a production of *Salomé* which had earlier been presented in Los Angeles. I had seen it there, and was so struck by it, and by Maria Ewing's performance, that I invited them on the spot to bring it to London. Before this we had discussed a new production of the *Ring*, but this was abandoned when he was invited to Bayreuth in 1983 to direct a production with Georg Solti conducting.

The *Ring* has featured prominently in Covent Garden's repertoire, and Götz Friedrich's arrival to direct it for the 1976 centenary opened a new chapter in its history in the House. From the beginning I asked that we should receive an overall plan for the *Ring*, with at least an outline from Josef Svoboda, Friedrich's designer, so that we could see how it was to be developed visually and could begin to have some idea of cost. Such a plan was never produced, and we moved from opera to opera without any idea of what the next would be like. One of the reasons for this was Friedrich's intention to pursue what he saw as a difference of mode between the dramas. It emerged that there was not to be visual unity. For example, Friedrich was unconcerned that in *Siegfried* Brunhilde woke up on a different rock from that on which she had gone to sleep in *Die*

Walküre. I remonstrated, but was told that it did not matter. Throughout, the stage represented the world, and a hydraulic platform a space on
which the action unfolded – with Wotan, Loge and Alberich addressing
the audience from outside it. It was just such an imaginative and original
approach as we had hoped for as we searched for a producer immersed
in Wagner but yet to produce his first *Ring*.

As the *Ring* was put together, some things occurred to which Friedrich
had difficulty in responding. I was concerned that Valhalla would be
invisible to a section of the audience in the amphitheatre, remembering
the bad reaction we had encountered with *Der Fliegende Holländer*
because of the ship being out of sight. Friedrich was unmoved by this,
and seemed to be content so long as the critics saw it. In *Die Walküre*,
Svoboda had designed a sort of catapult to transport the bodies of the
heroes to Valhalla. I told Friedrich that this would appeal to the British
sense of the ridiculous and provoke laughter. He disagreed, and insisted
on proceeding with it. I said that I would return to this issue if there was
any sign of mirth at the general rehearsal. There was, and I asked him to
reconsider this part of the production. This was on a Saturday. On
Monday he called the *Walküre* ladies to a rehearsal and talked to them
for an hour or so about philosophical aspects of the *Ring*, at the end of
which one of them came to my room to ask for an explanation of what
she had been listening to, because she had not understood. I told her,
and she expressed astonishment that Friedrich could indulge in a long
abstract argument about the correction of a practical problem. Unwilling to admit defeat, Friedrich was unhappy about having to make a
change and told me that I had wounded him.

It was a successful *Ring*. Indeed, some found it the most illuminating
they had seen, and there was a strong wish on our part to continue with
it for as long as possible. However, such epics ideally need the regular
attention of the original producer if they are to maintain their quality at
a desirable level, but producers are not necessarily keen on revisiting
earlier productions – and few can find the time in any event. Friedrich
had moved on to another view of the cycle, and it was becoming clear
that we needed to find another solution.

It was while he was working on *The Knot Garden* that Tim O'Brien
telephoned to tell me of a talented producer whom he had come across in
Oxford. He urged me to go and see a production of *As You Like It* which
Elijah Moshinsky had mounted at the Oxford Playhouse. It was excellent – imaginative, and well conceived and executed. I reported this to

Colin Davis, and we decided that we should offer Moshinsky an engagement as a member of the Royal Opera's production staff. He accepted, and so began a long association between him and Covent Garden. His first venture, in the 1974/75 season, was *Peter Grimes* – a critical and popular success indicating beyond doubt that we had in him the makings of an imaginative and important opera producer. *Lohengrin* followed in 1977 – again a low-budget presentation, which showed his ability to distil the essence of the work and make a production which was faithful to the music and at the same time illuminating in its statements. Moshinsky's intellect is sharp, and he has the ability to illustrate what he finds in a score and its text without offending against the spirit of the music or the composer's intentions.

One of the operas which Moshinsky was later to produce was *Samson et Dalila*, which he and I were keen should be designed by Sidney Nolan, with whom I had been discussing opera design for a number of years, including a plan for him to design the 1976 *Ring*. A Wagnerian and steeped in the *Ring*, Nolan had been enthusiastic, and I had been able to persuade Götz Friedrich to accept him, but when we reached the point of confirmation Nolan backed away. He cited other painting commitments, but I have always suspected that it was Cynthia, his then wife, who objected. She hated Wagner, and seemed intent on preventing her husband from becoming involved with a Wagnerian project.

The Saint-Saëns opera – produced in October 1981, with Colin Davis conducting – presented no problems, and Nolan happily accepted. However, at the time when we would have expected designs to be submitted Nolan was in Australia. He explained that he would soon be in England, but it transpired that his route to this country was via China and the Gobi Desert. Time for modelling and making the sets was running out, and there was no further news from him until Moshinsky received a phone call from the Gobi Desert – I have always had an image of Nolan in a red telephone box in the middle of the desert calling to explain his continuing absence. At the end of May, with the production opening in October, Nolan walked into my room with a swatch of silk tucked under his arm, saying, 'Don't worry, John, we'll make it – and here's the material for a couple of Dalila's dresses,' as he handed over the silk he had brought from China. Make it we did – and very successfully.

This production – shortage of time apart – was a good example of how a painter can apply his skills to the creation of scenery in conjunction with modelmakers who dictate the scale and help to translate the designs into three dimensions. In three or four weeks *Samson et Dalila* was ready for the workshops, and then in turn ready for the stage.

Sidney Nolan was to collaborate again with Elijah Moshinsky, on Mozart's *Die Entführung aus dem Serail* in November 1987. This had a less good outcome, because the scenic demands of the opera demanded a stage designer, who was Tim O'Brien, and Nolan was there only on the periphery, contributing act drops almost as an afterthought. The painting of these cloths was splendid, but it would have been better not to have had them and they were dropped on the opera's revival.

Nolan and Moshinsky spent time together and had started to plan a *Ring*. News of this reached me, and I was anxious to pursue it, believing that this could well be the answer to our problems following our inability to go further with the Friedrich production. However, on discussing it with Bernard Haitink, who would be conducting the next cycle, I found little enthusiasm. Haitink had not been happy with Moshinsky's *Lohengrin* production, which he had previously conducted – he felt the placing of the chorus impaired the sound – and wanted to look elsewhere. If we had stayed with the Nolan/Moshinsky team the story of the *Ring* over the last few years might well have been different.

Some years after this, and after I had left Covent Garden, I was lunching with the Nolans at their country house when the subject of an Australian *Ring* – a plan already mooted but previously abandoned – came up once again. This time it was a serious offer, from the Victorian State Opera in Melbourne, for Nolan to design it, with a young Australian director, Elizabeth Gail, producing. Nolan wanted to accept, but would do so only if I agreed to coordinate the whole operation for him. I said that I would, and looked forward to what could have been an exciting project. Sadly, it came to nothing, because the money was not in place and then Sidney Nolan tragically died. Australia now has a *Ring*, not in Melbourne but in Adelaide.

From early days, Elijah Moshinsky understood the need to create productions which were the product of sound research and of examination with fresh eyes and ears. He also realized that complicated stage settings and action would hamper the introduction of different casts in the future. This was certainly the case with operas such as *Otello* with a Domingo and relatively little rehearsal time. Complicated productions require more rehearsal time than is sometimes possible, with the result that they reappear underprepared and with singers poorly integrated into the action.

During the 1970s and '80s Covent Garden was accused of playing safe. In some ways we did – not unimaginatively, but in an attempt to create productions which would stand the test of time and permit us to engage the world's greatest singers to appear in them. The public want to hear these artists, and it has been our responsibility to make this possible from every standpoint. In this we succeeded, not at the expense of all innovation but with practical considerations in mind.

A high proportion of the year's work is dependent on the skills and dedication of the resident production team and the music staff. The latter are involved in the musical preparation of singers in advance of production rehearsals where this is requested by the singer or sought by the management. There is now less coaching of soloists by the Royal Opera staff than there used to be, because singers tend to be more self-sufficient and are frequently too busy to come into Covent Garden for rehearsal. There is a downside to this. Preparation of a role goes further than just learning the notes: help is often needed in interpreting the music and text, understanding the interrelationship of words and music, developing the characterization, and bringing the score and the role to life. This serious preparatory work was at the heart of the Royal Opera's policy, and its diminution must be rectified if the company is to regain lost ground and be again counted as one of the great opera houses of the world.

6 *Singers*

From the beginning it was the intention to form an ensemble at Covent Garden, to promote native singers and to integrate them in casts with foreign artists. In those early days there were few British singers with any operatic experience. For everyone the learning curve was steep, and every opportunity for improvement needed to be seized.

Although its future was uncertain for some years after its formation, Covent Garden Opera soon became the company with which singers wanted to be associated. Australians were joining in considerable numbers, and when Joan Sutherland arrived, in 1952, among sopranos alone there were four other Australians either already or soon to be there: Sylvia Fisher, Eleanor Houston, Elsie Morison and Una Hale. When Sutherland first sang in *Die Zauberflöte* in the autumn of that year, two other members of the cast were Australian, John Lanigan and Arnold Matters, and one was a New Zealander, Inia Te Wiata.

In addition to artists from the Commonwealth, there were singers from America, Germany, Austria, Italy and elsewhere in Europe to supplement the British company. The singing of opera in English limited the number of European singers who could be engaged, although there were occasions when a singer needed for a particular role could sing only in German, say. Then he or she would perform in that language and the remainder of the cast in English. The language policy was to change later, but it was realized in those first years that some operas had to be sung in German because of the impossibility of assembling suitable casts capable of singing in English. Operas which fell in this category included *Tristan und Isolde* and the *Ring*, although Kirsten Flagstad and Hans Hotter did perform *Die Walküre* in English in 1948. It was also a matter of enabling the public to hear certain famous singers who would not otherwise have performed in post-war London. Nevertheless, it is extraordinary to recall that singers such as Elisabeth Schwarzkopf, Ljuba Welitsch, Hans Hotter and Paolo Silveri were willing to learn roles in English and give a fledgling company the benefit of their experience as well as huge pleasure to audiences.

I was pleased to come across Silveri again a year or two before I left Covent Garden. I had been to performances of his, I had met him when he came to talk to undergraduates at Cambridge, and I had seen him subsequently – but many years ago. As I walked into my room at the opera house one day, I was greeted by an Italian. He asked me if I knew who he was. Rashly, I replied in the affirmative, to be met with the response, 'Tell me.' God was with me and I answered correctly. Silveri would have been so offended had I failed.

Singers were found from all over the British Isles, but, not surprisingly, the largest numbers came from Wales. These were men and women with music and singing in their blood, and this tradition continues in Wales today, even though the chapel is less of a force than it was. Singing comes naturally to the Welsh, and this, coupled with an emotional energy in their make-up, makes for great performances. Such was the strength of the Welsh influence in the company that we all dreaded the Saturday-night performance following a Welsh defeat in an important rugby match that afternoon. The depression was acute.

Even the most casual survey of the singers who have appeared at Covent Garden in the last fifty years reveals how comprehensive the list is, how few of the great singers of this half-century are missing, and the regularity with which many singers returned. However, it is interesting to note the differences in the patterns of the careers of two Welshmen, Geraint Evans and Bryn Terfel, one of whom started in the early days of Covent Garden and the other towards the end of the pre-closure period. Evans was very much a company member and personified that kind of singer – loyal, committed, giving the Royal Opera House priority in accepting engagements, and regarding Covent Garden as home. For Bryn Terfel and other stars of his generation – unattached to a company, in huge demand, and moving freely around the world – there is now a different order.

Geraint Evans made his Covent Garden debut as the Nightwatchman in *Die Meistersinger* in 1948. There is an apocryphal story about this. Intensely nervous as he was about to make his first entry for that all too brief appearance, he longed for encouragement and support. But all he heard coming from the pit was, 'Where the bloody hell are we?' This question is attributed to Sir Thomas Beecham – and might well have been uttered by him if he had been conducting that night. Beecham did lose the place from time to time, and players have told me that slashing the air with his baton as he frantically turned the pages of his score was a sure sign that all was not well. But what a musician and conductor!

Evans's career moved ahead rapidly, but, unlike today, British singers were then rarely offered roles overseas: it was not until the 1950s that their quality began to be recognized, and even then engagements were slow to follow. Geraint Evans was among the first to establish the British singer abroad, following his success in *Le Nozze di Figaro* at La Scala in 1960. Of course it was also at La Scala that Eva Turner had made her debut in 1924, and at Brescia where she had triumphed as Turandot in 1926, but her success was not followed by any upsurge of interest in British artists in general. Evans, on the other hand, became increasingly in demand, and so did many others.

Conductors had already furthered the cause of some singers. It was through Erich Kleiber, who had instilled self-confidence in singers at Covent Garden, that Constance Shacklock was engaged to sing Brangäne in Berlin in 1952. In the following year Kleiber took Sylvia Fisher and Edgar Evans to Rome for the *Ring*. The doors of Bayreuth were opened to Covent Garden singers by Jon Vickers as Siegmund in 1958. Amy Shuard, David Ward and Otakar Kraus were to find their way there, too, on the recommendation of Rudolf Kempe. In addition to these artists, others – Gwyneth Jones and Donald McIntyre, to name but two – were increasingly in demand overseas, encouraged and recommended by successive music directors – Georg Solti, Colin Davis and Bernard Haitink – as well as by others who were impressed by the quality and breadth of British talent.

What was started in 1947, and continued for many years, was not only a company awareness among singers and staff, but also the development of an ensemble in which roles were studied and performed at a steady pace. Singers working in these conditions gained immeasurably from coaching by an experienced music staff and from learning stagecraft from the resident producers and from each other. There was no make-up team available at first, except for character make-up, and singers did their own, often seeking advice from more experienced colleagues. There seems to have been an expectation that a singer would arrive equipped to do everything. That was unrealistic – and still is, although singers are better prepared for professional life than they used to be. There is much to be learned, and the days of the ensemble gave the singer the best chance of doing so and building repertoire and technique for a long career. The pressure on some singers did become too intense at times, however – as it did for Joan Sutherland – and the management then had to readjust casting and schedules to ease it. Money was short, and it took a huge amount of will to ensure that rehearsal time was not unreasonably cut in pursuit of economy.

Much though we may mourn the virtual demise of the ensemble and yearn for its return, it was not without its problems – not least in trying to satisfy the growing needs of singers as they developed their capabilities. Geraint Evans, for example, was often frustrated and angered by his inability to move from Schaunard to Marcello in *La Bohème*, and later by the absence of offers from Covent Garden of roles for which he felt suited and which were coming to him from other opera houses.

Finding sufficient performances of the right roles for singers within the company or closely associated with it presented many problems. Singers rightly have their minds set on new challenges, and the further they progress the greater their expectation of plum roles; but inevitably there may sometimes be doubt that a singer can perform a longed-for role to the standard expected and demanded by the management and the public. However, if there is sufficient faith that an artist can fulfil expectations, it can be a gamble but there must be no holding back. Frustration and resentment can bedevil an artist's relationship with the management when his or her wishes are not met. A delicate balance has to be struck between risk and potential fulfilment. Such problems were more often than not sorted out, but they created tensions and strained loyalties.

With the benefits of earlier working practice in mind, in the 1980s we introduced a scheme whereby two young singers would join the Royal Opera, sing small parts, and cover larger parts and eventually take them over. Outside engagements had to be vetted so that a sensible work pattern could be maintained – not to mollycoddle the singers but simply to protect young voices from overstrain. We were fortunate in finding a benefactor for this scheme – Jack Heinz, who had once asked me how he could help and who responded generously to this proposal – and the first two singers selected were Judith Howarth and Linda Kitchen.

On coaching, we knew that some singers would benefit if the excellent work of our music staff was supplemented by working on particular roles with other singers renowned for them or with other coaches in Europe. Again, we benefited from the generosity of well-wishers – this time the Astors. One example of the use of this scheme was sending Michael Langdon to Vienna to study Baron Ochs with a great exponent of that role, Alfred Jerger.

The Covent Garden chorus contained some fine voices, and it was no surprise that at quite an early moment in its life singers emerged who were to have very successful careers as soloists. Other soloists came from the chorus later, but as time went by fewer and fewer singers saw membership of the chorus as the route to a solo career. Opportunities for small parts and covering of roles diminished as soloists were engaged for them. While this was in pursuit of higher standards, I became increasingly aware of a feeling of hopelessness creeping into some sections of the chorus as they saw their chances of individual work disappearing. I was keen to change this practice in the interests of the choristers and in the hope of attracting good singers to the chorus through some solo opportunities. It is a difficult balance to strike, and only limited progress was made.

The year 1952, as well as seeing the arrival at Covent Garden of Joan Sutherland, who was to be launched on a great international career with *Lucia di Lammermoor* in 1959, also saw the Covent Garden debut of another distinguished soprano whose career was already under way: Maria Callas, in *Norma*. This was the start of an association with Covent Garden which continued until her operatic career came to a halt, her last appearance being as Tosca in 1964. She was fond of David Webster, who reciprocated her affection, and she found at Covent Garden an agreeable atmosphere and the right conditions for serious work.

She was renowned for her rows and tantrums, but these were rarely experienced in London. She was a perfectionist, and she became angry only when she felt her quest for perfection was being needlessly obstructed by management or by insensitive colleagues – particularly if they did not know their roles well enough. She was patient and understanding with young singers, and those who came into contact with her benefited from observing her and from the occasional comment which she might make. In *Tosca*, for example, Cavaradossi was sung by a young and inexperienced tenor from Elba, Renato Cioni, to whom she could not have been more encouraging.

Callas's presence in the opera house was always felt. It was not that everyone thought that they had to be on their best behaviour, but there was something in the air which made for alertness and a determination to live up to the standards which she set. Here, in our midst, was one of the very greatest singers and performers, who had opened up the bel canto repertoire and shown us how it should be sung. It was a revelation.

She was not a confident performer. The preparation for a performance and the waiting to go on were nerve-racking periods for her. As the moment approached, she would cling to Gertie Stelzel, her dresser, or to somebody else in the wings, leaving a bruise where she had pressed the hand or the wrist with her nails. She would then deliver a breathtaking performance. Like others at the top of their profession, she was aware of the public's high expectations and was terrified of not living up to them. It was a burden of which she was never to divest herself – in fact it worsened. When she was with Aristotle Onassis she did not perform for longish periods, and when she returned to the stage every performance became a first night for her.

There were times when she would let her hair down – not always to the delight of others. One Sunday afternoon there were rehearsals for the later live transmission of Act 2 of *Tosca* during a programme presented by Associated Television and entitled *The Golden Hour*, in which Callas was to feature more than once. I left after seeing the beginning of the rehearsal, but on arriving at my house I was telephoned by Bill Ward, the producer of the programme, who was in utter despair because Callas and Tito Gobbi had joked throughout the camera rehearsal and had left everybody in a state of uncertainty about where they were to be on the stage for the performance. This was in part to relieve their own tensions, but it also created an atmosphere in which everyone would be on their toes during the transmission. The performance which ensued was electrifying and has become a legend.

For another of these *Golden Hour* programmes Callas was joined by Giuseppe di Stefano, who was unwell on the day of transmission. The programme started at 8 p.m., and at that time di Stefano was not only not in the theatre but refusing to leave the Savoy Hotel. Callas decided that she needed a B12 injection, and some time was spent in finding a doctor. Meanwhile there was still no sign of di Stefano, and the clock was approaching 8.25. I was at the stage door telephoning the tenor once more when Lew Grade, the chairman of ATV, came to express his concern about the second half of the programme. We had already moved one artist from the second part to the first to fill the gap left by the tenor's absence. I rashly assured him that di Stefano would be with us shortly, and asked Grade to move all the commercial breaks forward to give more time before the singer had to go on. By some miracle I had persuaded di Stefano to come. He sang one song and immediately excused himself, to return later for a duet with Callas.

Later, Callas and di Stefano were to undertake a concert tour. Callas was singing poorly and the venture was a huge mistake, doing nothing to enhance her reputation. Many were dismayed by this, and regarded her career as being finished. I was less sure that this need be the case, and in 1973 I talked to her about returning to Covent Garden in the 1975/76 season to sing Santuzza in a revival of *Cavalleria Rusticana*, with Placido Domingo as Turiddu. Vocally the part was right for her, and with a strong cast to support her it seemed a secure way for her to make a comeback. She agreed, and all was set until a phone call came to tell me that she had thought more about it and that she needed a grander role with which to make her re-entrance. Tosca it had to be. I could not persuade her otherwise, though I warned her of the obvious problems for her if she persisted.

To give her encouragement, and to discover how things really were with her vocally, I sent Jeffrey Tate, then a member of the music staff, to Paris to work with her for a few weeks. All went well at the beginning, but then the phone calls started, telling me that she was not feeling well and that I should recall Tate to London. Nevertheless, she continued to work spasmodically with him until a photographer discovered that she was rehearsing at the Théâtre des Champs-Élysées. That was the end for her.

We spoke on the telephone from time to time, and I would see her when I was in Paris. An intensely lonely woman, she lived in a world of her own and could not recognize that anything worthwhile was going on operatically. When I took my leave of her, she would ask where I was going. I usually replied, 'To the Opéra,' which invariably produced an outburst to the effect that there no singers of any merit and that I was wasting my time. 'Much better to stay and have dinner with me,' she would say. The last time I spoke with her was in 1976, when I was at home recovering from hepatitis. She had heard that I was poorly and had rung to wish me well. As our conversation was finishing, she suddenly said, 'John, you were right about Santuzza. I should have taken your advice.' I never heard from her again.

While many singers who joined the opera company had previously been freelancing, there were a number who came from Sadler's Wells.

These included Amy Shuard, James Johnston, David Ward, Donald McIntyre and Peter Glossop, all of whom had benefited from learning and singing large roles in a smaller theatre and in a relatively unpressurized atmosphere. This stood them in good stead for the challenges of bigger theatres, both at home and abroad. The decision to move Sadler's Wells Opera from Rosebery Avenue to the Coliseum deprived British opera of a wonderful breeding ground for singers. The Coliseum – larger than the Royal Opera House – could not give young singers the same opportunities, and certainly not in big roles without the risk of damage. This gap has now been partially, if not wholly, filled by the regional companies. The move to the Coliseum was the only source of dissension between myself and Stephen Arlen, the managing director of Sadler's Wells, with whom I had otherwise worked for many years harmoniously and to the benefit of our two theatres. Sadly, he was taken ill shortly after the move to St Martin's Lane and tragically died.

It is worth reminding ourselves of the strength of the Covent Garden Opera of thirty or forty years ago. In 1957 *Les Troyens* was mounted in its entirety and cast solely from the company with the exception of Dido. In that cast, as Aeneas, was one of the great artists of post-war Covent Garden, Jon Vickers, discovered by David Webster two years previously in Canada. That country was the source of a number of other fine singers who found their home with us. In 1958, when *Don Carlos* was produced, Joseph Rouleau, a French Canadian basso cantante, sang the Monk, with Vickers as Don Carlos. Others who followed included André Turp and Louis Quilico.

Jon Vickers, one of the truly great heroic tenors of this age, was more sure of what he wanted and more determined to achieve it than any other singer I can think of. I admired him for his tenacity, for his deeply felt faith and sense of purpose, but I could equally be maddened by him as he went into one of his tirades and argued from a standpoint which was often impenetrable. But what mattered was that I and countless others were swept off our feet by his magnificent singing. There was an intensity in his performances which has rarely been matched, and he never failed to thrill and to move audiences.

Immensely careful of his voice, Vickers was wary of roles which he regarded as too heavy and potentially damaging, and ensured that his performances were well spaced. Once in London, he would stay here until the end of the engagement, perhaps going to Vienna to see his throat specialist if the need arose.

Vickers has no doubt that his voice is God-given, and hence thought has to be given to the content as well as to the vocal suitability of a role. Moral integrity was an ingredient which he sought in the make-up of all the characters he portrayed. He felt deeply about this, as indeed he does about every aspect of life. Nevertheless, it was hard to understand how he could come to terms with a role like Siegmund in *Die Walküre*, whose exploits leave a good deal to be desired. I can only thank God that Vickers apparently did not dwell on these for too long and that the world was blessed with truly great performances of that role. Later in his career I suggested Captain Vere in Britten's *Billy Budd* to him, but he rejected this out of hand because of that character's latent homosexuality.

A role which he did agree to sing, and for which he signed a contract, was Tannhäuser, in Wagner's opera of that name. We were surprised at his decision, because the tessitura of the role – particularly in the first act – is cruelly high and persuades many not to attempt it. A tenor once remarked to me that he would rather sing Siegfried than Tannhäuser any day. Some months before rehearsals were due to start, however, I was telephoned by John Coast, Vickers's manager, to say that the singer was withdrawing from his contract because he found that some words uttered by Tannhäuser were blasphemous and there was no way he could sing them. I remonstrated with Vickers as he called on me on his way home from Vienna a few weeks later. He remained intransigent, and at short notice we found a replacement in the American tenor Richard Cassilly.

Vickers never hesitated to make his views known about anyone and anything which caused him displeasure or which he considered wrong. Once he walked across Floral Street in costume and make-up to complain to me about a conductor. On another occasion, in 1983, when I had introduced him to Sir Charles Mackerras to discuss a new production of Handel's *Samson*, he was so angry at what he was hearing that he hurled his score of the Raymond Leppard edition of *Samson* on to the table with such vigour that everything else on it was thrown to the floor, proclaiming that Leppard's was the only version which he would perform. Later that day I went to his dressing room and was greeted with, 'I was a bit noisy this afternoon, wasn't I?' That was Vickers – convinced that he was right and that we were wrong, and unwavering in his opinion.

Vickers very much wanted to perform Handel's Samson again. The role suited him, and I wanted to grant him his wish. However, I was concerned about the version to be used, since performing style had changed a great deal since his performances in 1961. Even if Raymond Leppard had been willing to let us use his edition, I knew that Vickers and we would be heavily criticized for our seeming lack of awareness of progress in Handelian scholarship. But I could not shift him, and he remained adamant that decoration was out of order – that there was no historical evidence to support it, and that it was merely an invention of Mackerras and his like. I did point out to him that a decorated version of the da capo section of 'Where'er you walk', as sung by John Beard, Jupiter in the first performances of *Semele*, was written out in a score in the British Library. He was unmoved, and stuck to his beliefs.

In the end, I relented and decided to take the risk of the adverse critical reaction inherent in using an out-dated version, however discreetly re-edited. There was room in the repertoire for another Handelian work, other opera houses wanted to share a new production, and nothing would prevent its revival in a more musically authentic version at a later date. Elijah Moshinsky, who had worked with Vickers on *Peter Grimes*, was the producer, in 1985, and at Vickers's suggestion Julius Rudel was engaged to conduct. Later Vickers was to query why Rudel was there. It was not a happy experience, and Rudel suffered an undue amount of torment – sometimes in relation to tempi, but at others over things which were not of his doing. At one rehearsal Marie McLoughlin decorated an aria; Vickers saw this as provocation and clearly suspected a conspiracy on the part of Rudel and the cast. Of course, it was nothing of the kind – no more than a display of exuberance.

Jon Vickers, with a magnificent presence as an Old Testament figure, sang with his usual intensity, and in 'Total Eclipse' he left the audience moved and enthralled. But, good as the performances were within the context of an outmoded performing style, I decided that we could only revive *Samson*, as we had planned for the next season, if authentic performing practice was adopted. Roger Norrington was our choice of conductor, and we went ahead without Vickers, who had withdrawn, unwilling even to look at what this revival could mean for him. It was a sad ending.

During a conversation one evening in the early 1980s, Vickers and I talked about the dwindling number of world-class tenors. We recalled that twenty-five years earlier there had been at least twelve tenors of the highest quality to cover the whole operatic repertoire, whereas at the time when we were talking there was not much more than a handful.

Categories of voices do come and go, and nobody seems to know why. For years there has been a shortage of real Verdi baritones and of Heldentenors. This will no doubt change.

Of the Three Tenors, as they have become known, Placido Domingo and José Carreras have performed regularly at Covent Garden, with Luciano Pavarotti appearing less often. This led him once to remark that I had engaged the Spanish Mafia at his expense. It could have been otherwise. The invitations were there but were not always taken up, or, if accepted, were sometimes not fulfilled.

Some twenty-five years ago we had planned a new production of *Turandot* and had engaged Gwyneth Jones in the title role and Pavarotti as Calaf. Many months before rehearsals were to begin, Pavarotti telephoned to say that he had just sung Calaf at San Francisco and had decided to drop it from his repertoire because he found the role too heavy and was concerned about damaging his voice. His concern had to be respected, but I was curious and asked why he was giving up Calaf when he continued to sing Radamès in *Aida*. His reply was that you can sing Radamès lyrically, but Calaf demands heavy singing all the time. 'Listen', he said, 'to that greatest of tenors, Carlo Bergonzi, in *Aida*. He sings it convincingly but lyrically.'

It was not always easy to satisfy the demands of Domingo and Carreras, both of whom we wanted to have regularly. Both sought new productions, but often they had to settle for revivals. Furthermore, we were interested in Giacomo Aragall, who appeared less often than we would have liked. If only his nerves could have been calmed, I believe he might well have outstripped them all. He has a voice of an individual and lovely timbre, and is a convincing performer when he can cross the threshold of nerves. We also wanted to keep an association with Carlo Cossutta, Charles Craig and Carlo Bergonzi for the Italian repertoire, and with other fine singers such as Nicolai Gedda – the most elegant and appealing of artists, fluent in many languages and the possessor of the most beautiful *mezza voce*, which is still in place long after most singers would have called it a day.

Carlo Bergonzi is the most stylish singer of the Italian repertoire, having a natural feeling for phrasing and impeccable taste. Words, coloured by a slight lisp, are clear and in no way impede the flow of glorious tone. A baritone originally and largely self-taught as a tenor, he has become the epitome of Italian vocal art. A real Verdian in all respects, he opened a hotel near the composer's birthplace, in Busseto.

What has been pleasing about so many singers is their loyalty to Covent Garden and their wish to return. Throughout my years at the Royal Opera, Placido Domingo was generous in his allocation of time to us. It has been sad to see that reduced. Even though singers had come to regard Covent Garden as one of the opera houses which it was essential to visit regularly for the sake of their careers, they still needed to be wooed and tempted with interesting and stimulating proposals. Intensely musical and serious, Domingo has shown himself to be the most adventurous of leading tenors, with a wide repertoire and forever keen to explore new territory – in recent years the German repertoire, with *Parsifal* and *Die Walküre*, and the Russian, with *The Queen of Spades*. There is no other singer who can match this. It is a matter not only of range, but of the musicality and dramatic instinct which he brings to such disparate roles. Interestingly enough, he has only once said to me that he did not want to be asked to sing a particular role. That was Aeneas in *Les Troyens*, which he had been performing at the Metropolitan in New York and which he had experienced difficulty in learning and memorizing. The musical idiom was foreign to him, and he could not easily come to terms with it. This was a blow, since we had envisaged inviting him for this role.

Originally trained as a conductor and a pianist, Domingo conducts regularly, but not at the expense of singing. This is also the case with his direction of opera companies, first in Washington and now in Los Angeles, where he has been artistic adviser since the company's formation. This diverse activity has broadened his knowledge and has in many ways contributed to the strength and freshness of his performances as a singer.

Some time after I had left Covent Garden, I was with Placido Domingo in his dressing room when he began to talk about his desire to be the artistic director of the Teatro Real in Madrid. Plans were advancing for its restoration to a theatre, and Domingo was in the running for this appointment. He asked if I would be willing to join him in this and be responsible for the theatre's management. In principle I agreed. However, it came to nothing, because changes of government followed and the minister supporting Domingo went out of office.

Domingo's schedule has always been full – to some of us overcrowded and the cause of concern. When challenged, he replies that he alone must be the judge of what he can and cannot do. A singer's knowledge of his or her voice has to be respected. It was because of this that I rarely tried to persuade singers to perform against their better judgement. On the day of one *Tosca* performance his manager telephoned to say that Domingo was not well and begged us to find a replacement. It is rare for a singer to want to miss a performance, and I knew that we really needed to find another tenor. We failed to trace a singer of quality who was free and were on the point of cancelling the performance when the telephone rang. It was Domingo, to ask if we had found anyone. I replied that we had not. Without hesitation, he said that he would not let us down but would come in for the performance, provided that I personally made an announcement about his indisposition. I did, and he sang superbly. If I had called during the day to put pressure on him, I doubt that the outcome would have been the same.

A different situation arose when Michael Langdon withdrew from a performance of *Götterdämmerung* one Saturday night because of a bad cold. We had found a replacement, but we were suddenly faced with a huge problem because the singer in question thought that he was coming to sing Hunding, not Hagen, a role which he did not know. This news was relayed to me by Lies Askonas – an artists' manager in London, and familiar with Royal Opera House programmes – who happened to be sitting next to this singer on a plane from Germany and had expressed her delight at the prospect of hearing him as Hagen. I had no alternative but to call Michael Langdon, explain our predicament, and plead for his help. After brief thought, he agreed to sing in spite of feeling very unwell.

I have often been asked how it is that singers can perform up to their usual standards after an announcement of a cold or some other affliction. A sound technique is invaluable in this kind of situation, and will see a singer through all sorts of problems. However, the statement before the curtain that all might not be well makes the singer more relaxed, because the audience is prepared. It is a matter of releasing tension as much as anything else, and an awareness that there will be understanding if the voice cracks. Audiences are fascinated by disaster or near disaster, and like to be in the know. Once they are, they are in sympathy with the performer.

Since first knowing Placido Domingo in 1971, and having spent a lot of time with him in London, in opera houses abroad and on tour, the only subject over which I find myself in disagreement with him is the Three Tenors. In my view it is nonsense to pretend that these events attract people to opera. They are entertaining and bring in large crowds – or they used to – but that is as far as they go. They make huge money for the artists and the promoter, but they have continued too long and are falling into disrepute. The original plan and its objects were admirable, but there it should have stopped. The reaching out to large audiences in stadia is a negation of the art of singing. Pop singers, relying on the microphone, lose nothing by performing in arenas, but trained singers, used to singing with their natural voice and filling a theatre with sound without mechanical aids, downgrade their art.

Two brothers-in-law were frequent visitors to Covent Garden: Tito Gobbi and Boris Christoff. Peace having been made after the *Otello* débâcle with Rafael Kubelik, Gobbi, a true actor-singer, made a huge impression on audiences and on other singers alike through his complete involvement with a character and his ability to portray this person convincingly in his acting and glorious singing. His was a powerful presence on the stage, and his communication with the public was instant. In addition to singing many roles, he directed *Simone Boccanegra* in a conventional and straightforward production. There were no particular insights revealed and the outcome typified the problems which singers face as they turn from performing to producing: they know their own roles inside out, and often know others, but most seem to lack the means of directing singers beyond positioning them on the stage.

Some years after the first run of *Simone Boccanegra* performances, Boris Christoff was engaged to sing Fiesco. During early rehearsals he telephoned to say that he needed to talk to me. He explained that he had been through the production with his brother-in-law and had been assured that Fiesco's interests had been well taken care of. 'Not so,' said Christoff. 'Take his first entrance. It is through a doorway, out of sight to half of the audience. Fiesco's entrance is poor. Would you please have the door moved two metres towards the centre of the stage?' I replied that this was impossible. 'In any event,' I went on, 'you will make directly for a position near the prompt box, where you know that you will be heard to best advantage. There you will stay until the end of your aria. All of this will be in full view of the audience.' Roaring with laughter, he agreed and returned to the rehearsal.

A larger-than-life man, Christoff did create problems for others on the stage if he was not getting his way or if he felt there was a lack of cooperation with him. The death fall of Boris was a case in point. He once complained to me that the chorus nearly dropped him as he fell. At the next performance he stuck his elbows out and could have seriously harmed the choristers as well as preventing them from catching him correctly. It was then their turn to protest.

Christoff's reputation for being difficult was well known. When he had been invited to sing Russian opera arias at a BBC promenade concert with the Royal Opera House orchestra, the BBC telephoned to say that they did not want to negotiate the contract with him, because of previous experiences, and asked if I would act on their behalf. I agreed, and in a brief telephone call I fixed a fee with him. A few weeks later he called to say that he had received a contract from the BBC, but did not intend to sign it since his agreement was with me. He insisted on a contract with the Royal Opera House, which would collect the money from the BBC and pass it on to him.

In trying to place Christoff, I would describe him as a true successor to Chaliapin. He had remarkable histrionic abilities which, combined with a fine bass voice, enabled him to give vivid portrayals of a range of characters on the stage. In his performing capabilities, if not in his behaviour, he was unquestionably an object lesson to others, as indeed was his brother-in-law.

A number of black singers have contributed to the success of Covent Garden. No one present can surely ever forget Leontyne Price as Aida in the 1958/59 season. The role was magnificently sung, but equally memorable were her performance and her bearing, portraying the walk of a dejected people. Shirley Verrett and Grace Bumbry arrived at Covent Garden early in their careers and enjoyed huge success as mezzo-sopranos. Seemingly not content with this, they moved upward to soprano roles and lost something in the process, either in the higher parts or when returning to their original repertoire.

Another black singer, Martina Arroyo – only ever a soprano – was a great adjunct to the company, both as a superb singer and also as a joyous person to have around. Having seen the Visconti black-and-white *Traviata*, she one day exclaimed to John Copley, 'Cast me as Violetta, put me in a white dress, and I'll have a slap-up success!' She used to worry about her figure. Entering her dressing room with the wife of the tenor Carlo Cossutta, who had been angry with himself over an imperfect high C at the end of 'Di quella pira' in *Il Trovatore*, I sympathized with Mrs Cossutta over the difficult time I imagined that she had experienced since the last performance. She replied that it had not been easy and that she had lost weight. 'That's my answer,' said Arroyo – 'I must marry a tenor.'

A young black soprano grabbed my attention when attending a performance of Thea Musgrave's *Harriet, the Woman called Moses* by the

Norfolk Opera in Virginia. She was Cynthia Haymon. She had injured herself during rehearsals and was performing with one leg encased in plaster. Immobile she may have been, but that did not detract from the quality of her singing and her personality. I immediately thought of her for Liù in *Turandot*, which she came to sing with the Royal Opera on a Far Eastern tour in 1987. She was so touching and vulnerable in this role, even though in rehearsal she was smitten with doubt about her ability to live up to our expectations. She more than did so.

Grace Bumbry became involved in an extraordinary episode with Montserrat Caballé. For the 1977/78 season they had been engaged to perform the title role and Adalgisa alternately in Bellini's *Norma* – an idea which appealed to them. However, there are two versions of *Norma*: one in the original high key and the other in a lower key. According to which role they were singing, one wanted the key which the other did not. Unfortunately this had not been sorted out at the contract stage and we were faced with a dilemma and no sign of agreement. The two ladies argued, each deferring to the other but neither giving way. In the end, after days of toing and froing between them, I decided that I had to release Caballé after her performances as Norma and find another Adalgisa to Bumbry's Norma. It was not a happy solution in that Caballé was deprived of half her contract – Josephine Veasey took her place – but nothing else was possible.

The role of Norma is fraught with vocal difficulties, and few emerge from singing it unscathed. Even Maria Callas, the greatest Norma within living memory, never in my hearing scaled the heights in 'Casta Diva' in a public performance as she once did in rehearsal at Covent Garden. It was a momentous occasion.

Unperturbed by the experience of singers embarking on this role, and undaunted by what she had seen in the score, Margaret Price had set her heart on singing Norma and pleaded with me for the opportunity. She had applied the same pressure on Wolfgang Sawallisch in Munich, but encountered strong opposition from him because he was convinced that she could not satisfactorily negotiate the difficulties of the first act. He was being protective of her and did not want one of the greatest sopranos of our times to be wrongly exposed. In the end, he relented and presented two concert performances of the opera, only the first of which she sang.

I had decided to attend the second performance. Because I was travelling from Italy that morning, the Munich management was unable to reach me by phone and I arrived in Munich to discover that Norma was now to be sung by Susanne Murphy. However, I saw Sawallisch, who repeated to me his earlier warning to Margaret Price that she should keep well clear of the role.

I returned to Munich a few weeks later to try to persuade Price to give up Norma, but failed to convince her. An ardent admirer of her singing, and aware that the public did not understand why she was so seldom heard in opera in London, I did not want to present yet another obstacle to her appearance at Covent Garden. Reluctantly I agreed to Norma. As predicted, the outcome was a disaster – both for Margaret Price and for the Royal Opera. In recent interviews she has been generous to me, which I appreciate, but I wish that I had saved her from that catastrophe.

This 1987 revival was doomed from the beginning, with the principal protagonist often absent from rehearsal. We had engaged John Pritchard to conduct, because we knew that he, strongly supportive of Margaret Price, was best able to guide her through this taxing role. However, we were soon searching for replacement Normas. Jane Eaglen was covering the role and, although she had not sung through the entire opera, I was sure that we should take the risk of asking her to sing. Unfortunately Pritchard was not convinced, and wanted another singer, with whom he had worked previously. While inquiries about her availability were going on, I had to attend another engagement. On my return, I was informed that she was available and that, because of the need for immediate confirmation to enable her to catch the next plane to London, she had been engaged. I was furious about this and doubted the wisdom of the choice. The outcome proved disastrous, with the singer barely able to memorize the part and a thoroughly bad performance ensuing.

I was also disturbed by this decision of Pritchard's for another reason. I have never seen the point of having covers if they are not given the opportunity to sing when the moment comes. Furthermore, denial of this opening to a singer as talented as Jane Eaglen sends the wrong message both to her and to the public. She had cause to be disappointed, if not angry.

Margaret Price had made her debut at Covent Garden as Cherubino in 1963, and had displayed a beautiful voice – round, brilliant and flexible – and also a real talent for conveying meaning through singing. Working closely for many years with the conductor James Lockhart, then on Covent Garden's music staff, she soon became established as one of the finest opera and lieder singers to be heard anywhere. Who will ever forget her Desdemona in that legendary revival of *Otello* with Carlos Kleiber in 1980? With so much success, and potential for more, the failure of Norma was doubly hard to witness.

The paucity of Price performances at Covent Garden was due not to a lack of invitations but to other commitments – often lieder recitals – and to her dogs. The latter had become all-important in her life, and she could not bear to be separated from them for long. If the quarantine regulations had been relaxed, I believe we would have seen more of her.

Finding roles for Joan Sutherland beyond the standard repertoire was eased by the phenomenal knowledge of her husband, Richard Bonynge. He knew which operas would be good vehicles for her and of interest to audiences. Sutherland was the most popular singer to have graced the boards of Covent Garden, and I believed that we owed her and her immense following the chance of appearances in London in an unfamiliar opera. *Esclarmonde* by Massenet was the one selected. She had sung in this in San Francisco, and it was this production, by Lotfi Mansouri, which we used in autumn 1983.

It did not turn out to be the success for which we had hoped. Sutherland was not well and sang at far below her usual marvellous form. It was also an example of how a producer can trivialize an opera which is not strong dramatically and which needs every scrap of well-thought-out ingenuity to enable it to succeed. This kind of work has to be produced with conviction and without apology – anything less results in failure. It did on this occasion, although pleasure was still found in the performances – not least by some musicians, who revelled in Massenet's orchestral palette. The Scottish composer Iain Hamilton, who lived in Covent Garden and whom I would meet in the street, used to tell me of his delight with the score.

Joan Sutherland's huge popularity derives obviously from her heaven-sent voice and her spectacular use of it. But there is another dimension, which comes from her personality. Great diva though she is, she never behaves like one, with the result that people can identify with her. She is down to earth and easy in their company. It is a great gift, and has won her many friends and admirers.

The birth of a star is thrilling to witness. After the triumph of *Lucia di Lammermoor* there was no holding Sutherland, but, guided by Richard Bonynge, she quickly learned how to handle success, how to exploit it, which invitations to accept and which to reject. By the time of *Lucia* she had spent seven years with the company, her technique was well grounded, and she had learned how to be an opera singer. For another star, Kiri Te Kanawa, fame came about much more quickly. Cast as the Countess in *Le Nozze di Figaro* in 1971, with relatively little experience behind her, and enjoying a huge success with her glorious voice and winning personality, the world was wanting her. She had to be cautious and to spend time with the company and with her teacher, Vera Rozsa, developing her technique and broadening her experience and knowledge as well as building a repertoire. The pressures on a performer in this situation are colossal, and not easy to manage.

For the Wagner and Strauss operas, although not exclusively so, we were fortunate to have Birgit Nilsson and Gwyneth Jones for many years. The former made her debut in the *Ring* in 1957, followed by *Tristan und Isolde* in June 1958, sharing the role with Sylvia Fisher. Nilsson was considered the greatest Wagnerian soprano of her day, and possessed a voice of huge size, even throughout its range and with a free-ringing top. She gave much to Covent Garden and set standards not only for Wagnerian singing but for singing generally, which were an inspiration to all.

She had phenomenal strength and stamina. After a performance of *Elektra* I asked if she could sing it all again, because she seemed so fresh and full of energy. To this she said no, but that she would sing the Queen of the Night arias. She then started to throw them off as if the evening was just beginning.

Nilsson is a great trouper. We had invited her to be the special guest in Act 2 of *Die Fledermaus* on New Year's Eve 1980. Unfortunately she was unwell, and as she called me each day to report her condition it was clear that she would not be able to come. We invited her for the next New Year's Eve. This time her health was all right, but the weather was atrocious in Sweden and she was concerned about reaching London. The day before the performance she telephoned to report little improvement in the weather but that I should rely on her being there. Trusting her, I accepted what she had said and we waited. By curtain up she had not arrived, but fifteen minutes later in she walked, having left Sweden early in the morning and having travelled by car, rail, boat and air. This was so typical of her. She asked for a few minutes with the conductor in the interval, and went on in the second act to sing gloriously.

Gwyneth Jones first appeared at Covent Garden in November 1964, in place of Leontyne Price as Leonora in the Visconti production of *Il*

Trovatore. With her handsome stage presence and a commanding and vibrant voice, her career went ahead very fast – some would say too fast – and two years later she was at Bayreuth as Sieglinde. She is an exciting performer, and with her Welsh upbringing she brings a strongly developed emotional and dramatic force to the characters she portrays.

She sang Turandot in the new production which we first presented at the Olympics Arts Festival in Los Angeles in 1984. It was a triumph for her, and the product of serious study with Eva Turner, whom she brought to California so that she could have coaching right up to the last minute. Turner was a disciplinarian. Once when she was working with Turner in London and began to tire, Jones decided that she needed a break, only to discover that Turner had locked the door so that she could not escape. It was much the same in Los Angeles, where she was exposed to hours of work with her mentor. It paid off.

Along with Jon Vickers, there was also a soprano who was very willing to tell producers and conductors when she thought that they were wrong: Ileana Cotrubas. Slight in build, she is a wonderful performer – intensely musical, intelligent, and able to portray a character to perfection through her dramatic sense, her vulnerability and a highly distinctive and individual voice. In a way she frets too much about what is going on around her, but she cares and has to express her feelings and opinions.

In turn, you listen. She always has something important to say.

She first appeared at Covent Garden in February 1971, as Tatyana in the Peter Hall production of *Eugene Onegin*, conducted by Georg Solti. It was sung in English, in the David Lloyd-Jones translation, which caused her to greet me every time I went into her dressing room with the words she used on meeting Onegin again in the St Petersburg ballroom scene: 'I am pleased to meet you. I think we've met before.'

On one occasion when Cotrubas was singing *La Traviata* with José Carreras, there was a bomb scare in the first scene. I had no doubt that we had to clear the theatre, and I went on the stage to ask everyone to leave. Cotrubas never got over seeing me approach her as she was expecting Carreras. The performance continued after an interval while the theatre was searched, but, as she recalled, starting again in that situation is incredibly hard. The shock and the nature of the interruption drain you emotionally.

We enjoyed a cornucopia of mezzo-sopranos, and were fortunate to have such distinguished artists as Josephine Veasey, Anne Howells and Yvonne Minton in the company as well as Janet Baker as a guest. So strong was the list that for a time we could not find room for others such as Ann Murray.

José van Dam has accused me of obstructing his career in Great Britain. It is true that offers to appear at Covent Garden have been few, but the reason for this is not lack of regard for him but rather the protection of our own singers by ensuring that they have first choice of the roles for which they are suited. For example, two fine basses, Robert Lloyd and Gwynne Howell, have been given priority over foreign singers – not exclusively, but sufficiently to provide them with the opportunities needed for their development. Even so, we have not always avoided disappointing both them and others.

Baritones at Covent Garden, whether members of the company or closely associated with it, have presented a formidable line-up, beginning with Geraint Evans and the American Jess Walters, and progressing through John Shaw, Louis Quilico, Peter Glossop and Thomas Allen to Anthony Michaels Moore, just to mention a few to give a sense of the quality which we have all enjoyed since the reopening after the war.

When, at the request of Benjamin Britten, the Royal Opera House took over the management of the English Opera Group in 1961, it was hoped that one of the benefits would be the greater deployment of Covent Garden singers as casting opportunities for two companies became available. The theory proved to be more appealing than the practice, and the hoped-for opportunities for company singers to enlarge their experience and repertoire did not materialize. We had encountered the same thing when assuming the management of the Sadler's Wells Ballet four years earlier, but with singers having different work patterns and attitudes from those of dancers we had expected to achieve more than we did in integrating the two opera companies. This is not to suggest that we regretted the assumption of this responsibility – far from it. The concept of an opera house with a large and a small company brings important possibilities for cross-fertilization of artistic policy and endeavour. The fulfilment of this potential obviously depends on adequate funding, but also on a conveniently positioned smaller theatre or space, giving good and immediate access between rehearsal areas and stages. The redeveloped Royal Opera House has these facilities, which were previously lacking, and it must be ensured that they are profitably used. This will be achieved effectively only if both theatres are under the direction of one artistic director.

The benefit to the Royal Opera House in establishing a closer relationship with Benjamin Britten and Peter Pears, which this link made possible, was all-important to us, both directly on English Opera Group matters and indirectly through insights gained by regular contact. The managers of both companies – Patrick Terry and Keith Grant – kept this in mind as we worked to ensure that each company contributed whatever it could to the other and at the same time profited from the experiences of the other.

No opera company can survive without its team of *comprimario* singers – those taking small parts. Covent Garden has benefited hugely from having in the company a number of first-rank artists to assume these roles. Elizabeth Bainbridge, Paul Crook, Frank Egerton, Eric Garrett and John Dobson are but a few of them – and not confined to the smaller parts, but assuming larger roles when the opportunities arise.

For me, John Dobson is the personification of the ideal *comprimario* artist and company singer. Whatever the role or its size, it is treated with the same degree of seriousness and attention to detail in its presentation on stage, the defining of the character and the way that it is sung. Every performance is an occasion, and as each approaches there is just suf-ficient nervous edge at work to spur him on to his best endeavour. To have kept this approach fresh after so many years of performing is an achievement in itself and has been a source of inspiration and encouragement to others.

Going into the dressing rooms of these singers was always a pleasure. There was invariably a joke or story to be shared, and laughter was rarely absent until the moment of going on drew near, but there was a disastrous production of *Aida* in June 1984. Luciano Pavarotti was not giving Jean-Pierre Ponnelle, the producer and designer, what he was looking for and was being quite destructive around the soprano Katia Ricciarelli. Ponnelle had virtually given up, and left a shambles of a production. (He later wanted to restore it to his real conception, but tragically died before this was possible.) The public and critical reaction was hostile – with some justification. Dobson sang the Messenger, and on entering his dressing room one night he told me that he had come to the conclusion that he should carry a banner saying, 'Don't blame me, I'm only the messenger'.

Surtitles continue to be the subject of debate. Critics of surtitles have argued that audiences should do their homework more thoroughly and come better prepared, particularly to performances not given in English. Preparation certainly brings greater enjoyment, but it is doubtful if all the words of the recitatives in *Le Nozze di Figaro*, for example, will be recalled however much time is spent on preparatory study. In view of this, surtitles are helpful in that they have enabled many to understand the action and the interchange of dialogue more clearly. They are less helpful when they anticipate the expression of emotions. Laughter from the audience before the singer has made the point is disturbing and absurd, but such moments have been reduced, if not eliminated, by the introduction of more sophisticated projection equipment and experience in its operation.

Surtitles are now with us, and it would be foolish of anyone seriously to consider their abolition. Some still detest them as an unwanted visual intrusion. Their objections would be met by a screen in front of each seat, individually controlled, as at the Metropolitan in New York. This arrangement also deals effectively with sight-line problems, which in some theatres prevent sections of the audience from reading surtitles. Interestingly enough, Ubaldo Gardini, one of our Italian coaches, proposed such an idea to me years ago, and I attempted to interest Sir Clive Sinclair in it. His mind was on other things at the time, however, and I could find no one else willing to pursue it.

Poor enunciation of words by singers has become a huge problem, and there must be concern that surtitles only aggravate this deficiency. It is true that some music may have been written in a way which makes it impossible for the singer to put the words across, but my hunch is that an acceptable standard of articulation is generally not there in the first place. Words and music are interrelated, and a loss of verbal clarity diminishes the impact of the music. It is difficult to know why the trend to poor enunciation has occurred. Of course, there are exceptions, and some notable ones come immediately to mind – such as John Tomlinson and, from earlier generations, Heddle Nash and Richard Lewis. The problem must be partly due to teaching, where there is perhaps over-concentration on the production of beautiful tone at the expense of conveying the words and their sense. Whatever the reasons, they must be corrected. Too much is lost in a welter of sound, often lovely to hear but without true meaning.

The achievements of the Royal Opera in the fifty years of its life are truly astonishing. High though everyone's hopes for the future may have been at the beginning, no one could have imagined the speed with which success would come and the company's world standing be established. So many have played a part in this success, and the fact that it was the product of company effort gives hope for the future as the return to the Royal Opera House approaches. Ideals were established early on and were maintained and expanded over the years. Some have been abandoned, however, and these must be restored to ensure the future growth of the company, whose management's concern must be the well-being of the singers – soloists or choristers – to whom the debt owed is immeasurable.

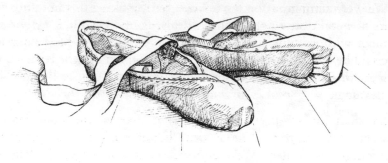

7 *The Royal Ballet*

I have often wondered if, when Ninette de Valois decided to accept the invitation of the Covent Garden Opera Trust to transfer her Sadler's Wells Ballet to the Royal Opera House in 1945, the real value of this company was fully understood by either theatre. Some of the Sadler's Wells governors had misgivings about allowing the company to go, but no action appears to have been taken to prevent it. Probably they realized that it would have been fruitless to intervene once de Valois had made up her mind. Negotiations between the two theatres – represented by their chairmen, Lord Keynes and Lord Lytton – were informal, and at their conclusion no formal agreement was exchanged. This was also to be the case when the later Sadler's Wells Theatre Ballet came under Covent Garden's management in 1957, and again with the English Opera Group in 1961, the only difference being that in these two instances the companies were actively seeking a new management, whereas Ninette de Valois and Sadler's Wells were not – or at any rate not at that moment.

Covent Garden acquired for next to nothing an immensely valuable asset, the true worth of which was to be revealed before much time had passed. It was a company with fourteen years of performing experience behind it, war-weary perhaps, but ready for new challenges, led by two stars of growing reputation, Margot Fonteyn and Robert Helpmann, under the visionary direction of Ninette de Valois, who had with her a highly gifted choreographer in Frederick Ashton and a fine musician and artistic adviser in Constant Lambert. The company had more than sixty ballets in its repertoire, of which a good proportion could be used at Covent Garden.

Ninette de Valois was later to write endearingly and vividly about this period:

We were setting out on the adventure of making this building extend its hospitality to us throughout the year, challenging it, at the beginning, with nothing more than a bedraggled war-weary company. It could be likened to a crazy nightmare, wherein I might be given Buckingham Palace, a few dusters, and told to get on with the spring-cleaning.

She had in fact been hesitant about making the huge leap from Rosebery Avenue to Covent Garden, though she knew that the company had outgrown Sadler's Wells and was ready for bigger challenges. She had already experienced sharing a stage with an opera company, and was apprehensive about repeating this. On the other hand, she was seized with the vision of a national lyric theatre in which opera and ballet would be presented all year round in a partnership of equal standing and opportunity. Eventual failure to realize this ideal came as no surprise to her – she is a realist – but she knew that without aiming for targets just out of reach the result would be acceptance of the second best. She set out with high hopes and colossal energy and courage to tackle the myriad difficulties and complications arising from the move and exacerbated by the aftermath of war. The country was exhausted and there was little money. A lesser person than she would not have found a way of making progress in such a barren situation, nor have stayed the course.

She moved her school, which she had always seen as a vital ingredient of her company, to Barons Court, in west London, and without further ado she established another ballet company, the Sadler's Wells Theatre Ballet (later the Royal Ballet Touring Section – 'the Touring Company' for short – then Sadler's Wells Royal Ballet and now the Birmingham Royal Ballet), to play at Rosebery Avenue and tour the regions. It was a risky venture, which ended with the Sadler's Wells governors being unable to afford it and the company moving to Covent Garden ten years later.

She wanted a grand opening for Sadler's Wells Ballet in its new home, and settled upon *Sleeping Beauty* – a ballet which was to become the company's calling card for many years, and which set visual and choreographic standards rarely surpassed in later productions. For the first time in its life the company was able to enjoy dancing to a full symphony orchestra playing Tchaikovsky's score as he had written it. Oliver Messel designed sumptuous scenery and costumes, and Frederick Ashton added some new dances. Rationing was still in force, and clothing coupons had to be found for the purchase of fabrics. Mounting a new production of a full-length nineteenth-century ballet is a gigantic undertaking at the best of times, but unimaginable in these conditions. Undeterred, de Valois pressed on and had the ballet ready for the reopening of the Royal Opera House on 20 February 1946. It was a triumph, and, as Alexander Bland wrote in his history of the company's first fifty years, 'The reopening of the Royal Opera House became a symbol of the beginning of peacetime, as opposed to the mere ending of the war.'

The company at this time had the theatre to itself, the opera company still being in the process of formation, and presented seventy-eight consecutive performances of *Sleeping Beauty*. David Webster had to earn money for Covent Garden, and demanded as many performances as possible while the next programme was in preparation. This included *Adam Zero*, a new ballet by Robert Helpmann, beginning to show his paces as a choreographer, to a score by Arthur Bliss. It was not a success, but it demonstrated de Valois's determination to build a new repertoire and showed the world how she was going to proceed, even in these difficult conditions of post-war London and in an opera house struggling to its feet. Obstacles – and there were plenty of them – were cast to one side.

She knew the directions in which she needed to take her company, but it was fortuitous that the next ballet, *Symphonic Variations*, choreographed by Frederick Ashton to César Franck's eponymous score and with designs by Sophie Fedorovitch, took audiences from the sumptuousness and grandeur of *Sleeping Beauty* to something on a smaller scale and different in style. It is a quintessentially English ballet, lyrical and poetic, and remains one of Ashton's masterpieces.

After 130 performances, the company's first season ended. It had been a success, and the dancers were coming to terms with the larger theatre. Now de Valois could assess the consequences of the move to Covent Garden and determine the next steps she needed to take for the company's advancement, in consultation with Ashton, Lambert and Webster.

She has often told me how much she and Ashton relied on Constant Lambert for advice and artistic guidance. A splendid musician and conductor, he was a thoroughly cultured man, with impeccable taste and a wide-ranging knowledge of painting and literature. A bohemian, who led a raffish life in the company of other musicians, writers and artists, he was a fund of ideas for ballets as well as being a composer of standing and a skilled and imaginative arranger of music for the ballet.

I have many memories of him and Hilda Gaunt accompanying the company on two pianos on tour in the early days of the war. At the New Theatre, with a tiny orchestra, he would wring the last ounce out of his musicians as they played Tchaikovsky's Hamlet Overture to the ballet which Helpmann had created from it. Few have equalled his conducting of Tchaikovsky. He also loved the music of Puccini, as he was to show in his conducting of *Turandot* with Eva Turner in 1947. Alcohol could get the better of him, however, and one night as he mounted the podium to conduct *Sleeping Beauty* at the Royal Opera House he turned to Thomas Matthews, the leader of the orchestra, and said, 'When the pas de trois becomes the pas de six, I know that it's time for me to go home.' I never knew him, but I recall that the last time I saw his unmistakable profile was in a bar in Paris in 1949, as he made his uncertain way to the counter. That was two years before his tragically premature death, prior to which he had created one of his masterly ballet scores from the music of Chabrier for Roland Petit's ballet *Ballabile*, and had composed an original score for *Tiresias*, another Ashton ballet.

Two observations need to be made about the company at this point.

First, the restrictions of the size of stage at Sadler's Wells and at the regional theatres had inhibited any real expansiveness in the company's dancing, and it was going to take the dancers time to adjust to the larger stage of Covent Garden and adopt a broader style. In fact the Royal Opera House itself is not the best of theatres for dance, and time and time again I have found the company revelling in the joys of dancing on the stage of the Metropolitan Opera House in New York and bemoaning their home stage on their return. This is a matter not simply of space but also of the relationship between stage and auditorium and how dancers look. In New York the dancers and the productions look magnificent – better than anywhere else. They also look wonderful at the Coliseum, although there are other drawbacks there. It remains to be seen how effective the opened-up proscenium and the enlarged stage at Covent Garden will be in showing off dancers to advantage.

Second, the way in which English dancers performed was governed by respectability. At the beginning, Ninette de Valois had to convince parents that ballet would offer their children a good and respectable career. This was particularly true of boys, whom it was hard to recruit anyway, for reasons other than parental opposition. Although less evident today, the effects of this respectability are still detectable in a certain primness among the girls and a lack of abandon in performance. Lincoln Kirstein, the founder of the New York City Ballet, though recognizing that de Valois needed to adopt the line which she did, used to tell me that this had left an indelible mark. This also accounted for the less than generous or polite comments which Arlene Croce, the former dance critic of *The New Yorker*, used to make about the company's corps de ballet.

Playing in smaller theatres did not encourage strong projection, and I still find the lack of real projection among English dancers a hindrance to the achievement of their full potential as performers. Svetlana Beriosova often complained to me about this, whether she was coaching or simply an observer, and encouraged dancers to be more open and expansive. When she was a member of the company she had only to stand on the stage to rouse an audience, and could never understand why anyone purporting to be a performer did not see the need to reach out to the public.

In the company's second year, one of Constant Lambert's long-held wishes was fulfilled: a production of Purcell's *Fairy Queen*, which was mounted in the autumn of 1946 in conjunction with the newly formed opera company. A complex work to produce, it was not a huge success, and its failure to please generally was a blow to Lambert. It was important, however, for the two companies to collaborate, and it is one of the disappointments of the post-war years that this was one of very few occasions when they did so.

In search of established choreographers with experience of large-scale ballets, to supplement the work of Frederick Ashton, Ninette de Valois turned to Léonide Massine, who both mounted and appeared in two ballets from the Diaghilev era: *The Three-Cornered Hat* and *La Boutique Fantasque*. Massine was to return many years later – still taking daily class – to re-create the latter for the Touring Company. When David Webster heard that Massine was returning, he made it quite clear to me that he did not want to see him and that I was to negotiate his fees. He explained that he had been exasperated by him on earlier visits. I came to understand why – he could be maddening.

In December 1948 an important event occurred which was to have considerable bearing on the future style of the company: the first original full-length ballet created for it was performed. It was *Cinderella*, choreographed by Frederick Ashton to the music of Prokofiev. This was the beginning of a series of full-length works, most of which would find a regular place in the company's repertoire.

Since coming to see *Sleeping Beauty* in 1946, the American impresario Sol Hurok had been discussing an American tour for the company. With her usual prudence, Ninette de Valois had decided that the company was not ready. Hurok bided his time. When he proposed a season at the City Center Theatre in 1948, as part of a dance festival, Webster and de Valois again declined, on the grounds that the theatre was too small – though privately thinking, I suspect, that the Metropolitan Opera was the only New York theatre fit for the company. There is a certain snobbery with managers the world over about the theatres in which their companies will appear. For many years the Royal Ballet did not visit Paris because access to the Opéra was impossible, due to its resident company's own needs, and the Théâtre des Champs-Élysées was regarded as unsuitable. Similarly, companies visiting London have waited for the Royal Opera House to become available, rejecting other venues in the meantime. In October 1949, however, the Metropolitan Opera House (the old theatre on Broadway, between Thirty-ninth and Fortieth streets) would be available, and another chapter in the history of the Royal Ballet began.

Ninette de Valois sought the challenge of New York, but was apprehensive about how an audience largely brought up on the one-act, non-narrative, pure-dance ballets of George Balanchine would react to a diet of full-length works: *Sleeping Beauty*, *Swan Lake* and *Cinderella*. She need not have worried. After a huge amount of pre-opening publicity, and with a box-office advance of record proportions, a nervous but excited company arrived in New York to a warm welcome and expressions of eager expectation. The dancers had experienced nothing like this before.

Their first New York season began on 9 October to a tumultuous reception, applause greeting Oliver Messel's opening scene of *Sleeping Beauty* even before a step had been danced, continuing at every chance throughout the evening, and rising to a gigantic climax at the final curtain calls. It was a historic moment – a turning point for the company and for Margot Fonteyn, as well as a personal triumph for her.

The richness of the spectacle made an immediate impact on an audience which was surprisingly undeterred by the relative absence of virtuosity in the dancing but quickly warmed to English understatement and lyricism. This style created an image of dance which was to remain closely associated with the company in American minds over the coming decades. Perceptive critics saw that the strength of the company lay in individual talent and in the nature of the ensemble: a well-integrated body of dancers under imaginative and visionary artistic leadership.

New York was followed by appearances in Washington, Chicago, Richmond, Philadelphia, East Lansing, Detroit, Toronto, Montreal and Ottawa. This was to be the pattern of subsequent North American tours: an opening in New York – essential for the publicity which it generated in those days – was followed by visits to cities across the continent. For example, the next tour started in New York on 10 September 1950, after which performances took the company to the West Coast and back to the East Coast, via Chicago for Christmas, before finishing in Quebec on 28 January 1951. This would be the shape and duration of tours for some years – featuring full-length ballets such as *Sleeping Beauty*, *Swan Lake*, *Cinderella* or *Giselle*, with one-act ballets the most popular of which was *Façade* – though later tours were to be shorter and, having begun in New York, would finish on the West Coast, with a final week in Vancouver before the return home.

These tours of nineteen weeks or more were soon found to be too long, but they were profitable, and Covent Garden needed the money. Attempts used to be made to deny that the Royal Opera House depended on this source of income for balancing its budgets and helping to fund London performances of opera as well as ballet. It did, though, and it would have been in even greater financial difficulties without it. In those days there were not separate budgets for opera and ballet, and income from whatever source found its way into one pot. If American tours had not happened, or had not occurred until much later, I doubt that Covent Garden would have survived. It was perpetually sailing close to the wind, and any significant reduction in its income would have sunk it.

These tours were made possible, practically and financially, by the railroad system then in existence. After New York, and with the exception of certain other big cities, a train was hired to take the dancers, staff, scenery and costumes to their destinations. The train was the hotel, and there everyone lived and slept. This arrangement enabled several towns to be visited in a week, with one- or two-night stands in each. The train would arrive at a town in the early morning. The dancers would take class there, perform that night, and return to the train to sleep – either in the sidings for another performance in that town, or while moving on to the next, where the same pattern would be repeated. It was tiring for the dancers and staff, and on later tours one-night stands were discontinued – much to the disquiet of Sol Hurok, who saw income being reduced, in his view needlessly.

For the first tours, Hurok was hired as the company's agent and was paid a weekly management fee. This gave Covent Garden the lion's share of the income, but it was not to last. With rising costs and diminishing margins, it was decided by the mid-1950s that it was no longer safe for Covent Garden to take the financial risks of touring, and the arrangement was reversed.

Another factor eventually contributing to the decline in profits was the collapse of the railroad network, which meant that long-distance travelling by train was no longer possible. By the beginning of the 1960s there was complete dependence on the aeroplane for moving the company and on the roads for the scenery. No longer could the dancers arrive in a city in the morning, take class, and perform that night. Moves between cities now took two days – one for travel and the next preparing for a performance – with consequent loss of performances and of income. Lost, too, were some of the camaraderie which flourished in life on trains and the making and breaking of relationships, which developed or unscrambled in the close confines of train life. The financial outcome of American tours became less secure, but with a carefully chosen selection of cities – geographically well placed and permitting sensible routing – there was still money to be made.

Sol Hurok had arrived in America from Russia in 1906, and, like many others in a similar situation, had found various ways of making a livelihood until he could achieve what he really wanted: to present performers and performing companies. He was to become one of the leading impresarios of post-war America, and by the time of his death, in 1974, he was really the last of them. He had a number of distinguished musicians in his care, including Arthur Rubinstein and Isaac Stern, but it was the promoting of companies which interested him most and to which he devoted much of his energy. The Royal Ballet owes a great deal to him, but equally I believe that it was his involvement with the company which finally established his reputation.

Speaking in fractured English, which he never did anything to improve, he could be difficult to understand, but as soon as you were on his wavelength all was well. Language oddities were not confined to English. For him, 'pas de deux' was always pronounced 'pas de douze', and I recall Frederick Ashton saying to me one day, 'Now that I have created a real pas de douze for the first act of *Swan Lake*, Hurok can get the pronunciation right.'

Hurok was totally trustworthy, and in all the years that I was responsible for touring we never had a contract for any tour, until he sold his company to another promoter, when there was a demand for formal agreements. Some months before each tour, he and I would meet for lunch in the Savoy Grill and discuss likely costs. There was a ritual. I would state our weekly financial requirement, which he would invariably say was too high. I always kept a decent margin up my sleeve, and after some argument I would quote a lower figure which he accepted. In the meantime he had done all sorts of sums on the tablecloth, in ink, and he then wrote down the finally accepted figure. That was it for the time being. The agreed sum was paid each week to the company manager, and some time after the tour we would meet again in the Savoy Grill. I would quote our final costs. We then agreed a final management fee for Covent Garden. We had an understanding about its level. It would never be less than a certain amount, but it could be more if the tour had been particularly successful. Having remonstrated with the waiter for having given us too few strawberries – which he always believed that the waiters were under instructions to count – Hurok would go to his room and return with a cheque for the balance owing. There was nothing in writing except for scribbles on the tablecloth at the beginning and end of each tour. Unorthodox though this system was, it never failed.

The only time we ran into trouble was much later on, with Hurok's successors, when there was a written contract. They absconded with the portion of our fee withheld on behalf of the IRS (the United States tax authority). No tax was payable by us, but, when we came to reclaim it, no refund was forthcoming. In the end we sued, and managed to recover the money not from Hurok's successors but from the IRS. Our lawyers, who were engaged on a contingency-fee basis, argued that Hurok's successors were acting as an agent of the IRS. They had defaulted, and therefore it was up to the IRS to make good the omissions of their agent. The IRS agreed.

Dancers have always found American visits stimulating, and the audience response has drawn that extra ounce of energy from them. The admiration is mutual, and has survived for fifty years, even during a low point in the 1970s. All in all, these tours have been good for the company. At the beginning they were effective in building dancers' confidence, and consecutive performances over longish periods gave dancers opportunities to consolidate roles. They did do some harm, however, when Hurok was taking increased financial risks and insisted on playing too safe with programming and casting. There was then too much dependence on dancers known to be audience favourites, and younger dancers had their opportunities to perform leading roles reduced, hampering their development as artists and preventing them from building their own audience following. I discussed this often with Hurok, but he was concerned only with immediate maximization of ticket sales, believing that the future would take care of itself. It was a short-sighted attitude, which was later to cost the company dear.

For twenty-five years Hurok was dependent for guidance about programming and casting on Martin Feinstein, who took care of press and publicity. Feinstein is a forceful character, and had strong views on what he thought was good and what would sell. In such cases there can be conflict between the promoter and the director of the company, whose prerogative it must always be to decide the final programming and casting. It was not easy to strike and hold a balance. Feinstein eventually left Hurok to become director of the Kennedy Center in Washington. On hearing the news, I phoned Hurok to express my sympathy on his losing a valuable member of his staff. He dismissed Feinstein's departure as a problem, but I sensed anger about it. When arranging a tour in 1974 and wanting to include the Kennedy Center, I asked Hurok to be in touch with Feinstein to negotiate a contract. He never did telephone him, and when challenged he asked me to deal with Feinstein direct. The tour was settled through telephone calls from London to Washington and from London to New York.

Hurok regarded himself as the leading impresario in New York, and jealously protected his position. He was concerned that Columbia Artists, his most threatening rival, should have as little exposure as possible in presenting the world's greatest dance companies, and to this end he rented the Metropolitan Opera House for the entire closed summer period, lasting some thirteen weeks, so that no other management could have access to it. It was a huge risk for him, but he managed to fill those weeks without too much difficulty until relations between the Soviet Union and the United States reached such a low point in the late 1960s that all cultural exchanges between the two countries were ended. Hurok was desperate, and pleaded with me to send the Royal Ballet to New York for an additional and unscheduled season in April and May 1970 in order to fill a serious gap in his Met programme. We owed Hurok a great deal and, inconvenient though it was to reschedule our London season, we did so and found ourselves going to America twice in twelve months. A deteriorating international scene was the beginning of the end for him. After selling his business, and even though he continued to run it, life was never the same for him or for us.

Soon after the first American tour, another important event in the artistic growth of the company occurred. As Frederick Ashton mounted *Les Illuminations* on the New York City Ballet, George Balanchine, that company's director, came to London in 1950 to reproduce *Ballet Imperial* on the Sadler's Wells Ballet. Set to Tchaikovsky's Second Piano Concerto and first performed in 1941, this work has a marked relationship with the classical traditions of the Mariinsky Theatre in St Petersburg, with which the Royal Ballet's style has affinities, but its idiom was foreign to the British dancers, who found the sharply etched steps difficult to execute after the softer style of Ashton. The dancers' exposure to the athletic and brilliant demands of this choreography was a stimulating, if frustrating, experience and demonstrated, not for the last time, that ballets created for American performers can never be exactly reproduced on other dancers. Differences in temperament, training and physique make that impossible.

With successful tours behind it and a growing reputation around the world, the company was attracting dancers from the Commonwealth as well as this country. Alexander Grant had come from New Zealand, and, before the war, Robert Helpmann had moved from Australia to London, as Elaine Fifield was to do later. Rhodesia and South Africa were to produce still more dancers – Nadia Nerina, Monica Mason, Deanne Bergsma, Vergie Derman, Maryon Lane, Merle Park and Gary Burne spring immediately to mind. These important sources of talent were open to the company because of the few opportunities which existed for dancers in their home countries at the time. However, as indigenous companies were formed or expanded, many dancers became inclined to join them, or to return to them after training at the Royal Ballet School. Furthermore, dancers' chances of working in Britain were severely restricted by the application to Commonwealth citizens of employment regulations originally designed to protect the British labour market from foreign competition.

The year 1956 saw a series of anniversaries: the twenty-fifth birthday of Sadler's Wells Ballet and of the reopening of the theatre in which it began, the tenth anniversary of the reopening of the Royal Opera House, and the twenty-fifth anniversary of the death of Anna Pavlova. The company celebrated its anniversary on 5 May with a triple bill, beginning with *The Rake's Progress* and ending with *Façade*. In between was sandwiched a masterly new ballet by Frederick Ashton, *Birthday Offering*, to music by Glazunov, arranged by Robert Irving. Intended as a *pièce d'occasion* and to show off the best of the dancers, the movements being created around the talents and style of each artist, it was so successful and so beautifully crafted that it has found a continuing place in the repertoire.

At the end of the performance, Dame Ninette de Valois made a speech in which she typically expressed gratitude to everyone for their support and encouragement, her pride in her companies, and her hopes for the future, all underlined with down-to-earth good sense and determination, but still the thoughts of a visionary. 'Twenty-five years old!' she said. 'That means we can take two paths. We can sit back and remember what we have achieved, or we can sit up and remember what we have still got to do.' There was only one choice for Dame Ninette, and everyone knew it.

The company was strong in talent and was well set for the future, with an experienced choreographer in place – Frederick Ashton – and two younger and immensely promising creative talents in John Cranko and Kenneth MacMillan. Dame Ninette herself had renounced choreography to devote her time and energy to the direction of the company and to the overseeing of her empire, which embraced the school, the Sadler's Wells Theatre Ballet and the company in Ankara which she had established at the invitation of the Turkish government.

With her inimitable foresight, de Valois had seen how vulnerable her companies were because of the way in which they were funded by the Arts Council. Grants were negotiated and paid to the theatres in which they performed. (The practice of paying one grant to Covent Garden was later changed, with separate, designated, grants being paid to each of the performing companies instead.) She was concerned about the future of her companies and the school, and wanted to protect them by establishing an independent body which would have ultimate responsibility for their well-being. In effect, this would license Covent Garden to manage the company, but if it failed to do so adequately the licence could be revoked. It was an ingenious scheme, put forward by Lord Waverley, chairman of the Royal Opera House, and was implemented under a royal charter in October 1956, announced the following January, with the title of The Royal Ballet, thus bestowing 'Royal' on both the companies – the Sadler's Wells Theatre Ballet being formally affiliated to the

Royal Ballet at the same time – and the school. It was a signal honour, but its intentions were practical and wise.

Dame Ninette has often commented to me how essential it is to look to the future and to ensure that the means of protecting the companies are in place. 'You never know when things might go wrong and you might want to move to another management,' she used to say. How close we were to the Royal Ballet governors revoking the Covent Garden licence during 1998's closure crisis we will never really know, but it is clear that this was the kind of eventuality which Dame Ninette had in mind forty years or more ago.

The royal charter is couched in flowery language. I recall visiting Lord Goodman to discuss a school matter as this document was being prepared and being told that he had been rebuked by the Privy Council Office for having inserted the name of Lord Waverley in the draft *tout court*, whereas, as a privy councillor, he should have been described as 'Our trusty and well beloved cousin . . . '. Goodman was highly entertained by this, and was equally entertaining on the subject.

Another twenty-fifth anniversary, two years earlier, commemorating the death of Diaghilev, had inspired Ninette de Valois to present her Covent Garden company in *Firebird* at the Edinburgh Festival of 1954. Natalia Goncharova's original designs were used and Serge Grigoriev, Diaghilev's régisseur, mounted the production. The conductor was Ernst Ansermet, the conductor of the Ballets Russes and a fierce musical disciplinarian, who instilled fear in dancers who queried his tempi. There was only one tempo, and that was what the composer had written and intended. For Margot Fonteyn, coached in the role by Tamara Karsavina, the production was a triumph. Lacking the jump the part really demands, she again showed how she could compensate with her musicality, her extraordinary glamour and her dramatic instincts.

Having produced *Firebird* successfully, de Valois turned to *Petrushka* – after some hesitation. She foresaw a British company having difficulty with the style of this work, based as it is on Russian folk dance. A great believer in the link between folk dance and a national dance style, she was equally aware of the problems of differing styles meeting each other. Her initial caution was justified: the crowd scenes turned out to be limp and unconvincing, and neither of the principals – Margot Fonteyn and Alexander Grant – scored the success for which all had hoped.

By 1960 Ninette de Valois had built up a considerable repertoire for her company, having taken in two new full-length ballets, *The Prince of the Pagodas* and *Ondine* in 1957 and 1958. Neither of these mammoth undertakings was completely successful, but they were essential to her plan for the company as she sought a judicious mixture of one-act and full-length works.

The Prince of the Pagodas, with choreography by John Cranko and a commissioned score by Benjamin Britten, suffered from a poor scenario and from the writing of the score largely in a vacuum. Britten told me that communication with Cranko was difficult, and often non-existent, to the point where, in the absence of clear directions from either the scenario or the choreographer, there was no alternative but to compose some of the music according to his own judgement of what was required. Composing for ballet – difficult at the best of times – is well-nigh impossible if musicians are not instructed by choreographers, and if the latter are not also reasonably available for consultation during composition. Failure to produce a detailed scenario is not uncommon, but it can have unhappy consequences in the making of the ballet in the studio and on the stage, by which time it may be too late to make the changes ideally required for the true success of the work. Britten, a great admirer of Tchaikovsky, had hoped to collaborate with John Cranko in the same way as Tchaikovsky had with Marius Petipa. He had studied closely the score of *Sleeping Beauty*, the layout of the ballet and the timings demanded by Petipa, and knew what was expected of him in general terms, but not in the precise detail necessary for the proper integration of music and choreography. Nevertheless, the music which he wrote must count among his best work.

Interestingly, Britten phoned me one day during a Kirov season in London some ten years later to ask if he could come to a performance of *Sleeping Beauty* with me, because he wanted to hear Tchaikovsky's orchestration again. He listened in admiration to the extraordinary range of colour and invention to be found in the score, and murmured with delight at everything which he was hearing. Viktor Fedotov was the conductor and was much praised by Britten, who asked to be introduced to him in the second interval, much to the astonishment and pleasure of the maestro.

Happily, *The Prince of the Pagodas* is now in the repertoire again, with a rewritten scenario by Colin Thubron and choreography by Kenneth MacMillan. It would be good to be able to say that it is securely there, but that is not so and more needs to be done to tighten the storyline and increase its dramatic intensity. That in turn means more musical cuts – decisions difficult for a composer's heirs to make, though I believe that they would give the ballet a greater chance of the real success that it deserves and would be no more than the composer recognized as essential. He longed for guidance in such matters and for the restoration of the work to the repertoire. I tried to provide him with that, but it was not to be during his lifetime. A meeting with Kenneth MacMillan in the early 1970s was unproductive, and unhappily led to even more frustration and anger over the work's dormant state.

Ondine, with choreography by Frederick Ashton and an original score by Hans Werner Henze, was a real collaboration between composer and choreographer, in the sense that the storyline was agreed and Ashton specified the duration and mood of each section. Yet, because of a conflict of style between choreographer, composer and designer, the work turned out not to be ideal. However, Margot Fonteyn, for whom the ballet was created, pulled the conflicting threads together around herself – it was a Fonteyn concerto, one critic suggested. Of course, there was much to admire and enjoy in it, but it is flawed and has not yet a secure place in the repertoire.

As Ninette de Valois looked to the make-up of the repertoire for the years ahead, she was also thinking about succession to herself. So that the next generation can have a sensible amount of time in which to develop its ideas and fulfil its aims and aspirations, she has always believed that no one should stay beyond a certain age – in her mind sixty-five. In 1963 she was to reach her retirement age. There was nothing to discuss: she was going. Having named Ashton as associate director in 1952, she had in her mind settled the succession. After all, he had been a close collaborator of hers almost from the beginning, and had been a major influence in making the company's policies and setting the directions in which it was to go. He was an obvious and natural choice to succeed her, and nobody better for the next years.

She also applied her usual vigour and common sense to the arrival of Rudolf Nureyev. The circumstances of Nureyev's departure from the Kirov company and defection to the West in June 1961 are outlined in Chapter 9. Shortly thereafter he was in Copenhagen, studying with Vera Volkova, when a telephone call came through to her from Margot Fonteyn asking if she knew the whereabouts of the Russian boy who had recently defected. Volkova was able to tell her that he was right there. An invitation was immediately extended to him to appear in a gala in aid of the Royal Academy of Dancing. There could be no fee, only expenses.

Having already met Erik Bruhn, the distinguished Danish dancer whose classical style and technique epitomized for him the ideals to which he aspired, Nureyev saw the chance of also meeting a ballerina whom he greatly admired, and he agreed to take part provided that he could dance with her. In the end he did not perform with Fonteyn, because she was already committed to dancing with John Gilpin in *La Spectre de la Rose*, Nureyev's favoured work for his London debut. Instead, and more importantly, Frederick Ashton agreed to create a solo for him to music of the dancer's choice: Scriabin's *Poème Tragique*.

Thus, within a short time, Nureyev met the three artists – Bruhn, Ashton and Fonteyn – who were most to influence his career, and the consequence of his gala appearance was an invitation from the Royal Ballet to partner Margot Fonteyn in three performances of *Giselle*, the first of which was given on 21 February 1962, in a torrent of publicity. He took the town by storm – as did Fonteyn, who in many respects was transformed by his presence. Giselle was not one of her greatest parts, but she suddenly found herself responding to his dramatic insights and intensity. It became a refreshed and important role for her.

For Nureyev it was a remarkable debut. His naturalness on stage and his ability through every gesture and movement to delineate the character and feelings of Albrecht gripped the audience, which in any event was spellbound by the prowess of his dancing, his ability to travel further than British dancers in his *cabrioles* and seemingly to pause in the air at their highest point. What came across was a committed performer, fearless and possessed of a fiery, sexual temperament which would leave nothing unexplored in quest of the most complete and compelling performance that could be delivered.

These performances initiated a glorious and famous partnership. At the same time they brought with them controversy and discontent, because of changes which Nureyev made to the choreography – arbitrarily in the minds of some, but in accord with what he had learned in the Soviet Union. The version used by the Royal Ballet was derived from the pre-war Vic–Wells production and, along with other ballets from that era, was regarded as part of the company's heritage and not to be tampered with – least of all by a newcomer.

Following his success, there was of course immediate discussion about his future involvement with the company, which at that time had some excellent male dancers, but lacked a virtuoso *danseur noble*. I had negotiated his contract for the *Giselle* performances as a guest artist, but the longer-term issue of his relationship with the company had to be settled if he was to remain with it. There was every indication that he would, and Ninette de Valois believed it hugely important that he should. Here arose the dilemma. She was adamantly opposed to the company becoming a vehicle for guest dancers, believing fervently in its integrity as an ensemble. There was concern that a dancer of a different background and style, with a reputation for being demanding and difficult – not to mention an explosive temperament – might be too destructive an influence in a carefully structured environment, particularly if engaged as a permanent company member. At the same time, however, such an artist represented a force which the company needed, for the energizing of British male dancing which his example could bring about and also for the disclosure of a repertoire unfamiliar to both company and audiences. The compromise of contracting him as a permanent guest artist was struck – an arrangement which was also intended to minimize the threat that male dancers were feeling – and so began a relationship which was to endure until the beginning of the next decade.

Nureyev was a wild, heady influence. Most could take it and respond to it; a few could not. What was confirmed by his arrival was that the Royal Ballet was strong enough to absorb an injection of different attitudes and methods and emerge the better for it. It was so typical of de Valois to see the benefits which would come from Nureyev's presence and to be wholly supportive of him.

Nureyev had been a late starter as a dancer – a fact which I believe had a strong bearing on his attitude to work and his need for a high frequency of performances. His technique was not perfect, and there is no doubt that some of his peers in Leningrad, for example, were better dancers per se than he. What they were not, on the other hand, was this incredible stage creature, capable of performing with an unrivalled force and intensity that left an audience shouting for more. It was in this respect that Nureyev was to prove an invaluable asset in portraying a nineteenth-century prince such as Albrecht in a different light: not as a cardboard figure, but as a living person with a soul and a heart.

Nureyev worked hard at his technique and was never satisfied with where he had got to in its development. He was critical of those who did not share his attitude to work, and was forever urging Fonteyn and those around him to take risks in performance which I suspect they had never previously considered or, if they had, lacked the courage to undertake. Though often appearing to be concentrating solely on himself in perfecting his performance, he was a persuasive and encouraging supporter of his partners. For him it was always a matter of pushing oneself beyond what one thought possible, of accepting challenges. That, coupled with a blazing cauldron in his belly, enabled him to give performances of rare quality and excitement as well as revealing a remarkable insight into the characters he portrayed.

His moods were unpredictable, and havoc could suddenly come out of nowhere. Margot Fonteyn, talking about his personality in her TV programme *I am a Dancer*, said, 'It's complex and very simple and always interesting. Very often he's very amusing, and one was never going to be bored with him. He has a lot of changes of mood. Sometimes they are bad, but they are not really serious. He does not mean it at the time, but in five minutes it's gone.' He did, however, develop a distressing habit of keeping people waiting before the beginning of performances or acts. This was a problem not only for audiences, who understandably became impatient as the minutes ticked away, but also for the other dancers, who responded promptly to their calls and did not understand why he could get away with doing otherwise, as largely he did. He simply said that he was not ready, and that was that. His dresser at Covent Garden, Michael Brown, struggled valiantly to persuade him to change his ways, but to little avail. I had several skirmishes with him over this, but rarely came out of his dressing room the winner. It was a matter of him wanting to reassure himself that he was in the best possible condition to perform. His timing in achieving that ignored much else!

Breaches of discipline on his part were a nuisance and caused discontent in the company, but his general influence on individual dancers – Fonteyn in particular – and on the company was evident. With Fonteyn and himself it was a matter of two exceptional dancers coming together and inspiring each other to greater and greater heights. They had a common goal – perfection – and each learned from the other in its pursuit.

There can be no doubt about the huge benefits which he brought to the Royal Ballet: in the development of dancers, in the broadening of the repertoire and in the enlargement of audiences through his sheer ability to attract and to enthral. New vistas were opened, and the public responded. But sometimes it seemed that too high a price was being paid for this extraordinary and incredibly talented artist – not in monetary terms, but in the concentration of audience attention on the Fonteyn–Nureyev duo and the clamour for their performances. Performances without them suffered at the box office; also, more importantly, other talented dancers were given fewer opportunities to perform, to develop artistically and to build their own following. This was a source of great concern and, try as everyone did to achieve a sensible balance in the distribution of performances, a number of company dancers felt hard done by. Strenuous efforts had been made to ease Nureyev into the company. David Blair, for example, who had succeeded Michael Somes as Fonteyn's regular partner, continued to dance with her on various occasions. But eventually he and one or two others could not cope with the pressure of this level of competition and fell by the wayside.

We also encountered strong demand for Fonteyn and Nureyev to appear in Royal Ballet tours of North America. Sol Hurok was now taking the sole financial risk in presenting the company in the USA and was naturally anxious to maximize his box-office take and to minimize his risk. The resulting balances struck in casting were not always that fair to the majority of dancers, and I have no doubt that the failure to present younger dancers to a desirable degree in tours during the 1960s made for difficulties in attracting a good public in the 1970s when the great partnership was over.

Before Nureyev had arrived in London, Margot Fonteyn, already an internationally acclaimed ballerina after her triumph in New York in 1949, and with a huge following of her own, had talked to me about giving up. She was finding it harder and harder to keep herself in trim for performances and to maintain her standards. After all, she was already beyond the age at which many would have retired. Rightly, she was concerned that the public might be left with an inferior impression of her talents and of the real quality of her dancing if she continued for too long. She saw the end in sight for her. But there would be no fuss around her departure from the stage: 'I will phone you after breakfast one morning, John, to tell you that this is it.' Happily, that call did not come until much later.

Forever an avid learner and seeker after knowledge and information, Nureyev showed that he had an extraordinary recall of productions and steps of ballets in which he had appeared or with which he was familiar through watching rehearsals and performances. When he arrived in the West, it was clear that he would cling to everything which he considered good from his past and adapt it for use here, at the same time assimilating new influences. It was a hard balance for him to strike, but what emerged was a real talent for reproducing ballets, from which the Royal Ballet was to benefit.

His first full-length ballet was *Raymonda*, which was mounted on the Touring Company for performance at the Spoleto Festival in June 1964, with designs by Beni Montresor and with Fonteyn and Nureyev in the principal roles. The designer, whose work I usually admired, had been chosen by the Festival. Unfortunately, he was unwilling to respond to Nureyev's request for the scenery and costumes to be re-created in a nineteenth-century style, believing that by adopting another approach he was enhancing the human elements in Fonteyn and Nureyev. This was a misconception, and the ballet never enjoyed the success for which we had hoped in this production. It was withdrawn after the Festival performances, although Act 3 was subsequently restored to the Touring Company's repertoire with new scenery and costumes by Barry Kay.

A further complication had arisen during rehearsals, when Fonteyn heard that an attempt had been made on her husband's life in Panama. He was gravely ill, and needed the medical attention that the Stoke Mandeville hospital could best give him. He was accordingly brought to England, and Fonteyn left Spoleto to be with him. There were anxious days waiting for news of his condition, and I was frequently in contact with both Fonteyn and the director of the hospital. Fonteyn, anxious to be in touch and keep me informed of progress and a likely departure date for Italy, went to great lengths to phone. One night there was a call from her, obviously from a telephone box. I suggested that I should ring her back. 'You must be joking!' came the reply. 'I'm on Aylesbury station and I've spent the last ten minutes trying to find five shillings' worth of change to talk to you. I am now going to spend it doing just that.' When the first night in Spoleto was approaching and it was obvious that she could not be there, her place was taken by Doreen Wells. Fonteyn was eventually able to leave her husband and dance in the last performance in Spoleto.

Fonteyn had been torn between being with her husband and fulfilling her commitment to Nureyev and the company. Performers are often faced with this sort of dilemma – not necessarily as dramatic as in this case, but nonetheless strongly charged with emotion.

One thing about which I have never been quite sure was our decision to engage Nureyev as a guest artist throughout his time with the Royal Ballet. To all intents and purposes he was in fact a member of the company, and naming him as that rather than as a guest might well have given him greater security as a human being, separated as he was from his country and family, and officially stateless. I also think that the potential harm to the company which it was thought would come from this would not have occurred. With hindsight, I believe we were too defensive and overprotective of the company, which was quickly to demonstrate its ability to handle the situation.

Around the time of Nureyev's arrival, another important influence was brought to bear on the company in the person of Nureyev's inspiration, Erik Bruhn. The coincidence of his engagement with that of Nureyev was accidental, it having been planned sometime before Nureyev defected. The impact of Nureyev's performances certainly dulled the impression which Bruhn was to make. Nevertheless, it was extraordinary to have two of the greatest male dancers in the world appearing at the same time and shifting public attention from the ballerina to the male dancer.

Bruhn, a seasoned dancer and the product of Danish training and discipline, was more easily accommodated within the company than Nureyev. Partnered by Nadia Nerina, he danced in *Swan Lake*, *Sleeping Beauty* and *Giselle*, in all of which he displayed immaculate style and bearing – an object lesson to all who watched him. Many dancers did, and learned much.

A school and gifted choreographers are the mainstay of any ballet company. The Upper School, at Barons Court, and the Junior School, at White Lodge in Richmond Park, were both under the watchful and perceptive eye of Ninette de Valois, who made a point of visiting them at regular intervals until a few years ago.

Two choreographers had emerged from the Sadler's Wells Theatre Ballet, which had quickly shown its value as a breeding ground for creative as well as interpretative artists. John Cranko, a South African dancer and the creator of *The Prince of the Pagodas*, *Lady and the Fool*, *Pineapple Poll* and *Antigone*, to name only a handful of his output, was not to stay. In 1961 he went to Stuttgart at the invitation of one of the most benevolent and far-seeing of German intendants, Dr Walter Erich Schäfer, who was intent on building a ballet company of international renown and would spare nothing to achieve it. In the majority of German opera houses the ballet takes very much second place and is allocated only a small number of performances each month, its principal function being to supply dancers for the opera. Schäffer wanted it otherwise, and saw in Cranko the choreographer/director who could give him what he needed for Stuttgart. He was right. In a matter of nine or ten years, Cranko lifted the Stuttgart company from relative provincial obscurity to a place among the leading ballet companies of the world. It was a huge achievement.

1 Sir David Webster, the creator of post-war Covent Garden and its General Administrator 1944–70

20 Sir Geraint Evans as Figaro in *Le Nozze de Figaro*

21 Plácido Domingo as Otello in 1980 discussing his costume with Ande Anderson, Janice Green and Sir John Tooley

22 Dame Joan Sutherland in *Lucia di Lammermoor* in 1959

23 Jon Vickers as Peter Grimes in 1975

24 Dame Kiri Te Kanawa as Desdemona in *Otello* in 1992

25 Sir Thomas Allen as Don Giovanni in 1996

Part of the secret of Cranko's success as a choreographer lay in his reliance on dancing to tell a story and to express emotions, whether serious or comic. He possessed a remarkable gift for the making of narrative ballets, in which his characters rang true and which he shaped and developed with extraordinary skill and perception. He also had a real feel for comedy, making situations funny in a way which leaves them fresh and appealing however often they are seen. His departure from Covent Garden was a real loss, but, as will be explained, he established a creative environment in Stuttgart which was to bring other returns to the Royal Ballet.

The other choreographer who crossed from Rosebery Avenue to Covent Garden was Kenneth MacMillan. He had already made something of a name for himself as a dancer, but his real talent lay in the making of ballets – often related to psychological aspects of life, matters not hitherto treated balletically. *Noctambules*, his first Covent Garden ballet, presented in March 1956, with music by Humphrey Searle and decor by Nicholas Georgiadis, who was to become a lifetime collaborator, was received with bewilderment by both audience and critics. While the meaning of the ballet may not have been understood, there was instant recognition of a rare and original talent which the company needed for its future and to complement the lyrical and poetic work of that greatest of choreographers, Frederick Ashton.

This early sign of promise was soon to be followed by greater achievements. Innovative and daring, MacMillan explored subjects for ballets which stretched the imagination and dramatic talents of dancers and which could not fail to provoke an audience to thought. He also turned to remaking existing ballets, the first of which was *Baiser de la Fée*, Stravinsky's homage to Tchaikovsky, in 1960. It had never enjoyed success, and MacMillan could not change its course. He triumphed with another Stravinsky ballet, however, *The Rite of Spring*, when he re-created this work in 1962, with Monica Mason as the Chosen Maiden and with scenery and costumes designed by Sidney Nolan.

The Royal Ballet now had two creative forces working within it, Ashton and MacMillan, totally different from each other and taking the company down separate paths of exploration and invention. This was just what the company required, and, with its dancing at a peak, it was able to profit from it and widen its repertoire.

The New Year of 1960 saw Frederick Ashton turning from an earlier romantic style to a bucolic comedy, set in a farmyard and with characters drawn from life. *La Fille mal Gardée*, a subject suggested to Ashton by Tamara Karsavina, one of the great and early interpreters of the role of Lise, is a wonderfully inventive ballet, a work of genius. The choice of Osbert Lancaster as designer was inspired, and John Lanchbery made a brilliant arrangement of the music, largely based on that composed by Ferdinand Hérold for an early version of the ballet.

Reluctant to take on another lengthy work, Ashton delayed and delayed starting it, much to the fury of Ninette de Valois, who, unwilling to wait any longer, simply announced the ballet in the next programme. She was delighted with this move, and telephoned to tell me what she had done. It certainly had the desired effect. Ashton responded to the challenge, and a masterpiece was created in a matter of weeks, ready for performance on the day announced.

The first performance at Covent Garden was a triumph, but in the regions and in New York there was not the same spontaneous response as in London. This piece has spectacle and romance, for which audiences crave, but it is countrified and removed from the high romance normally associated with ballet. When the out-of-town and overseas public was slow to take to it, there was a suggestion that the French title was not understood by many and therefore off-putting. Sol Hurok felt strongly about this and wanted an English substitute found. Ideas were passed around and Hurok even proposed a competition in search of a name which might make the work more saleable in American cities other than New York. Nothing came of any of this: we stuck to the original name, and in the end this felicitous and charming ballet won the affection of audiences everywhere.

Ninette de Valois's anticipated retirement in 1963 became public knowledge in March of that year, only three days after Ashton's masterly distillation of *La Dame aux Camélias* into a ballet for Fonteyn and Nureyev had received an ecstatic ovation. The excitement with which this had been greeted was replaced by disbelief that the founder of the Royal Ballet was giving up its directorship. Even though Ashton was named as her successor, and highly regarded as he was, some had doubts about the future well-being of the companies and the school without her. These doubts were misplaced, but many had expected de Valois to continue until a much greater age and could not envisage the company without her.

Having known and worked with Madam (as Ninette de Valois is known) for many years, I have always been conscious of her pride in her companies and her school, but also of her refusal to regard them as monuments to herself. She has never been interested in such a concept. Lilian Baylis gave her the first opportunities to present ballet at the Old Vic, in 1928, and three years later at Sadler's Wells. From then on her vision led her to fight ferociously for everything which she regarded as essential for the establishment of ballet as a serious art form in this country and for the advancement of her companies. Nothing deterred her.

Progress was not always in a straight line. As she saw an obstacle or stumbled across one, she was quick to find a way round it. She was a pragmatist, and capable of rapid changes of mind to achieve a particular objective which she regarded as important. There was an inconsistency and contrariness in her which could be maddening but was often endearing and the source of laughter as you realized what she was doing.

When she was leaving, I told her I would miss the enraged phone calls as she discovered what she saw as dastardly acts by the opera company against the interests of the ballet. I used to feel the phone lines becoming white hot as she talked furiously about a problem. Soon after arriving at Covent Garden I had become a buffer between her and David Webster, and I was to enjoy her good-humoured company much more frequently than the reverse. It was a wonderful initiation for me, and I owe much of my knowledge of ballet to her.

We have kept in touch over the years, and visits to Barnes for a chat over coffee have been moments to be treasured. Entertaining and informative, she will reminisce about Diaghilev and others with extraordinary recall and clarity. Never good with the names of those immediately around her, she will spend time trying to identify someone about whom she is talking, eventually producing a quite incorrect version of the name sought. This has occasionally led me to wonder if she always had the right name for a dancer whom she was recommending for a role or wanting to reprimand for some misdemeanour. You might question her, only to be told, 'You know whom I mean.'

She used to say that the spirit of Lilian Baylis lived on in her. In many ways this was true. Conscious of money and loath to spend it unnecessarily, for years she travelled from Barnes to Covent Garden by the No. 9 bus to Hammersmith and the Piccadilly Line for the rest of the journey, returning home in the same way. When visiting me in my office – which she did for years after she had retired – she always refused the offer of a taxi home. In the end we resorted to ordering one and practically pushing her into it. 'Taxis make me feel ill,' she used to say. 'I feel sick as I watch the meter clocking up the fare.'

Her official pension was miserly, and I was extremely concerned about her ability to make ends meet. I decided to supplement it with a regular additional payment in recognition of all the work which she was still undertaking – attending company rehearsals, visiting the Royal Ballet School, and being available to advise. One day, when I was calling on her at home, she remarked that a cheque which she had just received was for a larger amount than previously. I explained that this was because of a cost-of-living increase. She immediately retorted, 'You can't afford it and I do not need it. Please take it back and ask them to send me a cheque for the old amount.' We continued to pay at the new rate.

Her retirement was the end of an era, but, as she had said in an article written in 1932, ' It is the belief of the present director, and this is a point to be driven home, that if the Ballet does not survive many a director it will have failed utterly in the eyes of the first dancer to hold that post.' In fact so strongly had she laid its foundations and so surely had she set the succession that the company, under its new director and with its own huge momentum, could only glide smoothly and without fuss into a fresh chapter in its history.

Ninette de Valois remained on hand to advise, but used to say that she was determined not to interfere, unless her help was sought. Nevertheless, a presence as powerful as hers will always be felt, and there was a risk of decisions being taken with a glance over the shoulder in her direction.

Ashton left personnel and policy much as they were. Fundamentally a creative and sensitive artist, he wanted time to concentrate on his choreography. Unlike de Valois, he was not interested in the daily management routine, and he delegated this to three assistant directors: Michael Somes, John Hart and John Field. The last of these was in charge of the Touring Company, Somes was responsible for coaching and rehearsing in the studio and on stage, and Hart planned the rehearsal schedules and calls around programmes agreed with Ashton. It was an arrangement which worked well, in spite of some tension between Hart and Somes on the allocation of rehearsal calls, and little contact between Field and the rest of the team. Hart understandably wanted some stake in the rehearsing of the dancers, but often found himself excluded by Somes, a strong and forceful personality who, having been an early eminent dancer in the company, which he had joined in 1935, saw himself as the guardian of the Royal Ballet's heritage and tradition. It was not a situation in which Ashton was ever going to become involved, and they were left to sort it out themselves.

Naturally, Ashton wanted to put his own stamp on the repertoire, and he did so with his eye on the classical tradition and guided by his admiration for the works of choreographers such as George Balanchine and Bronislava Nijinska. Nureyev was keen to present the full-length *La Bayadère*, but there was doubt about its public appeal and hence its box-office potential. However, it was thought that Act 4, 'The Kingdom of Shades', would be a valuable addition to the repertoire, and, true to his instincts, Ashton decided to take the risk of entrusting this to Nureyev. There were doubts about the wisdom of handing such responsibility to this untried and difficult Russian dancer, but he was known to have an incredible memory and was already demonstrating his talents as a coach. With Margot Fonteyn, Merle Park, Monica Mason, Lynn Seymour, Nureyev himself and a superbly prepared corps de ballet, the production, in November 1963, was a triumph and quickly became an established addition to the repertoire. Russian style came naturally to the company, and Nureyev goaded the dancers into greater and greater achievements.

A revised *Swan Lake* followed, with production in the hands of Robert Helpmann. In preparation for this he had been looking at other European productions, and I was keen that he should attend a performance by the Stanislavsky company, in Moscow, which was supposedly close to the original and reported to be worth seeing. The only performance in the near future was merely days away, and a visa had to be obtained very quickly. I called the cultural attaché at the Soviet Embassy to seek his help, but was treated to a torrent of abuse over our engagement of Nureyev, whom he regarded as a traitor and whose performances at Covent Garden were an embarrassment to his country. Eventually the conversation – if it could be called that – ended with the remark that I had not helped him and he was certainly not going to help me. Helpmann did not get to the Stanislavsky Theatre.

The four-hundredth anniversary of the birth of Shakespeare occurred on 23 April 1964, and in celebration the Royal Ballet presented a programme of ballets based on Shakespeare's plays and sonnets. Helpmann's *Hamlet* was already available, and Kenneth MacMillan created a new work, *Images of Love*, based on lines from plays and sonnets, with music by Peter Tranchell and decor by Barry Kay. It did not fare well, and blame was partly laid at the composer's feet. I had commissioned the score at MacMillan's request, and had done so with enthusiasm at the prospect of newly written music for a ballet. Unfortunately, however, communication between choreographer and composer was to prove minimal and much of the score had to be written blind, in spite of several attempts on Tranchell's part as well as my own to start the necessary dialogue.

The last part of this celebratory programme was a new ballet by Frederick Ashton, soon to be one of his most popular: *A Midsummer Night's Dream*, based straightforwardly on the Shakespeare play and choreographed to Mendelssohn's incidental music, arranged by John Lanchbery. It won an immediate positive response from the audience, who revelled in the balletic treatment of the lovers, the fairies and the mechanicals, and have continued to do so.

In this ballet Ashton showed a remarkable facility for distilling a play into a shorter form which in turn could be reinterpreted choreographically, with little mime needed. This in itself was an achievement, but what emerged on the stage that night – a magical transformation of the Shakespeare play into lyrical and poetic dance – was miraculous. Furthermore, it displayed and exploited the outstanding gifts of two dancers who were to play an increasingly important role in the future of the Royal Ballet: Antoinette Sibley as Titania, and Anthony Dowell as Oberon.

Following a gala in honour of Dame Ninette de Valois, the Royal Ballet moved to the Theatre Royal, Drury Lane, for the summer of 1964, while essential repairs and alterations were carried out to the Royal Opera House. Performing separately from the opera company inevitably raised the question of the desirability of this becoming a permanent arrangement. De Valois, however, still believed in the concept of a national lyric theatre, with opera and ballet sharing equally in performance and rehearsal opportunities, and had no wish to break away from that, although she did welcome the periodic seasons for the ballet alone, either in the Opera House, on tour or in another theatre in London. Drury Lane was usually occupied by long-running musicals, and the only other suitable London venue was the Coliseum. A Royal Ballet season was held there in 1973, but regrettably this never became established as a regular event because of theatre availability and cost.

An important step towards reaching wider audiences for opera and ballet occurred in June 1964: the launching of a film by Anthony Havelock-Allen entitled *An Evening with the Royal Ballet*. This included

Ashton's *La Valse*, *Le Corsaire* and *Les Sylphides*, with Fonteyn and Nureyev, and Act 3 of *Sleeping Beauty*, with Fonteyn and David Blair. The Austrian film director Paul Czinner had pioneered the filming of opera and ballet as performed on the stage, with works filmed in a studio being presented essentially as stage performances. There are limitations in trying to make productions conceived entirely in theatrical terms viable on the screen, but this is not to underestimate the importance of the approach in furthering interest in these art forms, and Havelock-Allen's initiative was warmly welcomed.

By mid-1966 three of Ashton's wishes for the repertoire had been fulfilled: Balanchine's *Serenade* had been introduced in May 1964, Nijinska's *Les Biches* in December 1964, and her *Les Noces* in March 1966. *Serenade* was instantly popular with audiences. *Les Biches* was important for the company, as its wit and covert emotion needed to be subtly conveyed and demanded as much acting ability as dancing. Nijinska was a disciplinarian, and worked hard with the company to ensure a seamless join between the 1920s period style and the ballet's classical base. The public adored it.

In spite of protests from Lincoln Kirstein that three-act ballets had no place in contemporary life – a theme which he pursued with me from time to time – they continued to prosper in the repertories of the Royal Ballet companies and were the works most sought after by the public. After the visit of the Bolshoi Ballet to London in 1956, it had been agreed that there should be an exchange of choreographers: Ashton would go to Moscow, and Leonid Lavrovsky would mount his much admired *Romeo and Juliet* – one of the biggest successes of the Bolshoi season – on the Royal Ballet. This exchange did not happen. There was, however, a need for a production of this ballet.

Ashton had already created a production for the Royal Danish Ballet in 1955. It was a subject which had interested him for a long time, and he had previously proposed to Ninette de Valois that he should make a version of it to the Prokofiev score. She had disagreed, on the grounds that there was enough of Prokofiev's music in the repertoire already – a curious objection. When the invitation came from Copenhagen to mount it there, he naturally accepted with alacrity. He was not fond of the highly dramatic and grandiose style of Lavrovsky's production, and treated the work as an intimate chamber piece, concentrating on the two lovers. John Cranko had also choreographed a version, for the Stuttgart Ballet in 1963.

Ashton was rightly of the opinion that remounting his Copenhagen production was not an option – it would look lightweight against the massive and heavy Bolshoi version – and he turned instead to Kenneth MacMillan, believing in his ability to bring a freshness and perception to the work, despite the restrictions of the shape and construction of Prokofiev's score. There was another motive in Ashton's action. He was aware that MacMillan was restless, and that the Deutsche Oper was beckoning to him to be the ballet director in Berlin. A commission would not necessarily prevent him from eventually going, but it would secure another major work from him for the Royal Ballet. It did, and, with designs by Nicholas Georgiadis, *Romeo and Juliet* was the hit of the 1965 season and has been a staple element in the repertoire since.

However, for some of us the opening was marred by what I have always regarded as a wrong decision to allow Margot Fonteyn and Rudolf Nureyev to assume the leading roles, in place of Lynn Seymour and Christopher Gable, on whom the ballet was mounted. Sol Hurok was forever pressing for the appearance of the by then already famous duo of Fonteyn and Nureyev, and wanted the publicity of their performances in the London opening in preparation for their later performances in New York. Such demands should have been refused; however, artistic and moral considerations were discarded and the knee was bowed to the box office. I was as angry as most people about this, and upset that MacMillan was not supported more strongly in his desire to retain the original cast. Lamentable as this was, however, everyone survived the decision and brought more and more laurels upon themselves as they made their triumphant progress across the United States and Canada in the spring and summer of 1965, beginning in New York and finishing in Vancouver after visiting no less than seventeen other cities.

Ashton imaginatively added to the repertoire throughout his years as director, and was skilful in his construction of programmes – an art which has not been so successfully practised by others. There was an aura of excitement around. The company was strong and dancing superbly, fired by an interesting and innovative programme. The public responded enthusiastically.

If constantly performing routine programmes, with little new work, dancers can become stale. Their creative processes are unchallenged and lie fallow. This is not healthy for a dancer or good for choreographers. The human beings on whom ballets are created must be able to respond to direction from choreographers, and they can do so effectively only if their creative senses can be stimulated. The realization of a ballet is more than the slavish following of direction: it relies for success on the inter-action of ideas from both the choreographer and his interpreters. Glen Tetley, coming to create a ballet some years later, after a difficult time for the company, complained to me about the absence of a creative force in the dancers. It needed reawakening.

In 1964 Kenneth MacMillan announced his wish to make a ballet to Mahler's *Das Lied von der Erde*. This aroused instant horror in the boardroom when reported, and led to an unfortunate situation which should never have been allowed to develop. Some board members felt that Mahler's work was so complete in itself that nothing could be added to it and that damage might even be done. The debate continued for some time, and the opinions of distinguished musicians were sought. The latter were mostly opposed to the ballet, and swung the board to voting for rejection. Of course the board had the right – indeed the obligation – to discuss such an issue when in doubt about it, but their concerns should have been discussed with MacMillan, who in turn should have considered their objections and have had the opportunity to return for further discussion, when the board should have relented.

MacMillan took the idea to John Cranko in Stuttgart, who immedi-ately accepted it and arranged for its inclusion in his programme. The result was a hauntingly beautiful ballet, *Song of the Earth*, with MacMillan at his most sensitive and responding movingly and perceptively to the glorious music. It was a colossal success in Germany, and vindicated the matching of movement to Mahler's score. It had to come to London, and did so in 1966, when it was warmly received.

Doubts about basing ballets on self-sufficient musical masterpieces persisted, however. Music critics attended performances. Some shared the board's original view and were perplexed that the work had been staged; others argued that, as the standards of the musical performance were not of the highest, movement could be accommodated without further compromising an already compromised enterprise. If the musical standards had been those found in a concert hall, they went on, they would have rejected the ballet on the grounds of the self-sufficiency of the music.

A similar controversy was to befall another MacMillan ballet ten years later, this time based on Fauré's Requiem. Some board members were horrified at the prospect of such intimate and sacred music being performed in a theatre as the springboard for a ballet. Before the debate had gone very far, MacMillan decided that Stuttgart would again provide a better environment for the creation of his work, and took it there without further ado. Like the Mahler, *Requiem* also found its way back to London. Objections on this occasion were too subjective to be the basis of serious rejection in my opinion. But I am sure that if MacMillan had attempted to make the ballet in London it would not have been as successful. I do not believe that the Royal Ballet's dancers were ready for the creative processes which this work entailed in its beginnings.

Ashton persuaded a long-time absentee from London, Antony Tudor, to return to create an original work for the company in January 1967. A superb and original craftsman, Tudor was difficult and demanding. Intensely interested in Buddhism and responding to his faith, he created *Shadowplay*, to a score by Charles Koechlin, a composer of whom most of us knew little. The ballet described a young man's search for his own identity, hindered by all sorts of distractions. The subject matter was too obscure for it to be a popular success, but there could be no doubt of the ballet's individuality and distinction. It also had the big advantage of taking Anthony Dowell from his familiar roles into one quite different and which showed him in another light as a performer.

Nutcracker had been in the pre-war repertory of the Sadler's Wells Ballet but had not been subsequently revived. Its absence left a hole in Christmas programme planning, with *Sleeping Beauty* and *Cinderella* as the only seasonal fare. Nureyev had an imaginative idea for this ballet and was asked to mount a production for the Royal Ballet, following an earlier production in Stockholm. Nicholas Georgiadis, one of his most important collaborators, was to design it, but, because of a commitment to design *Aida*, the first night of *Nutcracker* was not to take place until February 1968, instead of the previous Christmas. One unusual feature of this production was a corps de ballet made up of children from the Royal Ballet Junior School, who revelled in the experience of working with Nureyev. The production made wonderful entertainment, and was an immediate favourite with the public.

Ashton's final years as director were marred by the tragic mishandling of his retirement. By 1967 David Webster was talking to me about his own retirement. The precise date was not mentioned, but, whenever there was reference to the subject, he invariably informed me that Ashton was going with him. Webster was far from well by this time, and had experienced some uncomfortable episodes arising from forgetfulness or occasional panic – usually the result of a misunderstanding. He was no longer himself, and found it hard to deal with many issues. These included his evidence to a 1967 House of Commons select-committee inquiry into the Arts Council, at which for unfathomable reasons he thought that the Royal Opera House would be criticized for overspending on a production of *Aida*. None of us could convince him that this was outside the scope of the inquiry, and that the matter – which in any case was not a huge issue – would not arise. He suffered grievously for weeks in anticipation of the meeting, but when it was over and there had been no mention of *Aida* the joy in his face and the relief which came over his whole being was wondrous to see.

Webster never explained why Ashton intended to leave at the same time as he; when questioned, he invariably replied, 'I just know that he does.' The Royal Ballet was dancing superbly, there had been important additions to the repertoire, and more were to come. I could see no sensible reason for change in the directorship within the next few years, in spite of some dancers' difficulties with Hart and Somes, Ashton's lack of interest in the Touring Company, and the unwillingness of the London directorate to embrace the Touring Company's director, John Field, on whose work they looked with some disdain. There was still much going for this team: the problems were not insuperable, and, for all its faults and weaknesses, it was surely folly to be ending a successful regime prematurely. I was concerned that we might fall inadvertently into a situation from which there was no escape.

This happened. Sir Donald Albery, director of the London Festival Ballet, announced his retirement in the early days of 1968, and an invitation to succeed him was received by John Field. Webster, not wanting to lose Field, and certainly not to a rival company in London, persuaded him to reject it – apparently on the understanding that there was change in the Royal Ballet's management in the offing and that it would be worth Field's while to stay. I never discovered what was actually said in this interview, which involved Webster and Field only, and of which Webster's account to me was brief and uninformative beyond the fact that Field had agreed to remain.

Kenneth MacMillan had left Covent Garden in 1966 to be the ballet director of the Deutsche Oper in Berlin, and had taken Lynn Seymour with him. I believe this was a reaction to the *Romeo and Juliet* casting arguments and because MacMillan wanted more opportunities for creative work than he thought were likely to come his way under the

Ashton regime. When he had left, it seems that Webster had indicated to MacMillan that he would succeed Ashton as director of the Royal Ballet.

To the best of my knowledge and in my view, despite his subsequent conversation with Webster, Field was never really the favoured successor: Kenneth MacMillan was most naturally in the line of succession. This was supported by Ninette de Valois, who was beginning to indulge in her familiar cry that the old should make way for the young – obviously directing it at Ashton, who, at sixty-four, was some twenty-five years older than MacMillan. Whether she ever talked directly to Ashton about making way for MacMillan I do not know, but her determination to achieve change sooner rather than later was apparent.

David Webster was keeping all of this close to his chest. Even though I was the favoured candidate to succeed him, he was curiously reluctant to talk very much to me about it and insisted on handling the matter himself. It was as though he saw his Covent Garden life coming to an end and believed that he should tidy everything up before handing over a newly packaged Royal Ballet to me. This was not the case with the Royal Opera, however, where discussions about a successor to Georg Solti were open, with all concerned being seriously involved. There was some mystique around the Webster/Ashton relationship which I never penetrated but which I can only attribute to the period in the 1930s when David Webster and Jimmy Cleveland Belle, his lifelong partner, became caught up with the Ashton fan club and other homosexual groups with whom they mingled on their weekend jaunts from Liverpool, where they both worked, to enjoy the theatre and the social life of London. Webster talked quite often about his earlier London life. It had left its mark.

Quite casually, one morning in April 1968 Webster told me that he was seeing Ashton later in the day to talk about the future; he suggested that I be present. I explained that I had a commitment elsewhere, but would join them when I returned if their meeting was still going on.

When I entered Webster's room some twenty minutes after they had begun to talk, I found Ashton glum and crestfallen. 'It's all over,' he said. When I asked what he meant, 'I've been sacked' was the reply. Whatever had taken place in the first part of the discussion, I am quite sure that Webster would not have mentioned sacking – although I can understand why it was construed as such. In any event, having reached this point, Ashton was going to dramatize the situation – sacking has a quite different ring to it from retiring, particularly when you are leaving against your will. After Ashton had left the room, I asked Webster what had happened. He had told Ashton that they were both leaving in 1970. He had not queried Ashton's wish to go with him, since he was quite certain of it, whereas Ashton was in fact longing to be asked to stay. The question of whether he wanted to go or stay when Webster left was never put to him.

The news of Ashton's departure quickly spread, and caused dismay among dancers, staff and loyal members of the audience, although it was some time before an official announcement was made. It caused an immediate rift between the company and the administration of the Royal Opera House, and, since I was in the theatre much more often than Webster, it was I who was on the receiving end of the abuse from Michael Somes. It was a disturbed and unsettling period for us all. I felt it keenly, because I knew that the affair had been badly handled and I was concerned that perhaps I had not done enough to prevent Ashton's premature exit, although what I might have done I am not sure. Webster was intransigent, and was so determined that this was the agreed plan that he was deaf to questioning on the subject, and I could do nothing but try to calm those who were upset.

I did not want Ashton to go, and believed that we would all have benefited from another two or three years with him as Royal Ballet director. It might not have been plain sailing – because of the unresolved difficulties between staff and dancers – but it would have been an infinitely easier situation for me to have handled than that with which I was left. More importantly, it would have given Ashton the chance to have rounded off what he wanted to do and there would have been a well-organized takeover by Kenneth MacMillan a year or two later.

Ninette de Valois was party to MacMillan's appointment. She was in Turkey at the time, and Webster talked often to her on the phone. I doubt that she would have queried Ashton leaving at the same time as Webster, given her views on age. However, she might not have demurred at Ashton staying longer, provided that MacMillan was his agreed successor and a date had been fixed for him to take charge. What is not known is whether Webster in that 1966 conversation had given MacMillan a date for his becoming director, which was causing him to keep resolutely to Ashton's leaving with him.

I put much of this confused and distressing episode down to Webster's poor health, but underlying it all I believe there was something else which persuaded Webster to cling so strongly to the idea that he and

Ashton would retire at the same time. Post-war Covent Garden was David Webster's creation. He dreaded the moment of going, and seemed not to want to leave behind a symbol of what had been so important to him. For Webster, Ashton was an idol for whom his respect and affection went back to those pre-war encounters. Now that they were of an age to retire, Webster seemed determined that Ashton should not outlast him at Covent Garden. They had to go together: there was no room for discussion. Hence his failure to ask Ashton the obvious question at that fateful meeting.

This left Ashton in despair, insecure and depressed. Nothing could console him. He felt he was a cast-off – unloved and rejected. Though this did not correspond to the attitudes of any of us at Covent Garden, his bitterness towards the Royal Opera House and those whom he thought had engineered his departure were understandable. It was to be a long time before anything like a normal relationship could be restored, and during this dreadful period there was no way of explaining the circumstances without betraying David Webster – although nothing could justify the ultimatum which Webster had delivered.

Later in 1968 Frederick Ashton was to identify himself with another British artist who had suffered neglect and private unhappiness – Edward Elgar. For many years the designer Julia Trevelyan Oman had been harbouring ideas for a ballet to the score of Elgar's *Enigma Variations*, and some time earlier she had left some sketches for Ashton to peruse. He now recalled these and, with Trevelyan Oman as his designer, he began work on a ballet which portrayed in the most realistic of terms the life of the creative artist and his loneliness, even though surrounded by friends. It was hugely successful, and showed off the company's dramatic dancing skills to perfection. It was to be Ashton's last full-scale ballet for the main company for eight years.

Aware that the *Sleeping Beauty* production with which the company had reopened Covent Garden was more than twenty years old and looking tired, Ashton decided to present a new production in the autumn of 1968 and chose Peter Wright to direct it. Wright, formerly a dancer with the Kurt Jooss company and then with the Sadler's Wells Theatre Ballet, had become John Cranko's assistant in Stuttgart. He had devised a considerable number of original ballets, but it was with new versions of the nineteenth-century classics that he was beginning to make his name. With sets by Henry Bardon, costumes by Lila di Nobili and masks by Rostislav Doboujinski, the period chosen in this case was medieval.

There were cuts, alterations and additions to what had become the firmly established view of how *Sleeping Beauty* should be, and the end result was not wholly successful, failing to win the universal acclaim for which we had all hoped. However, it did bring Peter Wright back into the fold. As events turned out, there was to be serious need of his talents and experience before much time had elapsed.

Two more visits to America were to take place before Frederick Ashton left. The American public adored him, and I am sure that their warmth and enthusiasm for his work and for him did something to raise his spirits and restore his self-esteem. Indeed, the 1970 New York season culminated with a gala in his honour. On the company's return to London, most of the remainder of the season was properly devoted to an Ashton Festival, ending on 24 July 1970 with a programme devised and produced by three of his closest colleagues: Michael Somes, John Hart and Leslie Edwards. Thirty-six of his ballets were represented, inter-linked by a dialogue written by William Chappell and spoken by Robert Helpmann. It was an evening of celebration of a truly great creative talent, heavily laced with nostalgia, and reminding us – if we needed a reminder – of the huge debt owed to him for the forty-eight ballets written for the company and the qualities inherent in them: poetry, lyricism, restraint and impeccable taste. The Ashton style had become the hallmark of the company, which was handed over to his successors enriched by his genius and raised to superlative levels of dancing under his stewardship.

In January 1970 an important announcement had been made about the appointment of successors to Frederick Ashton and about the reorganization of the Royal Ballet companies. Kenneth MacMillan had been appointed artistic director, with John Field as administrative director. Then, for artistic and financial reasons, it was decided to merge the Touring Company with the main company. Big productions would be confined to Covent Garden, and smaller-scale ballets – both existing works of a suitable scale and newly created ones – would be toured by a changing collection of twenty-two soloists drawn from the merged companies and to be known as the New Group.

This plan was taking a leaf out of the Bolshoi's book, and had been mooted on and off since that company's 1956 London season. As with other projects of this kind, the theory was wonderful, but the practice less so. The venture ran into early difficulties, which were not resolved by a variety of modifications, and eventually the New Group was abandoned and replaced by a larger company, later to become Sadler's Wells Royal Ballet and most recently Birmingham Royal Ballet.

Administration of a company was no more congenial to Kenneth MacMillan than it had been to Frederick Ashton, and MacMillan's experiences in Berlin had not changed his opinion of this aspect of a director's responsibilities. He wanted to concentrate on the artistic direction of the Royal Ballet and have time for serious creative work. John Field, however, revelled in all the elements of company direction, and following fifteen years of running the Touring Company as an almost independent entity he was well equipped for the task in hand and seemingly able to complement MacMillan. But this was to underestimate inherent difficulties in the changeover plans – partly historical and partly personal.

John Hart had left the company, but Michael Somes remained – very much in charge of the Ashton legacy and the Royal Ballet's traditions. He had always looked upon John Field with some disdain – a view shared by some others – and had regarded dancers from Field's company as inferior to those in the main company. It is true that Covent Garden tended to take most of the best dancers from the Royal Ballet School, but it did not take them all, and the Touring Company had some fine artists. In matters of finesse and ultimate style, there was certainly room for improvement, and there was no doubt that the Touring Company dancers would benefit from extended rehearsal free from the pressure of performance. Eight performances per week on the road, with generally poor rehearsal facilities, left little time to spare for improving standards. This was remediable, but attempts to transfer dancers from the Touring Company for limited periods rarely succeeded. Somes made these dancers so unwelcome, both before and after the merger, and gave them such a hard time that they found it hard to bear. The cross-fertilization which we had envisaged on taking over the Sadler's Wells Theatre Ballet in 1957, and which Ninette de Valois wanted and had seen as important, failed to all intents and purposes.

The other problem, which proved insurmountable, arose from Field's designation as administrative director, rather than co-director. Wary of two-headed ill-defined directorates as we were, and knowing of MacMillan's reluctance to accept Field as an equal and Field's unwillingness to accept any position other than director, this was the only solution open to us. I was uncomfortable with it, however: I was not convinced that Field could set his artistic ambitions to one side and concentrate solely on the management of the company, new and challenging though that job was because of the company's new guise. By Christmas the cracks in this arrangement had split wide open and Field had resigned.

Peter Wright, who had been engaged to direct the Touring Company and took on the New Group after the merger, was appointed in place of Field, but was described as associate director. It was to be the beginning of a long association between Wright and the Royal Ballet, all parts of which were to benefit from his artistic flair and common sense during the many years he spent with the organization. John Auld – former assistant director of the Festival Ballet and director of the Gulbenkian Dance Company in Lisbon – became assistant to MacMillan.

Kenneth MacMillan scored a coup near the beginning of his regime by persuading Jerome Robbins to mount *Dances at a Gathering* on the Royal Ballet in October 1970. Previously created for the New York City Ballet in 1969, it was a knockout – praised by critics and audiences, and a triumph for the dancers, who responded brilliantly to Robbins's challenging and demanding choreography and added individual dimensions to their roles. Robbins refused to settle on the first-night cast until twenty-four hours before opening, and laid down rigorous stipulations on future cast changes. It was not to be a simple matter of one dancer being replaced by another: rather, multiple changes of roles were to follow the introduction of a new body. Sheets and sheets of paper were filled with the permutations of casting he would allow.

The integration of two corps de ballet was a major undertaking, and was quickly put to the test with the transfer of Peter Wright's Touring Company production of *Giselle* to Covent Garden and later a revised version of *Swan Lake*.

It is worth recalling a conversation I had with Kenneth MacMillan before the second Bolshoi season at Covent Garden, in 1969. 'No doubt', he said, 'the most successful and sought-after ballet in their coming season will be *Spartacus*.' He was absolutely right: the public flocked to it and loved it. Impressed by the strength and virility of the dancing, some later questioned Royal Ballet standards (a criticism which was underlined by MacMillan himself when commenting unfavourably on British male dancing in a radio interview). During our conversation, MacMillan asked if I would support his plan to create full-length narrative ballets. The creative urge to do this was clearly in him, and my support was readily given. Like him, I was sure that this was the direction in which the Royal Ballet needed to go – not to the exclusion of the one-act ballet, but as a means of providing a more balanced repertoire which would have strong audience appeal. The outcome was the full-length *Anastasia*, followed later by *Manon*, *Meyerling* and *Isadora* as, during the 1970s, we began to fulfil that earlier and deeply held conviction of Dame Ninette de Valois that the English needed the experience of creating three-act ballets – 'the experiment in creative production of the more leisured approach'. In a paper read to the Royal Society of Arts on 24 May 1957 ('The English Ballet') she had made the following observations:

> We need contact with that forgotten part of the theatre in modern ballet – the part I can only describe as theatre sense; it lies at the core of these great traditional three-act ballets. The structure of the scenario alone is of immense importance, for never does it appear to be an obscure peg used to hang movement on; it becomes instead a *raison d'être* for movement itself, a return to the significance of drama in the theatre.

In Berlin in 1967, MacMillan had already devised a remarkable one-act ballet about Anastasia – the self-proclaimed daughter of the murdered Tsar Nicholas II – creating it on Lynn Seymour. He now decided to extend the story to cover some of the events in her troubled childhood, before the mental illness which had caused her to be hospitalized. In a brilliantly designed setting by Barry Kay, which incorporated the projection of silent film of pre-revolutionary Russia, MacMillan devised dances and movement evoking the period. The first performances, in the 1970/71 season, were imaginative and moving, but bedevilled by the length of the music for the first two acts, which were performed to two Tchaikovsky symphonies. Although fearful of time, initially we resisted the idea of cutting the symphonies, but in a recent revival this has been done, without critical comment and to the advantage of the work.

MacMillan was to set the pace in productivity and standards for the three-act ballet. Not all of his full-length works have held a regular place in the repertoire, but the record is an astonishing one. It is also encouraging that David Bintley – armed with his notebook full of ideas for ballets, both long and short – is creating a succession of ballets which are thoughtfully conceived, dramatic and fluent, and using the medium of dance as a means to express not only emotion but also fact, to telling effect and to the delight of audiences.

Bold moves in programming were important for the company, and the last ballet in the 1970/71 season made the point that there was a new directorate in place, intent on taking the company in a variety of artistic directions – though not abandoning its roots and its traditional idioms, as *Anastasia* had confirmed. The American choreographer Glen Tetley had made *Field Figures* for the New Group in Nottingham the previous autumn, to a score by Karlheinz Stockhausen, and it was now brought to London to close the season. The score is complex and presented the dancers with unfamiliar challenges in adjusting to non-classical dancing techniques. It was an important innovation, but its complexities have made it difficult to keep in the repertoire.

Having visited the United States every year between 1967 and 1970, the company enjoyed a welcome interval before returning for a six-week New York season in April 1972. This was a testing time for MacMillan, as he took his company to a city where Ashton had been acclaimed as a hero and where the latter's seemingly enforced retirement was resented in some quarters. New York was slow to warm to newcomers in such a situation, even though MacMillan's *Romeo and Juliet* had been well received. Unfortunately he was not helped by his late arrival, caused by the necessity of staying in England for a few weeks to choreograph his newest ballet, *Ballade*, for the New Group. (Having produced a small-scale work for Covent Garden, *Triad*, and now turning his attention to the New Group, he was to admit to me that it was the small ensemble which was beginning to interest him most, because of the scope it offered for experimentation.) The company's dancing was once again applauded, however, and it was gratifying that Antoinette Sibley and Anthony Dowell were now receiving favourable notice, in spite of the continuing dominance of Margot Fonteyn and Rudolf Nureyev in the public's attention.

Glen Tetley's *Field Figures* had stretched the company, but even greater demands were to be made on the dancers and, in its musical set-up, on the opera house itself by his next ballet, *Laborintus*, in July 1972, to a difficult and complicated score of that name by Luciano Berio. This was another important move into the contemporary scene. Regrettably, it was not followed by any similar works, and this was the furthest point to which the Royal Ballet was to go in this direction for many years.

The New York connections were being developed by MacMillan, with Jerome Robbins returning in November 1972 for a third ballet, *Requiem Canticles*, *Afternoon of a Faun* having been introduced the previous year. Then came a triple bill of Balanchine ballets: *Prodigal Son* (ideally suited to Nureyev), *The Four Temperaments* and *Agon*. This was an immensely important addition to the repertoire, and, with *Ballet Imperial*, *Serenade* and the 1966 *Apollo*, made a total of six Balanchine ballets with the company. Balanchine and Ashton were the two greatest choreographers of their time, and better representation of the former was essential for the Royal Ballet, which naturally had the greater concentration of Ashton works.

In March 1974 Kenneth MacMillan introduced one of his most successful full-length ballets, *Manon* – a mixture of drama and spectacle, with sumptuous scenery and costumes by Nicholas Georgiadis, successfully evoking the eighteenth century. As was his wont, MacMillan worked first on the pas de deux and created superbly imaginative and erotic movements for his dancers. These were soon regular showstoppers, as the drunk scene in Act 2, devised and originally danced by David Wall, was also to be. The success of these moments and the impetus which they create sweep the audience through the more routine sections. The work is firmly established in the repertoire, and remains a favourite with audiences.

One thing I do regret about *Manon*, however, is that we did not produce a different kind of musical score for it. When MacMillan first put the idea of *Manon* to me, we both hit upon Massenet – not his opera of that name, but his other music. My suggestion was that we should find someone to make a mélange of this in the way that Charles Mackerras had done with the music of Sullivan to create *Pineapple Poll* – by common consent one of the best ballet scores ever written. MacMillan agreed, and I proposed Leighton Lucas, a good musician and an experienced conductor of ballet. Unhappily, it was not to work out. MacMillan was understandably eager to start work, and I quickly realized that the musical plan was finished when he phoned to tell me that he had just received a glorious piece of music, not from Leighton Lucas but from his own assistant, Hilda Gaunt, and that he was well into his first pas de deux. At that stage I could not sensibly stem the creative flow to wait for Lucas's score to be written. I still think that the ballet would have been even better if the music had been as planned.

For a long time there had been discussion about advantages that would accrue to the Royal Ballet and its dancers if it could regularly appear in a season of its own for four or more weeks – either at Covent Garden or in another theatre in London, ideally the Coliseum, a superb venue for dance. Covent Garden could be free only if the Royal Opera was on tour, which was rarely the case, and so the Coliseum was booked for a season in May and early June 1973. It was a very successful experiment, enabling the whole company to be deployed in wide-ranging programmes. Dancers were given welcome opportunities to perform a role more than once within a matter of days or a week instead of the usual months. If we could maintain this arrangement, or something similar, each year, this would be an answer to dancers' justified complaints about their inability to consolidate roles. Another Coliseum season was booked for 1975, but sadly this was cancelled because of a dispute with the Coliseum staff about certain payments and was replaced by performances in Battersea Park. Then, as inflation took its toll, the finances of the Royal Opera House were such that seasons like this at the Coliseum could no longer be contemplated.

Presenting large companies in theatres out of London had always been a problem because of small stages and the necessity of major scenic compromise. There were also parts of the country without any theatre big enough to accept these companies in any form. The South-West was an example in those days. In view of this, I had been looking for a portable theatre, and concluded that a tent might be the answer – a more solid structure being beyond our means. Michael Tippett had come in for a chat one day in the early 1970s and casually mentioned that he had been listening to a string quartet in a tent and had been impressed by the sound quality. I sat up, and thought that this might well be what we were looking for. Tippett could remember no details of who owned the tent, but I asked Paul Findlay, who by then was my assistant, to trace it. He found that it belonged to a circus proprietor, and that it could be viewed in a field near Huntingdon. The tent – originally built for Cinerama film performances in Germany – was about to be sold for scrap. The owner, Robert Fossett, was asked to delay the sale while we examined its possible use.

We looked to the South-West, and settled on Plymouth as the right centre for a Royal Ballet season. The city council was enthusiastic about the tent, but turned down my suggestion of the Hoe as its site and sent us to the Plymouth Argyll football ground, where the company played for a very successful two weeks in July and August 1974. The Big Top, as the tent was christened, was not an ideal venue – its seating capacity was not large, it was noisy in wet or windy weather, and it had a generally makeshift air – but, with the regular support of the Midland Bank, it proved immensely useful for many years in enabling the companies to play to audiences otherwise unable to see ballet, throughout the country. This was also made possible by the tent remaining in the hands of the Fossett family, and consequently financially viable.

An extended tour of Japan had been organized for the Royal Ballet in April and May 1975 – the first since 1961, when the Touring Company had visited Japan and the Philippines. A believer in the importance and efficacy of cultural diplomacy, I have been dismayed by the little use which successive British governments have made of one of this country's greatest assets: its performing companies and orchestras. British Council money had been allocated to the 1974 tour, and I was concerned that an itinerary confined to Japan was not making the most effective use of this. By chance, at a Foreign Office lunch given in honour of a member of the Japanese royal family, Princess Chichibu, I sat next to the head of the Far Eastern Section of the Foreign Office, and expressed my disquiet about the expenditure of public money on visiting one country only. As we were about to depart, he asked if we would go to South Korea. I replied that we would, and so began the establishment of long-lasting cultural relations with that country – much to the delight of British businessmen, who were opening up that market and found our continuing presence valuable. It was not that we directly sold goods, but that we were helpful in persuading the Koreans to think British.

Thanks to the initiative of an outstanding British Council representative in Seoul, Colin Perchard, we quickly made headway in organizing our first visit, which was to be followed by many more from both Royal Ballet companies and the Royal Opera. Our loyal sponsor was Dr Kim Sang-Man, an Anglophile and a staunch patriot, who through his newspaper, *Dong-a-Ilbo*, gave us unstinting support and generous financial aid.

The Royal Ballet returned to London to join forces with the other company in a Big Top season in Battersea Park, hastily arranged following the cancellation of the planned Coliseum season. The financial backing of this by the Midland Bank at the last minute, in response to a cable from me in Korea, was an example of how close collaboration and trust between a commercial and an arts organization can work to their mutual benefit.

The New Year of 1976 saw the final performances at the Royal Opera House of Margot Fonteyn and Rudolf Nureyev together in a complete ballet. Contrary to all expectations, one of the most illustrious and fruitful partnerships in the history of ballet had endured for fourteen years at Covent Garden. At the start of the 1960s Fonteyn had occasionally been talking about giving up. However, after Nureyev's arrival in London, it was to be a long time before she again began to talk in a similar vein. A miracle had happened: a great ballerina, at an age when most would feel obliged to quit, had found rejuvenation with a younger partner of fiery and unpredictable temperament, who made huge demands on her. As she responded to him, so did he to her. They fed off each other in a unique way, and brought lustre to the company as their reputation grew and as they set higher and higher standards of dancing. It was a glorious era.

Frederick Ashton had been absent from the company for over five years. His creative influences were missed, and, difficult though his return might be, it was essential that he came back. He did, in February 1976 – and in triumph, with *A Month in the Country*, another of his superb distillations of a play, this time by Turgenev, to which he brought his familiar sensitivity and lyricism. The scenery and costumes were again designed by Julia Trevelyan Oman, who, with her acute sense of detail, created an atmospheric setting evocative of nineteenth-century Russian country life. On the advice of Isaiah Berlin, Ashton selected music by Chopin. The finished ballet, with Antoinette Sibley and Anthony Dowell taking the leads as they had done in Ashton's *A Midsummer Night's Dream* twelve years earlier, was exactly what the company needed – another Ashton masterpiece – and, as the public warmly welcomed it, so too did the company, with joy that its creator was back and with relief that they had found each other again.

Kenneth MacMillan's introduction to the directorship of the Royal Ballet had been fraught with problems as a result of the merging of the two companies and the resignation of John Field, and he was in any case never really cut out to deal with the administrative aspects of his post. He was shy and withdrawn, not given to saying much, but under a remote exterior lay charm and intelligence and a constantly churning creative energy. Much of what he had to do as director he saw as a hindrance to his real mission: the making of ballets and other theatrical projects. Peter Wright was a great support to him, but even so he needed more time for creative endeavour.

Nevertheless, MacMillan's output during these years was astonishing, with both full-length ballets and shorter works, many for the New Group, with which he developed a special affinity. He had successfully enriched the repertoire both with some of his own ballets and with those of American and other choreographers whom he had introduced. He saw the need for the company to adopt more contemporary-style works if it was to flourish and be stimulated by new creative and performing demands, and he made very positive moves in this direction. Even though the company was dancing well, he was well aware of the need to find ways of maintaining and improving its standards.

He was, however, aware of criticism levelled at him for his direction of the company. In New York, for example, Clive Barnes wrote hostile pieces about MacMillan's ballets and about what he saw as the deterioration of the company since Ashton's departure. I was infuriated by his strictures and, knowing him, I suggested that we meet after a performance at the Metropolitan Opera House to talk through his charges against MacMillan. This was in the spring of 1976. In the Bank Street flat of Ene Riisna, a friend of Barnes and later of mine, and over the consumption of more alcohol than was good for us, we talked until the very early hours of the morning. Little impression seemed to be made on Barnes, but I felt better for having attempted to fight MacMillan's case.

Given such criticism and his administrative burdens, everything was pointing to MacMillan's resignation, and in June 1976 it was announced. It was a blow, in spite of being predicted, and the search for a successor was far from simple. MacMillan had followed Ashton in the natural line of succession from Ninette de Valois. There was nobody brought up within the Royal Ballet who was ready to succeed him. We had to look further afield – and in any case there was a feeling that we should seek a director from a different background: someone who could persuade the Royal Ballet to look at itself through fresh eyes.

My thoughts turned to Nureyev. I knew that many would see him as a risky appointment, and it was more than likely that the staff – and certainly the old guard – would be appalled by such an idea to the point of actively trying to sabotage it. But the Royal Ballet was in need of dynamic and imaginative leadership, and Nureyev certainly had dynamism and imagination – though I realized that his desire to continue dancing would be a problem with the company. By this time his appearances with the Royal Ballet were infrequent, which was a source of much distress and anger to him. He wanted to perform often, and could not understand why space could not be found for him, failing to see that many others were clamouring for performance opportunities and that his presence would reduce their chances even more.

From that viewpoint the idea did not look promising, but I believed that all his other qualities outweighed this drawback and that it would be wrong not to sound him out. I did that, and my proposal was greeted warmly. The need for him to dance was soon on the table, however, and we spent time going over the issues. He was not convinced that my condition that he should not dance – or that he should dance on at most a limited number of occasions – was justified or appropriate, and asked me to reconsider it.

We met again and went over familiar ground, making little progress towards a solution acceptable to us both. I then decided to go to Paris for one more conversation, and we met in his dressing room at the Opéra. By this stage he was totally clear about things. 'If I give up dancing now to become director of the Royal Ballet and I fail at it, I will have nothing to do. If, on the other hand, I continue dancing, I reckon I have another five years. I can then direct a company after that. This is the most sensible plan for me.' I had nothing to say in reply to that. So we lost one of the most important figures to have appeared on the ballet scene – to the gain of the Ballet de l'Opéra, which was willing to grant him freedom to dance. Some price was paid for that, but the overall benefit to the Paris company was beyond doubt in the development of its dancers and the breadth of its programming.

The person we eventually appointed was Norman Morrice, a choreographer and former director of the Ballet Rambert, who had resigned from there three years earlier to devote himself exclusively to creative work. Kenneth MacMillan was to become principal choreographer. Starting work in 1977, thrust into the fray of directing a company several times larger than the one he had left – and one intricately bound up with the functioning of an opera company and an overstretched opera house – Morrice paused to analyse the company's problems before coming to any conclusions about its policies and the need for change. A quiet but determined man, he was not to be rushed, and those who had hoped for dramatic changes from somebody not from a Royal Ballet background were to be disappointed. He also had to win the support of a suspicious staff, who were justifiably upset by the lack of consultation before he was appointed. In principle, I would have welcomed such consultation, but, knowing the ingrained attitudes of one or two staff members, I believed that proposing Morrice's appointment would have resulted in destructive wrangling, and that the presentation of a fait accompli was preferable to this.

There was already dissatisfaction among dancers, which Morrice believed would be remedied by more performance opportunities, a greater variety of roles, and a complete breakaway from hierarchical attitudes, which were in decline but still prevalent. Courageously, he decided to dispense temporarily with guest artists, who had been dominating the scene for many years. There was, he believed, a need for the company to examine its own resources and find new strengths from within. It was a bold move, which raised the morale of the company but dampened the enthusiasm of the public. Some members of the audience understood the long-term merit of this measure; others felt deprived and resentful – particularly in the wake of the stars whom they had been watching in previous years.

MacMillan had eased out Fonteyn and Nureyev and had brought on younger dancers, but Natalia Makarova was a regular guest artist and Mikhail Baryshnikov was also appearing. These were all dancers whom the public wanted to see, and they had a contribution to make to the company. Nevertheless, the balance between guests and resident dancers – difficult to strike at the best of times – had been uncomfortably weighted in favour of the former. A factor in this, of course, had been the huge popularity of the Fonteyn–Nureyev duo and the quest for more and more performances by Nureyev himself, whose appetite for dancing was insatiable and incompatible with the needs of the company.

Morrice faced the first major challenge of his new policy with a revival of *Sleeping Beauty* by Ninette de Valois in the autumn of 1977. She wanted to return to the 1946 version, with some additions, and chose David Walker as her designer. In many ways the results were successful, with an admirable pair of principals in Lesley Collier and Anthony Dowell, and with Lynn Seymour as Carabosse. But comparisons with the past were inevitable, and I fear that nostalgia led some to recall the 1946 production and to make dubious critical comment.

Kenneth MacMillan, always in search of a contemporary reworking of the nineteenth-century format for a full-length ballet and intrigued by the balletic representation of historical fact, hit upon the idea of a ballet based on the neurotic behaviour and eventual suicide of Prince Rudolf, son of the Emperor Franz-Joseph. This was a powerful story of sex and violence, far removed from most previous ballet subjects, and yet in February 1978 *Mayerling* proved that in the hands of a MacMillan it could make for enthralling, if disturbing, dance. It provided real opportunities for performers to display their dramatic talents, and was warmly received.

The autumn of 1978 saw the departure of Lynn Seymour, to become ballet director in Munich, and of Anthony Dowell, to join American

Ballet Theatre and to broaden his horizons and his experience. The loss of an amazing dramatic dancer in Seymour and a *danseur noble* nearing the peak of his career was hard for Morrice and the company to swallow. However, as Morrice knew, the status quo cannot be maintained, and it is often undesirable that it should be. Your most coveted talent cannot be expected to stay still, but may eventually return to you refreshed and invigorated, as Dowell was later to do.

The spring of 1979 saw a special performance in honour of Margot Fonteyn's sixtieth birthday. After *Birthday Offering*, the guest herself appeared in a solo deftly choreographed by Frederick Ashton to include steps from many of the ballets he had created for her. Dressed by William Chappell and looking so glamorous, she was approaching the end when the choreographer himself entered and, having paid his respects, took her by the arm and led her off. So loud and so prolonged was the applause that it had to be repeated. Nostalgia was strongly in the air and a sense of a passing era was felt by many.

Margot Fonteyn was to appear once more on the Covent Garden stage: in May 1990, when, at my urging, a gala was mounted to raise money for her. By then she was very ill with cancer, and I knew that her medical insurance was not to be continued for much longer. She had little money, and was likely to be faced with huge bills as she continued treatment in the Houston hospital where she had been a patient for some time.

Fonteyn had telephoned me a good deal from Panama to talk about her financial predicament. There has not been a world market for dancers in the same way as for singers. Until Nureyev arrived in the West, dancers rarely travelled without their companies and, when they did, there were few fee comparisons on which to draw as contracts were negotiated. Consequently fees tended to be relatively low, and Fonteyn was of a generation which was unlikely to benefit greatly from their later escalation. Caring for her paralysed husband and maintaining their farms in Panama was a huge drain on her modest resources, which more than once could not take the strain. She would call me to ask if there was anything I could do to help. We were keen that she should coach dancers in her roles periodically. This would have been of benefit to the company – though it did not eventually prove possible – and it enabled me to ease her immediate distress by sending her money on account of agreed fees.

After the May gala I was not to see her again. We talked on the phone several times, and then in December 1990 came what was to be our final conversation. She called to say that she could not endure any more treatment and had asked the doctor to end it. She then went on to ask that Bonaventura, who had looked after her husband for so long, should be given extra money from her estate and that she should be taken to Panama as soon as possible so that she could die in the country she loved. This was my farewell to a truly great ballerina and a divine woman, to whom we all owe so much.

In 1980, two years after guest artists had been banished, some were to return. Natalia Makarova appeared in a production of *Giselle* revised by Norman Morrice, and Mikhail Baryshnikov in *Romeo and Juliet*. Baryshnikov was also to appear to stunning effect – unmatched by any successor – in *Rhapsody*, a new ballet created by Frederick Ashton in honour of the eightieth birthday of Queen Elizabeth, the Queen Mother.

Another guest was to appear with the Royal Ballet for the first time that year: Gelsey Kirkland. Insecure, unpredictable and unreliable, she is one of the really great dancers of the world and worth all the time and trouble which inevitably surround her engagement. Like the opera singer Teresa Stratas, her personal chemistry had to be absolutely in balance to enable her to perform. If it was not, she could not perform well and was convinced that she would short-change the public. She appeared in *Romeo and Juliet* with Anthony Dowell, and her passion, fluency and portrayal of a woman's progress from childhood naivety to adult tragedy in that role have not been equalled in my experience. She was breathtaking, and wondrous to watch as the character unfolded.

The following year, 1981, was the fiftieth anniversary of the first performance by the Vic–Wells Ballet, on 5 May 1931. It was celebrated with a performance of *Sleeping Beauty* and by the publication of a book by Alexander Bland, giving a well-balanced and graphic description of the growth of the companies from their modest beginnings to world renown.

Kenneth MacMillan's newest ballet, *Isadora*, was included in the programme of another American tour in June and July 1981, this time successfully managed by the Metropolitan Opera House. This was a welcome innovation, because no successor to Hurok had emerged and our two recent American tours under other managements had been less than rewarding.

Norman Morrice continued to promote the interests of company dancers. He had by now won their confidence and was found to be both accessible and straightforward in his comments. A person of integrity, he was unafraid to confront dancers with the truth, disconcerting though it could be. A choreographer himself – and of course recognizing a company's dependence on new work if it is not to become moribund – he was quick to spot and encourage new creative talents. One, from within the company, was Ashley Page; another, from Sadler's Wells Royal Ballet, was David Bintley. Quite unjustly, in view of his record, however, the fact that Morrice was not of the Royal Ballet somehow told against him.

Finding opportunities for untried choreographers presents serious problems for a director. The public is rarely receptive to experiment, and the cost of failure on a large opera-house stage is considerable. The close proximity of a studio theatre in the new Covent Garden complex will be a great asset in developing creative talent, but the decision when to give someone their head and move them to the main stage will be no easier to take. The transition from the small to the large stage is a huge step, and sometimes the gulf between them cannot be bridged. Nevertheless, Morrice presented six ballets by young choreographers from within the company in the 1984/85 season. The initiative itself was welcomed, although the response to the individual works was mixed.

After eight years as director, in 1985 it was understandable that Norman Morrice wanted to move on – particularly after a bout of ill health. Managing a ballet company is a huge responsibility and, for somebody as sensitive and conscientious as Morrice, very stressful. What we had hoped for from him – an analysis of the company, a period of self-examination, greater use and encouragement of its own dancers, a sensible balance in the engagement of guest artists, a broadening of the repertoire, and the development of creative talent – had been a tall order, but he had delivered it.

After a period with a director from outside the Royal Ballet's traditions, it was felt that the performance style of the company needed the attention of a director brought up within its orbit. There was no one in the original line of succession and there was no choreographer in sight. Peter Wright was enjoying success with Sadler's Wells Royal Ballet, which had become an important force in the land, and we did not want to move him from there. Thoughts turned to dancers. The most obvious choice was Anthony Dowell, the most elegant and stylish of performers, immersed in Royal Ballet tradition and, because of his standing as an artist, capable of winning the confidence of both staff and dancers. He was revered and respected, and could take the company on from where Morrice had left off.

He accepted our invitation, and became director in September 1986. We only had two years together, but in this time he was addressing matters of dancing style and was active in the pursuit of the highest standards. Sloppiness was spotted and dealt with as he meticulously attended performances. A presence both in the studio and on the stage, he urged the company onwards.

Although a respecter of tradition, Dowell did not want to stick slavishly to conventional designs for the nineteenth-century classics and sought contemporary solutions when the occasion arose. His designer for *Swan Lake* was Yolanda Sonnabend, whose work I much admired and whose engagement I welcomed and supported. What appeared did not win universal acceptance, and Dowell has tended to remain subject to grumbling about programming, the choice of versions of ballets, and the selection of choreographers.

The musical standards of the Royal Ballet have been hard to maintain. Repetition of familiar ballets leads to routine performance unless there is a conductor who has something to say and can lift the orchestra. Musicians do not want to give poor performances, but there are times when they need help. Constant Lambert set the highest standards, and upheld them. Robert Irving, his successor, was a brilliant conductor for the ballet – understanding well the relationship of movement to music – but even he failed to prevent what is a source of endless irritation to musicians: the setting of steps to wrong and inappropriate tempi. To ensure that a choreographer understands what the composer intended and is not altering tempi to accommodate steps, it is essential for a conductor to be present at all initial rehearsals. To leave this to the rehearsal pianists is not good enough: it is unreasonable to expect them to intervene over tempi and matters of musical style. Hugo Rignold once queried a tempo adopted by Frederick Ashton in *Cinderella*. He was firmly put in his place and told that there could be no change, however wrong it might be, because the steps could not otherwise be fitted in. This should have been sorted out in the early days of putting the work together.

An essential difference between playing for the ballet and playing for the opera is the absence of any feedback, aural or visual, from the stage to the pit in the former. In opera, musicians hear the singers and are closely involved in accompanying them, responding to any rubato or changing nuances which reach them. In ballet there is nothing of this sort, so there is an even bigger obligation on the conductor to mediate between the two.

Finding conductors such as John Lanchbery or Ashley Lawrence willing to devote their lives to ballet is hard. Some cannot face the degree of musical compromise which they see as being involved; others have been worried at being typecast. Both views are exaggerated, as plenty of evidence makes clear. What has been encouraging in recent years has been the willingness and the desire of music directors of the Royal Opera to conduct ballet. The first was Colin Davis. It worked well at the beginning, but later he fell foul of Michael Somes, who felt that his musical authority was being usurped. Bernard Haitink has enjoyed a successful relationship with the dancers, and has conducted some superb performances.

Understandably, dancers are wary of wayward conductors. They need their support and depend on them to be constant, but also to be aware of dancers' frailties and to note when they are labouring or when the music needs to be slower. One conductor whom I have always regarded highly is Barry Wordsworth, and I was maddened by the long time it took the company to accept him as music director. He delivered consistently good performances, but the dancers appeared to feel insecure with him.

I have never understood why dancers have to be so reliant on counts and seem unable to feel the music to the point where they can discard these and rely solely on the music and its pulse. For me, counting encourages rigidity rather than a natural response to the music's flow, and this detracts from the final impact of the performance. But I am not a dancer!

The adverse publicity which has bedevilled the Royal Opera House for several years has inevitably influenced press attention towards its performing companies. Minor difficulties have been inflated into crises, with catastrophe being anticipated. Much of such coverage is unfair and unhelpful, but unavoidable with a press which revels in bad news and by and large gives little exposure to good. A case in point was the recent departure of five boys to Tetsuya Kumakawa's company. It was, of course, a blow to the company to lose them, and dented its pride, giving the impression that things are so bad within it that there is mass defection at the first opportunity. Their departure can be described as a PR disaster, but not much more. It should be seen as an opportunity for internal promotion, which can otherwise be frustratingly slow for some, and for the engagement of other male dancers.

For years the Royal Ballet rarely imported dancers but relied on the Royal Ballet School to meet its requirements. This policy severely restricted recruitment, although it helped to preserve a purity of style. Other companies throughout the world have long been drawing on talent from wherever they can find it, but the Royal Ballet has been slow to respond. Chances to use dancers from other traditions are there and must be seized if the Royal Ballet companies are to achieve the highest standards and maintain their hard-won place on the world stage.

Classical ballet companies do face difficult artistic decisions today. For years the nineteenth-century classical ballet and its modern equivalent have attracted the biggest audiences in this country, but I sense that interest in them is now waning and that there is a search for more thought-provoking spectacle among the ballet-going public as well as those who stay away. Christopher Gable, before his untimely death, was intensely interested in finding new approaches to the presentation of nineteenth-century ballet, both to suit the size and strength of his company, Northern Ballet, and to attract new audiences. He had already re-produced *Swan Lake* on his company. I do not think that he had quite found the right formula, but he was moving in the direction of one which would instil new life into a much revered format. Whatever changes are made, however, when companies like the Royal Ballet have the means, the preservation of the original choreography and its accepted variations is essential. There is a risk that too much tampering will destroy the fundamentals of a tradition on which classical ballet is based.

The one-act ballet, which makes up the greater part of the Royal Ballet's repertoire, has mostly failed to attract the high average ticket sales on which successive budgets have depended, and will continue to do so. At the same time, it is with work on this scale that a company will largely find its artistic soul and permit the growth of creative talent.

What a ballet company needs and what an audience expects is a rich and varied repertoire of stimulating versions of the nineteenth-century classics, modern narrative ballets and a good smattering of short ballets, assembled in imaginative and well-presented packages. The Paris Ballet de l'Opéra has it right. It has wide-ranging programmes of ballets by the world's leading choreographers, presented in a way to attract audiences, and danced by a company at the top of its form. There is much to learn from this source alone.

What is undeniable is that this costs money. Paris enjoys high government support – far in excess of Covent Garden's subvention – but without it the kind of programming which stimulates dancers and audiences cannot be achieved. Even if the diet was confined to endless performances of *Swan Lake*, *Sleeping Beauty* or *Romeo and Juliet* – just to name three ballets which have regularly been successful at the box office in the past – I do not believe that this would hold audiences, and I am sure that the Royal Ballet would die on its feet.

Somehow we have to find a way forward which will ensure the growth of the Royal Ballet companies and their audiences. It is a huge challenge, demanding artistic vision and know-how, but also financial cunning and ingenuity.

8 Birmingham Royal Ballet

Having decided to take the Sadler's Wells Ballet to the Royal Opera House, Ninette de Valois began to think about the consequences of this move for Sadler's Wells itself. This was, after all, the theatre which had nurtured her company from its beginnings and which was the source of its name. A following of loyal ballet-goers had been built up there, and it would have been folly to abandon them. There was also the question of touring and serving the regions. De Valois saw that her enlarged company at Covent Garden would find opportunities to tour the regions restricted by stage sizes and cost, and yet she believed it was important to preserve and extend this connection with the country as a whole. What better way of dealing with these issues and of providing Sadler's Wells Opera with dancers than to found another company? This is what she did, and so Sadler's Wells Theatre Ballet was born – initially not under that name but as Sadler's Wells Opera Ballet.

At its launch, in October 1945, Ninette de Valois announced that she would be the director of the companies at Covent Garden and at Sadler's Wells, and that Sadler's Wells Opera Ballet would have Peggy van Praagh as its ballet mistress. Seeing this company as a potential breeding ground for young dancers and, because of its smaller size, as useful for experimentation and for allowing young choreographers and their collaborators to show their paces, de Valois believed that overall control by her was essential, at least in those early days.

The relationship between the two companies was easy to explain, but in practice it proved difficult both for audiences and for the new organization itself. The first name of the Sadler's Wells company is an example. This was considered misleading in that it did not reflect the complete activities of the company, which was a performing group in its own right as well as the provider of dancers for the opera. A further complication was that this company was financed and managed by Sadler's Wells Theatre. It was an independent unit, yet under the final control of Ninette de Valois and seen as part of the Sadler's Wells Ballet at Covent Garden. Its status was held to be equal to that of the big company at the Royal Opera House, but at the same time it was a training ground for young dancers.

It proved hard to find a title for this company which did not belittle its status and which defined its purpose, until, having left Sadler's Wells to come under the management of Covent Garden in 1957, it returned to take up residence at Rosebery Avenue in 1976 and then happily adopted the title of Sadler's Wells Royal Ballet. This was later to be changed to Birmingham Royal Ballet on its removal to that city.

In the beginning, the pattern of the company's work at Sadler's Wells was dictated by the opera company's requirements, with usually one or two performances of ballet each week and several weeks of touring. The repertoire was made up of one-act ballets – many newly created – interspersed with single acts of nineteenth-century classics, *Nutcracker* Act 3 and *Swan Lake* Act 2, followed later by *Coppélia*. Dancers who were later to make their names with the Covent Garden company were blossoming and winning a following. These included Svetlana Beriosova, Elaine Fifield, Maryon Lane, David Blair, Stanley Holden and Pirmin Trecu, in addition to three other dancers who were to emerge as distinguished choreographers and directors: John Cranko, Kenneth MacMillan and Peter Darrell. The company was truly fulfilling the purposes which de Valois had had in mind.

In 1955 changes occurred which were to influence the company's future course. First, Peggy van Praagh, who had been directing the company since 1953, resigned. A woman of authority and with a real understanding of dancers, she had led the company with energy and enthusiasm through its formative years and established its independent character. She was succeeded by John Field, a senior principal of the Covent Garden company now of an age when he was ready to forsake dancing for another career.

As Ninette de Valois had foreseen when setting up the smaller ballet company, touring of the regions became more and more difficult for the Covent Garden company. An answer to this was found in enlarging the Sadler's Wells Theatre Ballet, as it had been called since 1947, so that it could tour major works such as *Swan Lake* and *Sleeping Beauty* in their entirety. As a consequence of this change of policy, the Sadler's Wells company was unable regularly to provide dancers for the opera. This was solved by the introduction of a group of dancers to work with singers, under the direction of Peter Wright, who had joined the organization in 1949 and whose role in the future development of the Royal Ballet was to be of critical importance.

John Field's appointment coincided with deterioration in the finances of Sadler's Wells Theatre, which had prompted David Webster to remark to Field that he might well be joining a sinking ship. Webster's assessment was correct, and by the beginning of 1956 the governors of Sadler's Wells had concluded that they could no longer support the company. On the company's return from a successful Spanish tour, which had ended with the mounting of a new production of *Giselle* at the Santander Festival, the contracts with Sadler's Wells were at an end and the company's demise seemed imminent.

Webster had earlier indicated to Field that Covent Garden would take over management of the company, and by the summer of 1956 the Royal Opera House board had agreed to this. The next question was what to do with the company, there being no money available in Covent Garden's purse and none extra forthcoming from the Arts Council. We could not allow this group of talented dancers to disperse and lose ten years of growth and a rapidly developing repertoire of ballets, many created by John Cranko and Kenneth MacMillan. We had to take the plunge and find work for them, in the hope that additional public funding would be available within a reasonable space of time. The latter did not happen, however, and the acquisition of the company remained financially unrecognized by the Arts Council for years.

David Webster never asked me to take on the responsibility of organizing the company's transfer to Covent Garden and putting together a season for it: in his inimitable style, he simply assumed that I was doing it. In fact, I had started work on this when one day he came to my room and asked what on earth we could do to find additional money. I replied that the only way forward was to arrange a year's work at home and in Europe, anything else which might be profitable being impossible at such short notice. This, I proposed, should be followed by a foreign tour as far away as possible and for as long as possible, to give ourselves time to sort things out in London. I had already heard from Alfred Francis at the Old Vic how successful that theatre had been in touring drama in Australia and New Zealand, and I thought that a similar tour for

Sadler's Wells Theatre Ballet might prove to be its salvation, at least for a year or two.

Unfamiliar with touring conditions in the Antipodes, I sought advice from Alfred Francis and others. My first plan, to tour under more than one Australian management, to ensure that the company played in the most desirable theatres, proved too risky. I then turned to J. C. Williamsons, an old-established theatrical management based in Melbourne and the owner of theatres in most of the cities we wished to visit. Williamsons were experienced in touring, and had previously assembled seasons of Italian opera in Australia. Their senior management was in the hands of the Tait brothers, one of whom, Nevin, lived in London. It was through him that I negotiated a thirty-four-week tour of Australia and New Zealand, beginning in Sydney and ending in Wellington. Nevin Tait was a smoker and always had cigarette ash on his lapels, which prompted Robert Helpmann to refer to him as Ashes Tait. His brother, Frank, was in charge in Australia and proved to be a tower of strength to us.

It was a mammoth undertaking for everybody, but it saved the day for the company, which returned to London with a trail of successes behind it and with all its salaries and expenses paid and a profit of £15,000. Robert Helpmann was appearing in Noël Coward's *Nude with Violin* in Sydney at the beginning of the tour and joined the company at the end of the play's run, much to the delight of audiences. Margot Fonteyn and Michael Somes joined the company in New Zealand and enjoyed tumultuous receptions wherever they performed or went. In Australia the company was strengthened by dancers from the other company: Svetlana Beriosova, Anya Linden, Donald MacLeary and David Blair.

Before the company left London, in September 1958, there was much discussion and negotiation of daily food allowances – a familiar prelude to most foreign tours. Information had been produced to illustrate living costs, which were the basis of the management's offer. Agreement seemed far away, and eventually I decided to talk to the company myself. After an exchange of views, a voice was heard from the back of the studio saying, 'What are you all fussing about? It's better to starve in Sydney than in Hanley!' It was Lynn Seymour. Shortly afterwards agreement was reached.

The tour was long and arduous and not without its problems. Foundations for the appreciation of classical ballet had been well laid in Australia by Edouard Borovansky, who had founded the Borovansky

Australian Ballet – later to become the Australian Ballet – in 1939, and continued to direct it until the early 1960s, but we were concerned about selling tickets for a company which was to be perceived as merely the touring company of the Royal Ballet, and for eight-week seasons in Sydney and Melbourne. Our contract with Williamsons stipulated dates by which an advertising campaign would be implemented. On walking down a Sydney street on the day on which our posters were to be displayed, I came across a billboard carrying an old poster. I asked Harry Strachan, the Sydney manager of Williamsons, to come for a walk with me. Grudgingly he agreed, and when I pointed out the offending poster to him he replied, 'John, what are you fussing about? Tomorrow will do.' This was my first exposure to the procrastination which seemed to be endemic in Australia and the cause of many unnecessary problems for us.

John Lanchbery, the principal conductor of the company, had been traumatized by an earlier flying experience and asked if he could travel to Australia by ship. I agreed on condition that he used the journey to make a reduced version of *Swan Lake* for the size of orchestra we were to have on the tour. Lanchbery arrived in Sydney and began rehearsals with the orchestra, which unsurprisingly turned out to be not very good. He and I pleaded with Williamsons to change some of the personnel. They agreed, but finding other musicians was easier said than done – not least because of the inadequacy of Williamsons's file of musicians. As we went through the dog-eared card index, we would pull out name after name only to be told that the player had either retired or was dead. We did make some improvements in the end.

The company was flown between cities, and, because some of the charter planes had limited pressurization, a maximum flying height was imposed in the contract. This was all right until the company took off for Brisbane and struck bad weather, which persuaded the pilot to climb above the agreed altitude in a vain attempt to reduce the discomfort. The dancers and staff were nervous and were suffering the ill effects of poor pressurization. As they looked to the stewardesses for help, they found them passing out one by one. However, the day was saved by Alan Beale, a member of the company and a Royal Navy-trained nurse, who dealt with the situation brilliantly. The plane eventually landed safely, albeit with a disorientated and shaken company.

As the companies were drawn closer to each other through shared overall management and the single banner of the Royal Ballet – a title granted under royal charter with effect from 1957 – two difficulties arose. One was confusion in the public's mind about which of the companies they were seeing – a problem partially solved by describing the smaller company as 'The Royal Ballet (formerly Sadler's Wells Theatre Ballet)'. This was a mouthful, however, and soon the company was being called the Touring Company or the Second Company – which was frowned upon officially, but useful shorthand. Inability to differentiate between the companies did lead to complaints from the public, who felt that one was inferior to the other and that they had been short-changed when they attended Touring Company performances. Time and experience brought a clearer understanding.

The other difficulty was more serious. Ninette de Valois had long believed that an interchange of dancers between the companies would be advantageous, at both soloist and corps de ballet level. The first real experiment with this took place in the summer of 1959, when the companies joined forces for a Covent Garden season. It did not work well, with each company mainly performing its own repertoire. Exchanges of corps de ballet occurred without noticeable gain – in many ways the reverse, given the difficulty of integrating newcomers into an established corps and the feeling of superiority prevailing in the Covent Garden company. The interchange of soloists fared no better, and, apart from desultory exchanges of soloists over the next few years, the idea was abandoned until the complete integration of the two companies in 1970.

In the autumn of 1959, *Sleeping Beauty* was added to the repertoire of the smaller company – a faithful reproduction of the 1946 version – and was warmly welcomed by audiences up and down the country. It was at this stage that the complementary function of the two companies came into play, with the smaller company providing a means for dancers from the main company to extend their experience in principal classical roles and for younger artists to gain experience away from the pressures of an opera house. None of this was at the expense of the Sadler's Wells company's own dancers, many of whom established themselves as ballerinas and principal male dancers in these ballets and became firm favourites with the public. Most prominent of these were Doreen Wells and David Wall.

In 1960 the company left for a tour of South Africa. This followed much heart-searching – not least because it was clear from the start that we could not take a Cape Coloured dancer, Johaar Mosaval. However, the final view of Equity, the Commonwealth Office and the Covent Garden board was that there could be political benefit from undertaking a tour which had been so arranged that we could play to mixed audiences in Pietermaritzburg and to black and white audiences at different times in Cape Town. In Durban and Johannesburg we were unhappily confined to white audiences. It was a struggle to get to this point, and there was no way of making further inroads into apartheid at this time. In spite of audience restrictions and racial disturbances in Durban, the tour was a success and worthwhile. Audiences and the company also benefited from the presence of Antoinette Sibley, making her debut in *Sleeping Beauty* and *Giselle*.

Protocol on the opening night needed close attention. On talking to Sir John Redcliffe Maude, the British high commissioner, it was obvious that he wanted the British national anthem played at the beginning, but he was quick to add that we must play 'Die Stem van Suid-Afrika', the South African anthem, as well. The opening came and I found myself next to the mayor of Johannesburg, who, on hearing 'God Save the Queen', nudged me and said, 'Hm, I haven't heard that tune much here recently.'

The need for caution in the playing of national anthems was brought home to us on a visit to Damascus in 1961, following performances at Baalbeck. The orchestra, which we had brought from London, was having a seating call, and time was used to rehearse the Syrian anthem – or what we thought was the Syrian anthem. As we started, an Arab rushed through the theatre exclaiming that we were playing the anthem of the last regime and that we must perform the newest one. Obviously we had to do that, but, needless to say, there was no orchestration of it available in Damascus, or probably anywhere else. Richard Temple Savage, the Covent Garden librarian and clarinettist, had to take down the tune from the protesting Arab and orchestrate it then and there in time for the evening opening.

In managing the company and in coaching and rehearsing dancers, John Field was in his element. Touring – with eight performances each week, and Sunday usually spent on slow trains moving from one destination to another – was exhausting, and dancers and staff needed inspired leadership if standards were to be maintained. Field had a knack of jollying people along, not by cutting corners and easing the workload, but by encouragement and praise where it was due. He was a trouper, and showed others how to be one through example. Field had a lot to offer – his taste may not always have been impeccable, but he was a man of the theatre and knew how to get a show on its feet and on the road. I was saddened by the way he became separated from the Royal Ballet team of Ashton, Somes and Hart after Ashton had succeeded de Valois in 1963. Ashton took little interest in Field's company and left Field to his own devices. This split was not of Field's making, and he wanted relations to be different. However, the gulf between the companies became wider, and they were to operate independently for the rest of the decade.

The smaller company spent most of its time in touring, at home or abroad, interspersed with seasons at the Royal Opera House. Its popularity was evident, but the duplication of some programming between the two companies – albeit in different versions of works – raised questions of the validity of financing two companies with this degree of overlap. The regions were being well served and the differentiation between the companies was now clearer, but this did not prevent some of the non-metropolitan public from insisting on their rights as taxpayers to see the Covent Garden company in their home town. This coincided with a deteriorating financial situation at Covent Garden itself. Financial and artistic considerations were pointing to a review of where we were and of the directions in which we should move in the next decade, when Ashton would have retired.

Of course new works had been added to the Touring Company's repertoire, including MacMillan's *The Invitation*, Cranko's *Sweeney Todd*, Nureyev's full-length *Raymonda* (in Spoleto), Tudor's *Knight Errant* and Ashton's *Two Pigeons*, *Sinfonietta* and *A Midsummer Night's Dream*, the last of which had originally been created for the other company in 1964. But preparation time for new work was at a premium, given the necessity to fulfil demanding performing and touring plans to maximize revenue.

The year 1970 was immensely difficult. David Webster and Frederick Ashton retired. The Royal Ballet was reorganized as described in Chapter 7, and a financial crisis was impending. The relationship between Kenneth MacMillan and John Field as, respectively, artistic director and administrative director of the merged company was shaky – the result of compromise and Webster's overreaction to Field's earlier threatened departure for the Festival Ballet. In September I took over from Webster and was keen to calm the Royal Ballet and to have the reorganization implemented as quickly as possible.

The adopted plan – of one large company of 122 dancers – seemed set to bring artistic and financial benefits. The New Group, which was to replace the Touring Company, consisted of twenty-two soloists drawn from the company who were to be regularly replaced by others from Covent Garden and augmented when programming required. There was no corps de ballet. Peter Wright, who had previously been invited to replace Field before the decision about the New Group had been taken, agreed to direct it. It was intended that it should concentrate on one-act ballets – some established and some experimental – with opportunities for young choreographers to work free of London pressures and the high cost of failure at the Royal Opera House.

The New Group's first visit was to Nottingham. The outlook was promising, with an excellent opening programme of Balanchine's *Apollo*, Ashton's *Symphonic Variations* and Glen Tetley's *Field Figures*, to which was later added Tudor's *Lilac Garden*. Meantime, MacMillan, who was showing increasing interest in the New Group as a vehicle for his own ballets, was creating *Checkpoint*, which was to have its first performance in Manchester a few weeks later.

John Field's sudden departure at Christmas 1970 meant a rearrangement of the Royal Ballet management, with Peter Wright taking over the administration of both companies from Field. Peter Clegg, who had been with the company since the end of the war, was appointed ballet master of the New Group.

There was a sense of pioneering in launching the New Group. With programmes containing none of the classical ballets which the public wanted more than anything else – particularly from the Royal Ballet – the box-office risks were obvious. Nevertheless, with reduced costs of touring it was hoped that inroads could be made into audience taste without breaking the bank and that a public for more adventurous programmes would be forthcoming. Wishful thinking perhaps, but we had the responsibility to try. More new and experimental work was introduced, but by the summer of 1973 the New Group was running at a strength of forty dancers and performing a repertoire – Macmillan's *The Poltroon*, *Las Hermanas* and *Checkpoint*, Hans van Manen's *Grosse Fugue*, Ronald Hynd's *In a Summer Garden*, Glen Tetley's *Field Figures*, Joe Layton's *The Grand Tour* and Herbert Ross's *The Maids* – which was removed from its first intentions. This trend continued until spring 1975, when, after two years' absence, the New Group was back at Covent Garden performing *Coppélia* and *Giselle*. Market forces had won and there were two companies performing the same kind of programme. The experiment had failed.

In September 1976 the New Group was succeeded by Sadler's Wells

Royal Ballet, which presented a gala to mark this change and to commemorate the twenty-fifth anniversary of the death of Constant Lambert. This also marked a homecoming. In addition to regular seasons at Sadler's Wells, the company – with Peter Wright as its director – would be based there, with rehearsal rooms, offices and wardrobe accommodation readily to hand. It was what was needed, and ensured the future of a company which already had many achievements to its name, had largely retained its distinctive character in programming, and was to find a performing style which complemented that of the Royal Ballet at Covent Garden. This was to become even more the case after the move to Birmingham in 1990.

The company continued with its pattern of touring at home and overseas, interspersed with London seasons, but, firmly settled in Rosebery Avenue, it now had a greater sense of security than hitherto. This was probably illusory, but by then I was clear that the future of the Royal Ballet and of Covent Garden itself depended on the sinking of deeper political roots than we had so far achieved, with a greater presence outside London, and our key to this lay with this company.

New work was created, and March 1978 saw the debut of a young dancer and budding choreographer whose career was eventually to be with the Birmingham Royal Ballet: David Bintley. The ballet which he had devised was called *The Outsider*, and was the product of a rapidly developing imaginative and inventive mind. Both Ninette de Valois and Frederick Ashton thought highly of his work, but somehow the Royal Ballet did not immediately discover a way of using a remarkably gifted choreographer as well as character dancer. I had little doubt that he would be an ideal successor to Peter Wright, but there was continual anxiety about him going elsewhere because of the then limited opportunities with the Royal Ballet and a failure to cherish him enough. The world is crying out for choreographers, and we came near to losing this one.

The move to Birmingham, which was the fulfilment of endeavours over many years to find the right home for the company, is discussed in Chapter 11. Logically it could be said that Sadler's Wells Theatre represented this home, and so it was argued by opponents of the Birmingham plan. I had some sympathy with those who took this line, and I was aware of the huge domestic upheaval which the Birmingham proposal would entail for dancers and staff. But, looking to the future of the company, and the political gains which would accrue, I had no doubts about the need to persuade the company that it was in everyone's interests to go along with the move. I believe that none of those who made the decision to stay with the company and settle in the Midlands has regretted it.

In 1995 Peter Wright was approaching retirement, and the decision was taken to appoint David Bintley as his successor. This was warmly welcomed, and I have no doubt that Bintley is the right person for the next decade or so. Wright had been an excellent director, and a colossal debt is owed to him for this and for fulfilling the many responsibilities which he was asked to assume as we picked our way through the morass of problems in the early 1970s.

Wright is a strong upholder of Royal Ballet traditions and standards, and his productions of nineteenth-century ballets have shown his ability to shed new light while still remaining faithful to the original. This has been of great importance to both companies of the Royal Ballet. While these large-scale works continue to attract a loyal public, however, there is a desire in the wider world for more thought-provoking and intellectually stimulating works, and it is here that Bintley's different and more progressive approach to the subject matter and creation of ballets is so important.

The arrival of the company in Birmingham was the beginning of a new era for ballet in the regions. A bigger and bigger following for the company and its work will surely come, and audience loyalty for ballet at the Hippodrome will match that which Simon Rattle built up for the City of Birmingham Symphony Orchestra at Symphony Hall. Peter Wright laid the foundations, and David Bintley is rapidly building on them.

As an independent company, based in its own theatre and pursuing its own artistic policy, the Birmingham Royal Ballet has come full circle since its inception as the Sadler's Wells Opera Ballet. It is larger than it was in those days, and in its artistic and technical standards it is able to hold its own on the world stage and to maintain all that is best in the Royal Ballet's traditions. Its journey to Birmingham has not been straightforward. It has embraced different sizes of company and purposes en route. Now, however, the company is set on course, with its identity clear and a well-defined artistic policy to guide it into the next century.

9 Russian Influences

One of the characteristics of working with David Webster was the rarity of instructions about what to do. He believed that you would know what was expected of you and that knowledge and intuition would take you to the next most important task. Often he would wander down the passage to my room for a chat and to ask about this and that. Occasionally it would be with a specific request. One, in January 1956, concerned a possible visit to Covent Garden by the Bolshoi Ballet, with the then Sadler's Wells Ballet visiting Moscow and Leningrad in return. He asked me to assume responsibility for completing negotiations and looking after the Bolshoi company when it arrived in London. It was a huge and daunting challenge, which broadened my experience in a short time and opened many doors for me – not least through getting to know Russians and developing a rapport with them. That was to give me much personal pleasure, and prepare me well for future adventures.

Plans to bring the Bolshoi company to London had been mooted as early as 1944. A film of *The Fountain of Bakhchisarai* had been seen in the West and had given audiences here their first sight of the company, and particularly of that greatest of ballerinas, Galina Ulanova, in a role which she was to repeat twelve years later when the Bolshoi finally reached Covent Garden. Meanwhile, Lord Keynes had seen the ballet in Moscow and had reported to Webster that it was 'not quite first class but well worth seeing'.

A little later Sir Anthony Eden had proposed a visit by the Bolshoi, which was the subject of a report from the British ambassador in Moscow, Sir Archibald Kerr, to Lord Keynes early in 1945:

Eden's suggestion was made and Molotov's consent given in that glow of brotherhood that comes with food and wine . . . No answer means 'no' – a polite form of saying no. And I think that the reason is probably a physical one – the business of moving the corps de ballet from Moscow to London would be very formidable, and, so long as everything in the Soviet Union is set aside in the interests of the Red Army, I don't think that there is any chance of getting your attractive plan on foot. If Hitler is finished this year it would not be impossible to get it moving next year.

So the whole idea was dropped. The practical difficulties could have been surmounted, but I suspect that the refusal of the Russian government to pursue it at that stage was probably much more to do with doubts about exposing their elite to Western life and culture and the threat to their own social and political stability that could have ensued.

In 1955 the Bolshoi Ballet had been to Paris, but the outbreak of the French Indo-China war persuaded them not to stay. They returned to Moscow without performing but having been involved in a typically French episode. Soon after their arrival, the French technicians had staged a strike – to the consternation of M. Georges Hirsch, the director of the Opéra, who was heard to ask Mikhail Chulaki, the director of the Bolshoi Theatre, why the technicians should be striking at this moment, when most of them were members of the Communist Party. Chulaki paused and replied that they were clearly a different kind of communist!

The idea of Sadler's Wells Ballet performing in Moscow and Leningrad was daunting, and it was daring of a company just twenty-five years old to be venturing into the Bolshoi and the Kirov theatres, with their long tradition of classical ballet. However, encouraged by its success in New York in 1949 and in subsequent visits to North America, the company was ready for this huge challenge, and Ninette de Valois particularly wanted to show off her dancers at the Kirov, to whose company English ballet owed much in the development of its own style of dancing.

Preparations for both companies' visits went ahead quite smoothly, with few serious difficulties but with many points needing close watching. The payment to Sadler's Wells Ballet was to be in non-convertible roubles – at the time, the only method of payment available to visiting artists. Some of that would be spent in daily allowances to the dancers and staff and in the running of the company while there. Nevertheless, there would be surplus cash to be left behind on our departure, and opening a bank account in Moscow became essential for that as well as for the safe keeping of money during the tour. Quite a healthy balance was to stay in that account until a tour by the English Opera Group in 1964, when some convertible currency was available and we could conveniently spend those roubles in the bank. Non-convertible currency was a nightmare for performers appearing often in Russia. There was no way of spending all your earnings, and useless cash accumulated there. One solution was thought up by a pop singer, who bought round-the-world air tickets for his entire family and invited them to Moscow to set off on their journeys. It was ingenious but inconvenient – and of course condemned them to fly by Aeroflot.

We and the Russians had decided that the scenery and costumes of both companies should travel by sea, which was less expensive than the overland route, the only viable alternative. Accordingly, we chartered a small steamer to carry the Royal Ballet's equipment to Leningrad and sent a stage carpenter, Cyril Hyam, with it to oversee the unloading at the other end and begin preparations for the arrival of the company in Leningrad some weeks later.

For reasons which will shortly become apparent, Hyam remained in Leningrad alone for many more weeks than anticipated. Although we kept in touch with him by phone, he became increasingly lonely and one day told me that he was so desperate to talk to somebody that on getting up in the morning he would go to the mirror and exchange greetings with himself. Food was also a problem for him. Suspicious of most dishes which were put before him, he rejoiced at soup being brought and thought that this would be his salvation – until he saw a raw egg being broken into it. Cyril Hyam became something of a hero, and is certainly part of the folklore of Covent Garden.

Tickets for the Bolshoi season were sold as quickly as the staff could handle the applications. Activity was feverish, the box-office telephones never stopped ringing, and letters from disappointed customers and those containing personal requests for tickets swamped the mailbags. Never had the staff realized that they had so many friends! Tickets were unobtainable through legitimate channels, and many behaved quite shamelessly in their quest for them. The prospect of the Bolshoi performances had seized the imagination of a public far wider than that which normally attended ballet performances. There was an expectation in the air, and this was not to be disappointed by the dancing and the spectacle, even if the latter was achieved by old-fashioned and often crude means.

Excitement grew as the opening night approached, only to be dashed by a totally unexpected event: the publication of a letter in *Izvestia* on 21 September signed by the the majority of the Bolshoi artists, including Galina Ulanova, and staff. In this they sought the cancellation of the tour for fear of being subjected to treatment similar to that which had been meted out a few days earlier to a Russian athlete by the name of Nina Ponomerova, who had been charged with shoplifting when she was allegedly seen by a store detective picking up hats at C & A in Oxford Street and not paying for them. It was an unfortunate incident, clumsily handled by the store managers, who were overhasty in taking the action they did. There was doubt that the athlete was really stealing hats, though the temptation to do so may have been strong: rather, the language barrier had given rise to misunderstandings as she was apprehended. The incident of 'Nina and the Hats' was reported extensively in the daily press.

We were within ten days of opening, and there was no time to lose if the season was to go ahead intact. Assurances had to be given to the Bolshoi company that they had nothing to fear in London. David Webster was at his best and, following discussion with the Soviet Embassy, wrote a letter to the Bolshoi setting out all the reasons why it was safe for them to come to England. The British Embassy and the British Council in Moscow were similarly attempting to persuade the Bolshoi management and artists that all would be well.

Meanwhile, the steamer carrying the Bolshoi's scenery and costumes was due to arrive in London. It docked on time and was met by our shipping agent, who was immediately informed by the ship's master that he was under strict orders from Moscow not to discharge his cargo but to return to Leningrad without delay. The agent telephoned as I was leaving home for Covent Garden and urged me to take a taxi to the Surrey Docks as quickly as possible, for fear of the boat leaving before any action could be taken to prevent it.

When I arrived, the master told me that his orders were clear and irreversible. The situation looked bleak, but vodka was flowing and I found that he was becoming more and more amenable to reason. He eventually agreed that I should talk to the cultural attaché at the Soviet Embassy, with whom I was friendly and on whom I believed that I could rely for help in some kind of damage limitation. After a long conversation with me, and a further call to Moscow, the embassy said that they would accept my proposal that the scenery should be unloaded and stored on the dockside – but not moved – until the Bolshoi's intentions were clear.

That was one obstacle removed, and we did not have long to wait for the main problem to be rectified. In a statement released in Moscow on 26 September, Mikhail Chulaki confirmed that he was of the opinion that the visit must go ahead and that he personally would take responsibility for ensuring that it did. This was repeated to us in London, and on 28 September we were able to announce that the season was secure, although two days shorter and with some rearrangement of the programme. The opening was to be on 3 October and the final performance on 27 October, with the same previously agreed programme of *Swan Lake, Giselle, Romeo and Juliet* and *The Fountain of Bakhchisarai*. The conductors and technical staff were due to arrive the next day and to start work immediately.

While the scenery was being brought from the docks, Yuri Fayer, the principal conductor of the Bolshoi Ballet, and his assistant, Gennady Rozhdestvensky, began rehearsals of *Romeo and Juliet* with the Covent Garden orchestra. The musicians, displaying their usual skill at sight-reading, played through this difficult score superbly – so well, in fact, that after the sword fight, played in tempo at a furious speed, Fayer threw down his baton and expressed his amazement to Rozhdestvensky that anybody could sight-read that particular number so accurately. He could not believe that they had not seen the parts previously.

Yuri Fayer was an outstanding musician. Having first been a violinist, he was chief conductor of the Bolshoi Ballet from 1924 until 1968. He had a profound knowledge of ballet and the relationship of movement to music, and a real understanding of choreographic design. All of this was coupled with an extraordinary memory, which stood him in good stead as his eyesight faded. He had always conducted without a score, and by the time he came to Covent Garden he could not read one and could see only vague shapes on the stage. Jokingly, he used to tell me that this was good, since he could not see the dancers and so they had to follow him. I have subsequently wondered if Fayer's experience persuaded Rozhdestvensky that it was preferable to stand on the floor of the pit when conducting ballet, rather than on a podium, so that he could see only the dancers' knees and not their feet!

Fayer was also passionately interested in horse racing. Having discovered this, I introduced him to Robert Irving, then music director of Sadler's Wells Ballet and himself a racehorse owner. They struck up an instant friendship and – obviously without the knowledge of the Bolshoi management – Robert took him to race meetings. Even though he could not see much, Fayer revelled in the atmosphere and returned to conduct in the evening ecstatic with joy and bestowing even more than usual wet embraces on me! He was the most loveable of men, and what a conductor!

Meanwhile we were preparing for the arrival of the company, and the next day we were at London Airport to meet them. The weather was bad and was not improving, which began to raise doubts about the ability of the Russian aircraft to land. By this time many planes had been diverted and we had already witnessed an accident. A Vulcan bomber, piloted by an air marshal, was overflying the airport and had suddenly exploded, crashing to the ground in plumes of smoke. Fortunately the pilot and crew managed to use the ejector seats and landed safely. An unnerving experience for us, it increased our feelings of uncertainty about the arrival of the Bolshoi – and, as it turned out, not without reason. In the wake of this we received a message that the Russian planes were being diverted to Manston Airport in Kent, a former Battle of Britain station. This was an inconvenience more than anything else, but nonetheless likely to heighten tension within the company and lead to delay in settling them in their hotels. That was protracted by the refusal of the pilots to disembark the company without permission from Moscow. This took time to obtain, and the dancers and staff were left sitting in their planes at Manston for the best part of two hours. They eventually boarded coaches which we had ordered and arrived at the Royal Opera House in the early evening, to be formally greeted by David Webster before going to their accommodation.

The lead-up to opening was not without incident. The dancers, tired after a long journey, felt hampered by the relatively small size of the stage and were anxious about the lack of time to adjust. The scenery, too, had been constructed for much larger stages, and, while there had been some modification, it had often not been sufficiently reduced in size to fit comfortably. Adjustments to the scenery meant frequent changes to its hanging and the focusing of lamps. Everything had to be finished within a very tight schedule. The atmosphere was tense, but the Russian technicians remained good-humoured and passed on their requirements to the Covent Garden crew through interpreters and sign language. I never cease to wonder at the way in which theatre people do communicate with each other in the absence of any common language.

The last straw – and this usually happens at the most inconvenient moments – was the arrival of the fire inspector, who rejected such primitive fireproofing of the scenery as there was. All the old tricks for dealing with this kind of situation were brought into play – dowsing sets with size, and wetting parts of the scenery likely to be tested – and eventually the inspector, reassured by the presence of additional firemen on stage to deal with any emergency, agreed that the performances could go on. For a time, however, it had seemed that the season was in serious jeopardy. Whatever precautions you take to ensure that visiting companies understand British fire regulations, it is rare that the fire inspector does not find something to query as he applies his match to the scenery. The Russians have been the worst offenders – owing to their lax fire precautions and their easy solution of bringing in extra firemen during performances.

The season opened on 3 October as planned, and from the very first moments it was clear that it would be a triumph for the Bolshoi. And as the opening performance progressed the excitement grew. In many ways the audiences did not know what to expect. Of course they were immediately struck by the magnificence and authority of the dancing, which usually led to the kind of interval comments often heard when no one is quite sure what to say: 'So, this is the genuine thing!' or 'Wasn't that something?' The quality of the dancing was there for all to see – the strength and pliability of the girls' backs, the fluidity of their arms and hands, the virility of the men, the height of their jumps, the softness and control of their landings, and an extraordinary sense of discipline and commitment pervading the entire company. Headlines in Soviet newspapers on the following days proclaimed 'Triumph of Soviet Art' and 'London applauds Soviet Ballet'. Nearer home, Dame Marie Rambert enthused, 'The Italians have bel canto and the Russians bella danza. They sing with their bodies.'

There was, however, an occasional oddity – at least for Western audiences unfamiliar with Russian productions. For example, a jester was substituted for Benno, the Prince's friend, in *Swan Lake*. For some this was a misguided change, but objections evaporated when the part was performed superbly by one of the Bolshoi's magnificent *demi-caractère* dancers. The recognition of the importance of the *demi-caractère* dancer in the Bolshoi hierarchy was illuminating, and led to a change of attitude towards dancers in that category here, who had hitherto not received the recognition that was their due. Another feature of the Bolshoi company was the retention on the payroll of older dancers, past their prime but essential in giving weight and authority to the playing of older characters and in large scenes where a mixture of old and young gives authenticity. *Romeo and Juliet* is an obvious example of a ballet which gains immeasurably from this.

The corps de ballet was magnificent throughout the season, rising to every demand and demonstrating the advantages the Russians have in attracting talent from a huge population and enabling it to be intensively trained in ideal conditions. There was an extraordinary moment in a performance of *Giselle*: in Act 2, when the Wilis cross with each other and hop in arabesque, their dancing was so remarkable, with their back legs extended and absolutely still, that the audience could not contain itself and burst into applause in the middle of the movement. It was an unusual interruption – the spontaneous response of an audience marvelling at what they were seeing.

The soloists, without exception, opened the eyes of everyone to what could be achieved technically, if not always artistically. Everywhere you looked there was always some facet of dancing to fascinate and admire. Galina Ulanova was, of course, the outstanding member of the company from every viewpoint, and displayed her remarkable talents to the full in *Giselle* and *Romeo and Juliet*, expressing the full gamut of emotions with her face and her whole being. Her portrayals were so complete that you could only rejoice that a dancer, through the medium of her art, could create such totally rounded portraits. Breathtaking!

In a review of this Bolshoi season in the December 1956 *Dance and Dancers*, Richard Buckle referred to a conversation with Alexandra Danilova in which she suggested that most Russian dancers had lost the true style of classical ballet and lacked that distinction which comes from giving every movement its full value. This was a subject for much debate, and in this instance it was important to remember, as I am sure Danilova would have remarked, that these dancers were mostly Moscow-trained, whereas she came from St Petersburg. London audiences were to have the chance of seeing what that meant five years later, when the Kirov Ballet came to Covent Garden for the first time.

What also had to be borne in mind at this time was the complete isolation of Russian companies from Western culture and from social and political developments beyond the Soviet Union which were themselves influencing artistic trends and ideas in the West. The Bolshoi's scenery looked old-fashioned, heavy and obviously artificial. Costumes were often poorly designed and badly made, usually with synthetic fabrics and unsubtle colours. Wigs were crude, and make-up was primitive. Everything had a provincial look about it. But at the same time it was essential to recognize the extreme control that the Soviet government exercised over all aspects of life and to understand the price paid for what might be perceived as political incorrectness in the eyes of an authoritative and all-pervasive power. What was on display in 1956 was unlikely to cause offence in Moscow. It is worth recalling that even thirteen years later, in 1969, a new production of *Swan Lake* which the Bolshoi was to have brought to Covent Garden was cancelled at the last moment and the old one substituted. The new production was apparently an abstract design, and on seeing a rehearsal Mme Furtseva, the then Minister of Culture, decided that it was too outlandish for anyone's good and forbade its further use. According to Gennady Rozhdestvensky, who was conducting during the 1969 visit, her problem was that she couldn't catch fish in the lake!

As the Russians swept all before them through the magnificence of their dancing, you could not help thinking that the performances would have been still better with more imaginative and inspired artistic direction. There was an abandon and carefree spirit in that dancing which cried out for another dimension to be added to it.

The company went about its business in an atmosphere of fear and suspicion. The commissars were omnipresent, holding sessions with the dancers and staff on communist doctrine, and watching the movement of every member of the Bolshoi – aided and abetted by trusty members of the company who were constantly observing and at the ready to report any deviant behaviour. Nobody walked alone, and all were under surveillance. It was disagreeable to see this, but heartening to find a dancer occasionally escaping the net, even if it meant admonishment and the threat of an early return to Moscow.

Mikhail Chulaki, the director of the Bolshoi, was a composer, and I felt he was ill at ease with what was required of him, although he made a success of his appointment. He and I met daily, sometimes alone and on other occasions with a group of staff whom I always referred to as the Presidium. These meetings were normally uneventful and were a convenient way of keeping track of what was happening, planning rehearsals – which were constantly changing – and anticipating problems.

We were approaching the end of the second week of the season when Chulaki requested an urgent meeting. I went to the Waldorf Hotel, where he was staying, to be told that there was concern about the company's return to Moscow, as Russian aircraft had mysteriously become unavailable. On questioning this curious state of affairs, I was informed that the only planes that were free were being used to take Russian athletes to the Australian Olympics. Unconvinced, I nevertheless undertook to make inquiries of British European Airways. Three Viscounts could take the Russians on the appointed day, but only against sterling or dollar payment in London. This was reported to Chulaki, who in turn had to refer to Moscow. The next day there was the inevitable response: that it was disappointing that payment could not be in roubles. Nothing more was heard of this for some days, when I was again asked about aircraft. BEA repeated their offer, only to have it rejected. Chulaki returned to this once again. I didn't bother to phone BEA but simply repeated their original offer. There was then silence, and nothing more was said about the journey home until departure plans were disclosed at the end of the season.

There were often niggling difficulties to be sorted out, especially around stage availability for rehearsal and catering in the hotels, but one incident did provoke a major crisis. Chulaki phoned and asked me to attend a meeting at one of the hotels immediately. Pieces of glass had been found in a portion of ice cream. Of course there were instant accusations of a conspiracy to injure members of the Bolshoi and a total unwillingness to accept that the glass might have been the result of an accident – which it was, and which should have been attended to at the time. Threats to cancel the remaining performances were bandied around, and it was only after a great deal of talking that the Bolshoi management could be persuaded to continue with the season.

The success of the visit gathered momentum daily with the public, and the scramble for returned tickets became fiercer and fiercer. By the time we were halfway through the season at Covent Garden it was obvious that we needed more performances if we were to begin to satisfy public demand. The Bolshoi agreed, and wanted to give them in a popular and more accessible venue than the Royal Opera House. The Davies Theatre, Croydon – a poorly equipped but large theatre, often used by companies wanting to perform away from the West End – was available on the days required. This was acceptable to the Bolshoi, and arrangements were made for three extra performances in November. The planning of this short season was going ahead smoothly when Chulaki demanded that a large number of tickets – almost the capacity of one house – should be reserved for the Russian Embassy. I refused, explaining that these performances were being mounted for the benefit of the public at large and that to deprive the public of that number of tickets was unacceptable. The conversation ended on a very sour note, with no concession being made by either side. Later that day, Chulaki, who was suffering from lumbago and was being treated by Beryl Gray's husband, Set Svensen, asked me to see him in his hotel. When I went into his room, he acknowledged that I had a point and said that the embassy would settle for a much smaller allocation. That concluded, he went on to tell me that there was no way that we could part that evening without drinking to each other's health. A lacquered drinking vessel was thrust into my hand and filled with Georgian brandy. At the end of a convivial session I was told that to seal our friendship I should keep the cup and the remainder of the brandy. I was glad that we did that. We were to meet often in the future.

The day of departure drew near, and there was an extraordinary silence about how the Russians were going to travel home. Eventually it was announced that there would be three Soviet planes on the Saturday and that take-off would be early. On arriving at the airport we found that few planes were flying, because of atrocious weather over Europe. The Russian air attaché was there and was becoming more and more agitated at the prospect of serious delay, murmuring from time to time that the company must go that day. Eventually three Ilyushin 3s arrived – fair-weather planes by any standards, and so unstable that, according to the chief executive of BEA, who drew my attention to this, they needed a stabilizing fin to keep them upright. These were insufficient to take the whole company, and it was decided that they would take half of them to East Berlin immediately, returning later to collect the remainder. The weather did not improve, and those dancers must have had the most uncomfortable journey.

The next day revealed the reason for the inquiry about planes and why there was such urgency to the Russians' departure. That fateful Sunday saw Soviet forces enter Budapest to quell the Hungarian uprising. John Peter, the *Sunday Times* theatre critic, was a student in Budapest at the time, and, as far as he and I could remember dates, we believed that certain events there coincided with the request for planes in London.

The Bolshoi certainly left its mark. Some of the public began to say that the only worthwhile ballet was Russian and that British dancers paled before their Russian colleagues. These were unhelpful remarks, and were not heard for long. In the meantime, our own dancers – many of whom had been at Bolshoi classes and rehearsals, if not perform-ances – were benefiting from what they had seen and experienced. At the same time, they had been preparing to go to Moscow and Leningrad as part of the exchange agreement, only to realize that events in Hungary were likely to bring about its cancellation. That was shortly confirmed by the Foreign Office as part of its protest against the Soviet invasion, but even if that confirmation had not been forthcoming I believe that none of us would have had the heart to go on with the exchange. The Royal Ballet had to wait five years to visit the Soviet Union.

On looking back at that period, there can be little doubt about the significance of the Bolshoi visit for ballet and its audiences in this coun-try. Britain was still emerging from post-war disillusionment and uncertainty, and struggling to find a real sense of direction. A growing interest in ballet was given a huge boost by the Bolshoi performances. This, coupled with the rapidly developing success of the Sadler's Wells Ballet in New York and London, boded well for the future.

It was interesting to compare the repertoires of the Bolshoi and the Sadler's Wells companies. The three-act ballet, so much the strength of the Russian companies, had made little progress here, where there was a far greater concentration of creative energy on the one-act work – important in the development of choreographic talent and very much the hallmark of both the Sadler's Wells Ballet and the Sadler's Wells Theatre Ballet, but not making for a completely satisfying repertoire, successful as the one-act literary dramatic ballet had become. The companies and the public now needed the full-length narrative ballet. The balance of the Bolshoi and Kirov repertoires was the reverse, with a need there for concentrated one-act ballets to leaven the diet of three-act works.

The visit to the Soviet Union finally took place in 1961, and brought a further enhancement of the company's fortunes and reputation. As the company – by then the Royal Ballet – performed at the Kirov Theatre in Leningrad, that theatre's company appeared at Covent Garden for the first time. This was an agreeable concurrence, since there is a close affin-ity between the two companies, English style owing much to that of the Kirov (now happily reverted to its original title of the State Academic Mariinsky Theatre). It was also from here that Nicholas Sergueyev had come. He had been régisseur at the Mariinsky and had left Russia in 1918, bringing with him an invaluable collection of notebooks, from which he was able to reconstruct many ballets, including *The Sleeping Princess* for Diaghilev in 1921. Ninette de Valois was not slow in enlisting his aid for her then Vic–Wells Ballet, and in 1933 she engaged him to mount *Coppélia* on her company. This was to be followed by *Nutcracker*, *Giselle* and *Swan Lake* in 1934 and *Sleeping Beauty* in 1939.

Other influences were to come from that city in addition to Sergueyev, arriving in England via Shanghai in the 1940s and being snapped up by de Valois. They were the dancers Vera Volkova, who had been trained by Agrippina Vaganova, and George Gontcharov. Later were to come Serge Grigoriev and his wife, Liubov Tchernicheva, who mounted *Firebird*, *Petrushka* and *The Good-Humoured Ladies* on the Sadler's Wells Ballet. Another important influence was that of Bronislava Nijinska, invited by Frederick Ashton to produce *Les Biches* in 1964 and *Les Noces* in 1966.

Important and essential as these influences were, and stimulating to the company as was its rapturous reception in Moscow and Leningrad, nothing was to be like the bombshell which hit the company in 1962 with the arrival of Rudolf Nureyev. At the conclusion of their Paris season in June 1961, the Kirov Ballet left for London. The management already knew that Nureyev was not coming, because of instructions from Moscow that he was to return to the Soviet Union for a very spurious reason – a special performance at the Kremlin – following which he would supposedly rejoin the company in London. This was casually explained to him by Konstantin Sergueyev, the company's artistic director, at Paris airport as the company was about to leave. Many of his friends in the company, aware of his troubles, weighed up what was happening and what could well have been going through his mind. They urged him to do nothing rash.

What they soon discovered was that he had given his minders the slip and was seeking asylum from the French police. It was a dramatic and sudden decision by Nureyev to jump, because he quickly realized that to return to the Soviet Union in these circumstances would probably mean that he would never come to the West again and almost certainly would even be denied performances in Leningrad and Moscow. He had already been sent away from Leningrad twice for misdemeanours and breaches of discipline, and envisaged himself condemned to perform in provincial cities for the rest of his career – an intolerable prospect. He knew that he had to find freedom and the artistic stimulus essential to his development and well-being. He believed that the West would give him those, but it was a leap into the unknown.

I was at Heathrow to meet the Kirov company, and the image of downcast dancers and managers is indelibly set in my mind – the dancers aware that they were to be without a colleague and friend and likely to face more severe restrictions on their movements in London than usual, and the management realizing that they were destined for Siberia or its equivalent. The director of the Kirov Theatre was removed from his post on his return and was demoted first to a clerical job and then to the management of a small theatre. Konstantin Sergueyev and his wife, Natalia Doudinskaya, were reprimanded.

A worse fate was to befall them when Natalia Makarova defected from the company during its 1971 London season. For reasons I have never discovered, Sergueyev believed that I knew where Makarova was hiding. I did not, but I had the utmost difficulty in convincing him of that. There were telephone calls and visits to my office, in which he pleaded with me to reveal her whereabouts, at the same time reminding me of the serious consequences awaiting him at home if he returned without her. I could not help, and I felt for him because I knew that he was destined for demotion and ostracism. And that was what happened – to both him and his wife – leaving its mark to the point that, when during a visit to Leningrad in 1988 I asked the director of the Kirov Theatre if I could see them, they came but would not enter his office. We stood outside to talk – an unhappy memory.

The Kirov season was a triumph, in spite of the absence of Nureyev, and audiences responded warmly and excitedly to a rich display of lyrical and expressive dancing. The Kirov lack the brashness of the Bolshoi, and it was possible at moments to sense a disappointment in some parts of the audience that they were not once again experiencing the extrovert virility and near-circus turns of the Moscow company. What was recognized, however, was that the Kirov style is much closer to that of the Royal Ballet, and the public revelled in the familiar.

What also emerged was the quality of the Kirov's music-making. As had been the case with the Bolshoi, the sounds from the pit were glorious. Tempi could differ from those with which we were familiar, but the music came across with an invigorating freshness and rightness in relation to the movement on the stage. I recall only one doubt: about the unbearably slow speed of the Vision Scene in *Sleeping Beauty*, which almost destroyed its lovely tune. You could also find fault with the extent to which variations could be mauled musically to accommodate dancers' needs or perhaps their wishes and moods.

In the meantime, Rudolf Nureyev had acquired a *carnet* from the French government, which enabled him to travel. This usually involved the inconvenience of visas, but nevertheless the world was open to him. For his first appearances with a Western company he had accepted an engagement with the Grand Ballet of Marquis de Cuevas, and he danced in *Sleeping Beauty* with them on the same night on which he might have made his London debut with the Kirov.

Russian ballet companies have continued to come to London. Some have been of dubious origin, and have mostly toured the regions. It is important that the great companies should continue to visit. While the excitement of the earlier visits is harder to find in performances today, there is still much to admire and we have much to learn from each other, in addition to the benefits of stimulating interest in ballet as a serious art form. Individual dancers from Russia, too, have continued to appear with the Royal Ballet. The most influential of these has been Irek Mukhamedov, who left the Bolshoi permanently, joined the Royal Ballet, and settled in London with his family. Another Russian has sadly been seen much less frequently in London. This is Mikhail Baryshnikov, a hugely gifted and stylish performer from the Kirov, who was for a time director of American Ballet Theatre and has sought his fortune in film and dance.

Makarova was to dance often with the Royal Ballet, and later mounted her production of *La Bayadère* for the company. Among the many qualities she brought to her performances were lyricism, spontaneity and radiance. My only complaint was her tendency to be musically lax. I once asked her why she was so frequently behind the beat, to which she replied, 'That's my spontaneity, darling!'

For opera the situation has been different. As far as London audiences are concerned, it was only with the visit of the Kirov Opera to Covent Garden in 1987 that there was first-hand acquaintance with a Russian company. The singing and orchestral playing were of a high order, but production standards were another matter. That these were the result of the company's isolation from the rest of the world for so many years was all too clear.

One important contemporary Russian opera, by Dmitri Shostakovich, was heard in London for the first time some years after it had initially been banned by the Soviet authorities under its original title of *The Lady Macbeth of the Mtensk District*. Permission was granted for performances of a revised and renamed version at Covent Garden in the 1963/64

season. The opera was to be called *Katarina Ismailova*, and it was performed in the presence of the composer, with Marie Collier in the title
role and Edward Downes conducting. It was a triumph, and an early
opportunity to hear an opera composed by a contemporary Russian
musician.

What was to emerge from Russia in post-Gorbachev days was a
colossal flow of the most gifted singers. We were already familiar with
a few Russian singers and many instrumentalists, but it is only in the last
decade that the real nature and extent of the singing talent has become
clear. It is breathtaking, and it is difficult to believe that it has been there
and largely unknown to us in the West for so long. Apart from the
freedom of movement that all now enjoy, it is very much owing to Valery
Gergiev, the illustrious conductor and director of the Mariinsky Theatre,
that this has happened. He has been a magnet in attracting talent from
all over the old Soviet Union and has channelled it in all directions, but
especially into his own company, where singers are benefiting from
first-rate coaching and performance experience.

Gergiev has conducted too infrequently at Covent Garden, but when
he is there the sheer force of his musicianship is all-pervading. This is a
view shared by many musicians, and is reflected in a remark that Bernard
Haitink made to me after listening to Gergiev conduct *Eugene Onegin* at
the Royal Opera House a few years ago: 'I have never heard the strings
play so well.'

In addition to Yuri Temikarnov, who conducted memorable performances with the Kirov in London, two other Russian conductors have
brought their considerable talents to bear on Covent Garden. One, who
conducted *The Queen of Spades* in the 1961/62 season and *Aida* two
years later, was Alexander Melik-Pashayev, a fine Verdi conductor, highly disciplined and knowing exactly how to use rehearsal time to maximum advantage. For *Aida* he had one three-hour rehearsal with stage
and orchestra – not long enough to play the whole opera through. But he
had a clear idea of what to cover and what to leave out, and not a second
was wasted. By the end everybody was amazed at what had been
achieved – it was a tour de force which left a lasting impression on us all
and led to splendid performances.

A fine musician of a quite different kind is Gennady Rozhdestvensky,
who has appeared too little at Covent Garden but again brought a very
individual approach to music-making and left his mark. Possessed of a
supple and fluent stick technique, he would mould performances as they

progressed, using little rehearsal time and enjoying sending the orchestra home early. His argument was that the good player would sort out any technical problems and needed no help from him. The less good player, on the other hand, probably couldn't do any better, and there was nothing the conductor could do to help. So why waste the time? In difficult works this practice leaves the players too much on a knife edge, but the results were often magical and so spontaneous that you could only marvel.

Another distinguished Russian artist to come to Covent Garden was Andrei Tarkovsky. *Boris Godunov* had been scheduled for a new production in the autumn of 1983, with Claudio Abbado conducting. At the beginning we did not have a producer in mind, but in the early part of the year Abbado telephoned to ask if I had seen the film *Andrei Rublev*. As it happened, I had. I was immediately asked if I thought that its director, Tarkovsky, would be a good choice for our production of *Boris*. I did, and then embarked upon the longest saga I have ever experienced in bringing an artist to the point of starting work.

Tarkovsky was working on a film in Rome – a joint venture between the Soviet Union and Italy. The Soviet authorities, it seemed, regarded him with some suspicion – largely, I believe, because they could not understand his films and what he was about. At this time he had made only six films in a career of twenty-one years. He was keen to direct *Boris*, but was most anxious that his engagement should be negotiated through official channels. He was in touch with the Soviet Agency in Moscow, and so was I, but no reply came to either of us. On one of several visits to Rome, where he was filming at Cinecittà, I proposed that he and I make an agreement and then tell the authorities what we had done. At this he became uncomfortable and expressed his fear that he would be arrested by the KGB. In the end he agreed. Our next meeting had to take place in an editing room, where he felt more secure and free, but even there I remember a door opening and panic setting in that he had been discovered. It was quite pitiful, and I felt so deeply for this great film-maker.

Eventually a contract was agreed. Meanwhile he had chosen a designer, a Soviet painter, Nicolas Dvigoubsky, who was married to a Frenchwoman and living in Paris. Dvigoubsky was, of course, free to come and go, but it was only in July that I managed to get Tarkovsky and his designer together. Tarkovsky was concerned about seeing anyone in Rome, and I had encountered difficulties with his English visa, which delayed his arrival in London. The first problem was that he was nervous about going to the British Embassy in Rome to have his passport stamped, because of his fear of being picked up by Soviet agents on leaving. I phoned Lord Bridges, the British ambassador, to ask if he could be granted a visa without going to the embassy. I was told definitely not – much though Bridges wanted to help. A further phone call from me persuaded Tarkovsky that it was safe to go. It was then discovered that his passport was so full of visas and stamps that there was scarcely room for another. He could not return to Moscow, so there was no way of obtaining a replacement document for him, short of buying an illicit one, which was not a valid option. Another call to the embassy confirmed that the visa had to be stamped on an existing page and could not be affixed to a separate sheet, as I had hoped might be possible. There was now nothing left but to appeal to the visa clerk to be really ingenious and squeeze the visa on to the edge of a page. That is what he did, saving the day for us.

Tarkovsky and Dvigoubsky met in London on a Wednesday later in July. They talked and argued for two days. On the Friday night, Tarkovsky was having a drink with me in the Crush Bar and remarked that I looked preoccupied. I replied that I was, because he had been in London for two days, had not agreed any designs with Dvigoubsky, and was leaving twenty-four hours later. I explained that we were already extremely late and that the workshops would have difficulty in completing the work in time. 'Don't worry, John,' said Tarkovsky – 'you'll have everything by tomorrow night.' We did, but it was the beginning of a tense relationship between designer and director, with Tarkovsky feeling that he was not getting what he really wanted. Given the pattern of his life, I suspect that he felt rushed and had had insufficient gestation time, although Dvigoubsky was convinced that he was providing what he had been asked for. Whatever Tarkovsky's reservations about the set may have been, the production was a huge success and later found its way to St Petersburg for some performances by the Kirov.

It was an unnerving if exhilarating experience working with Tarkovsky. Never having made a stage production before, it took him some time to discover what was needed by way of direction to the singers and supers. In fact a fortnight went by without too much evidence of a production; but with the help of a staff producer, Stephen Lawless, one began to take shape.

I was so struck by what eventually emerged that I was determined that

Tarkovsky should return to direct another opera. He was keen to do so, and liked the idea of *Der Fliegende Holländer*. We met in Berlin in early 1985 to discuss it further, and immediately ran into a problem: the colour of the skin of the singer engaged for the Dutchman. He was black. Tarkovsky was adamant that he could not accept this casting, because a black person had no connection with European legend. Things did not look good. We talked and talked until the early hours of the next morning, when suddenly he relented. Tragically, the production never took place with him. He had been ill in Stockholm before coming to Berlin, and cancer was diagnosed shortly after.

What is so promising for the future is the cross-fertilization between Russian and European cultures, made so easy by the freedom that artists now have to move between Russia and the West, and vice versa. There is a rich Russian heritage to be explored still more widely and deeply, to the advantage of us all.

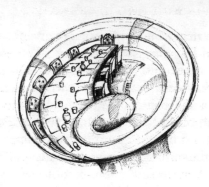

10 *Finance and Governance*

If war had not been declared in 1939 and the resulting national government had not laid the foundations of public funding of the arts, I often wonder when this principle would have been adopted. It is impossible to believe that the unopposed introduction it received then could have been achieved so easily in peacetime, or in time to have secured the reopening of the Royal Opera House at a moment when the lease could be retrieved from Mecca Cafés.

By the time the war had come to an end, the Council for the Encouragement of Music and the Arts (CEMA) had shown that there was a continuing role to be fulfilled in making the arts accessible to the population at large, and this was confirmed by Sir John Anderson, the Chancellor of the Exchequer and later chairman of the Royal Opera House, in a statement in the House of Commons in June 1945. The government, he announced, had decided that CEMA should be succeeded by the Arts Council of Great Britain, which, unlike its predecessor, would be responsible to, and financed by, the Treasury rather than the Ministry of Education. Lord Keynes, who had been chairman of CEMA, declared that the new body would aim 'to carry the arts through the countryside and maintain metropolitan standards'. Tragically, he died before the royal charter incorporating the Arts Council was promulgated, in 1946, but he had lived long enough at least to see the government's continued acceptance of the principle of public funding of the arts.

The independence of the Arts Council from government was firmly established by the articles accompanying the Council's royal charter, and this independence was maintained for many years. Unfortunately this was not to last, and in recent times ministers have been unable to resist the temptation to interfere. The arm's-length principle was sound and, in spite of it being used by successive ministers as an escape route when faced by awkward questions about arts funding in the House of Commons, it has been seen as a reliable way of securing government money – mostly in a difficult financial climate – and of ensuring its distribution free of political intervention. While the Arts Council's fortunes have ebbed and flowed according to the state of the economy and the influence of the minister in office, the general consensus is that, disappointing as funding levels are – often not even keeping pace with inflation – the arts community has probably fared better under the Council than it might have done if tied directly to a ministry of culture, when fluctuations could have been more severe.

Two notable examples of ministerial influence come to mind. One occurred when Jennie Lee was Arts Minister in the mid to late 1960s. She had threatened resignation over a proposed increase in prescription charges. Dissuaded from this, she remained in office, and in the following April the Arts Council was awarded the biggest increase in grant it had ever received. Another example came much later, in 1992, when David Mellor had inflated the title of his office to that of Secretary of State for National Heritage. This followed a period as Chief Secretary to the Treasury, where he had obviously learned a thing or two. By whatever means, the Council's next grant saw a huge increase.

Mellor once told me that he found it hard just to allocate a sum to the Arts Council and not in some way to be able to influence its spending. This reflected the feelings of a man passionately interested in music, and with ideas about the areas in which he believed money could profitably be spent. He was not slow in letting these ideas be known, nor in finding the necessary money from the Treasury and the Foundation for Sports and Arts – on which bodies I can only conclude that he leaned heavily to enable English National Opera to purchase the freehold of the Coliseum in the 1990s. It was an important decision for ENO, for the future of which Mellor has high hopes, but I could not help seeing it also as a reflection of political expediency. An election was in the offing, and a gesture to those living in the South-East who were ENO regulars and Tory Party supporters would not have gone amiss. I had not thought about this connection until Lord Gowrie, when Arts Minister between 1983 and 1985, telephoned one day, as he did from time to time, to talk about the funding of opera in London. In the course of this conversation, he suddenly said that he could not contemplate the closing down of ENO for many reasons, among them the risk of offending his party's supporters in Tunbridge Wells and its environs.

Although there has been change in recent years, for far too long the Arts Council allocated grants without having a strategic plan in place. The result was that funding was too thinly spread and the Council was unable to depart from a policy of equal misery for all. The time in the 1960s when Jennie Lee was in charge of the arts for the government and Lord Goodman was presiding at the Arts Council is often recalled as the Council's most prosperous period. The two of them were a powerful and influential duo, and dispensed money on a scale hitherto unheard of in this country. The increase in arts funding was applauded – and rightly so – but the way in which grants were distributed is, in my view, at the heart of some of the problems we face today. Funds were handed out with largesse to all comers. There seems to have been little discrimination in the selection of recipients, and there was encouragement of new companies and organizations without any awareness of how they fitted into a plan – unsurprisingly, because there was no strategy in place. Awarding grants was a reactive process, which was encouraging a large amount of uncoordinated activity without much thought about its future.

I discussed this with Lord Goodman, and found his response worrying, but typical of him. He firmly believed that response to activity was right, and that an Arts Council strategic plan would discourage initiative and restrict the flowering of talent. There was, of course, good sense in this, but it ignored the ill effect which the limitation of funding, and its resultant thin spreading, was having on existing organizations – which was to be exacerbated by inflation in the 1970s. Somehow, he thought, the future would take care of itself – with his intervention if need be. Hence the remark he once made to me when I queried a union settlement which he had negotiated for ENO: that he would bail me out when Covent Garden was in similar difficulties. I am sure he would have found the means of doing so – a phone call here or there never seemed to fail him.

The Arts Council for far too long remained reactive, when there were two simple questions which should have been asked and answered: what do we need and what can we afford? The resulting rationalization of funding might well have ended in some organizations being deprived of public money, and this would have been regrettable, but, given the slowness in the growth of funding levels in the face of impregnable political attitudes, it would surely have been better to have grasped the nettle years ago and ensured that at least what activity was thought essential for the cultural well-being of the country was reasonably financially secure, while holding some reserves for new and interesting work.

Every pound of public money spent on the arts has to be justified, and there is no divine right of access to any of it. Accountability and transparency are essential. Roy Shaw, secretary-general of the Arts Council from 1975 to 1983, once cited me as an example of someone who rejected this principle. Nothing could have been further from the case. What I had queried was the way in which it was implemented, since it was my belief that the Arts Council at the time was ill-equipped to do so effectively.

I have always thought that greater openness about the means by which funding levels are assessed would be helpful both to applicants for grants and to the Arts Council itself. Too often the fixing of grants has been shrouded in mystery and explanations have been unsatisfactory. This situation could be rectified through targeted funding – subsidizing selected elements of an organization's budget at agreed percentages of estimated cost, perhaps with matching funding against box-office returns, to encourage maximizing of revenue. Grant allocations would then be attached to items of expenditure, and overspending on one item could not be rectified by the transfer of unspent funds allocated for another item except with the consent of the funder.

The 1984 Priestley Report on a government-sponsored inquiry into the affairs of the Royal Opera House and the Royal Shakespeare Company strongly advocated this system, and I have tried to persuade a succession of arts ministers to adopt it – but to no avail. Somehow the myth has become established that it contains an in-built inflation factor. In fact, however, it has the potential to achieve the opposite.

Various methods of calculating funding have been adopted over the years, some with such adverse results that they could not be continued. One was based on a percentage of cost alone, with a maximum limit. Another, based on a matching of box-office income, was more beneficial but still produced inadequate subvention and was also abandoned. Grants were then based on an overall assessment of programming, its cost and income.

The hand-to-mouth pattern of grant allocation, from which the Arts

Council has valiantly tried to break away, has been imposed by the annual cycle of government tax policy. However, an opera house needs to plan at least three years in advance if it is to be able to engage the singers, conductors, directors and designers it wants when it wants them, and it therefore has to do so in the hope that the subsidy it needs will eventually be available and that the budget can be balanced. Planning on this basis has involved huge acts of faith on the part of boards and managements. Fortunately, change has come about and organizations now receive forecasts of future grants and advance warning of adverse funding. In the present case of the Royal Opera House, funding for two years is in place, with that for a third year to be confirmed but with a guaranteed minimum.

I have long wished that artistic planning could be on a shorter-term basis, but competition by other opera houses has prevented this. When Joan Ingpen was at the Metropolitan Opera House, five-year planning cycles were adopted there. Anthony Bliss, the Met's general manager at the time, regarded this as a virtue and took comfort from knowing that everything was in place for years ahead. However, it made a change of mind impossible, and prevented the ready means of accommodating new talent as it appeared. It also had the added disadvantage of putting unwanted pressure on Covent Garden and other opera houses.

During the early 1960s, those of us involved with touring were increasingly concerned about the lack of coordination of regional touring schedules. Seasons by subsidized companies – particularly ballet companies – were too often haphazardly bunched too close together in the same town, or in towns within close proximity to each other, with an adverse effect on the box office. To the public, this appeared to be chaotic – which it was – and not a sensible way of spending taxpayers' money. It was beginning to bring the subsidized theatre into disrepute, and something had to be done. Moreover, companies would benefit from longer stays and more settled conditions for rehearsal and for preparing new work than were feasible with weekly stands. Stephen Arlen, the managing director of Sadler's Wells, and I, looking on this situation with dismay, went to see Nigel Abercrombie, the then secretary-general of the Arts Council, to draw his attention to the problem and to seek his help in rectifying it. No help was immediately forthcoming and, after listening to expressions of concern, Arlen and I left, determined to found our own coordinating organization.

To all the subsidized companies committed to touring, we proposed the setting up of an organization to coordinate and direct touring plans. There was obviously a cost involved, and there was unanimous agreement to contribute to it. A person was to be engaged to undertake the planning of tours, which were to be based on seasons combining opera, ballet and drama where these could be sensibly accommodated and promoted. A good geographical coverage of the country was essential. The body was called the Dramatic and Lyric Theatre Association (DALTA), and was charged with a wider remit than just touring, so that it would embrace other areas of common interest to the participating companies, such as publicity, purchasing and the coordination of union negotiations.

The first pilot scheme was launched in Bristol in March 1966, and was followed by seasons in Glasgow, Manchester and Leeds, with performances by Sadler's Wells Opera, the Royal Ballet and the Royal Shakespeare Company. The results in Manchester and Glasgow were sufficiently good to encourage us to continue with this venture, although we had to recognize that in presenting these extended seasons we were asking the public to buy tickets for more performances than usual in a particular period. It was an important experiment, but the lengthy seasons proved difficult for local audiences to sustain and companies reverted to single-week patterns of touring. However, the value of coordinating tours was proved, and eventually the Arts Council accepted responsibility for this. The regularity of visits, and particularly of visits at the same time of year, was also found to be important. Such experiences were later embraced by the Arts Council in establishing areas of influence, which demarcate the parts of the country in which a company will operate.

Over the years, the arts communities have relied on the Arts Council to persuade, and if necessary battle with, successive governments to raise the levels of public funding. In turn, the Arts Council and the arts communities have expected that arts ministers will respond to the cry. The extents to which the Council and successive arts ministers have striven for better arts funding have varied – in relation not necessarily to the state of the economy but more to the clout exerted by a particular minister or Arts Council chairman and their willingness to fight to persuade ministers and officials of the value of the arts to the nation – morally and culturally, and also as a revenue earner through the encouragement of tourism and the payment of VAT. It has been infuriating to watch opportunities to obtain more money for the arts being lost – for example, when the government's search for a new chairman of the Arts Council has been unsuccessful, an incumbent's agreement to stay on should have been conditional on increased funding.

The Arts Council has lost its way in recent years and has become a body to which arts companies turn to gripe rather than for help and advice. The market-forces policies of Margaret Thatcher did not help, and her unwillingness to believe that arts companies were often well managed and that they were run by anything other than a bunch of irresponsible luvvies set a gulf between the source of funding and its ultimate recipients. The Arts Council seemed powerless in the midst of this, and resorted to bureaucratic procedures which bedevilled its relationships both with its immediate clients and with the regional arts boards, to which increasing money and responsibility had been delegated.

The Council became too large, and its running costs became disproportionate to the money it dispensed and to the functions it fulfilled, which had multiplied unnecessarily. I have always thought that the Council should be a compact body, responsible principally for the strategy of arts funding, the implementation of which should be devolved to the regional arts boards, with only the direct funding of the four major national companies – the Royal Opera House, the Royal National Theatre, English National Opera and the Royal Shakespeare Company – being the responsibility of the Council itself. It is to be hoped that under a new chairman, Gerry Robinson, and secretary-general, Peter Hewitt, a less expensive, more straightforward and more transparent method of dispensing public money will be adopted. As devolution expands, however, regional arts boards must show themselves capable of exercising increased responsibilities and of distributing public funds without political quirkiness and correctness.

Because of the pressures arising from inadequate arts funding and the consequent spreading of subventions too thinly, the four national companies have felt themselves penalized by an Arts Council struggling to make ends meet and to ensure an equitable distribution of funds to all clients. This has prompted consideration of allying these companies to the Department of Culture, Media and Sport, so that their funding would be freed from the maelstrom of country-wide allocations of grants and could be increased without any impact on the Arts Council's own funds. The conclusion of all the discussions to which I have been party has been that, attractive though the idea may appear, the resulting direct exposure to government public-expenditure policies, and political whims and interference, could prove to be even less beneficial than the current arrangements.

During Roy Shaw's time as secretary-general of the Arts Council, relations between performing companies and the Council were strained by both sides' lack of appreciation of what this relationship should be – non-bureaucratic and based on partnership – and by a failure to understand companies' operating methods and hence their needs. However, there was one important matter on which agreement did emerge, and that was education. Roy Shaw rightly argued that part of the philosophy of arts funding involved accessibility – which meant not just reasonable admission prices, but also the opportunity for as many as possible to be introduced to what companies had on offer and to see if they liked it.

During the 1970s, arts education plans were in embryo, some being more advanced than others. The importance of this work was recognized, but cash-starved organizations found it hard to allocate funds from their general budgets for this purpose and usually depended on sponsorship to finance education schemes. Such schemes began to attract money from a number of sponsors, who turned from supporting productions and performances in search of less ephemeral projects.

Imaginative schemes were introduced for both young and old, and increasingly these were accepted as an integral part of a performing company's life – not an add-on, but an essential by-product of the performance of opera and ballet on stage. This status can finally be confirmed only by the inclusion of education in annual budgets – as it is now – still attracting sponsorship, but not completely dependent on it, and as deserving of public funding as the rest of a company's activities. Education is not a marketing tool, however, and any attempt to make it one will weaken its integrity and effectiveness, and erode its fundamental relationship with its performing company. But if future audiences do grow because of education projects, all well and good.

What has been heart-warming about the education work at Covent Garden – where we have been fortunate in having a group of inspired and committed men and women in charge of diverse activities, including wig-making, make-up and costume-making, as well as performers and musicians – has been the response of the children as they have been exposed to singing and dancing, often taking part alongside the professionals, who have themselves reaped huge enjoyment and benefit from such projects. For many singers, instrumentalists and dancers, working with young people, and discovering their response to music and dance has been a revelation, and has added a dimension to their performing skills.

The age of populism is with us, and high culture – for want of a better term – ranks low in the present government's rating of the arts scene. This is denied by ministers, but a contrary attitude needs to be demonstrated by actions, not words, to dispel this view. More resources have to be found to support the cultural ingredients which go to make a healthy, civilized society to which all can feel they belong. Dumbing down and setting standards by the lowest common denominator are not the way forward. The arts have been one of the success stories of Britain since 1945. Arts organizations' ingenuity in finding solutions when in tight corners have created an impression that all is well, and that life in the arts world can go on as hitherto. The truth is that it cannot, and already the essential arts infrastructure of the country is crumbling – indeed, in some instances it has collapsed.

From its beginnings the Royal Opera House has rarely been free of financial difficulties, but, like other arts organizations up and down the land, it has found short-term answers and, with expertise and resolve, has made do to produce work of the highest quality. This has made Covent Garden the envy of the world, and the object of astonishment at how it has been possible to create so much work of the highest standards with such small resources. It was the Covent Garden family spirit, embracing the whole organization, which drove it forward and which saw it through the peaks and troughs of the post-war years. Against the background of an extraordinary array of talent among artists and staff, there was the determination to succeed, never to rest content with the achievements of today but to aim still higher for tomorrow. That was my guiding principle, and I never ceased to advocate it.

Wartime austerity was still prevailing when the first governing body of the Royal Opera House – the Covent Garden Opera Trust – met in the autumn of 1946. It was a gigantic act of faith to embark on the reopening of Covent Garden as an opera house, and colossal determination was required to overcome obstacles which were especially forbidding immediately after the war. Money was short, with the first Arts Council grant amounting to no more than £25,000.

Shortly after the formation of the Covent Garden Opera Trust, its chairman and its principal inspirational and driving force, Lord Keynes, died. He was succeeded by someone of quite different personality and background: Viscount Waverley, a former Home Secretary and Chancellor of the Exchequer.

Waverley was a man of stature, who knew his way round government corridors and was never slow to exploit his connections. He believed that a direct link between Covent Garden and the Treasury was vital, and when the Covent Garden Opera Trust was replaced by a company limited by guarantee – Royal Opera House, Covent Garden Ltd – in April 1950, he invited Dennis Rickett, a senior Treasury official, to be secretary to the board. It was a shrewd move, and was the beginning of a tradition of Civil Service mandarins, mostly very elevated, servicing the board and its committees. The quality of minute-taking has been impeccable, and the writing of the minutes stylish and lucid. Two Cabinet secretaries – Lord Armstrong and Lord Butler – were previously secretaries to the board, and today's board secretary, Andrew Edwards, was formerly a senior Treasury official. They and others have contributed hugely to the good order of the board and its affairs.

Although Covent Garden's subvention was paid by the Arts Council, there was active lobbying of the Treasury about funding levels for many years. It was a fascinating exercise, but I was never sure how successful it really was in obtaining more money. I had little direct contact with Lord Waverley, but when I did, and when it was about money, he invariably asked with which official at the Treasury I was in touch. His reply was always the same: 'Not nearly senior enough! Talk to so and so.'

The Treasury link was looked upon with scepticism by some arts bodies, but without good cause, since, in making officials aware of the needs of the arts community, it was in reality an important service to others beyond Covent Garden – and one without strings. Another much more bizarre tie-up, which would never be tolerated today, or even thought remotely feasible or desirable, was the appointment of Douglas Lund, an accountant in private practice, as secretary and chief accountant to the Royal Opera House, Covent Garden Ltd, in April 1950, at the same time as he was accounting officer of the Arts Council. Lund was a man of integrity and would never have taken advantage of his dual role, but nevertheless he had insight into the workings of the Arts Council from which it must have been difficult to divorce himself when dealing with Covent Garden matters. It was a curiosity of Arts Council workings which should not have been permitted.

The Royal Opera House, Covent Garden Ltd was incorporated with its articles and memorandum of association in line with those adopted by most arts companies in this country. Each director's financial liability is limited to £1, and the terms of their appointment have been varied in the course of time. Although the approval of the Arts Minister and the chairman of the Arts Council has been sought for the appointment of a chairman, his selection, until the recent arrival of Sir Colin Southgate, has been by the board members, as has also been the case with directors. This has led to the accusation that the board is a self-elected and self-generating oligarchy, which is unfair and unjust in the light of its track record over much of its existence. However, recent events – discussed in Chapter 11 – and the desirability of transparency must lead to different methods of selection in future.

Over the years there has been a good mix of business- and arts-orientated men and women on the Covent Garden board, which has shown great skill in balancing artistic endeavour against financial restriction. There is a danger of arts boards becoming talking shops, and I cannot pretend that Covent Garden has always escaped this. Naturally, board members want to express views about choice of repertoire and singers, but there have been occasions when this has gone too far. Musician board members have tended to remain silent; on challenging one about his silence, I was told that he was unhappy with the way that other directors aired their likes and dislikes of singers and dancers and so refused to join in.

Covent Garden has been fortunate in having many board members who have made important contributions to the development and well-being of the organization. For me the board was an important forum in which plans could be proposed and tested or grievances and doubts be shared with others. I found it a good sounding board. On the other hand, David Webster used it as little as possible, preferring to keep his own counsel and to divulge the minimum of information to the board – much to the fury of its then chairman, the Earl of Drogheda, a man passionately committed to Covent Garden and bent on its success. Drogheda would telephone me frequently to ask what was happening or what was really in Webster's mind. These were not comfortable moments as I defended Webster and attempted to reduce the tension between him and the chairman.

Desirous of strengthening the artistic make-up of the board, and at the suggestion of a fellow director, Lord Donaldson, Lord Drogheda invited Walter Legge to become a director in 1958. Following his pre-war involvement with Covent Garden as Beecham's assistant artistic director, there is no doubt that Legge would have liked Webster's job. The latter, aware of this, deplored his appointment and was constantly on guard against any sinister move by Legge to unseat him. Legge was never slow to express his thoughts on repertoire and casting, and, close as he was to musicians such as Otto Klemperer, he would not miss a chance to snipe at Webster – usually for his dilatoriness in answering cables or letters. It was a difficult period for Webster, and was eased only when Legge resigned in 1963.

For all Legge's acerbity, there was an approachable man behind it, possessed of a sharp and imaginative mind and an extraordinarily developed sensibility to music, particularly where voices were concerned. He and I became friendly, and during his London visits we took every opportunity to meet. These were stimulating occasions, and I came away from them both better informed and wiser. After a period when for one reason or another we had not met for some time, I received from him a letter which began, 'If the governments of Iceland and the United Kingdom had been as successful as you and I in not meeting, there would have been no cod war.' Others in similar vein appeared from time to time, and always with information about singers and conductors whom he had just heard.

Lord Drogheda had an extraordinary eye for detail, and little escaped his attention. When he detected any blemish, there would be an immediate phone call or a 'yellow peril' (as notes written on the yellow paper used for all internal messages at Covent Garden were known) – such notes soon becoming known as Droghedagrams. He would react angrily to a bad notice or inaccurate newspaper comment about the House, and the editor of an offending paper who lived near him would find a note from Drogheda on his breakfast table, delivered personally by his lordship in his pyjamas and dressing gown. Drogheda's interventions could be infuriating, but they arose from a determination that Covent Garden should succeed and that nothing should obstruct or tarnish its progress.

In 1974 Lord Drogheda was followed as chairman by Sir Claus Moser. A Berlin-born Jew, non-aristocratic and, at the time, non-Establishment, Moser was quite unlike his predecessor. An academic and chief government statistician until 1978, when he became vice-chairman of N. M. Rothschild & Sons, he had been introduced to the board ten years earlier, by the distinguished economist Lord Robbins. Since then he had made his mark as somebody who happily combined artistic judgement with financial prudence. At the beginning of his chairmanship I sensed that he did not quite know where he stood in relation to the management and where his responsibilities started and stopped. This was sorted out with little said, and then began a happy collaboration which was to last for thirteen years.

Moser is himself a sensitive and first-rate pianist, and one of his strengths is a passionate interest in music, opera and ballet, which is infectious and rubs off on all who come into contact with him. A warm and approachable man, his presence in the House was always welcomed and appreciated by staff and artists; he is at ease with them, and they are comfortable with him. A strong emotional streak in his make-up could occasionally get the better of him, leaving me with awkward situations to be disentangled, but this was a small price to pay for his presence – and far preferable to a lack of feeling.

There were strong and colourful personalities on the board through-out my years at Covent Garden – cultured men and women who were rarely slow to express their opinions. Particularly during Claus Moser's chairmanship, there was a fondness on the part of some to shoot from the hip, which resulted in the pursuit of some ideas which you knew from the beginning were of little value, although deference to fellow board members meant that time and money had to be spent on their examination until they were proved impractical, or occasionally the reverse. Of course, good could come out of this, but a willingness to discard some suggestions at meetings would have been helpful.

Try as we would to allocate a good proportion of time at board meet-ings to the discussion of subjects other than money, such discussion all too rarely took place, because Covent Garden has seldom been without financial problems and the strain of balancing the books. Finance is one of a board's principal responsibilities, and it behoves the management to keep its members well informed and prepared for any likely mishaps – or worse. It took time to find the most effective methods of presenting financial information as we developed our management reporting and control systems. In the early days of Covent Garden – in fact for a long time – budgets were based on the previous year's experiences and con-tained good safety margins. As inflation took over in the 1970s, the slimming of margins coincided with the introduction of increasingly sophisticated financial-management techniques, and the reality of where we stood in relation to budgets was more apparent than ever before. This led to detailed board discussion with greater purpose. Obviously, discussion about money was inextricably linked to artistic considerations, and some discussions would lead to painful artistic conclusions, with the postponement or cancellation of a new production, or of some performances, when it was demonstrated that a change might at least ease our monetary difficulties, even if it could not rescue us from them altogether.

In these areas I welcomed the board's help and advice. In those days the board contained sufficient members with artistic knowledge and experience to prevent money from dominating every decision. However cold the financial climate – and it has rarely been warm – artistic considerations must be kept well in focus and artistic ideals cannot be jettisoned at the first obstacle. The board recognized this, and was supportive of the management in the quest for programmes which were artistically sound and yet consistent with financial reality.

Lord Sainsbury succeeded Sir Claus Moser in 1987, and he and I had a year together. When he had been a director between 1969 and 1985 there had been a number of spats between us about money, during which I believed (and I know of at least one board member who felt the same) that the board, led by the chairman, should have been more supportive of me. These earlier experiences resulted in a certain guardedness between us on his appointment as chairman. As it turned out, this was unnecessary, and I found him supportive and considerate around me. I could not have asked for more.

The composition of arts boards is now more open to scrutiny than ever before, and, though boards may remain self-electing, there is greater attention to meeting an organization's needs by appointing men and women with specialist knowledge. In the past the approach was more generalized – which is not to say that those appointed did not have a particular contribution to make, but the requirement today is more specific. At the same time, what is on offer from the widely cultured individual cannot be ignored, and a board without such leavening will be the poorer for it.

Boards can be tiresome to managements, and attendance at board and committee meetings can be a nuisance, but it is my belief that having a non-executive and well-constituted board working closely with management is the most effective way of running an arts organization in this country. Managements may think how good it would be to function without a board, but there is no doubt in my mind that the support and advice which boards can provide are invaluable. To some, boards may have looked like mere clubs, but this is a distorted view of their present reality – we are long past the days of old chums and cronies being invited to join them. The good ones are made up of like-minded men and women dedicated to the organization which they represent and determined to find the means of ensuring its progress. Membership is a highly responsible assignment, not to be undertaken lightly.

11 *The Years since 1988*

My contract as general director was due to end in July 1989. There had been talk about extending it, largely as the result of the appointment as music director of Bernard Haitink, who asked that my contract should run in parallel with his. That was a request which could not be met for many reasons – and one which had been made by other conductors in the past, but similarly rejected. It was flattering for me, but impossible for the organization.

In any event, it was time for change. I had spent most of my working life at Covent Garden, and had been general director (initially I was called general administrator) since 1970. Some would argue that this was too long for one person to be at the head of an organization, whether it be Covent Garden or anywhere else. But this is to overlook an important factor in the building and development of opera and ballet companies, one from scratch and the others from relative infancy: continuity in the overall direction of the theatre managing them.

David Webster had been in office for twenty-five years, and through his personal authority and skills, and through the talents and commitment of the hundreds of men and women who joined forces with him, he had brought the Royal Opera House from nothing in the immediate post-war years to being respected as one of the truly great opera houses of the world – and all achieved with a fraction of the public funding enjoyed in most of Europe. In my judgement, a break in his sequence of direction could have delayed that progress. In my being appointed to succeed Webster, the importance of continuity was made clear. There was every chance that I would continue his tradition, albeit in different ways, reflecting my personality and style.

By the beginning of 1987 the board had decided not to renew my contract. While I was sad that a lifetime at Covent Garden was coming to an end, I was also relieved to be giving up institutional responsibilities and to have the prospect of time to do other things that were coming my way. By then I also wanted a life that was free of the everyday demands and pressures of an opera house. Those are not considerate of private life, and there is no question that my family had paid a price for my attachment and commitment to the Royal Opera House. The balance between public and private responsibility is difficult to strike, and I suspect that few ever really get it right. I did not.

Once this decision had been made, I urged Claus Moser, the chairman, to start looking for a successor as quickly as possible. Finding those with the right experience and qualifications to manage an opera house is difficult and time-consuming, as I had witnessed elsewhere – even in Germany, where, with over sixty opera houses, you would imagine there to be a plentiful supply of suitably qualified men and women. In 1976, for example, Günther Rennert, the intendant of the Bavarian State Opera in Munich, was retiring. I was with him a few months before the date of his departure. No successor had been found, and he was adamant that he would not stay beyond the end of that season. In the end, the only solution which the Bavarian Minister of Culture could find was to persuade August Everding to leave Hamburg, where he had been intendant for only a short time. Everding was happy to return to Munich, his city of adoption, where he had previously been director of the Kammerspiele Theatre. However, it was a move that brought a degree of odium on his head. Entering the Hamburg auditorium just after the announcement of his new appointment, he heard shouts of 'Traitor!' being addressed at him. Changes of management as rapid as this are undesirable.

The post of Webster's successor had not been advertised but instead a group of likely candidates had been invited to apply. Later, some disagreed with this, believing that all public-appointment vacancies should be made known, and a question about the absence of an advertisement was asked in Parliament, by Robert Strauss. Lord Goodman, then chairman of the Arts Council, let his views be known, not doubting that I would still have been appointed but arguing that my position would have been strengthened if I had been put through the advertising hoop. That is a matter of opinion, and there was a typical skirmish between him and Lord Drogheda, the then chairman of the Royal Opera House, on this subject. What was not understood in the late 1960s was that appointments of this kind were not being generally advertised – and certainly not in Europe. Now, however, my successor was to be advertised for. There were also discussions about possible candidates with a wide-ranging group of people, including Sir Georg Solti.

I was not involved with the selection process, and was happy not to be, although with my considerable experience of managing an opera house I could have made a useful contribution to the questioning and discussion. The selection panel – Sir Claus Moser, Lord Gibson, Sir Denis Forman, Colette Clark and Brian Nicholson – was faced with a formidable task in choosing the right candidate. There were a few applicants with opera-house experience, and those eventually considered were Hugues Gall, the then director of the Grand Théâtre in Geneva and who had not applied; Brian McMaster, the director of Welsh National Opera; Michael Hampe, the intendant of Cologne Opera; Cesare Mazzonis, artistic director of the Teatro Communale in Florence; Paul Findlay, assistant director at the Royal Opera House; Anthony Russell-Roberts, administrative director of the Royal Ballet; and Henry Wrong, director of the Barbican Centre and formerly assistant to Rudolf Bing at the Metropolitan Opera House in New York. There were also a number with television and arts management backgrounds, and these included John Drummond, Jeremy Isaacs and Humphrey Burton.

The most experienced and suitable of these candidates would have been Hugues Gall. Having worked initially in the French Ministry of Culture, Gall became Rolf Liebermann's assistant when the latter took over the management of the Paris Opéra in 1973. He understands ballet and opera in a way few others do, and would have been ideal but for one thing: the differing French and British cultures, expressed both in the levels of subsidy in the two countries and in personal and managerial attitudes. I talked to him about this at the time, and have done so again recently. He continues to believe that a Frenchman would not fare well here as intendant. Gall is shrewd, and declined to go to Paris until he thought the moment was appropriate. In London he could not see the time ever being right, and decided not even to come for an interview.

Jeremy Isaacs had been appointed to the board in 1985, and at that time it had occurred to Claus Moser that he might be my successor. Moser had mentioned this possibility to Denis Forman alone among board members. Now, at the conclusion of the interviews, Isaacs was appearing as the front runner, but not with the unanimous support of the panel. The final decision, it seems, was formed by what was described by one panel member as 'the Moser–Forman axis', determined to achieve Isaacs's nomination. They won the day.

Just as Jeremy Isaacs was being offered Covent Garden, he was asked if he would let his name go forward as a candidate for the post of director-general of the BBC, following the sacking of Alisdair Milne. This is a job in a million, and Isaacs felt that he could not let the opportunity go by. Accordingly, he asked Covent Garden if they would wait while he went through the BBC interviewing process. That was agreed and the outcome was awaited – which did not turn out in Isaacs's favour, contrary to many predictions. So he accepted Covent Garden's invitation. The fact that he put Covent Garden in second place and that his real interests appeared to lie elsewhere did not go unnoticed. Frankly, it was not a good omen.

I was disappointed that my successor was not a man with opera house or theatre experience. This is not to say that opera houses are so unique that they cannot be well managed by anybody without this experience, but it is a huge advantage to know how they operate and to be aware of the pitfalls which lie around every corner. This was very much the case with Covent Garden, as it faced a huge redevelopment programme and an uncertain financial future.

Isaacs had indicated to Channel 4 that he would remain there until the arrival of his successor. However, when this was announced as being Michael Grade, Isaacs was so enraged by the choice that he left immediately, threatening all manner of repercussions if Grade dared do anything to downgrade Channel 4's programmes or to change its policy in a way that departed radically from its original aims and aspirations. So, instead of being available to come to Covent Garden in 1988, with the possibility of operating in tandem with me until a date nearer to the expiry of my contract, he was around from the autumn of 1987. There was no way that we could both be there for two years, and I agreed that I would leave in July 1988.

It is true, of course, that Jeremy Isaacs had been a board member for a short while and had some insight into the difficulties besetting Covent Garden, but this is obviously not the same as experience of facing and handling them directly. Isaacs's television career had been very successful and he had shown real flair for assembling talented teams around him for creating such programmes as *The World at War*. The establishment and early years of Channel 4 were nothing short of a triumph and again demonstrated a serious gift for putting together and making television programmes of high quality and interest. Isaacs's entrepreneurial skills were undoubted, but what had reached my ears from a variety of sources raised a question mark over his managerial abilities. The Royal Opera House needed both, and as much as I wanted him to succeed, for the sake of a great institution as much as anything else, I was unsure that his approach to its direction would provide it with what was required. There is a big difference beween the working of a Channel-4 type of organization and an opera house. What suits one may not be right for the other.

Departing in 1988 was increasingly suiting me. John Pritchard had earlier telephoned from San Francisco to ask if I would be willing to let him propose me as Terry McEwan's successor as director of the opera there. He was keen to work with me, and pressed me hard to agree. I declined, because I did not want another institutional function, much as I would have enjoyed being with Pritchard, a musician I greatly admired. That would have come to naught anyway, because he tragically died. Sometime after that the president of the Netherlands Opera sought my advice about a new director for Amsterdam and in the course of one conversation asked if I would allow my name to be put in the ring. Again I declined, for the same reasons, but argued strongly for the engagement of Pierre Audi, who happily was engaged and is proving to be an imaginative opera-house director as well as stage director.

Looking back over this period reveals an extraordinary kaleidoscopic sequence of events and the role that networking plays in our lives, with one event leading to another. For example, Audi's appointment to Amsterdam required the board of the Almeida Theatre to seek new directors. These were to be Ian McDiarmid and Jonathan Kent, who were determined to turn the Almeida from a receiving to a producing house – something which they have achieved with conspicuous success. In their early days there they sought a new chairman, and in the course of a conversation with Martha Clarke, the American choreographer and a mutual friend, my name came up. Martha urged them to approach me, which they did, and I accepted their invitation. Thus began one of the happiest periods of my life.

I was more and more realizing that all sorts of opportunities were open to me and that it would be an advantage to be free to say yes to those that appealed. Proposals came from several directions, some pro bono and some paid. The result has turned out to be a happy mix of the two. It was also encouraging that some two years after I had left Covent Garden the mayor of Zurich and a member of the opera-house council flew to

London to invite me to be the intendant of the Zurich Opera. This was too good to be true, and I asked for time to consider it, because by now I was beginning to miss regular theatre life. While there was plenty to do, I sensed the danger of some vacuum developing. I talked to Swiss friends, who gave me mixed advice, and to Georg and Valerie Solti, who were enthusiastic and urged me to accept. After prolonged consideration, however, I declined for the same reasons as before.

When I first expressed my doubts to the mayor, he immediately told me that I need not be at every performance but could take reasonable time off: I could do the job differently from Covent Garden. I explained that I could not imagine how that could be, and that in any event the theatre needed strong leadership from a director who was more often there than not. For me, physical presence and direct knowledge of all that is going on are prerequisites for a director of an opera house.

One of the conditions that Isaacs made on his appointment was that he should remain a board member. I regarded that as a mistake. I had rejected a place on the board for myself some years previously. At that time Sir Joseph Lockwood was very much around Covent Garden, raising money for a first phase of proposed redevelopment, and as chairman of the board of the Young Vic he had recently appointed Frank Dunlop as director of that theatre, with a seat on the board. Sir Joseph considered this as essential for the effective functioning of a chief executive. He lobbied for my election to the board, until he was convinced that I did not want it or believe it to be right – a view shared by the directors.

The articles and memoranda of association of arts organizations generally provide only for unpaid directors. These can, of course, be amended, but they originally were drawn up in this manner because boards were seen as non-executive bodies, largely comprising men and women with a serious interest in the art form their organization presented, and working without remuneration. Lack of remuneration is also a stipulation of the Charity Commissioners for the boards of charitable organizations, which most arts institutions are. Directors were to be an organization's watchdogs, concerned with financial control and propriety, public taste, and a sound artistic policy which reflected well the organization's aims and which did not put the enterprise at unreasonable financial risk.

Boards could and should call into question the management's artistic plans and financial judgements when there is doubt about their validity. A work might be queried on grounds of artistic merit or potentially poor box-office returns, or the whole season's plans might be questioned for

lack of good balance. In any of these instances it behoves the management to re-examine its plans and report again to the board, either
acknowledging its views and offering changes, or arguing for the original
proposals. If the latter, then the board should accept those and fully
support the management in their implementation. For this procedure to
be effective, the independence of the management from the board is
essential. If it is otherwise, discussion and the asking of searching questions by a group of men and women who are largely not arts professionals will be inhibited. The delivery of faits accomplis is much easier,
too, in that situation. The challenging of artistic and financial proposals
must be open and constructive if it is to be effective. No obstacles should
be put in the way of that. Above all, accountability and transparency
must not be jeopardized.

(I should say that some management consultants take a contrary view
and argue that a management is strengthened by board membership and
that ideally the key senior managers should all be board members. In my
experience, this is not desirable.)

There is the risk that board meetings will be taken by their members as
a forum to express likes and dislikes, to advocate this or that performer,
and sometimes to inhibit the artistic aspirations of the management –
perhaps unintentionally but nevertheless effectively. Artistic policy, both
its establishment and its development, must be management-led, but the
board must share in that process and have the opportunity to comment
and criticize. Boards concentrating solely on finance and management –
as nowadays seems too often the case – cannot be true guardians of the
institutions which they represent. Board members have to be motivated
by an artistic vision and be participants in its realization if they are to
respond imaginatively to the financial demands of the programmes
created by their artistic directors. This is no sinecure: board membership
is demanding of time and commitment.

Surprisingly, Covent Garden directors seemed not to appreciate these
finer points of board–management relationships in agreeing to Jeremy
Isaacs's request. Or perhaps they did, but felt unable to refuse. He was,
after all, *in situ*. But they would have been well advised to have acted
differently.

When I left in July 1988 and Jeremy Isaacs had taken my place, it
was perhaps inevitable that he would say that the House was in the
doldrums and needed revitalizing. In such situations, memory is short

and selective. Certainly an injection of more cash was needed, but that had always been the case, and there was a need for a greater rate of new productions than we had felt able to achieve regularly during the previous few years. Apart from a determination not to engage in deficit budgeting – which the Arts Council would anyway not have permitted – we had restricted the number of new productions in favour of engaging the best singers and conductors whom we could assemble, and giving good rehearsal time to revivals as well as to new productions. Such a policy does not come without a substantial price tag, but there is no alternative if Covent Garden is to remain a centre of excellence. Principles of casting, rehearsing and performing had been well tested over the years, and it was its adherence to the *stagione* for the opera that set Covent Garden above most other opera companies. Departure from that would result only in a long-term decline in standards and make Covent Garden little different from the majority of European opera houses.

Unquestionably the opera and ballet repertoires needed enlargement, and some elderly productions needed to be refreshed. The recurring question was how to achieve this with a declining public subvention, in real terms, and likely audience hostility to greatly increased seat prices. As for the latter, the board and management were in any case wedded to a policy of affordable tickets and believed that it was incumbent on them to maintain this. That did not prevent some seats being sold at whatever price the market would bear, to enable a substantial number of seats to be offered at lower prices. Even so, the number of high-priced seats was restricted in order to give reasonable access to a broad section of the public. For example, premium-priced stalls seats – tickets for which were bought largely by companies for regular attendance each week – were limited to 10 per cent of the theatre's capacity.

In the 1970s, sponsorship was beginning to be a regular source of extra funding, but at that time nothing of the order expected in the late 1980s and 1990s could be anticipated or realized from this source. There was a concern that public funding might be at risk if private fund-raising proved too successful – with a danger of loss of continuity of funding if private sources declined – and in any case commerce and business were not yet ready to support the arts on the scale enjoyed in recent years. There was one person, George Whyte, a Hungarian settled in England for a long time, a trained musician and formerly chairman of the furniture store Maples, who believed that more could be done to stimulate the interest of the business community. To achieve this, he proposed to the

Covent Garden board the establishment of an enterprise board, composed of artistically inclined businessmen working in conjunction with the management and the main board. He also had strong views about the plans and strategy for the proposed redevelopment of the House, considering them ill-conceived. Anxious to find extra money, and warming to him and his ideas, I urged Lord Drogheda, the Covent Garden chairman, to see him. Unhappily – and perhaps typically of a board which regarded itself as self-sufficient and was at times overprotective of itself – Whyte was seen as an interloper, seeking board membership in an unaccustomed and unacceptable manner. His proposals were rejected virtually out of hand, which I thought a mistake. There was nothing to be lost and possibly much to be gained, at least with private funding, given the likely and necessary change in the balance between sponsorship and public funding. Interestingly, it was not long after this episode that a separate fund-raising body was set up, the Royal Opera House Trust, in 1973.

For years it had been recognized that the Royal Opera House was in serious need of modernization and enlargement. It had not been built for the intensive use to which it was being put in post-war England, and there was a limit to what it could contain and to what men and women working in confined areas and outmoded conditions could continue to achieve. Peter Moro, the architect responsible for the design of the Nottingham Playhouse and the interior of the Royal Festival Hall, had redesigned the upper part of the House during a modest modernization programme in 1964, when the gallery and amphitheatre had been joined together and equipped with comfortable seating. At the same time the theatre had been completely rewired and the stage floor had been replaced; apart from that, no other major work had been done since 1902. In that year the stage lifts had been installed, and since then they had continued to be driven by motors originally designed for submarines. The motors' date was stamped on them, and they were removed only on the closure of the theatre in 1997.

The announcement in 1964 of the intended removal of the Covent Garden fruit and vegetable market to a site at Nine Elms in Battersea meant the release of land on which the Royal Opera House could expand, and was the signal for action – strongly encouraged by the chairman, Lord Drogheda. He first advocated that Gollins, Melvin & Ward – the same firm of architects as the Covent Garden Market

Authority was employing for the new market buildings – be engaged to plan the modernization and enlargement of the House. They had a fine reputation (the P & O and Commercial Union buildings in the City were just two examples of their work at the time), but the logic behind the chairman's advocacy escaped me and most others. In fact, the architectural community was annoyed when Gollins, Melvin & Ward were appointed without competition or selection procedure.

It was decided to conduct the modernization programme in two stages. The first was to deal with the pressing need for an opera production rehearsal studio on site (full-scale rehearsals were previously held in the old Troxy Cinema in the Commercial Road, wasting time, money and energy in travel), a proper chorus rehearsal room to replace an inadequate and ill-equipped space, and opera dressing rooms, with wardrobe and make-up areas. Two studios for the Royal Ballet were also to be included. This extension was completed in 1982 – paid for by private donations for the greater part, with the balance covered by grants from the Greater London Council and national government. A fine example of neoclassical design by Edmund Ward, it won many plaudits for its appearance and for its functional interior design.

The second, and much larger, part of the redevelopment programme was intended to rectify inadequacies of the stage and technical areas, and to provide sufficient studios to enable the Royal Ballet to work entirely at Covent Garden and abandon its studios at Barons Court, with the endless and tiring journeys on the Piccadilly Line which their use involved.

From the beginning it was realised that government funds were unlikely to be forthcoming for this stage, and such was its scale that payment by private donation alone was unrealistic. Attention turned to commercial development of part of the site to generate a substantial part of the necessary money, and areas for this purpose – including new shops along the James Street frontage – were earmarked as the design progressed. It was this, as much as fund-raising generally, which had led George Whyte to think about ways of raising money for this project other than through partial commercial development of a site which, in his view, should have been wholly given over to arts activities. How successful his ideas would have been we will never know, but we lost an opportunity of exploring a different approach to the solution of a persistent problem.

In 1983, at the behest of the government, an inquiry into the affairs of the Royal Opera House and the Royal Shakespeare Company had been led by Clive Priestley, director of the government's Management and Efficiency Group (the Rayner Unit, otherwise known as Rayner's Rangers). In 1982 representations had been made to the Arts Council and the government about the inadequacy of public arts funding, which caused the Prime Minister, Margaret Thatcher, to ask what happened to all the money currently granted. Contrary to her expectations, the inquiry concluded with a report commenting favourably on the management of both institutions and recommending increased funding. Though the Priestley Report set out its views and recommendations in uncompromising and forthright terms, and those believing in the importance of the arts in national life could only applaud it, the government took another view. Nevertheless, it was embarrassed and discomforted by the report's content, and decided to increase funding for one year – apparently described by Richard Wilding, the Permanent Secretary of the Office of Arts and Libraries, at a meeting as a 'blip'. That was to be it. Priestley was put on the shelf, and efforts to interest subsequent governments in it have failed. However, it remains a landmark among arts reports and a source of reference on principles of public funding, including the important view that the index for the annual increase of grants should be based on a mixture of RPI (Retail Price Index) and AEI (Average Earnings Index) figures.

The increased subsidy for the year 1984/85, although not to be repeated, helped a great deal, and by judicious budgeting and accounting we were able to spread its benefits beyond that year. What has to be recognized, however, is that there is still no political will to support an adequate level of funding of the arts in the United Kingdom. Many pay lip-service to it, but few will go to the stake. In part, this lack of commitment lies in the absence of a long tradition of public funding – a principle which has its origins only in the Second World War, being established as continuing government policy in the immediate post-war period.

On one occasion when Mrs Thatcher came to a performance at Covent Garden, she was entertained to dinner during the intervals and I found myself seated between her and the Duke of Norfolk. As the Prime Minister turned to talk to the person on her left, the Duke, in a voice loud enough for her to hear and with a twinkle in his eye, asked me how arts funding in the United Kingdom compared with that in Europe. I started to reply, but before I could get very far Mrs Thatcher, having picked up the question, joined in to explain that, because the UK economy was not as strong as that of much of Europe, there was no way that we could match European levels of subsidy. When I suggested that this was a matter of priorities, the subject was changed. As we left the table, the Duke said he hoped he had not embarrassed me, but he had found the opportunity to provoke her irresistible.

On another occasion, New Year's Day 1981, the Prime Minister was in the Royal Opera House and was questioning Sir Claus Moser, the chairman, about a forthcoming television broadcast of *Les Contes d'Hoffmann*. I was to join the party, but had been detained backstage and was late. As I entered the royal-box ante-room, I was greeted by an agitated chairman and urged to talk to Mrs Thatcher because she was being difficult with him over fees for this broadcast. After a greeting, we became engaged on the same subject, and when I had told her what our fee was to be I was rebuked for accepting what she regarded as a derisory amount. I contradicted her and explained that this was the highest management fee ever paid by a broadcasting company. She continued to argue, and I told her that she did not understand the economics of broadcasting. We were summoned to our seats, and as we entered the box I whispered to Moser that I had wrecked our relations with the government and that we should expect the worst. The interval came and, much to our surprise, Mrs Thatcher was beaming. She talked about many things over dinner, but never once mentioned television. My point had gone home.

In spite of this flicker of understanding, there was always the feeling that Mrs Thatcher distrusted arts managers and believed them to be profligate, incapable of controlling expenditure, and ignorant of good business practice. She probably went further than that and believed that they were really uninterested in sound management and expected to be feather-bedded, which is not the case. The theory of market forces so dominated her thinking and that of her government that the true purpose and significance of public arts funding were lost on them. Financially, these were immensely difficult years for the arts, and ministers seemed reluctant to come to terms with the real issues. The amount of money at stake was trivial, and a willingness to listen and to join in a dialogue in quest of solutions would have made a big difference to all of us in our attitude towards the government.

No one in the arts looks for a blank cheque, but there is an expectation and need of more than has so far been provided. Plural funding has been with us for many years, and it is the commitment of business and private sponsors that has ensured the continuation of much that we take for granted. The problem today is that the balance between private and public funding is too heavily inclined towards the former. Not only does this arouse resentment among supporters, who believe that they are being asked to carry too much of a burden which government should share more equitably, but it can result in a waste of money through artistic resources not being fully exploited in an uncertain financial environment. For example, an opera company requires an orchestra and a chorus of a certain size to meet the demands of programming. If financial stringency forces a company to perform fewer works than normal, and to choose for part of the year's work operas with small forces, then players and singers will be underused. Furthermore, the public will feel short-changed if there is a reduction in repertoire. Standing performers off is not the answer. Success is to be found through developing and working with an ensemble of well-judged size. Reducing its numbers one day and increasing them the next will destroy the very basis on which lasting excellence is to be found. We are drifting fast from these ideals, and I fear that my successors at Covent Garden may not have understood the necessity of sustaining the means to these ends. None of these means has come about by chance. Funding obviously counts for a lot, but not for everything.

New productions are the lifeblood of a performing company, and when financial stringency restricts the number it is essential to find other ways of injecting creative energy – such as taking an existing production, stripping it down musically and dramatically, and reassembling it within a lengthy rehearsal period. A supreme example of the success of this approach was the November 1979 revival of *La Bohème*, with Carlos Kleiber conducting and a cast which included Ileana Cotrubas and Giacomo Aragall, all of whom knew how to use the extended rehearsal time to the fullest advantage, resulting in performances of extraordinary quality.

Where this attitude has not been taken, such as in Vienna, it is interesting, though saddening, to see the results. When Ioan Holender became intendant on the death of Eberhart Waechter, in 1992, he succumbed to the demands of the Ministry of Culture to reduce expenditure and live within smaller budgets. There are now few new productions, and the list of singers, conductors, directors and designers appearing there is a pale shadow of what it used to be. The consequences are a depressingly low average standard of performance.

*

In spite of a bleak monetary outlook, we mounted seven new productions in my final season: four in the financial year 1987/88 and the remainder in the following year. The straddling of a season across two financial years eases the financial burdens of production and programme planning, in spite of the untidy accounting it can create.

My successors wanted more new productions, and set out to finance them by greatly increasing sponsorship. The view was that money needed to be spent to make money – a wholly acceptable theory if initial and essential expenditure can be satisfactorily covered. John Sainsbury, by now chairman and intent on selling the House at a premium, not a discount, led the way. He asked Alex Alexander, a genius at raising money and then overseeing sponsorship at Glyndebourne, to be chairman of the Royal Opera House Trust and to head the fund-raising for Covent Garden. It was a difficult decision for Alexander to make, but both he and his wife, much as they were committed to Glyndebourne, also loved Covent Garden and were as devoted to the ballet as to the opera. He accepted the invitation – much to the gain of the Royal Opera House, but greatly to the fury of George Christie at Glyndebourne. When this plan was first mooted, I told John Sainsbury that Christie's anger over the loss of Bernard Haitink as music director in the previous year would be as nothing compared with that over the departure of Alex Alexander. I was right! It was a shrewd appointment, which made a huge difference to Covent Garden's immediate financial standing, although Alexander was to be perplexed by the House's changing financial demands. 'They keep moving the goalposts,' he once said to me.

By the time of my departure, Jeremy Isaacs was well prepared for his first season. For the time being he was keeping most of the staff who had worked for me, although this was not to be for long, and one by one my closest associates were to be replaced. But for the intervention of Bernard Haitink, one early casualty would have been Paul Findlay, who by then had become opera director. Haitink insisted on Findlay's retention, and threatened his own resignation if that did not happen. At breakfast one morning at the Savoy, Isaacs spoke to me of his dilemma. I said that the choice was simple: 'Keep Findlay and you have Haitink, or you lose both. That you cannot afford.'

Findlay proved invaluable to Jeremy Isaacs in his first years, not only in managing the opera company, but also in providing an essential element of continuity in the affairs of the House. This was warmly acknowledged by Isaacs in a phone call to me during his first season, and later publicly and generously.

Unhappily, the relationship between Isaacs and Haitink never flourished. It is hard to know whether this was because of impatience on Isaacs's part in dealing with a reticent musician or because of a failure to realize that the music director needed regular time for discussion and the formulation of plans. The end result was that Haitink felt increasingly isolated and decided to concentrate on his own performances in the House, leaving all other performers and performances to their own devices, and later to another uncommunicative person in Nicholas Payne, who was eventually appointed as Findlay's successor. If the music director is not involved in meetings to discuss and agree programming and casting for the whole season, I cannot see the point of having him – rather call him principal conductor and let him legitimately devote his time and energy to his own performances and the orchestra. This is what happened, but it is not what Haitink or I expected when he first joined us. Having established a good working practice with Colin Davis, whereby he was intimately involved with the artistic administrator and myself in deciding the choice of operas and casting, either at regular meetings or by phone and fax if away, it never occurred to me that the involvement of the music director would not be a prime consideration of the new management.

I had been a hands-on and omnipresent director, who had created certain expectations over the years. I had grown up at Covent Garden, knew everyone, and had acquired considerable knowledge and expertise in the presentation of opera and ballet, and in the managing of an opera house. Opera houses are complex organizations. This is particularly true of the Royal Opera House, at which opera and ballet are uniquely equal partners, although equality of opportunity has often been difficult, and sometimes impossible, to provide. Goodwill is an essential ingredient in the successful functioning of any institution. This in turn must evolve into consent, because it is by this that an opera house can best function. This process does not come about by itself: it requires constant attention from the top.

I was fortunate in inheriting from David Webster a House imbued with what I can only describe as an immensely strong and vibrant family spirit. Having been there for many years, I understood how much this – as well, of course, as the talents of artists and staff – contributed to Covent Garden's uniqueness. The Royal Opera House had become hugely admired and respected throughout the world, and performers wanted to appear there. They appreciated and enjoyed its serious but relaxed and intrigue-free working atmosphere, and felt themselves part of a family. Many of the staff used to say that they had come to work at Covent Garden for only a few months but had stayed for years, if not a lifetime. When silver medals were introduced in 1971 for those with twenty-five years' service, 10 per cent of the payroll became eligible – a startling commentary.

Not to understand this, or to ignore it, could only change the environment and lead to a situation where performers and staff would see Covent Garden merely as a place to work. Being there would lose its pleasure: it would be just another job. Their professionalism would compensate for this, at least for a time, but more than professionalism is needed to make great performing companies and opera houses, as Covent Garden had demonstrated.

I am sure the House was ready to respond to a new general director, but there had to be a meeting point between Isaacs's expectations and those of the artists and staff, and I think that there was misjudgement about where that should be. Those who work there do expect you to know who they are – maybe not immediately, but early recognition by a greeting would always have been appreciated. I had told Jeremy Isaacs that he needed from the beginning to set expectations of his presence at a level that he would be comfortable with and which he could sustain. I believe that he did, but the level was not what everyone had been used to.

Opera houses are what they are. Unless you are familiar with them, they are baffling because of the complexities of their operation, the hundreds of strands of activity that go to make a performance, the rigorous discipline of curtain-up every night (often in more than one theatre), considerations of money, the unpredictability of the box office, human failure, technical blips, the insecurity of performers and their need of real and regular support and encouragement, the last-minute crises through illness or injury putting the show at risk, and so on.

Coming from the hugely successful creation and establishing of Channel 4, it must have been a shock for Jeremy Isaacs now to find himself in charge of a cash-starved organization, with responsibility for three performing companies and the presentation of some five hundred performances each year. This is not to say that Channel 4 was overflowing with money, but it had sufficient to meet its immediate needs and to deal with daily demands. Not so at Covent Garden, where it must have been frustrating for Isaacs not to be able to respond positively to many of the requests for authorization of extra expenditure, however justified.

Telephoning some months after I had left Covent Garden, Isaacs told me that the job was much more difficult than he had ever thought it would be, and that shortage of money was his biggest problem. I can understand why he saw it from that perspective, but those of us accustomed to such a state of affairs would strive to find good solutions within the constraints of what was available as well as fighting for more. We had known nothing else, and lived with the reality of it – much though we wanted it to be different. We let our views be known where it mattered – not necessarily from coffee-table tops, as was Peter Hall's way, but quietly and persistently. We aired comparisons with the funding of European opera houses on innumerable occasions, but found that they cut no ice with government and that in the end they were counterproductive. Arguments that stood a better chance of striking home had to be put forward, although, compelling as they might be to us, few seemed to hit their target.

One important issue which the last ten years do raise is the wisdom of appointing those without opera-house or theatrical experience to the most senior positions in opera houses. Artistically there have been substantial gains at Covent Garden and the Coliseum in this decade, but much else has not been right and the price paid has been unacceptably high. Of course, underfunding has been a serious problem, but not everything can be blamed on that, and deficiencies in financial and human management cannot be lightly set aside.

Directors of opera houses must possess a wide knowledge of opera and, in the case of Covent Garden, ballet as well – not just in the sense of knowing about them, but from a deeper understanding. Musically and technically, they should be so equipped that they can discuss the finer points of works and their productions with conductors, directors and designers, aesthetically and practically. The ability to challenge ideas and demands from a well-informed standpoint is essential, and it is necessary on occasions to be able to persuade people to accept other, usually less costly, solutions than those proposed – a simpler set for a director and designer, for example, or less rehearsal time for a conductor. Whatever the situation, the general director must be able to argue with the conviction that comes from knowledge and experience.

Of course, there are musicians and technicians in an opera-house management team who will also be involved in these processes. Indeed, it will be their responsibility to start them and to see them through. At some point, however, the director may be called in to arbitrate. Then his skills in assessing what is acceptable and in bringing about consensus and agreement with all parties will be put to the test.

One method of reducing cost which had long been adopted was to run the entire opera house at less than its full establishment, usually twenty-five or so under strength. That was not ideal, but with careful selection of the areas in which it was applied the problems were containable, although in some instances they placed an unduly heavy burden on those immediately affected. There was also a policy of non-automatic replacement, so that when a vacancy occurred it had to be reviewed by the head of department and the director of administration before action to fill it could be taken.

Isaacs, it seemed, took a different view and concluded that working under strength was unacceptable – at least at the beginning of his time, until financial stringency drove him to other conclusions. With an increase in new productions in prospect and a heavier workload for the stage, he agreed to the introduction of a night gang to strike the scenery of the evening performance and set that needed for the next morning's rehearsal. Hitherto, that task had been undertaken by a day shift working late after the show and finishing the setting in the morning. Because of the cramped space on the stage and poor access to the main storage in the adjoining Floral Hall, however, this was not a foolproof operation and there were occasions when the stage was not ready in time for rehearsals. This caused consternation, and did not help in maintaining discipline – particularly with the orchestra and chorus, who were present on time and knew the price of being late. Nevertheless, night crews are costly and are an extravagant solution to this difficulty. There is not always sufficient work to fill their scheduled hours, and there is no guarantee that even they will deliver in the morning. I admit that this is an intractable problem, but Isaacs' was an easy solution – attractive in theory, but expensive in practice.

For many years we had discussed the appointment of a dramaturgs, and this had again become an issue soon after Colin Davis's arrival as music director. This is a key post in German opera houses, although it was only after the First World War that the dramaturg became the person with special responsibility for texts and versions of operas, and who edits programmes and writes explanatory articles as well as keeping an eye open for new work. In the eighteenth and early nineteenth centuries the dramaturg had fulfilled the role of producer, a function which did not then otherwise exist.

In the early 1970s we had identified a possible candidate for this post, but financial considerations prevailed and we concluded that we could not afford to go ahead. This was a pity, and I have little doubt that we would have benefited from having somebody in that position. Jeremy Isaacs had the same thoughts and went ahead with the appointment of Patrick Carnegy, then music books editor at Faber, as dramaturg. For anybody to be effective in this role a profound knowledge of opera and current performing practice is essential, and it is difficult to understand why another person with wider operatic experience was not sought.

Examination of annual reports from 1988 onwards reveals a sharp increase in numbers on the payroll: from 1,053 in the 1987/88 season to 1,152 in 1990/91. Twenty of this increase was attributable to the engagement of the night gang, fifteen to marketing, and fourteen to front of house. The Sadler's Wells Royal Ballet strength was increased by thirteen as the company moved to Birmingham and became dependent on its own management and technical resources. Those Birmingham appointments were essential and unavoidable, but there was doubt in the minds of some about the absolute necessity of the remaining additions and the ability of the House to sustain the extra cost. Indeed, as financial pressures grew, the numbers decreased from that peak to 1,000 in the 1995/96 season. There was much talk, and indeed action, about redundancies, as though radical pruning was being undertaken. It was not that, but the restoration of numbers to roughly what they had been in 1987/88, and a little below that figure in 1996/97. There had been miscalculations of the cost implications of the enlarged staff, desirable though it might have seemed in attempting to improve the efficiency of the House and to ease the workload in some areas. There was not the money to carry it.

The move of the Sadler's Wells Royal Ballet to Birmingham was politically and socially immensely important. As long ago as the early 1970s, I had been exploring the possibilities of basing this company out of London. One possibility had been to merge it with Northern Ballet and to establish Manchester as the base for the combined company. I talked to Simon Townley, the chairman of Northern Ballet, about this. We were so concerned that no one should be aware of our discussions that we met on a park bench to go over the advantages and disadvantages of such a move! The outcome was not at all straightforward, and it eventually became clear that the timing and circumstances were not right for such a plan to win support. The idea was dropped, and the companies remained separate.

Joining forces with another company was not practical, but I continued to believe that Covent Garden needed a regional foothold. We were under attack for not touring the regions with the Royal Opera and the Royal Ballet. The last occasion when the opera company had been on the road was in 1964, when the Royal Opera House had been closed for essential repairs and alterations. The Royal Ballet had continued to tour, but at high cost and often at a disadvantage because of the inadequacies of theatres (a situation now partially remedied).

As an alternative to touring our big companies, I believed that we could begin to serve the needs of the taxpayer better if we chose one location which would have regular visits by both of them. Manchester was the obvious city to be explored, with an excellent cultural tradition and a population of 10 million within an hour's drive of the centre. Encouraged by the Arts Council and by Bob Scott, who was managing Manchester's Opera House and the Palace Theatre, in the late 1970s we persuaded the Greater Manchester Council and Manchester City Council to support our proposal to make Manchester the second home of the Royal Opera and to assist in its realization by endorsing the enlargement of the Palace Theatre. Progress was slow, and an injection of private enterprise became necessary to bring the whole operation to a point where work on modernization could begin and a cash flow be guaranteed. It was a local businessman, Raymond Slater, and his company, Norwest Holst, who brought energy and money to this venture and ensured its completion. They did this because of their conviction that the project would be good for Manchester and the North-West by enriching the cultural life of the region. A huge debt is owed to them, and it is a sad commentary on local and national attitudes that their generosity was never publicly recognized.

The first Manchester season by the Royal Opera, in 1981, was reasonably successful, but those who lived in that area needed to demonstrate more convincingly that they really wanted a metropolitan company to visit their principal city regularly, by supporting it much more strongly than they had done so far. Nevertheless, there was enough evidence to support another season in 1983 and to justify the investment in the Palace Theatre. In any event, it would have been irresponsible to abandon the venture at that early stage and not to take advantage of the initial public response: the building of a regular audience takes time. However, others were soon to determine our fate in Manchester. As the second opera season was ending – with audiences of 66, 82 and 97 per cent of capacity for the three works presented (*La Clemenza di Tito, Il Trovatore* and *Madama Butterfly*) – I heard from the Arts Council that it would no longer provide funds for seasons there. I phoned William Rees-Mogg, who was the chairman of the Arts Council at the time, to protest angrily at this decision and its timing. Our heated conversation ended with Rees-Mogg putting the phone down on me. True, the costs were high, but we believed it was money well spent and that, given regular visits, a substantial and loyal audience would have been established. This was a serious attempt to develop a regional base for a metropolitan company and to meet the demands of taxpayers who contributed to Covent Garden's costs and yet could not attend performances in London. Unhappily and misguidedly, it was never given the chance to demonstrate what might have been achieved.

Undeterred, and still determined to find a way of giving Covent Garden and at least one of its companies regular exposure in the regions, I was encouraged by Norman Buchan, a former Labour shadow arts minister, to ensure that our political and social roots became sunk more deeply than they were, in and out of London. He was clear that a wholly metropolitan-based operation would eventually be at risk from a public-funding viewpoint if it concentrated solely on its home operation.

By this time, 1982/3, Simon Rattle was beginning to make his mark as principal conductor of the City of Birmingham Symphony Orchestra, strongly supported by the city council and its chief executive, Tom Caulcott, a cultured and civilized man determined to persuade his political masters to make Birmingham an important cultural centre. Already the Hippodrome Theatre was being modernized under the guidance of the trust which now owned it, and which wanted to provide first-rate facilities for larger companies. So it did not take a big leap of the imagination to see that Birmingham could become the home of the Sadler's Wells Royal Ballet. Through the untiring efforts of Jack Phipps at the Arts Council and Paul Findlay, my assistant, a plan was put together which won the support of Birmingham City Council and the Arts Council.

The Sadler's Wells Royal Ballet did not look upon the idea with much favour at the beginning. In fact there was serious hostility towards it, and it was obvious that a huge amount of time and effort would be required to bring the dancers and staff round to seeing the benefits of the move –

splendid facilities for all aspects of the company's work and the prospect of a much needed injection of cash towards everyday expenditure. To bring an independent and unprejudiced view to the discussions, I recommended that Dave Allen, a member of the Priestley team and by now well informed about ballet, be engaged to write a report on the projected move. This was helpful in clarifying the issues and in bringing the debate to a head.

This occurred after I had left. By the autumn of 1988 the City of Birmingham had offered £2.55 million for enlarging and improving the Hippodrome to provide tailor-made facilities, and up to £500,000 per annum for five years for revenue purposes, to be matched by the Arts Council. In addition, the Hippodrome Trust was to give £1 million towards removal expenses.

In the meantime, objections to the move continued to be heard. It was seen as a rupture with history, and there was concern about removing the company from the centre of artistic activity, London – little aware that there is life beyond the metropolis, as dancers and staff have subsequently discovered to their delight. Eventually, reason prevailed: the advantages were beginning to be understood, and most were willing to give the scheme a fair trial. This they did, and no one has looked back since going to Birmingham in 1990. It was the right decision of Jeremy Isaacs and the board to continue to encourage this and finally to bring about removal of the company to Birmingham by a resolution of the board in November 1988.

Peter Wright, the director of the company for many years, was initially reluctant, but was soon to understand the advantages and became a powerful force in leading the company to its new home. He has been succeeded by David Bintley, a rare creative talent, who is opening up new vistas for the company and I believe is beginning to create an audience loyalty for ballet such as was developed by Simon Rattle for music. How fortunate Birmingham is, and how brilliantly the city's vision and investment in talent have paid off!

The company retained its links with Covent Garden for a while, even though it had a separate board. Now, however, it is totally independent, which is admirable in many respects, and gives the company an essential sense of freedom in building its own future; but it does negate that Covent Garden–Birmingham link, which I had considered politically important.

*

As the move of Sadler's Wells Royal Ballet to Birmingham got under way, the two-year closure of the Royal Opera House for modernization and enlargement, then planned to start in 1993, became a pressing matter of discussion, including how best the Royal Opera and the Royal Ballet could be deployed during those two years. Naturally, first thoughts were towards the Theatre Royal, Drury Lane – a theatre well sited from the point of view of audiences familiar with Covent Garden. With some adaptation, it would be capable of taking both companies – not in repertory but separately, as was more than likely to be the case with any existing theatre. There was a major snag, however, and that was *Miss Saigon*: a highly successful musical with heavy advance bookings and a long run in prospect. Cameron Mackintosh, its producer, had a run-of-the-show agreement which allowed him to remain there until bookings fell below a certain level. At that moment there was understandably no question of him or the theatre's owners, Stoll Moss, giving up a lucrative production, although Mackintosh did later offer to transfer *Miss Saigon* to the Lyceum, provided that any losses on the move were made good by Covent Garden. It was not to be.

Some years earlier, in anticipation of redevelopment and the need for a temporary home for the Covent Garden companies during the inevitable closure, I had started to investigate the possible purchase of Drury Lane. Along with others, I was also interested in establishing a theatre devoted to dance in all its forms. One auditorium would not satisfy all dance requirements, and an advantage of Drury Lane was the huge backstage area, which could accommodate another performing space. Its purchase, with Sadler's Wells being used for mid-scale companies, would have satisfied present and future demands. However, I soon discovered that Robert Holmes à Court, the owner of Stoll Moss, was adamant that he would neither sell the theatre nor let it on a long lease, which for us would have been the more practical and realistic alternative. His wife, Janet Holmes à Court, attached great importance to its ownership and regarded it as the flagship of their theatre holdings.

In 1983, attention then turned to the Lyceum, a renowned theatre in the same area but derelict and up for sale by the London Residuary Board. Though better than most existing London theatres, it was not ideal for Covent Garden's needs. The stage is shallow, with no prospect of deepening because of the street immediately behind, which the local authority was unwilling to close. The wing and storage space is limited. The absence of a pit and rehearsal rooms could be rectified, and

additional dressing rooms could be built along the Exeter Street frontage. There was also the matter of internal decoration. The Lyceum had
been built as a family theatre, and Bertie Crewe, its designer, had decorated the auditorium in garish colours which if restored, as was likely to
be required, would not necessarily have suited it well to opera and ballet
performance.

In spite of these limitations, it seemed worth backing one of the
syndicates bidding for the Lyceum. The one chosen was led by Stephen
Hetherington, a theatrical agent, who had discovered a rich source of
money through the owners of the *Washington Times*. On further
inquiry, I discovered that this came from Sun Myung Moon and his
Unification Church organization. The 'Moonies' were the subject of considerable newspaper interest at the time, and I was not happy at the
prospect of being caught up with this dubious body, and of the Royal
Opera House being used for its propaganda purposes. It eventually
emerged that we could be distanced from the money's origins through a
laundering process. I remained uneasy, but was sufficiently convinced to
allow Hetherington to add Covent Garden's name to his bid. However,
the laundering process was never put to the test, because the London
Residuary Board – instructed by government to accept the highest bids
for all its property disposals – sold the Lyceum to George Walker, chairman of the property company Brent Walker, for an astronomical sum,
far outstripping all other offers.

Having lost this round, and really wanting Drury Lane, a year or two
later I came to the conclusion that the way forward could be through the
government purchasing the Lyceum from George Walker, who was by
then in difficulties, and offering it, refurbished and ready for use, to Stoll
Moss in exchange for Drury Lane. The latter has the larger seating capacity, but the stage is much bigger than any musical production requires,
resulting in wasted and unprofitable space which I knew that the owners
had been looking at ways of exploiting. The ballet and opera, on the
other hand, would benefit from that.

There was logic in this scheme, and I tried to persuade successive arts
ministers (there were several at this time) to pursue it as a real solution to
a short- and long-term need. None took it up, usually protesting that
the Treasury would not look at such a proposition. Hayden Phillips, the
Permanent Secretary at the Department of National Heritage, as the
Office of Arts and Libraries had by then become, took a more favourable
view and said that he would call a meeting to discuss it in detail. In spite

of reminders, it never happened. A possible way into the Theatre Royal was lost. Of course it might not have been acceptable to Janet Holmes à Court, who now owned Stoll Moss, following the death of her husband, but the failure to pursue it at all demonstrates a lack of foresight on the part of the ministry and caused the abandonment of a plan which could have avoided the catastrophe which later overwhelmed the Royal Opera House, at least as far as the housing of the the Royal Opera and the Royal Ballet during closure was concerned.

In the course of these discussions with Stephen Hetherington, I telephoned Dame Ninette de Valois to ask what she remembered of the Lyceum during the Diaghilev season of 1926, in which she had appeared. Her long-term memory remains remarkable, and her response was immediate. She recalled that Diaghilev played there only because he could not find another theatre free; he did not like it, and at the end apparently vowed never to return.

While I was still at Covent Garden, Stephen Hetherington produced another plan: for a theatre to be devoted eventually to dance, but which in the short term might be used by both Covent Garden companies. He had found a site at Waterloo which could be made available for the construction of a 2,000-seat auditorium with spacious backstage areas. It was a good plan, and was again to be funded largely from money channelled through the *Washington Times* – a source of concern, though I decided we had to live with this if we were to achieve any of our objectives. Progress in bringing this scheme to fruition was slow, and there was nothing in place by the time I left. The plan was to re-emerge at a later date, and was to be listed among the options being considered by the management and board for housing the Covent Garden companies during closure. However, it later fell by the wayside.

In discussions in September 1989 about the deployment of the companies during the redevelopment closure period, three options were put forward:

1 Performances should continue in another theatre just as at Covent Garden.
2 Activity should be reduced. To what extent it is not recorded.
3 Opera should be abandoned for the duration.

Rough costings were mentioned: £40 million for the first option, £32–35 million for the second, and around £20 million for the third. Other theatres discussed were the Palladium, the Cambridge, the Lyceum and the Dominion. A suggestion for a temporary theatre at Canary Wharf was also put forward by Alex Alexander.

With closure then proposed for 1993, secure plans were urgently needed. It was agreed that there were to be a progress report at the November board meeting, detailed proposals at the January meeting, and decisions taken in March. Neither the year nor the months were to be maintained, with the whole development programme slipping to 1997, although preliminary work would be undertaken before that. Decisions about the deployment of the companies were to be made at a dangerously late moment.

The redevelopment plans were by no means complete when I left in July 1988. Objections to our proposals had come from a number of quarters, and so much time and energy had been spent in firefighting and persuasion that there was a danger of momentum being lost and the whole scheme becoming a lost cause. It was also taking its toll on the management, part of which – including myself – was devoting an inordinate amount of every week to it at the expense of running the opera house. (This has become a huge problem for managements up and down the land as they struggle with rebuilding programmes and Lottery bids.) None of us anticipated the extent of these demands at the beginning. Even though we were not content with the point we had reached in our plans, in 1986 we had decided it was sensible to apply for outline planning consent. Then at least the world would know that we were serious about the project, and we would have a chance to test the water more thoroughly than hitherto possible. The City of Westminster's response was favourable, though guarded and with some reservations.

The financing of this scheme was initially dependent on a substantial injection of money from commercial exploitation of part of the site and a public appeal. The government had made it clear that there would be no help from public funds, although the first phase of the redevelopment programme, completed in 1982 on time and on budget, had been partially financed by grants from national and local governments, which gave some hope that more might be found from these sources for the remainder of the programme, in spite of a warning to me by David Eccles, the Arts Minister at the time, that the decision to buy the land needed for the extension did not guarantee public funding.

There was no question that the Royal Opera House needed modernization – not least to provide better working conditions, to comply with health-and-safety regulations, and to ensure the safety of the whole theatre. For example, the last occasion on which rewiring had been undertaken was during the modest modernization programme in 1964, which had been prompted by the theatre being closed by the Lord Chamberlain on safety grounds. The timbers supporting the gallery had been found to be in a poor state and there was an order to replace them. A huge amount of work had to be undertaken in a few months, but it was superbly planned and was finished on time. A special grant was negotiated from the government for this. In its inimitable way, the Treasury decided that it could not pay the whole amount in one year and urged us to arrange a loan from Coutts against a Treasury guarantee. Our bankers agreed, and once more saved the day for us.

It is important to record how much Covent Garden and a number of other theatres owe to Coutts. Without their earlier willingness to take considerable risks in granting unsecured overdrafts to impoverished companies, some might not have survived. That is true of the Royal Opera House, both in its early days and latterly. It is an amazing record, on which I was surprised that Edna Healey did not comment in her admirable history of the bank.

For Jeremy Isaacs's first season, 1988/89, a deficit of more than £600,000 was forecast, taking into account a contingency of £400,000 and an Enterprise Funding Award of £250,000. No account had been taken of an accumulated deficit of £500,000 from earlier seasons. The programme was to include new productions of *The Prince of the Pagodas* (later postponed because of Kenneth MacMillan's illness), *La Bayadère*, *Il Trovatore* and *Prince Igor* – all large-scale works. Expenditure was predicted to rise by 13 per cent over the previous year, with sponsorship increased by a massive 42 per cent to £7.5 million. With an unbalanced budget and a large unknown in income, much was at risk.

The corporate plan for the three years 1988–91 contained year-on-year seat-price increases of 5 per cent, 7.5 per cent and 5 per cent. The Arts Council grant was predicted to cover 41 per cent of expenditure in 1990/91, compared with 58 per cent in 1985/86, and sponsorship to cover 15 per cent, compared with 8 per cent in 1985/86, reflecting shifting funding emphasis. In turn, box-office revenue was forecast to increase its coverage of costs from 38 per cent to 41 per cent.

In January 1989 another corporate plan was presented to the board. This predicted further losses on a 85 per cent paid attendance after an estimated break-even in 1989/90: a loss of £600,000 in 1990/91 and

of £1.2 million in 1991/92. There was also to be a reduction in performance numbers – from 271 in 1990/91 to 245 for the following two years
– although new opera productions were to rise from seven in 1989/90 to
eleven in the following year and to eight in 1991/92. At this stage only
four new ballet productions were apparently under discussion.

Cost increases for 1989/90 were stated to be 14.6 per cent – a once and
for all increase for that year, according to Jeremy Isaacs – and payroll
costs were likely to show a 9 per cent increase by 1990/91. As costs were
rising, so inevitably were seat prices – at an alarming rate. For the four
years 1988/89 to 1991/92, the RPI forecasts were 7 per cent, 4.5 per
cent, 4 per cent and 5 per cent. The Arts Council grant was expected
not to increase above an annual forecast level of 2 per cent per annum,
although it did increase by 11 per cent in 1990/91. Increases in opera
seat prices were to jump from 7 per cent to 13.5 per cent, followed by
12.5 per cent and 10 per cent. Ballet prices followed more or less the
same pattern.

The board aired its worries over these increases, foreseeing the ill effect
that they would have on audiences and believing that Covent Garden
would become a place for corporate entertainment rather than a theatre
for opera and ballet lovers. Seat prices should ideally increase by no
more than the Retail Price Index, but to keep to such increases without
compensating uplifts in Arts Council grants and private funding, or
reduction in expenditure, would only add to the deficit.

In a further endeavour to combat deficits and rising prices, heroic
assumptions were made about the £4.6 million raised in sponsorship in
1988/89 being increased to £7.6 million, £8.8 million and £9.6 million
in the following three years. These gargantuan amounts had to be viewed
against a fall in Arts Council funding as a proportion of costs from 42
per cent in 1989/90 to 34 per cent in 1991/92. While there was a fall in
the value of public funding in real terms, of course, the decline in the
proportion of expenditure covered by such funding was exacerbated by
the steep rise of expenditure itself. Sponsorship could not be obtained at
the levels needed for balanced budgets and the avoidance of ever growing deficits. For example, in the 1989/90 season projected income from
private sources was to amount to £4.9 million, against a target of £7.1
million. Hope then lay in making good some of this loss in a benefit
performance of *L'Elisir d'Amore* with Luciano Pavarotti. Meanwhile the
Arts Council, it seems, was reconciled to a deficit of £2 million,
although Isaacs mentioned a much higher figure at the time.

Understandably, there was growing concern about sponsorship as a regular and reliable source of funding as that scene became more and more uncertain. Smaller units of giving in support of individual performances were to be sought, and Jeremy Isaacs proposed that new productions should be mounted only against known funding – a statement to be reversed at a later date. This proposal and the seeking of smaller units of giving had been tried before, but their context was now a more difficult financial situation than previously experienced. Not for the first time, the idea of an endowment was aired – raising a large capital sum, interest on which would provide an annual income to supplement other funding sources, as at the Met in New York. However, I suspect that the improbability of an endowment coming on stream in time to provide a rapid answer to Covent Garden's financial ills was soon recognized.

At board meetings around this time, worsening financial forecasts dominated the discussions, and at the first meeting of 1990 insolvency was aired, but found not to be an immediate issue. Nevertheless, it was recommended that the management consultants Peat Marwick be engaged to undertake an independent review – a prudent safeguard in public relations, and crucial to discussions with the Arts Council.

In spite of a deteriorating financial position, ten new opera productions were still included in the budget for one season. Their retention was probably justified on the grounds that production expenditure was still only 5.3 per cent of the total budget, compared with 4.9 per cent over the past three years.

Desperate measures were taken to improve income. Here a serious error was made in the decision substantially to increase amphitheatre prices. For years these had not been subjected to the same level of increase as the rest of the theatre, because of our conviction that a high proportion of the House should remain at truly affordable prices. Socially and politically, this was an essential policy. Substantial increases in amphitheatre prices would be contrary to an inherent element of public-funding philosophy, through allowing access to fewer people. In the 1990/91 season, prices for opera rose by 14.3 per cent on average and for ballet by 20 per cent, whereas in the amphitheatre there was an even bigger leap of 19 per cent for opera and 25 per cent for ballet. The shortage of money was creating untold problems and ways of improving revenue had to be found, but even so it is difficult to understand how the board and management could have decided to take this course. Conscience apart, the consequences could only be to the detriment of the

House's standing as well as of those unfortunate people no longer able to afford tickets.

As grand-tier prices rose to £112 and amphitheatre prices to an unprecedented height, a moral issue began to emerge: whether the use of public money was justified in underwriting seats of the high face value by then prevailing in the stalls, stalls circle and grand tier. Formerly an argument could be sustained that high-priced tickets were helping to subsidize lower prices elsewhere in the House, as was indeed the case. But when the differential between top and bottom prices is reduced to the extent that it then was, another situation prevails. It can then be argued that top-priced seats should recover their full cost without any element of subsidy, thereby releasing public funds to increase the number of tickets at affordable prices.

With a production of *Prince Igor* in the offing, needing dancers for the Polovtsian Dances, the perennial problem of the engagement of Royal Ballet dancers for opera performances arose. With opera and ballet companies appearing regularly in the same theatre, most would assume that singers and dancers would be available to perform without question in each other's productions when necessary. Not so. Singers appearing with the ballet – mostly as chorus in the pit or auditorium – received extra payment for each appearance, because the Equity standard chorus contract did not provide for this eventuality. This was similarly the case for dancers. Both chorus and dancers saw these situations as opportunities for increasing earnings, and exploited them to the full. This round of Royal Ballet wage negotiations failed to resolve the difficulty, and ended with a 5 per cent increase in salaries and £100 for each dancer per performance of *Prince Igor*.

The board was critical of this settlement, and complained of a lack of good information about progress in the negotiations and of other options for the acquisition of dancers. Little did they realize, it seems, that Equity would unquestionably have prevented the engagement of dancers from elsewhere. There was also concern that the House's credibility with ministers and the Arts Council might be damaged by a level of wage increase above that then considered acceptable for the public sector.

Around this time, early in 1990, there were further discussions about closure, still being planned to begin in the summer of 1993. The Waterloo project, likely to be ready by the autumn of 1993, was recommended as the best solution. It would give both companies a home base, which was seen as essential. While there was uncertainty about the future of the chorus as a full-time body during closure, there was no doubt about the orchestra. What was considered the most practical way forward in this situation was short separate seasons of opera and ballet. It was even suggested that this pattern of performance might be adopted when the House reopened – an arrangement that would destroy the very basis of the *stagione* system on which the opera company had risen to fame, although some advantages to the ballet could accrue from it.

What was emerging was the impossibility of avoiding deficit budgeting if a full programme of new productions was to be maintained without a marked increase in revenue from whatever source – ideally the Arts Council. In the autumn of 1989 John Sainsbury had written to the Prime Minister urging improved funding for the arts, and in May of the following year he had sent a letter to Peter Palumbo, the chairman of the Arts Council, confirming a conversation in which the latter had given his support to the Royal Opera House proceeding with an unbalanced budget. Without that letter, it is clear that the board would not have approved the budget for 1990/91. Meanwhile, there were strenuous attempts to bring down expenditure, including a reduction of night working. This was to have the undesirable effect of reducing stage rehearsal time.

By now Westminster City Council had approved revised redevelopment plans. These contained a redesigned fly tower and an extension of the Floral Hall to three and a half bays in depth – a welcome addition. By the end of 1990 it was clear that substantial money would be needed to complete the scheme, which prompted Sir Martin Jacomb, the chairman of the development board, to draw the attention of the main board to the huge risks involved. At this stage, construction costs of the theatre were expected to be £130 million and those of the commercial sections £35 million.

In spite of Jacomb urging that closure be delayed to Easter 1994, the board recommended that a timetable of closure in July 1993, and reopening in the autumn of 1996, should be adhered to, even though there was some thought that *Miss Saigon*'s run might be finished in time to release Drury Lane from January 1994. For good measure, Battersea Power Station was thrown into the discussion as a closure venue, as Earls Court and Olympia were discarded because of limited availability and suitability.

By the middle of 1990 it was recognized that there were too few ballet performances at Covent Garden and insufficient time to mount new ballets planned, particularly one by William Forsythe. Because it was deemed that opera was making the larger contribution to overheads, as a result of the higher prices that could be charged, the ballet was beginning to be denied its fair share of performances and rehearsals. The consequences of restoring the balance in face of massively adverse financial pressures were discussed. Also, the Arts Council was now denying having approved deficit budgeting and seeking information about the outcome of reducing the £3 million deficit. It was an increasingly uncomfortable time for board and management, although Jeremy Isaacs was to report on the success of the policy of a substantial number of new productions and good revivals with an air that seemed to imply that such successes had not happened before. There ensued debate about artistic desiderata versus financial savings and stringency – one that was not to be resolved.

Relations with the Arts Council were not easy, and the most recent of its periodic assessments of the Royal Ballet, revealing concern about performance opportunities, had indicated a new degree of intervention. The Secretary of State for National Heritage, by now David Mellor, was seeking a new approach to funding. As mentioned in Chapter 10, he told me on one occasion that he was increasingly frustrated by not being able to influence, or perhaps even control, the way in which public money was being spent on the arts. I reminded him that targeted funding would go some way towards achieving that, and would ensure more efficient use of funds. It is also worth noting a remark by Anthony Everitt, the then secretary-general of the Arts Council, to the effect that the Council's new role was that of setting the terms by which the funder would judge its funding for the funded. Further intrusion into the affairs of Covent Garden was to come through the setting up of an Arts Council appraisal team under the chairmanship of Baroness Warnock.

With a worsening financial outlook, in 1990 Jeremy Isaacs was to report that some opera prices had risen by 90 per cent in three years, and ballet prices by 70 per cent over the same period, in an attempt to combat a declining Arts Council grant in real terms and lower private funding (a direct consequence of a downturn in business confidence). Other measures to deal with a worrying deficit were a reduction in staff and in overtime, which would have an immediate bearing on the availability of the stage for rehearsal, and changes to the programme, producing expected savings of an estimated £1.1 million and increased revenue of £2 million.

Then suddenly, amid talk of cancelling a new production of the *Ring* and a poor revival of *The Barber of Seville*, the victim of under-preparation, David Mellor announced an increase in grant to the Arts Council of 11 per cent. That was obviously welcome news, and coincided with an approach to the minister in which John Sainsbury had remonstrated that the present level of activity could not be continued on present funding levels without a deficit; that comparisons with the funding of European opera houses showed this country in a poor light; and that, in any event, Covent Garden's share of the total grant given to the Arts Council by the government had fallen from 12.1 per cent to 8.7 per cent.

In spite of the Arts Council insisting on a balanced budget for 1991/92 and the elimination of the accumulated deficit by March 1994, the wage bill was to be increased by 11.3 per cent, offset by staff economies of forty-seven (eleven posts to remain unfilled and a reduction of thirty-six in the establishment). Savings of £1 million had also been found in the new production of the *Ring*, thus securing its place in the programme.

Cash flows were understandably causing anxiety, but the ever loyal Coutts again came to the rescue, with an increased borrowing facility of £3 million, in addition to an existing £1.5 million, although this time it was coupled with a letter of caution. The board, too, was troubled by difficulties in arriving at balanced budgets and sustaining them to the year end. As early as July 1991 an estimated loss of £830,000 was being forecast for the 1991/92 year, against a budgeted surplus of £723,000. This prompted the board to stress the need for firm control of expenditure – an obvious point, but one which it was thought needed to be emphasized.

At the January 1991 board meeting John Sainsbury had announced his decision to retire at the end of the season. On accepting the chairmanship in 1987, he had said that he would stay for only a limited period, but there had been an expectation that he would remain longer than this. He argued that his business commitments were making greater demands upon him and that he could not continue to find the time that Covent Garden needed. He had taken a strong, upbeat attitude towards the Royal Opera House and, with the artistic success that was largely in evidence, he must have had hopes of persuading the government, probably through the Prime Minister, to write off deficits and to improve funding so that the planned programmes could be maintained without incurring further losses, thus ensuring that the House could progress on a firmer financial footing. This was a wholly laudable ambition, but unrealistic in that it did not take into account the adverse image of Covent Garden, financially and managerially, which was emerging and which could only provoke a negative reaction, particularly from a government which was critical of organizations apparently unable to manage their affairs, however good in this instance the artistic record.

While the 1990/91 financial year had ended with a small surplus, the prospects for the following three years were not encouraging if grant increases were to be limited to 2.5–3.5 per cent. Already, by July 1991, a deficit instead of a budgeted surplus was looming for 1991/92. The box office was feeling the pinch of inflation, and the whole situation was not helped by a dispute with the orchestra over pay and conditions – always an unsettling situation.

It had been decided not to renew Paul Findlay's contract after 1993. This enabled Jeremy Isaacs to achieve his ambition of bringing Nicholas Payne to Covent Garden as opera director and finally to divest himself of the remnants of the old guard.

John Sainsbury was to be replaced as chairman by Angus Stirling. This was a surprising appointment, because of the demands which Stirling's current assignment as director of the National Trust were making upon him and which were unlikely to give him the degree of freedom that Covent Garden would require and expect. It was this selfsame reason which had persuaded him to decline the invitation to succeed Claus Moser in 1987. His acceptance of the Covent Garden role must have raised eyebrows at the National Trust, and left him exposed to undue pressures in both organizations. These were to weigh heavily on him, particularly as the fortunes of the Royal Opera House deteriorated and the need for greater involvement and decisiveness grew. This is not to say that he did not bring many qualities to the House. He did. From his earliest involvement with it as deputy secretary-general of the Arts Council, and later as chairman of the Friends of Covent Garden and as a member of the board, he had demonstrated a real understanding of the workings of the House and an empathy with it, along with a passionate interest in opera and ballet. It was perhaps this devotion which persuaded him to accept the offer – and a belief that it might not come again. After all, it is not every day that you receive such invitations.

He did not arrive at a propitious time, with the box office hit by recession and a generally worsening financial situation, exacerbated by the orchestra dispute and an expected profit of £100,000 on a Wembley

Stadium production of *Turandot* turning to a loss of £27,000. There was also the difficulty that a £10 million loan from Coutts, for the redevelopment of the James Street shops and the building of temporary dressing rooms under the Floral Hall, had to be repaid by September 1992. This loan was in addition to the overdraught facility of £4.5 million on the revenue account already granted to meet likely year-end demands.

The shops were seen as a revenue earner and were expected to produce a surplus of £6 million from the sale of leases. This was much needed, but in pursuit of it one of the finest post-war buildings, designed by Edmund Ward of Gollins, Melvin & Ward, the architects for the first redevelopment phase, has been spoiled. Some of us protested at the time, usually to be told that it was always intended that shops should be part of that site. Two shop units were indeed included in the original plans, but they were small and largely there as a sop to Westminster Council. The size of shop that now exists there was never envisaged, and certainly not the spoiling of the detail of the original design at street level.

Angus Stirling recognized that Covent Garden had lost the argument with government and the Arts Council over its financial position: its high fixed costs, with salaries and wages rising broadly in line with other organizations, but reliant on public funds which were not increasing in step with inflation and on sponsorship which was uncertain in a time of recession. The companies were performing well, in spite of the loss of that earlier spirit which had been so much a feature of the Royal Opera House. Their professionalism would endure even in the more difficult times to come. Yet, funding bodies failed to respond positively. Financial difficulties were acute, and there seemed to be no way forward except through further increasing ticket prices, in spite of adverse public reaction, and exercising more stringent control of expenditure. For the 1992/93 season seats would cost 7.5 per cent more, the chorus was to be reduced from seventy-two to sixty, and staffing levels were to be thoroughly reviewed. With these measures and a good box-office return, it was hoped that there would be a surplus of £1 million.

In addition to the ever present financial difficulties, the two matters that dominated most board discussions were redevelopment and plans for the closure period during reconstruction. By January 1992 there was government consent to a scheme which met all Covent Garden's needs and would cost £89 million. This was thought to require an appeal for £46 million, but could well have created an operating gain of £5.2

million. More modest options were considered, with fewer facilities but with lower costs and with the consequent need for less appeal money; however, at the same time potential revenue gains would also be diminished. The most ambitious scheme was considered to offer the best value for money and was the one to be pursued, in spite of an anticipated closure of more than three years. It was thought that that length of time, and the construction cost, might have been mitigated by proceeding in stages, although it is not clear how that might have worked. In any event, it was hoped to have the Royal Ballet operating entirely in Covent Garden by 1995.

Given the length of closure, the cost of reconstruction and the uncertainty about venues for the companies during this period, this would have appeared to be the time to give serious thought to abandoning the redevelopment of Covent Garden and to building a new opera house on a different site. Many would have been shocked by such an idea, but it was an option to be explored. From the beginning it was obvious that, whatever else was done, the auditorium of the House would remain much as it was, with improvements to the seating and sight lines but no appreciable increase in seat numbers. When Edmund Ward and I were considering ideas for a reconstructed Covent Garden twenty-five or more years ago, and the Greater London Council had plans to open up land to the west of the Royal Opera House, we examined the possibility of building another opera house immediately behind it, with the stages of the old and new theatres joining each other. One of the advantages of this would have been a larger seating capacity – not as big as the Metropolitan in New York, but significantly greater than the present House. Social and financial pressures create this need, and you ignore them at your peril, even though many of us might prefer the intimacy and acoustic ideal of a smaller theatre. If we had been able to realize this plan, the new house would have been for large-scale productions, and the existing theatre (with the upper part of the amphitheatre closed off) for smaller works. It was a good project, albeit idealistic, but it went no further because of the GLC withdrawing its plan for the open space.

Nobody would willingly abandon Covent Garden, but there are factors beyond our control which point to another opera house in another place. Even after the collapse of our first idea, I continued to think about the desirability, and perhaps the necessity, of building elsewhere. The opposition of the local communities to reconstruction on the existing site was strong, and I was concerned about the increased cost of building in a restricted area, value for money, and public reaction to high expenditure with next to no gain in extra seating, even though other facilities would be improved beyond recognition. There was also the matter of the House's elitist image, which has worsened dramatically in recent years for reasons not totally connected with the nature of the building, but which could have been dealt a heavy blow by a move to a new auditorium. Building costs would have been lower, and the result would have been an opera house better suited to the needs of the next century, socially and financially. Having said this, I would not deny that there are few modern opera houses which provide a good environment for audiences to enjoy opera and ballet. One exception in this country is Glyndebourne, designed by Michael Hopkins. This, of course, has the advantage of being medium-sized and intimate. It is very successful, and a pleasure to be in as well as to look at.

In 1983/84, as we searched for architects to undertake the second phase of development, we had no thoughts for anything other than Covent Garden, but privately I did sometimes wonder whether those we were selecting would also be capable of designing a completely new theatre if the opportunity ever arose. If it had done, the nightmares of the closed period would have been avoided. Later, by the time a new site might have become an issue – particularly when there were difficulties in coming to conclusions about the deployment of the companies during the closure – it was impossible to change course. There was also the matter of the accumulating debt, which stood a chance of being cleared only through the completion of the present scheme. Public opinion, too, might well have been against a new building.

At the beginning of 1992 it was decided to renew Anthony Dowell's contract. I had originally been very supportive of his appointment as director of the Royal Ballet, and hoped that, in spite of his private and introspective personality, he would be right to lead the company through a rapidly changing and difficult scene into a modernized opera house and beyond. The company by then needed a Royal Ballet-trained dancer at their head, and somebody whom they respected and admired. Dowell, after a most distinguished career as one of the Royal Ballet's greatest dancers, was just such a person. In dealing with the dancers he has been good, but his touch with programme-making and choosing new works has been less sure. He seems not to be well informed of what is going on in the rest of the dance world, and has made some surprising choices of choreographers and versions of nineteenth-century ballets as well as of designers. His re-appointment must surely have been questioned.

Bernard Haitink's contract was also extended. By now he was feeling completely on his own, and I suspect that it was only his loyalty to the orchestra and to the Royal Opera that persuaded him to accept a renewal, which was of immediate importance to Covent Garden and would prove to be even more so as the House slipped into greater chaos and uncertainty. As this was agreed, Edward Downes was invited to be associate music director, to help Haitink with everyday matters and to relieve him of administrative worries. His return to Covent Garden with a formal appointment was warmly welcomed. A fine and immensely knowledgeable musician, he spanned virtually the entire post-war life of the Royal Opera, as horn player, répétiteur and conductor. Another welcome addition to the music staff was that of Terry Edwards as chorus master. A good singer himself and widely experienced in chorus work as performer and coach, he was to bring new life to a chorus which was in urgent need of an injection of self-esteem and satisfaction.

The decline of public funding for Covent Garden continued to be a subject of debate. Once more it was demonstrated that there was a serious slippage in the proportion of Arts Council money coming to the Royal Opera House, which had received an increase of 41 per cent (11.1 per cent in real terms) between 1984/85 and 1992/93 against a 76.9 per cent increase to the Council.

A Cabinet Review – as periodically conducted of organizations in receipt of public funds – generally indicated a belief that Covent Garden should continue to receive the same proportion of the grant-in-aid given to the Arts Council, whose conviction was clearly that (1) 'It must remain an essential part of the general provision for the Arts in Britain to maintain a national opera house of high international quality,' and (2) 'The Royal Opera House should provide a greater number of opera productions in the future, and . . . this should not be regarded as the right area in which to make economies in expenditure if that becomes necessary.'

The view of the chairman of the Arts Council on the level of funding was that the grant should remain for the foreseeable future the same in real terms and in the same ratio to the Council's total grant-in-aid as in 1983/84 – conditions that prove incompatible if the Arts Council's total grant-in-aid has changed by something other than the rate of inflation.

The Cabinet Review also commented on the purpose of subsidy: (1) 'The function of subsidy is to preserve and promote the activities of a performing company on behalf of the nation and to make it accessible to the public at the box office,' and (2) 'The fixed costs of the company, whether of the payroll or other costs, should – once they are shown to be reasonable – not be allowed to impact too heavily on seat prices.'

A paper prepared early in 1992 indicated that box-office receipts were expected to increase from 35 per cent of the total budget in 1985/86 to 49 per cent in 1992/93, and sponsorship from 12 per cent to 15 per cent, whereas the grant was to decline from 53 per cent to 36 per cent.

As the financial problems grew and more drastic measures were taken to counter a worsening deficit, at an April 1992 board meeting it was decided to announce the closure for the summer of 1997, though this was not done immediately and the date continued to be uncertain. Meanwhile the Warnock Report had been completed. Lady Warnock was to appear before the board at its September meeting, and was later to tell me of her anger at the way she was treated, which she considered insulting and offhand. Knowing how courteous Angus Stirling is, I was surprised by her outburst.

The report, though supportive of a major theatre for opera and ballet in London, was critical of some areas of the operation and detected weaknesses in management efficiency and structure, which it recommended should be corrected. It viewed the redevelopment plans as the best possible in an ideal world, but cost and the absence of government money indicated that the scheme did not relate to the real world. It urged that work should be confined to modernizing and repairing the existing house. This – costing £25 million without significantly improving facilities for performers or the public – was not a realistic proposal. At the same time, the note of caution which the report contained was worthy of consideration and should have led to a further review of the scale and the expense of the plans proposed by the management and sanctioned by the board.

Angus Stirling was critical of the report's stress on the need to break even each year, which did not recognize the need to improve on the artistic standards obtaining when Jeremy Isaacs had taken office and that this could be achieved only at a cost. I am the first to agree that there was a lot of work to be done at that time, but that had always been the case. No one should ever be satisfied with the achievements of any particular moment; what is done today has to be bettered tomorrow if standards are to rise. Achieving this is not entirely a matter of money. However, the Warnock Report roused Isaacs to outbursts about the past, and he seemed oblivious to many fine performances and productions in the 1970s and 1980s as he recalled memories of drab and unexciting performances emerging from a deficit-ridden and dispirited organization. There were, for example, in the 1983/84 season eight new productions: *Turandot*, a double bill of *Le Rossignol* and *L'Enfant et les Sortilèges*, *Esclarmonde*, *Andrea Chénier*, *I Capuleti e i Montecchi*, *Boris Godunov* and *Aida*. He went on to describe work as underfunded and under-rehearsed. The former could be the case, but the latter was quite untrue. It was by concentrating much of its resources on rehearsal that the House had achieved what it did and thereby attracted the world's finest conductors, directors and artists to it. What happened during the 1990s was another matter, as changes of cast were introduced with next to no rehearsal and occasionally none at all. Justification of overspending – and of high seat prices to combat it – seemed increasingly to rest on selective and uncertain recollections of the past.

A hoped-for surplus of £1.65 million in March 1993 was rapidly becoming a loss, with box-office receipts and sponsorship down by £1.5 million, resulting in a likely accumulated deficit of £3.3 million, which it was argued was 50 per cent of the RPI shortfall in public funding. The auditors were warning that provision must be made for a box-office decline, and the board, aware of a precarious cash situation and the need for a larger overdraught facility at Coutts, was stressing the necessity of better financial forecasting and earlier warning of rising costs.

It was a grim situation, and not helped by the knowledge that advance-booking receipts were drying up and that there was no financial provision for the closed period, although the Secretary of State for National Heritage, by then Richard Luce, was to give an undertaking of a special grant to meet closure costs. Plans for the deployment of the companies were still unconfirmed, and the board urged contingency planning.

Bar sales can be a good guide to public mood. In the summer of 1992, champagne sales were down by 19 per cent and House white wine by 16 per cent. These reflected an audience decline of 7.5 per cent, which was most marked in the higher-price seats.

Early in 1992, David Mellor, now Treasury Secretary and in a dialogue with the chairman, had expressed his desire to see Covent Garden's less than fair share of Arts Council funds corrected, but said that nothing could be done before the arrival of the Warnock Report and a report commissioned from the management consultants KPMG. There was also the usual warning of a difficult year ahead for public expenditure, but at the same time a government grant to Covent Garden's redevelopment was not ruled out. Mellor was, however, concerned about the elitist image of the Royal Opera House and the board's self-election procedures, both of which he had mentioned to me in an earlier conversation. He stressed the need for the House to create a climate to help itself before he could do anything.

Later in 1992, KPMG, who had been engaged the same year to review the management and financial operation of the House, reported their belief that there could be savings of 4–5 per cent per annum, resulting in a cash advantage of £150,000 in the first year, rising to £1.5 million at the end of the fourth year. They also took the view that the quest for economy needed to be instilled in everyone's minds and should pervade the entire House.

The management responded to this call by deciding that the House could no longer be repertoire-led and that artistic costs must be contained within limits set by realistic forecasts. It is surprising that such an approach had not been adopted before, and does raise the question of what financial controls were in place.

Aware that loose methods of financial control would no longer suffice, in the 1970s and 1980s we had established financial-reporting systems which were to become an essential tool of those concerned with planning and cost control. Adrian Doran, the then finance director, originated these processes, and they were developed by his successor, Philip Jones, and improved still more by the Priestley team. Covent Garden was the first opera house in the world to introduce such methods of forecasting, information and cost control. As a programme was being planned, it was possible to show quickly the fixed and variable costs of a choice of operas and ballets and the net contributions to overheads. The financial consequences could thus be viewed at the same time as the artistic mix was considered.

No such system can be effective if it is ignored, or if artistic decisions are taken without knowing the financial consequences, or vice versa. It took time to instil the discipline that our system required. For example, I would refuse to answer queries, or deal with problems, without both the artistic and the financial information. Until both were available – and to begin with this took time – no decision was made. In the end, this system was accepted as an essential part of life and a device which made decisions easier to take and more reliable. What it also demonstrated was that financial control (and financial stringency for that matter) need not be the enemy of artistic endeavour and enterprise – frequently the reverse was the case.

The Metropolitan Opera in New York became interested in our systems and wanted to introduce them. Adrian Doran went to America for a few weeks to instruct staff in their use. Interestingly, they were found difficult and, after a trial run, were dropped.

In the early 1990s the financial fortunes of the House were to follow a familiar pattern of some optimism, with the forecasting of modest surpluses, followed by pessimism as box-office returns declined and it became difficult to maintain sponsorship at required levels through the years until closure in the summer of 1997, which by now had been established as a firm date. There were also unexpected events, such as writing off the cost of Covent Garden's contribution of £200,000 towards the Kirov's production of *War and Peace*, which was rotting in the open air in St Petersburg and could not be performed in London as had been intended. There was equally the wonderful surprise of a donation of £2.5 million, to be paid in five six-monthly instalments, from Dr Ho, a Hong Kong businessman. That was manna from heaven.

Redevelopment proposals were regularly under discussion, with the board and management believing that the most comprehensive plan was the one to be adopted, though the Arts Council and government advocated a lesser scheme. The repayment of the Coutts loan was pressing, and could be achieved only through the sale of property, now valued at £14.5 million against an earlier estimate of £19.9 million in the redevelopment plans. At a meeting on this subject in early 1993, it was reported that the bank took a statesmanlike view: it looked for reimbursement by the end of March 1993!

Of the four options for the future under consideration by the board, two could be dismissed speedily: to do nothing or to repair and refurbish the theatre in its present form at a cost of £25 million. The benefits of the other two were the subject of analysis and discussion, in which it was shown that the larger of the plans would have revenue and social gains, with twelve extra evening performances and forty extra matinees, some midweek. It was also demonstrated that there could be savings through more efficient operation of the stage and the resulting abolition of night gangs and Sunday technical rehearsals. Some of these revenue advantages and cost reductions would also apply to a reduced scheme, but on a smaller scale. What did not seem to emerge at this point was the actual cost of running a greatly enlarged building in terms of services and staffing apart from the stage. Equally, it is hard to discover the justification for the size of the stage spaces and who approved them.

The impact of restricting the closed period to two years and a few months was to be felt in shortening the two previous seasons for logistic reasons, resulting in losses of £2.9 million, and a further loss of £2.4 million in the months leading to opening. All of this was unavoidable, and help was sought from the Arts Council to deal with exceptional closure costs of £9.4 million.

By now – January 1993 – it was decided that continuous work needed to be found for the Royal Ballet during those two years, but that the Royal Opera would be restricted to eighty performances per season. The Drury Lane position was looking more promising, with the Theatre Royal being thought to be available at an annual rent of £2.6 million from July 1997 for two years.

Another report had appeared a few months earlier, this time from Price Waterhouse and commissioned by the board. In its introduction, it referred to a comment made by the Arts Council in 1952 as it had launched a rescue operation for the Royal Opera House with a special grant of £50,000: 'These are lottery economics – betting on 95 per cent attendance and American tours. We should like to see our national home of Grand Opera secured on a less sporting basis.' That was such a true assessment, and successive governments have done little to correct its continuing relevance.

Price Waterhouse recommended that the Royal Opera House should seek a fresh understanding with the Arts Council, based on a new and clear statement of purpose. Through the endeavours of Covent Garden and a special grant – this to be accompanied by a public commitment to manage well – this should lead to a clearing of the deficit by the end of the 1992/93 year.

Restructuring of the board was urged, to include the finance director and the opera and ballet directors in addition to the general director. It was suggested that the chairman should be appointed by the Prime Minister, and that three other board members should be nominated by the Prime Minister and the Department of National Heritage (later the Department of Culture, Media and Sport).

In an attempt to improve the financial situation by £1 million per annum, which the report believed was possible through either savings or bigger income, it was suggested that the general director, having spent the past four or five years encouraging artistic development and building a stock of good productions, should now place greater emphasis on stronger management and internal discipline. Full costing of everything was essential – with further examination of the repertoire mix and the commissioning of work – to develop an improved model of the factors driving stage costs. Little came of these recommendations.

The budget for 1994/95 was showing a deficit of £5 million, whereas 1992/93 was ending with a surplus of £349,000, thanks to half a million from Dr Ho. The projection for 1993/94 was still positive, though down by some £500,000 at that point. In their report on the 1992/93 year, the auditors made the obvious point that fundamental difficulties prevailed. They also made it clear that the House could not be financially insulated from the redevelopment and that the accounts were predicated on the assumption that public funding would be available during closure – a point already confirmed by the Arts Council, subject to an agreed number of performances being given.

The management had rightly agreed to give the artists and staff two years' notice of the closure, and the time for that was rapidly approaching, but with nothing firmly in place. The options were now regarded as Drury Lane, the Lyceum, the Dominion or the Docklands Arena. As far as the first of these was concerned, the technical director was estimating £10–15 million for alterations. This was a large sum and, as a guide, far too vague to be of real value.

The relationship of ballet to opera performances was again on the agenda. In 1992/93 there were 107 and 154 respectively, and this was to worsen to 97 against 162 in the following year, with both declining in 1994/45 to 95 and 113, and then rising to 105 and 114. This discrepancy alarmed the governors of the Royal Ballet, and was to lead to a protest by its chairman, Mark Bonham-Carter, to the Covent Garden board on a later occasion. Apart from the unbalanced ratio of ballet to opera, what was disturbing was the admission that it was conventional wisdom, not serious analysis, that said that the opera contributed more to overheads than did the ballet. It was agreed to reinvestigate.

Then came the announcement that the BBC was to create a series of television programmes about Covent Garden, entitled *The House*. In agreeing to this, I have no doubt that the board and management believed that the programmes would be an effective way of showing the public how an opera house functions, but it was a rash decision, with inevitably no editorial control, a roaming camera and crew, and Covent Garden already the source of a good deal of criticism and unfriendly chatter. The result, broadcast in 1994, was first-rate television, which won many plaudits for its director, Michael Waldman, but brought derision on a hapless Royal Opera House. The board emerged in a poor light, expressing opinions which were not always relevant, and casting aspersions in the wrong directions.

One example of this occurred during discussion of the close juxtaposition of two large productions, *Sleeping Beauty* and *Katya Kabanová*, both with the same designer, Maria Björnson, and each incurring excess expenditure in addition to considerable extra overtime. These productions were not originally planned to be so close, but even then it was unwise to have the same designer working on two productions in the same season, and even more so given that she was also involved with the musical *Sunset Boulevard*. Time and availability are of the essence in controlling cost, and divided loyalties between one production and another are to be avoided. Performance scheduling brought about this dangerous situation, but it should have been managed differently. Knowledge of Björnson's involvement with a large-scale musical should have made the management cautious about engaging her for one production at Covent Garden, let alone two. There is no way that a designer can work on two productions so close together, give each the time needed, and arrive at artistically and financially viable solutions. The management should have been taken to task for this, but instead it was Trevor Nunn, the director of *Katya Kabanová*, who came in for the criticism.

In the four BBC programmes, the theatre seemed in chaos much of the time, and there seemed to be little control over what was going on. Exposure which it was thought at the beginning would be beneficial turned out to be exactly the opposite in most respects. On the other hand, there was a certain gain in that the series became the subject of endless dinner-table talk. I doubt if the Royal Opera House has ever been on so many lips quite so often. A sequel, broadcast in 1998, was feeble and did nothing to correct past impressions.

The closure period and the final design of the modernized Royal Opera House understandably featured prominently in management and board discussions in 1994 and 1995. It was realized that the planned deep excavation to the south of the House would be time-consuming and costly, and was financially hard to justify in terms of gain, not least because it was to house scenery workshops which could be more economically situated on a less expensive site elsewhere. As the result of a review of the project commissioned by the board from the property developer Stuart Lipton, it was agreed to drop the excavation in favour of rejecting office development, on the basis of mutual cost cancellation, thus providing the House with a greatly improved area at ground level and above for its own use.

Drury Lane re-emerged as a possible runner for the closure, following Stoll Moss's proposal to take over the lease of the Lyceum and contribute 50 per cent of the cost of refurbishing the Theatre Royal. However, this would leave £10 million to be found, and Vivien Duffield, the board member leading the Covent Garden Appeal, expressed concern that a Lottery bid for that work could well prejudice Covent Garden's own bid. The timing of this was uncertain, and a decision would be made only in April 1995. A fall-back option was needed, and attention turned to the Dominion in Tottenham Court Road – an unattractive venue and a poor substitute.

Financially, things were going better, in spite of overruns on productions (£150,000 on a budget of £500,000 for *Sleeping Beauty*, for example). With the 1993/94 year ending with a surplus – the second year running to do so – and with the aid of Dr Ho's generous gift, the accumulated deficit could be reduced to £1.5 million. Even so, Jeremy Isaacs saw no alternative but to increase seat prices once again.

By the spring of 1994 there was still no firm decision about deployment of the companies during the closure. Drury Lane was still the best option, but access remained problematic. Moving *Miss Saigon* to the Lyceum was regarded as a possibility. To that end, a tripartite agreement between the Royal Opera House, Stoll Moss and Cameron Mackintosh was proposed. One snag had come to light, and that was that the valuation of a restored Lyceum apparently amounted to £8 million only after an investment of £2–3 million on purchase and £18 million on refurbishment. Without public funds or the injection of large sums by a private investor, this was beyond the reach of the House. By now there were also other bidders around: The Really Useful Group, Apollo and Disney. To muddy the waters further, English National Opera, then wanting to close the Coliseum for repair and modernization at the same time as Covent Garden, had its eye on the Lyceum. As Robert

Gavron, chairman of St Ives Press and a member of Covent Garden's board, was to remark, 'The Lyceum is the queen of the chessboard.'

Despite these obvious difficulties, the board charged Jeremy Isaacs to continue to pursue Drury Lane in tandem with the Lyceum, keeping the Dominion in mind if these options failed. Meanwhile, the pressure to come to terms with the final redevelopment plans was growing, with Westminster City Council and English Heritage welcoming the latest revised scheme and preferring it to its predecessor. This would permit a closed period of two years, against the earlier three, and the dates involved were again reconsidered: 1997–9 or 1998–2000. The earlier option was chosen. At least one decision had now been taken, and it was further agreed that closure plans must be settled by April 1995.

In June 1994 deficits were again looming, with £500,000 forecast for 1994/95 and £1 million for the next year. Inroads into expenditure were being made through a new agreement with the technicians' union, BECTU, which provided more flexible working in all stage areas but which in turn required well-trained, all-round technicians to fulfil a greater number of functions than hitherto. Eradication of demarcation lines had been negotiated many years earlier, but a totally integrated workforce – trained to undertake all stage functions – was the final goal. This has since been achieved.

The closure options were beginning to change, with the Lyceum now owned by Apollo and access to Drury Lane becoming less likely. Apollo was willing to sign an agreement with Covent Garden for the two seasons, 1997/98 and 1998/99. It was estimated at the time that 200 performances could be given each year at the Lyceum at a gross cost of £49.7 million for both years, or £20.5 million after taking account of box-office income. Sadler's Wells was now also in the running, with a rebuilt theatre likely to be open by the autumn of 1998. One of the handicaps which the House faced was uncertainty about the funding of the closure. There was a serious need for a better understanding with the Arts Council about this, as well as about things in general.

By the beginning of 1995 Jeremy Isaacs was expressing anxiety about closure and what to do with the companies. The Lyceum was seen as an expensive option, with relatively restricted usage. The idea of a temporary structure then appeared on the scene. John Harrison, the technical director, had been in discussion with the architect and acoustic engineers Arup's about the feasibility of constructing a temporary theatre with

2,500 seats. It would take fifteen months to build, at a cost of £8.5 million, and would have some residual life after Covent Garden's occupation. The board welcomed this as a highly imaginative solution and discussed possible sites: Hyde Park, Jubilee Gardens and Battersea Park. The Arts Council, on the other hand, was not in favour and preferred the Lyceum.

What followed was to be the beginning of the end of sensible planning of the closure, at least for its first year. It had transpired that a site close to Tower Bridge, known as Potters Fields, had been transferred to Southwark Council as planning gain by St Martin's Property Corporation Ltd. This was considered an excellent place for the temporary theatre, and such use had the backing of Southwark Council. Capital funding remained a problem until a consortium led by Crédit Lyonnais was set up, with Covent Garden and Disney as potential and successive tenants. Unfortunately the consortium was unable to come to an agreement with Southwark Council and withdrew its planning application.

As luck would have it, another body appeared on the scene, called GLE Properties, owned by a group of London boroughs and in possession of bank finance for a more permanent theatre. Time was running out for this building to be operating by the autumn of 1997, but if a planning application could be made for consideration at Southwark Council's December meeting and work started by January, all would be well. It would need fast-track planning consent and no obstacles in the way. If this failed, the House was to fall back on the Lyceum or the Dominion.

By the October board meeting, which was attended by GLE Properties and Southwark Council, Apollo's patience in waiting for Covent Garden to reach a decision had been exhausted and the Lyceum had been let to The Really Useful Group. To make things worse, the Dominion had by then agreed to a production of the musical *Grease*. With the Docklands Arena having been rejected, the House was now totally dependent on the Tower Bridge project coming off if it was to have a permanent home for its companies throughout closure.

What then transpired was an alarming display of naivety on the part of the board and management. I had first heard about this scheme from John Harrison one night in the crush bar, and immediately had doubts about its viability. Harrison had already persuaded Jeremy Isaacs and the board to accept his recommendation to put up a building for long-term scenery storage in Wales. It is true that the project was made financially attractive by a grant from the Wales Development Agency, but Wales is a long, long way from Covent Garden and transport costs are high. The Welsh scheme did not make sense for me. Now here was another proposal which seemed flawed at the outset, for two principal and quite different reasons. First, Disney were not fully on board, and in any event they are notoriously fickle partners, capable of withdrawing at the drop of a hat, as they had already demonstrated elsewhere. Second, it was impossible to see how planning consent could come through quickly enough for the theatre to be ready for occupation when needed. Southwark Council was aware that it would have to refer the application to the Department of the Environment, but hoped that it would be approved without the calling of an inquiry. It is difficult to understand how this was thought possible, given the sensitivity of the site, which was once designated for housing and is alongside Tower Bridge. Furthermore, the Environment Secretary's brother, Peter Gummer, was chairman of the Arts Council Lottery Panel (and later to be chairman of the Royal Opera House), from which Covent Garden was seeking money. This was potentially good *Private Eye* material: there was surely no way in which planning consent could be rubber-stamped by John Gummer. There had to be an inquiry, and the resultant delay would mean that even a favourable outcome would come too late for Covent Garden's needs. How anybody could have thought otherwise is beyond comprehension.

The inquiry set up by John Gummer was a major setback, with all other options for a single-theatre occupation now gone. Even so, I suspect that there was relief in some quarters that the Covent Garden Lottery bid would no longer run the risk of being compromised by a bid for the Tower Bridge scheme and that the main project of modernizing the Royal Opera House would remain the focal point of fund-raising. There must have been a realization that, once a Potters Fields theatre was to be more permanent, there was a danger of that replacing Covent Garden as the object of giving.

The concentration of time and effort on the Royal Opera House project was necessary without doubt, but in its wake it did strike me that buildings were being regarded as more important than people, ignoring the fact that it is the latter who make opera and ballet companies. As things have turned out, I was right to have had those thoughts.

For the 1996/97 year there were to be £3 million of repertoire-related savings. At this stage there was no contingency provision, and a £1 million shortfall was expected – the result, according to Vivien Duffield, of a larger budget than agreed. Again there was to be reliance on a successful gala – this time with Placido Domingo, in December 1996, in celebration of his twenty-five years' performing at Covent Garden. It was his wish that this gala should be held at the Royal Albert Hall, in order to give the maximum number of people the chance to attend. This was music to the ears of Duffield and her helpers as they considered the fund-raising possibilities there. However, it was not to be. A date had been pencilled in at the Royal Albert Hall, but apparently it was not confirmed by Covent Garden and the hall management lost patience and let it elsewhere.

So much could have been achieved in that venue, whereas at the Royal Opera House we were treated to an evening's entertainment, entitled *Gold and Silver*, which was an insult to everyone who has worked, or continues to work, at Covent Garden. There was no chorus, and the first plans included no British singers – an omission subsequently corrected by the accident of choice of arias and ensembles to be performed, and by the sudden departure of the American singer James Morris. There also were two singers who had never appeared in the House before. The entire show was poorly presented and reflected ill on what was once a great opera house. No doubt a great deal of money was raised – and thank heavens for that! – but this was an appalling and shameful way of doing it. It was described by Nicholas Payne as a commercial affair, as though that should justify its artistic shortcomings. It was also intended as the launch pad for the development appeal. It was a poor advertisement for that, but perhaps those concerned were not bothered by its deficiencies. Hasty apologies were forthcoming, and it was promised that amends would be made at the gala planned for the following July and intended to mark the closing of the present House. Sad to say, little was done then to correct the errors of the previous gala and to restore some credit to the House, on which the final curtain fell with little to remind us of its great past.

The July event could have been glorious and truly celebratory. It required more than just stringing together a series of ballet and opera excerpts. It was the occasion to have invited the participation of some-one like Patrick Garland, with whom I worked on galas to celebrate the entry of this country into Europe and, in collaboration with Thames

Television, to mark the Queen's silver jubilee. Both were hugely successful because a thread ran through the evening binding together well-
chosen arias and ensembles and using the spoken word to tell a story.
The last gala in the old House could have been similarly constructed,
recalling important events of post-war Covent Garden and combining
ballet and opera. It was an opportunity missed, and perhaps never even
thought about.

By January 1996 the board and management were assuming that the
companies would lead a nomadic life during the first year of closure. For
the second year there was still the hope that Sadler's Wells and Tower
Bridge might be available. For the 1997/98 season the Royal Ballet
planned 150 performances in a mixture of venues: the Royal Albert Hall,
the Royal Festival Hall, the Barbican and the Coliseum. In addition,
there were to be thirty-three performances overseas. The Royal Opera
proposed six months at the London Palladium, six weeks at the Barbican
and the remainder of the season on tour in the regions and abroad.

These facts were reported to the board in the spring of 1996. But it
transpired that none of the venues had so far been contracted. This
raised concern about the well-being of the orchestra in an uncertain
future and about how the plans were to be managed and financed. The
regional-touring content of the Royal Opera plan would be very expensive, but it seems that costings of both sets of plans – for the opera and
ballet companies – were not ready for discussion at that meeting. However, a month later it was said that the touring plan would cost £6 million more than a season at Tower Bridge. It was also argued that the
latter would have cost £3.5 million less than the Lyceum. Since neither
was available, these were entirely academic points.

A major change to the board occurred in the summer of 1996: the
appointment of Peter Gummer (later Lord Chadlington) as chairman, in
succession to Angus Stirling. He had joined the board earlier in the year,
relinquishing his Lottery Panel post, and some directors, believing Angus
Stirling to have been indecisive and seeking a change, had tried to
nominate him as chairman then and there. Approval of this was sought
from the chairman of the Arts Council, Lord Gowrie, and the Secretary
of State for Heritage, Virginia Bottomley. The latter urged caution over
this appointment, because of obvious conflicts of interest, but her views
proved unacceptable to those seeking change – particularly to two
of Covent Garden's benefactors, who threatened to withdraw their

committed donations if this proposal was not given a fair wind. Mrs Bottomley relented, but Angus Stirling rightly objected and insisted on seeing his time out. In any event, many eyebrows were raised by the appointment even as a board member of Peter Gummer, who only a few months before, as chairman of the Arts Council Lottery Panel, had delivered £78 million of Lottery money to Covent Garden for its redevelopment and now crossed over to become its recipient. When seen in that light, the appointment was a bad move and another example of public perception and reaction being ignored by those who should have been most alert to it.

In the midst of uncertainty over closure plans, it had been decided that Jeremy Isaacs should be asked to leave at the end of the year, six months before the expiry of his contract, in order that a successor could be appointed who would be in position to see the companies out of the old House, through the closure, and into a modernized Royal Opera House. This made sense, but it is a pity that this was not explained at the time. It can be reasonably assumed that Isaacs's *Cold War* television series had been commissioned by then and that Isaacs must have been spending time with his own production company in setting that up and actually starting to make programmes. This may have had some bearing on the board's decision. Opera houses require all the time and energy that their directors can give them, and there is little room for much else – particularly when in crisis, as Covent Garden had been for some years. Isaacs was not happy about his early departure, insisted on the continuation of programme and other credits, and remained a board member until the AGM in July 1997, as well as being paid until September, the termination date of his contract.

The search for a successor followed a familiar pattern: a mixture of pleasurably anticipating the discovery of an outstanding candidate and frustration at seeing no more than familiar names, with no one really capable of delivering what was wanted. But suddenly the scene changed on the appearance of Genista McIntosh. Here was a person steeped in the theatre, having spent her working life with the Royal Shakespeare Company and the National Theatre. She had no experience of opera and ballet management, but nevertheless was so aware of what was needed to make a performing-arts organization function to the highest standards that she immediately became the obvious successor to Jeremy Isaacs. She would bring to Covent Garden a true sense of theatre and the human qualities that staff and artists had been missing from the management. McIntosh cares passionately about her fellow human beings, and is easily offended by what she sees as injustice or brutish behaviour.

I suspect that she was to witness some of this quite soon after her arrival, but in a more general sense she would have found herself face to face with a culture that was quite foreign to her. As the board had once feared, and others were to remark upon, Covent Garden had become a place for corporate entertainment, no longer a theatre primarily for opera and ballet lovers, many of whom had been squeezed out by high prices or had drifted up to the less expensive parts of the House. The whole nature of the Royal Opera House had changed: the audience in the stalls, the stalls circle and the grand tier was largely different, and, backstage, the former unique and inimitable spirit had evaporated.

There was a huge amount of work to be done in dealing with these issues, as well as the vital and immediate question of the closure plans, their cost and viability. The challenge was immense, but one which I believe that McIntosh could have overcome with support from the board and a real willingness on their part to face the problems squarely and directly. The House had been lacking involved and strong management, and, coupled with the absence of information about closure and uncertainty about redundancy, this was causing it to lose direction and a sense of purpose. Morale was low, but professionalism still enabled high-quality performances to be delivered. What went on for the rest of the time was another matter, with rumours multiplying and anger and resentment building up at the way the House was being managed and the artists and staff treated.

The Royal Ballet closure plans were upset by the decision of the Royal Albert Hall to cancel their booking for the autumn of 1997. The reason for this was the hall's sudden view that there would be an overexposure of ballet there with the Royal Ballet in the autumn and English National Ballet earlier in the year. In my judgement this was not a valid excuse, and it is probable that ENB's sponsors had some say in this decision. A further blow was to come when the management of Sadler's Wells rejected a lengthy booking for both Covent Garden companies, deciding to maintain its preferred policy of receiving companies for short seasons. This decision was later to be reversed, with the acceptance of crippling terms by Covent Garden. Whether desperation had by then set in and there was fear of losing an important venue it is hard to know, but such exorbitant financial demands should have been refused.

In the end, the Sadler's Wells season was largely cancelled for want of money. The outcome of that fiasco is an interesting comment on the way that botched-up deals have a habit of turning out. The object of cancellation was to save money, but nobody seems to have taken into account the cost of compensation and how that was to be met, let alone informed the Sadler's Wells management before the event. The cancellation of several months of performances by the Royal Opera at a late stage left Sadler's Wells with a huge gap in its schedules and an even bigger hole in its pocket. Ian Albery, the chief executive of Sadler's Wells and a combative figure, naturally wanted to know how this was to be put right, and was on the point of litigation. A meeting between the two managements and the Arts Council was called, and ended with agreement to pay compensation against the broken contracts. What appeared to remain unsettled was who was to foot the large bill and where the money was to come from. This has since been resolved, but lack of clarity bedevils situations like this and in this case dealt a further blow to credibility already at a low ebb.

The Royal Ballet's autumn 1997 gap was to be filled by a season at the Labatt's Apollo in Hammersmith. This was formerly an Odeon cinema, with 3,400 seats and a stage for live performances. However, like most cinemas-cum-theatres, the stage is shallow and there is no pit for a ballet orchestra. Curiously enough, we had inspected this theatre many years earlier when searching for venues in Greater London in which to present the Sadler's Wells Royal Ballet. It was decided not to use it, because of its huge size and unsatisfactory ambience. Since then improvements have been made, and it is used continuously for live shows. *River Dance*, for example, has enjoyed great success there, and it was thought that the Royal Ballet could take advantage of that in attracting a new audience, and one unfamiliar with ballet. Nevertheless, my heart sank when the season there was announced.

The financing of the closure period remained difficult and uncertain. There was an understandable desire and need to maximize revenue from the box office, but if prices were pitched at an unacceptable level in pursuit of this there was a serious danger of losing an opportunity of bringing in a new public. In the case of the Apollo, there was also the sheer volume of seats to be filled. Choice of programmes was crucial to success in achieving two objectives: high box-office take and new audiences. Unfortunately, little imagination was shown here, with a surfeit of performances of full-length ballets, which looked indifferent on the shallow stage and which may have attracted some newcomers but repelled the regular ballet-goers. The cause of ballet was poorly served by this venture.

Further London seasons were planned at the Coliseum, the Barbican, Sadler's Wells and the Royal Festival Hall. The last of these had more free time than previously, as the result of English National Ballet's decision to desert the South Bank after many years, in favour of St Martin's Lane and the Royal Albert Hall. Overseas tours were to fill further weeks, including performances in New York under the aegis of the Lincoln Center Festival, and were likely to bring home some much needed cash.

The Royal Opera was to take itself off to the Barbican for the opening weeks of the 1998/99 season, and to follow those with performances at the Royal Albert Hall, Symphony Hall, Birmingham, and the Shaftesbury Theatre, in addition to appearances at a number of festivals, including those at New York's Lincoln Center, Baden-Baden, Savonlinna and Edinburgh.

The costing of this mixed bag of fare must have presented many difficulties, not least in forecasting box-office income at venues of which there was little or no experience. In attempts to balance budgets, it is probable that income was overstated and expenditure the reverse, with reduced contingency allowances. This seemed to have been the experience of *Turandot* at Wembley.

These were some of the many problems with which Jenny McIntosh had to grapple as, even before she took up her post, she also looked to the reopening of Covent Garden and examined the cost of running the vastly expanded building. There were figures around, but it was doubtful that they were realistic. Investigation brought little comfort to board and management.

Unquestionably, seat prices could not be maintained at their previously high level, but any reduction had ideally to be financed from public funds. Furthermore, the image of Covent Garden had to change: the House needed to become once more a theatre for opera and ballet lovers. Here arose the conflict that exists between social conscience and financial survival, the latter being heavily dependent on commercial support, which can carry with it a social price.

In an endeavour to provide firmer control over income and expenditure and to come to terms with exactly where the House was financially, before Jenny McIntosh's arrival and following Peter Gummer becoming chairman an executive board had been established under the chairman-ship of the latter (later to be succeeded by McIntosh). Gummer was a hands-on chairman, who clearly intended that he and the board should be more closely involved than ever before with the running of the House. To that end he was to have an office in the Royal Opera House – the first, and I hope the last, chairman to do so.

Estimates presented to the board in December 1996 for the 1997/98 year – all but four months of which would be during the closure – were indicating a deficit of £4.3 million and a Lottery grant of £3.9 million for special items. Strenuous efforts were being made to achieve savings of £3.3 million, but up to this point only £1.3 million had been identified.

The board also had figures for the first full year's operation in the new House. A deficit of £7.1 million was forecast, assuming twenty-two opera productions and fourteen ballet programmes, with a staff of 915, some expensive new productions and a 5 per cent wage increase. Despite lower current attendance, an increase in box-office receipts of £5.2 million was anticipated, with private funding hitting £6.5 million and Arts Council funding showing no increase. What also emerged was the cost of running the new theatre – staffing, maintenance, electricity, cleaning, etc. – then put at £8 million per annum.

It was already evident that, on the strength of these figures, the new House was not financially viable. It would be damaging to the appeal if this became known, but the board took the view that it was not a problem since they were determined that the House would be made financially sound.

In January 1997 Jenny McIntosh joined the Royal Opera House and quickly reviewed costs of the remainder of the last season in the old House and the first year of closure. Savings of £2 million were found, and there was the possibility of another £1 million through reordering of the programme. Deficits at the end of 1996/97 and the following year were thought to be hovering around £1 million.

What was becoming more and more obvious was the importance of Sadler's Wells in the second year of closure. Plans for the Royal Opera and the Royal Ballet in the first year were not hanging together, and it needed one location for both companies to give any sense of unity to the programming. Much was at stake, and ways had to be found of preserving and enhancing the companies' artistic reputations.

Uncertainties around the closed period persisted, and it was recognized that financial outcomes could vary considerably as a result of box-office shortfalls and overruns on expenditure arising from working in largely unknown locations. A proposed 'Dance Bites' season had been reduced from four weeks to two and had found a sponsor in Wellcome Glaxo. These weeks had been accepted by the Arts Council as a substitute for touring by the Royal Ballet itself, and thus relieved the financial pressure. This was a bonus for the Royal Ballet management, already concerned about numbers following the withdrawal of support for two corps de ballet dancers by the Linbury Trust. However, apart from the Dance Bites tour, it was expected that the Royal Ballet's performances would be profitable. Furthermore, the Royal Ballet governors were assured that no dancers would be lost during closure and that numbers would be increased on reopening.

Pressures on rehearsal time were being felt. Deborah MacMillan – Kenneth MacMillan's widow, and a member of the board – had already complained about inadequate stage and technical rehearsals for her late husband's ballets. Later *The Prince of the Pagodas* was to suffer from the dress rehearsal being the first full orchestral rehearsal – and in front of a paying audience. *Pagodas* has one of the most difficult scores in the ballet repertoire, but, in any case, this was a situation which should not have been allowed to happen.

Meanwhile the Arts Council Covent Garden monitoring committee was seeking reassurance about artistic and financial viability during closure and afterwards. At this stage the Council had not paid the second tranche of money owing to Covent Garden for its continuing programme – funds badly needed – and had made it plain that this would be forthcoming only on production of a break-even budget for 1997/98.

Access was on everyone's lips, and broadcasting by radio or television featured prominently in discussion. In February 1997 Jeremy Isaacs, still on the board, was right to emphasize that there was no point in winning broadcasting concessions from artists and staff if broadcasters could not, or were unwilling to, find airtime. There is a popularly held view that broadcasters are crying out for performances to relay. They are not to any great extent, and the present Covent Garden management may have fallen into the trap of wringing concessions from the unions which they cannot adequately use, although lower cost as the result of these will open more doors than hitherto.

During the 1980s I almost negotiated a deal with Texaco for the regular broadcasting of operas from Covent Garden – not on the scale of the Met/Texaco Saturday matinee relays, but more frequently than had been the case. Scheduling proved a problem, because regular slots of the required length were rarely available and there was concern about the balance and content of programmes overall, which could make opera an unwelcome intruder. Even so, the BBC was enthusiastic and, through the help of Aubrey Singer, managing director of BBC Radio at the time, a laundering process was negotiated to handle sponsorship money. This was within the bounds of BBC practice and permitted sponsorship credits on air and in the *Radio Times*. It had the makings of a splendid collaboration, but it was never put to the test because an oil crisis caused Texaco to abandon any new sponsorship.

Later in 1997 Peter Gummer was to make much of a plan for opera and ballet performances to be relayed by television to selected centres up and down the country, as a means of improving access. Such relays are no substitute for the real thing, but in the early 1970s I did have a similar idea. I had persuaded Midland Bank, who were then looking for arts ventures to sponsor, to put up the money. They were keen on this project because of its national coverage and the excellent exposure it would give them. Unfortunately the project had to be abandoned because of the high cost of land-line rental and the absence of sufficient specialized projectors to make it worthwhile. The country lost out, but promenaders gained as Midland Bank agreed to sponsor the Covent Garden Proms instead. Early in their life, Archie Forbes, then chairman of the bank, took me by the arm one prom night and said, 'John, it's good for you, it's good for us; let's stay together.' The bank remained the proms' sponsor for twenty-five years.

In the months after her arrival, Jenny McIntosh was making good progress in rationalizing programming, in providing more reliable financial forecasts, and in establishing good relationships between management and artists and staff. It was an uphill struggle, but she appeared to be getting the better of the mammoth problems besetting the organization and was winning the congratulations of the board. Unfortunately that was to change. In April 1997 she was telling the chairman of her unhappiness in the job, arising from managerial and structural weaknesses and what she described as 'a mismatch between me and the organization'. She found the board's attitudes excessively proprietorial, and she believed these would make certain changes – in management structure and style, and towards less elitist pricing – very difficult. By 7 May she had resigned, leaving immediately.

Against her better judgement, ill health was the explanation given by the board, but this cut little ice with the outside world and left Covent Garden unnecessarily exposed to gossip and speculation about the real reason. It is surprising that Lord Chadlington, an experienced PR man and chairman of a PR company, should have indulged in such a feeble cover-up. McIntosh was not ill, and two days before her supposed illness was reported she was undertaking a rigorous appraisal of the Nottingham Playhouse. What she did say, however, was that she might have been ill if she had stayed much longer. So, Covent Garden lost the very person it most needed.

Aware from the April conversations with Genista McIntosh that the House might soon be without a chief executive, Lord Chadlington went directly to the person whom he had initially wanted in preference to her, Mary Allen, secretary-general of the Arts Council. Although she had felt that there were several reasons why she could not accept an invitation to be interviewed for the post when Isaacs was leaving, she believed that she could now be free to take up the appointment if that was what everyone wanted.

There then followed muddled proceedings to obtain permission for her release from the Arts Council. The need for an immediate appointment because of the critical situation at Covent Garden was later emphasized by Lord Chadlington as the reason for the unusual course of subsequent events, including failure to advertise the post. On 7 May the Secretary of State for National Heritage, Chris Smith, who had barely taken office after the general election on the 1st, was rushed into a meeting with the chairman and Robert Gavron, who had requested the discussion on behalf of the Royal Opera House but had not declared its purpose. Baffled by being asked to sanction Mary Allen's appointment to Covent Garden, and probably wondering why this request was being addressed to him rather than to the Arts Council chairman, Lord Gowrie, Smith ended the meeting by saying that he had no objections to Allen's appointment. Chadlington reported that Smith was happy with it; that was hardly so. It was only after this that Lord Gowrie, Mary Allen's employer, was told of her wish to accept the Covent Garden offer. In his words, he was gobsmacked by the news.

The irony of the fiasco of the method and the unseemly rush of Mary Allen's appointment was that, despite her immediate departure from the

Arts Council, she did not arrive at Covent Garden until 1 September 1997, because Chadlington believed that an insulation period was essential to avoid conflict between her old and new responsibilities. It is difficult to see how that could have made much difference to anyone's perception of the situation, given the confusion that preceded it, or, if he had thought this to be essential at the beginning, why there was such rush and mystery around the whole exercise. None of this was conducive to the increased credibility which Covent Garden so desperately needed.

During this period without a chief executive, Lord Chadlington and another board member, Sir Kit McMahon, took turns to be in the Royal Opera House each day between 9.30 and 11.30 and to chair senior management meetings. Chadlington had already displayed his executive intentions, and here was a further demonstration of them – perhaps unavoidable at this stage, but fundamentally changing the relationship of board to management.

It was becoming an increasingly difficult time, with cash-flow problems and finances generally in a precarious state. By June 1997 there was an accumulated deficit of £5 million and larger losses were expected through the closure period, although there was cheer to be found in the halving of the likely deficit in the new House and in the news of the development appeal having raised £64 million. Nevertheless, the position was grim and the threat of insolvency hung over the House.

A further blow to the House's standing occurred over the last-minute cancellation of a new production of *Macbeth* scheduled for performance in June 1997. Apparently, warnings had been given six months earlier that pressures on the stage, exacerbated by restrictions arising from preparatory building work for the redevelopment programme, meant that there could be serious difficulties in mounting this production. These predictions proved to be right, and concert performances were substituted. It seems to have been typical of the organization in recent years to ignore information which was inconvenient, and to go blithely on in the hope that things would be all right in the end. On this occasion they were not, and much discredit to the Royal Opera House resulted. Such events do not go unnoticed around the world, and they also have an adverse impact on budgets – in this case a possible loss in excess of £200,000 due to expenditure already incurred.

By the summer of 1997 alarming news was coming from the box offices of the various venues to be played in the autumn. The Labatt's Apollo, for example, was showing only a 10 per cent advance, and at the

Royal Albert Hall there was an adverse forecast of £125,000 for *Otello*. This resulted in re-examination of capacities and forecasts – mostly downward. If that was not enough, there were budgetary difficulties with the Edinburgh Festival performances: *Platée* was over budget by £175,000, and *Macbeth* was looking financially unhealthy because of the earlier cancellation and substitution of concert performances.

The Royal Opera House was described as out of control on a number of occasions – a comment substantiated by these illustrations alone. Public reaction was hostile at one level, and at another there was bewilderment that a great opera house could find itself in such a state of disarray. The Arts Council, too, was unhappy about its relationship with the House. It felt that Covent Garden did not take it seriously, and that proper procedures were not being followed, bringing discredit to the principles of public arts funding. On another occasion the triumphant response of the board and management to the news of the award of a £78 million Lottery grant caused adverse reaction in the arts community. Of course there was reason to rejoice, but the tone was wrong – raucous and insensitive.

None of this was to be helped by the intemperate remarks of Gerald Kaufman MP in the autumn, following his chairing of meetings of the House of Commons Culture, Media and Sport Committee, at which all those immediately concerned with the Royal Opera House had given evidence and had been subjected to close questioning by committee members. The method of Mary Allen's appointment came in for much discussion and criticism, concluding with the remark that the committee was entirely unconvinced by Ms Allen's convoluted explanation of her actions in bypassing Lord Gowrie and insisting on her appointment to Covent Garden being referred to Chris Smith. At one session Lord Chadlington was to tell a startled world that Covent Garden was bankrupt and in need of an immediate injection of funds. These were to be forthcoming.

The recommendations of the committee were lengthy and comprehensive, and sought radical and fundamental changes to the regime. Lord Chadlington came in for his share of criticism and took the view that he should resign immediately as a matter of honour. The remainder of the board was also taken to task, and their fitness as a body to receive and administer public money was called into question. The same strictures were applied to the chief executive. The committee urged the appointment of an administrator in their place for the remainder of the closed period – an unrealistic proposal which the Secretary of State mercifully did not pursue.

The board complied with the committee's suggestion that they should resign, but the chief executive did not. She was surely right in staying, because her departure would have precipitated yet another crisis, with the House drifting still further into chaos without a person solely in charge.

In the midst of these select-committee meetings, the Secretary of State announced an amazing and totally unrealistic proposition: that the Royal Opera, the Royal Ballet and English National Opera should share Covent Garden on its reopening. Interestingly, Mark Fisher, the then Arts Minister, had put this idea to me during the course of an earlier private meeting, when he had said that there was only enough money for one and a half opera companies in London and new solutions for the presentation of opera in the metropolis had to be found. I told him that it would be unworkable: there would be insufficient performance opportunities for three companies, identity would be lost, and artistic integrity would be compromised. In his view, touring would make up the rest of each company's season – a suggestion indicating a lack of aware-ness of the huge cost of moving large companies around the country. Hearing of this nonsensical scheme again surprised me. But, reflecting on the timing – the day before Chris Smith himself was to appear before the select committee – I could only conclude that, aware of the roasting meted out to other witnesses, he was determined to avoid similar treat-ment for himself by putting forward some radical proposal.

Shortly after this, the Secretary of State was to say that he had come out with this idea as a means of starting serious discussion about opera and ballet, and that he had asked Sir Richard Eyre, former director of the Royal National Theatre, to report on the future of the lyric theatre in London. What emerged was a thoroughly researched and seriously con-ceived report, dealing not only with the immediate subject but comment-ing profoundly on the role of the arts in society. The companies were to be left in their respective homes, but all needed to define clearly their artistic visions and to promulgate them. On artistic leadership at Covent Garden, Sir Richard wrote in the Eyre Review:

> The Royal Opera House needs visionary leadership by an artistic director of international repute in the opera and ballet worlds, under-pinned by sound financial and management expertise. I exhort the

Royal Opera House, while having regard to proper process, to exped-
ite the appointment of its new Artistic Director.

In relation to the Royal Ballet, he went on to say:

> If the Royal Ballet stays at Covent Garden, the Royal Opera House
> needs to commit itself to closer parity of the Ballet's status with the
> Royal Opera, including performance patterns between the Royal
> Ballet and Royal Opera.

The sentiment expressed here was to be welcomed. My only quarrel
with the last paragraph was over the 'if'. Opera and ballet are integral to
the working of the Royal Opera House as a lyric theatre, and it is
inconceivable that one should be separated from the other if the standards of both are to be maintained and enhanced, and funds are to be well
spent. The operation of the *stagione* system is a key to the success of the
opera, but if followed strictly it prevents the generation of sufficient
performances to fill every night when opera alone is being performed
over any length of time. La Scala, one of the few European theatres
working to this principle, has many dark nights. If, on the other hand,
the ballet is an integral part of the planning, this is avoided. Similarly,
when the ballet is mounting new productions and would benefit from
fewer performances for a time, the opera can be scheduled to perform
more often for a limited period. All of this becomes even more possible in
a modernized theatre with facilities for rapid scenery movement and the
availability of the stage for three sessions each day.

The Eyre Review was not published until 30 June 1997, which left Sir
Colin Southgate, the new chairman of the Royal Opera House – and,
significantly, the first to be appointed by a Secretary of State – in something of a dilemma as he set out to put Covent Garden on its feet again,
since he understandably felt the need to await the Eyre recommendations
before making new appointments of chief executive and artistic director.

Few would have considered Colin Southgate to be the most obvious
choice for this role. He had not shown particular interest in music when
we were on the South Bank board together, and he appeared to be
uncomfortable with performers – as was borne out by later events. What
he is, of course, is a quite different kind of person from his predecessors,
and I suspect that that was what Chris Smith was looking for: a tough
businessman, free of nostalgia, and able to clear away unwanted bag-
gage from the past in sorting out the mess. A passion for opera and ballet

might have been considered another important quality, but perhaps that had not occurred to anyone. He had assembled a small board, which included two members of its previous incarnation, Vivien Duffield and Michael Berkeley, who was also to be chairman of the opera advisory board. Lord Eatwell, a newcomer, was to be chairman of the ballet advisory board. Both of these boards were subsequently to be abandoned.

Contrary to the advice of Mary Allen – who was advocating the engagement of a chief executive, with artistic directors for opera and ballet – Southgate was of the opinion that an intendant should be sought: a single person having overall direction of the entire operation. This would have left Mary Allen without a job. Lack of agreement over this issue was the final cause of her departure, although she was already feeling uncertain about her future at Covent Garden, given the arrival of Pelham Allen, an accountant from Coopers Lybrand, as a condition of the Floral Trust – a private body of well-wishers – making available essential money to save the Royal Opera House from bankruptcy. On Mary Allen's resignation in March 1998, Pelham Allen was to become chief executive until the arrival of a permanent replacement.

As secretary-general of the Arts Council, Mary Allen had been well acquainted with Covent Garden's difficulties, and she had therefore brought with her a good prior knowledge of what was at stake when she became chief executive in September 1997. Her arrival had been welcomed by artists and staff, and expectations were aroused – though not as strongly as on the occasion of Genista McIntosh's arrival, when hopes of recovery and stability based on a person with theatrical-management experience ran high. Those hopes were dashed by McIntosh's premature departure. Allen did not have that aura around her, or serious practical experience and knowledge of managing a large theatre. However, at the beginning she displayed a real virtue of listening and was able to distil effectively what she was hearing. This won her support – not throughout the House, but sufficient to give her emotional resilience to cope with the endless crises that came tumbling into her lap. She worked hard to stabilize the situation, but she was handicapped by the lack of reliable financial information and spent an inordinate amount of time in firefighting. To take on an organization as large as Covent Garden in a senior management role is a formidable task at the best of times, but when the organization is in serious crisis, and with little practical management experience behind you, it is well-nigh impossible.

*

After Mary Allen's departure Sir Colin Southgate began the search for a senior management team to pull the whole enterprise together and prepare it for the reopening of the Royal Opera House in December 1999. This was a huge task, for which Southgate sought the help and advice of the chairmen of the opera and ballet advisory boards and some others, including myself. I could see what was needed and I had previously told Colin Southgate that I would be happy to make suggestions if he wanted that. He made it clear that he did. At this juncture the focus was on an intendant, and with this in mind a list of candidates was drawn up. It was so small as to be almost useless, in the sense that none would be quickly available because of existing commitments and few would be interested in coming to Covent Garden in its present low and insecure condition. Nevertheless, there were one or two people who had good track records as intendants and whom I thought should be approached. To the best of my knowledge, this never happened. In looking abroad, I am well aware of the differences in culture which could make the Covent Garden position unworkable for some, even for the most highly qualified foreigner; but there are exceptions, and these should have been explored more thoroughly.

Sights having been set on the appointment of an intendant, I was surprised to learn that the board then decided to appoint two people to senior management positions instead: an artistic director and an administrative director, with the former in the superior position. This, in my view, was not a good idea in that leadership and direction need to be clearly defined, and having two people at the top can lead to divided rule – the last thing needed by any organization, and certainly not one as run down as Covent Garden has become.

I had already thrown the name of Michael Kaiser into the ring as the result of a conversation with Deborah MacMillan, who knew him well as administrative director of American Ballet Theatre, a company which he had pulled back from the brink of disaster and set on its feet again. I knew him only by reputation, but understood from Deborah MacMillan that he was keen to face the Covent Garden challenge. What was clear in pursuing him was the need of an artistic director – a role which he himself acknowledged he could not fulfil. Sarah Billinghurst was a name which came up in discussion several times as the supremo. This is not a position she has ever occupied, and some of us had doubts about her making this move from being artistic administrator at the Metropolitan Opera in New York, and previously with the

San Francisco Opera. However, the combination of Billinghurst and Kaiser attracted Southgate, who had already been in touch with her. What apparently had not been made clear in the first instance was the presence of Kaiser and, subsequently, the agreement of the board to his demand that he should report direct to them, effectively bypassing the artistic director and what she regarded as her superior position. Not surprisingly, she believed that the goalposts had been moved too far for her comfort. It was not what she had envisaged, and she withdrew her name.

Pelham Allen was continuing as chief executive, but made no bones about longing to get out. The need to appoint a permanent chief executive was obvious for every reason, and Kaiser was offered the post, which he readily accepted. A large gap in the senior management has thus been filled, but by going down this route the engagement of an intendant figure is surely ruled out for the time being. I believe this to be a serious drawback, since the two companies have become very separate organizations in recent years, negating principles governing the ideal concept of a lyric theatre. Mary Allen discovered this to her cost, and rightly attempted to change it, while still favouring separate artistic directors. However, overall artistic direction is required to rectify this. That comes from a real intendant who has both vision and the authority to implement it. Without such direction the House is in danger of becoming a quasi-receiving theatre, with the companies going their separate ways and with real integration of activity lost and money mis-spent.

Probably the most worrying aspect of recent years has been the absence of anyone with knowledge and experience of running an opera house at the helm of Covent Garden. An accountant, Pelham Allen, was appointed chief executive on the resignation of Mary Allen in March 1998. He did his best to plug a gaping hole in the management structure, and won support in the House through his honesty and lack of pretence about his knowledge of opera and ballet, which he proclaimed to be minimal. He kept everybody informed of developments through a weekly bulletin (described to me by one staff member as 'the parish magazine'), and he sorted out financial reporting and control systems, although I suspect that there was overreaction to the critical financial plight of Covent Garden by bringing in too many accountants. I did warn Colin Southgate of the dangers of a surfeit of accountants crawling over the theatre and of the establishing of future work patterns and procedures by those without real awareness of what is needed to create a successful opera house, unburdened by bureaucracy and yet strongly managed. His reply was that the board had complete confidence in the management.

Richard Jarman, formerly general manager of English National Ballet and later managing director of Scottish Opera, was engaged as artistic director for two years, to assist with artistic issues and in rationalizing plans for the rest of the closed period and the opening months of the new theatre. His experience of opera and ballet companies brought an air of realism to the management, even if circumstances limited what he could achieve. It was not an enviable position for him to occupy, and I suspect that he often found himself falling between several stools.

Covent Garden's finances remained critical, and Colin Southgate was increasingly frustrated by the lack of positive response from the Secretary of State or the Arts Council to his demands for increased subsidy for the companies during the remainder of the closed period and then to see them into the new House. In September 1998 a letter to Chris Smith indicating the need to double the present subsidy to enable the Royal Opera and the Royal Ballet to perform adequately in the modernized theatre was leaked and caused a furore. It was ill judged, and, as John Sainsbury had found when rebuffed by Mrs Thatcher on a previous occasion – albeit in different and better circumstances – ministers do not take kindly to such demands.

Colin Southgate was rebuked by Chris Smith, but, angered and undeterred, he sought to strike a bargain with the Secretary of State based on the proposal of closing down the whole operation, with the exception of the ballet, and starting it up again in time for the reopening. It was announced as a strategy to ensure the future of the nation's premier opera and ballet house and to guarantee a host of better practices, including affordable ticket prices. 'The days for fudging are long past. The board is sad at the pain this will cause our workforce but only a total restructuring will achieve real results,' stressed Sir Colin. 'We cannot afford the present situation, and yet we must not lose the Royal Opera House.'

Following a review of the previous six months, and in the light of the Eyre Review, in the summer of 1998 the board had agreed with the Arts Council and the government the following plan to preserve the artistic excellence of the performing companies:

1 The closure of the Royal Opera House in its present form on 18 January 1999.
2 A reduction in the number of performances by one-third, resulting in 120 and 100 opera performances in the first full season, increasing thereafter.
3 Staff and service agreements to be renegotiated in line with a reduced workforce, structure and programme.
4 Subject to the outcome of these negotiations, the Royal Opera House will reopen in December 1999.
5 The appointment of artistic and executive directors.
6 A commitment to increase access by a range of means including lower ticket prices, access to tickets by the general public and broadcasting.
7 A reaffirmation of the board's commitment to education and audience development.

In a letter of 7 September 1998 to Sir Colin Southgate, the Secretary of State wrote, 'I feel confident that, with the managed route of restructuring you have proposed, alongside the commitment from Government and the Arts Council we have outlined, you should feel able to enter the next phase of the redevelopment at the ROH with optimism.' He went on to say, 'I would expect the Arts Council to make available to the ROH substantial additional funding when it makes its allocations in December.'

While the news of increased funding was welcome, the rest of the letter sent shock waves through the House. Once again jobs were on the line, and failure to agree new terms and conditions of employment by 18 January would mean redundancy and the possible closing down of the House. A drastic situation required drastic solutions – I don't think anyone doubted that – but the way in which this was presented was unfortunate and caused great resentment among the staff and artists. They felt that they were being blamed for Covent Garden's problems and were being penalized accordingly, whereas those truly responsible for the appalling situation in which they found themselves were escaping unscathed. Time for negotiation was short and was in fact the statutory notice period for redundancy. It was surprising that the board approved this approach, since in the same breath they were saying that they had inherited an outdated culture of confrontational industrial relations which they implied should be abandoned. If that is what they thought, why did they continue with it? Fortunately agreement was reached in time.

For inexplicable reasons, Bernard Haitink was neither informed nor consulted about this turn of events. Richard Jarman and Pelham Allen had talked to him the previous week, but apparently failed to explain what was proposed, as Colin Southgate thought had happened. Instead, Haitink received a copy of the press statement with a note from the chairman to the effect that he thought that he would be interested to read this. Naturally Haitink was furious, and wrote a letter of resignation on the Sunday after the announcement. He and I spoke three times that day as he expressed his concern about keeping the orchestra together during the first six months of 1999 in the absence of a serious amount of work. While he wanted to resign in protest, he was aware that he was the one person who could keep the orchestra in place and that the orchestral musicians and chorus were looking to him for help. His loyalty to them was real and touching.

The letter went off. But, after discussion with the chairman, and later with Chris Smith, to whom he had also written, Haitink agreed to with-hold his resignation while other plans for performances by the Royal Opera were examined. The decision to cancel the whole Sadler's Wells opera season in 1999 had always seemed rash and to have been made without proper consideration of the consequences, artistic or financial. There were costs in whatever was to be done, and there must be doubt that these were ever properly weighed up. The Sadler's Wells contract alone was a huge financial burden for Covent Garden, and it is hard to understand how such terms and conditions were accepted, except that negotiations were handled by a number of people, including board members, who were unfamiliar with theatre practice. Interestingly, when I talked to Richard Jarman about an alternative plan for that six-month period, he revealed that he was working on various ideas but had to do so without the aid of accountants, because Pelham Allen had decreed that the decision had been made and that no more time was to be spent on reviewing the situation. This was a short-sighted attitude.

While Colin Southgate did not talk to Bernard Haitink about these proposals, he did phone me before they were announced. I was on a brief holiday in Cornwall, and he sought me out there to tell me of the plans. I was pleased to be informed, but it demonstrated a curious sense of prior-ities and confirmed my opinion that Southgate is so uncomfortable with artists that he goes out of his way to avoid them.

Michael Kaiser arrived at Covent Garden in November 1998, and created an immediate and good impression. He is up-beat and optimistic, and leaves you in no doubt that, while things are difficult, they could be worse, and in any event they are capable of solution. He has brought an air of confidence to an institution at a low ebb, and he is clear that he and the management are there to serve the artists. A former singer himself, and the son of a musician, he knows about performers and understands them. This was a refreshing discovery, and bodes well.

The quest for an artistic director continues, with Kaiser keen that a suitable person be in place at an early date. From conversations I have had with a number of people, there appears to be uncertainty about the kind of candidate that is being sought. The role has been identified: that of opera director, primarily an administrator but with some artistic responsibilities, who, with the music director, the ballet director, the chief executive and the finance director, will be answerable to the board. It is not a desirable arrangement, and will not solve the fundamental artistic and management problems, which are centred around the need to make a cohesive whole of the opera and ballet operation within one theatre. Furthermore, it is contrary to the recommendations of Sir Richard Eyre, who urged the engagement of a single figure to achieve just that.

There have been discussions with a conductor and a producer for the role of opera director, but I believe that neither is right. The task is to manage the company and implement the plans agreed with the music director. This requires the full-time engagement of a non-practising musician or somebody with management experience and artistic leanings and knowledge. Once again the board and senior management's lack of experience of how opera houses operate is disturbing.

Everything had remained in suspense for some weeks following the cancellation of the Sadler's Wells season, and it took the threatened resignation of Bernard Haitink to bring about a plan by which enough performances were found to keep the orchestra in place and to provide the chorus with some work until the beginning of rehearsals in the autumn for the reopening of the theatre. The very successful production of *Paul Bunyan* was revived for a season at Sadler's Wells in the spring of 1999, and Verdi's Requiem and his *Un Giorno di Regno* were performed at the Royal Festival Hall in May and June. It was a thin and meagre programme, which it seems was all that could be salvaged from the wreckage of the cancelled Sadler's Wells season. The Royal Ballet fared better with a Far Eastern tour and a season at Sadler's Wells.

The cancelled Sadler's Wells opera season had been dependent on a high box-office take. A shortfall on income, combined with the penal terms of the theatre agreement, would have created further difficulties if this season had gone ahead in its entirety. Even the eventual short season made a substantial loss, as *Paul Bunyan* did not attract good audiences – although the results might have been better if it had been presented in its original context of a varied season.

Anyone who said, as Jeremy Isaacs did, that the closure plans were admirable could have had no idea of what was at stake for the Royal Opera House and its companies, nor any understanding of the implications of what had been set in motion. To have relied so much on the Tower Bridge project, flawed as it obviously was in terms of timing, and to have allowed options other than those of a nomadic existence to have slipped away, is unforgivable, and responsibility for this rests solely with the board and management. The outcome – the near destruction of the Royal Opera House – should weigh heavily on their consciences.

In the years since 1988 much has been achieved artistically, and there has been plenty to admire in standards of performance and in the range of the repertoire. In the case of the former, however, I do not believe that these have been any higher than previously, and it is not the case that more rehearsal time has been allocated than before. In some instances it has been less. Where there has been gain in the last few years has been in the wider choice of operas and a greatly increased number of new productions. These are possible only if there is money available to pay for them, and the repertoire would have been enlarged much sooner if the same level of money could have been found in earlier years.

If a year had turned out well financially, it used to be the case that the ensuing surpluses were not rewarded with plaudits from the Arts Council and the encouragement of enhanced funding, but penalized with reduced grants because the organization had shown that it could manage with less. This was one of several absurd contradictions in Arts Council policy, and led companies to avoid surpluses or to conceal them.

To have taken the risks which the board and management have done since 1988 has bordered on the foolhardy. Too often money was not in place, production budgets were seemingly ignored, and larger deficits were incurred. Covent Garden has rarely been without deficits, but remedial action was previously taken in good time – not always with complete success, but enough to lessen the damage. Even in the most financially deprived times, opportunities did arise to permit one more new production or major revival than was first thought possible. But, in pushing the boat out further than prudency might normally have dictated, we found it essential to have an escape route in the event of the tide turning.

Jeremy Isaacs's first season, 1988/89, inevitably contained elements already planned during my time. One of these was a production of *Das Rheingold* with Yuri Lyubimov. Lyubimov had directed *Jenůfa* at Covent Garden in 1987, and had shown an original and distinctive, if eccentric, flair. At the same time he could be difficult, and he had a habit of upsetting artists and staff – often unnecessarily and as a result of language difficulties. At the end of each day I would spend time with him to go through problems and allay his anxieties. It was time-consuming, but justified in the light of what he had to offer as a very gifted director, not well versed in opera. Failure to have done this would have ended in catastrophe.

During *Jenůfa* rehearsals we talked about the *Ring*, which he said that he would be interested in producing, particularly if he could work with his *Jenůfa* design team, Paul Hernon and Claire Mitchell. Hernon created a remarkable and simple design concept for the whole *Ring*, which I believed could have been of immense value during the closure. Sadly, that was not to be, because *Rheingold* emerged far different from what had originally been planned – largely, I suspect, because Lyubimov was left too much to his own devices. I found rigorous overseeing to be essential with him.

Bernard Haitink, who had initially agreed to proceed with Lyubimov, was understandably appalled by what did emerge with *Rheingold*, and wanted a change of team for the *Ring*. Isaacs abandoned Lyubimov and his *Rheingold* and sought other solutions for the return of a complete cycle in later seasons.

Following this came a misjudged decision to replace a long-standing, beautiful and apt setting by Sophie Fedorovitch of *Madama Butterfly* with a new production by the distinguished Spanish actress Nuria Espert, based on her earlier Scottish Opera version. This did nothing for the opera, and seemed to be an example of change for change's sake. There must also have been a lack of awareness that Espert's real success as a producer occurred when working with her husband – alas no longer alive – otherwise she would surely not have been engaged at the same time to direct two other operas, *Rigoletto* and *Carmen*, without first seeing the outcome of *Butterfly*. Neither was a success, and perform-ances have been few. Furthermore, *Carmen* does not necessarily prosper in the hands of a Spanish director. It is a French opera, with Spain seen through French eyes.

Another example of rash commitment was that to Piero Faggioni to produce *Il Trovatore* in the summer of 1990, in sets, designed by himself, which would also be viable for two other Verdi operas in future seasons. Designing multi-purpose sets is not a new idea, but it has never worked satisfactorily. There was also a more worrying aspect of his engagement, which was that his recent track record was not reflecting his earlier immense promise. Something had gone wrong, as I was to discover when in Salzburg some years after *La Fanciulla del West* to see his production of Verdi's *Macbeth*, with Ezio Frigerio as designer. Disenchanted as he was with the designs, Faggioni failed to have the production ready, which turned out also to be the case with *Trovatore*. He had met me in Salzburg just before the performance, warmly welcoming but expressing his dismay that I had come and hoping that I would not stay but would return next year, when the production would be ready. This was said half jokingly, but with a strong streak of seriousness. Sadly, his doubts and fears were justified.

In the 1993/94 season, lack of judgement was again to be revealed over the details of the engagement of Valery Gergiev to conduct *Eugene Onegin*. That was, of course, admirable in itself, but it was tied to a new production, because it had become Gergiev's wont to demand this. This might have been tolerable if a new production had been required, but that was not the case. In any event, in mounting a new production it is essential to ensure that conductor, director and designer are available for all rehearsals if the full potential is to be realized. Everyone in the busi-ness knows that Gergiev – albeit one of the world's most talented con-ductors – is notoriously late in arriving for rehearsal, because of his overcrowded diary and huge number of commitments. To have sacrificed an outstanding production in these circumstances – and, to make matters worse, to replace it with a grossly inferior one – was a serious error. The musical results were excellent, but Russian style was not imprinted on the production as it could have been if Gergiev had been present from the beginning.

In an attempt to meet Gergiev's demands, a compromise was struck whereby John Cox would reproduce the opera in new sets by Tim O'Brien but with the previous production's costumes by Julia Trevelyan

Oman. All of this was planned without reference to her until twenty-four hours before the press announcement of the season's plans. Rightly, she protested vigorously, including telephoning me for sympathy and support, and withdrew permission for the use of her costumes.

John Cox had brought many improvements to an unsatisfactory 1987 production of Massenet's *Manon* by Rudolf Noelte. We had striven for a long time to bring this distinguished stage director to London, and were at last successful – only to be disappointed by the results. He certainly failed to win the confidence of the principal singers. Maybe the opera was wrong for him, although he was keen to work on it.

I cannot say that Cox had the same effect on *Die Fledermaus* in the 1990/91 season. By then production director, he coarsened and demeaned an earlier successful production. Although it had been created under difficult circumstances by an eminent Viennese director, Leopold Lindtberg, who appeared to have lost his nerve and needed endless encouragement to give directions, it had opened to acclaim on New Year's Eve 1977 and remained a popular and staple part of the repertory. It needed refreshing, but no more than that. It is also interesting to note that what resulted was billed as a new production, which it was not. Increasingly it was the habit to denote revivals as new productions when the sets and costumes remained as before but the content was changed.

An answer to the *Ring* problem following the Lyubimov decision was found in the production which Götz Friedrich had mounted at the Deutsche Oper in Berlin. This, he believed, was dramatically an improvement on his earlier London production. Visually, however, it was inferior – even on the large Berlin stage, where, dependent on space for its real effect, it could be set to a far greater depth than was possible at the Royal Opera House, but still failed to make its point. If it had been seen in Berlin by the Covent Garden management, and they had remembered their theatre's stage limitations, it is difficult to understand why it was chosen. Time was pressing, it is true, and there were difficulties in trying to revive the previous production, even though it had been hugely successful. Friedrich has never been enthusiastic about returning to old productions, and Haitink would have understandably wanted a new one – or at least one not seen in London before. Another solution should have been found, to match Haitink's remarkable musical results, first heard in *Walküre* in 1989 as Friedrich's production was introduced over three seasons. It has been said that there was disappointment in some quarters that the *Ring* could be produced at all – inability to do so because of insufficient money to make a new production was to have been a plank in the board's argument to government for a larger subvention. It is hard to believe that this would have had much effect.

Later, beginning in the 1994/45 season, a new production of the *Ring* was to be presented with Bernard Haitink, with Richard Jones and Nigel Lowery as director and designer. This was to be another example of a lack of communication between those concerned – in this instance the music director, the opera director and the production team. What emerged was an unconventional view of the *Ring*, often illuminating and stimulating, but too frequently accompanied by maddening episodes which detracted from the overall quality and message. Haitink had clearly not understood the nature of what was to be presented and was uncomfortable with the results. Musical standards were of the highest order, but there was conflict between the surreal stage pictures and the musical aspects of the performances. For a production truly to succeed, there must be unanimity of approach and style and a way must be found of matching the stage to the pit – music being the dominating force, from which all else should flow.

New productions came thick and fast, and the repertoire was extended from time to time with welcome and important additions: Rossini's *Guillaume Tell, Il Viaggio a Reims* and *Mosè in Egitto*, Verdi's *Attila* and *Stiffelio*, Mozart's *Mitridate, Re di Ponto*, Prokofiev's *The Fiery Angel*, Meyerbeer's *Les Huguenots*, Gershwin's *Porgy and Bess*, Massenet's *Chérubin*, Janáček's *Katya Kabanová* and *The Cunning Little Vixen*, Birtwistle's *Gawain*, Gounod's *Roméo et Juliette* and Hindemith's *Mathis der Maler*. *The Cunning Little Vixen* saw Simon Rattle make his Covent Garden debut, almost to the day that he and I decided several years previously would be the right moment for him to do so. In that conversation he had explained that he wanted to concentrate on the symphonic repertoire for the time being, with occasional excursions into opera, largely provided by Glyndebourne, but that by 1990 he would be ready for another adventure, ideally Janáček at Covent Garden.

The Verdi Festival, a project originally proposed by Sir Edward Downes, to perform all the operas by 2001, the centenary of the composer's death, was imaginative and gave a real and long-term sense of direction and purpose to the programming. Sadly, it was not to be realized in its entirety, nor wholly in the manner first conceived. Shortage of funds and planning mishaps prevented that.

These were fruitful years for the Royal Opera in the extension of its work, but much less so for the Royal Ballet, which suffered from a decline in performance opportunities at Covent Garden and, as a result, in the ability to extend its repertoire significantly. Touring, while stimulating for the dancers in presenting new challenges, makes impossible that essential requirement of any performing company: new work.

These years exacted a high cost, not only in monetary terms but also in other aspects of life at Covent Garden. From all accounts it is clear that the family spirit which had pervaded the Royal Opera House for so long had evaporated and that it was solely the professionalism of artists and staff which drove them to give of their best. Professionalism is a strong motivation in itself, but it is not enduring. What Covent Garden had established, even in its early post-war days, was an atmosphere and an ethos of work which made it a theatre to which artists and staff wanted to come. To work there, in whatever capacity, was more than just a job: it was a way of life, to which many made a strong commitment.

For performers, Covent Garden was one of the handful of opera houses which really mattered in the development of their careers. It was a stage on which you needed to be heard and seen, and it was a place where preparation for performance was thorough and enjoyable. For many, appearances at Covent Garden were essential not only from the point of view of building a following but in growing as an artist. Many a singer has come to London for coaching in roles which they were not necessarily performing there, to take advantage of the first-rate music staff assembled at the Royal Opera House and to profit from the working conditions if engaged to perform.

That so much has been achieved in fifty years is testimony to the talents and commitment of hundreds of men and women: performers, technicians, craftsmen and staff. The Royal Opera House was reborn after the war with ideals not all of which were to be fulfilled but which were altered to meet changing circumstances and needs. In its extraordinary growth from modest beginnings to world standing, as its companies increasingly won international recognition and acclaim, there was at work an indefinable force which bound the whole enterprise together and urged it on to greater and greater achievement. With David Webster, there was always present a quiet and sometimes virtually invisible but nevertheless effective authority. He was tolerant of artists' egos and insecurities, and from a distance he encouraged singers and dancers – rarely on the stage after a performance, but on the telephone the next day or in conversation in Floral Street. I found myself much closer to performers and staff than Webster, and it was increasingly my habit to visit dressing rooms regularly and to be around during and after performances. When I became general director, there was an assumption that I would often be in the theatre during the day and evening. That is how it turned out, and that proved to be the only way that I could direct the whole operation.

What this amounted to was visible and present leadership, to which the House became accustomed and the absence of which seems to have been felt on my departure. Jeremy Isaacs, fresh from a quite different world and with a different attitude to performers, was clearly unwilling to be wedded to Covent Garden in the manner that I had been and was much less tolerant of performers' egos. He did not see the necessity of being there all the time – in fact he thought it highly desirable not to be. There were other things to be done, to be seen and heard. That is true, but, in spite of my commitment to Covent Garden, there were many other performances of opera and ballet, as well as theatre and concerts, which I attended – sometimes with a Covent Garden connection, such as a concert with one of our conductors, but often not.

Apart from its public image having been severely dented, there is no doubt that the inner nature of the Royal Opera House has changed in recent years. It has been a much less happy institution, and the Royal Opera and the Royal Ballet have become separate entities to a dangerous degree. Part of this is attributable to overconcentration on the opera company, because of its financial potential at the box office as market forces were increasingly allowed to dominate the scene. The ballet began to feel more and more the poor relations in every sense – with fewer performances in London and at the bottom of the pile as far as distribution of resources was concerned. Market forces also influenced pricing policy to a point where audiences changed, largely to the exclusion of the genuine opera and ballet lover in the lower sections of the theatre.

Another factor in the separation of the two companies lies in the failure to understand how opera and ballet can work in tandem to their mutual advantage. Planning to that end is complicated, and, because of differing timescales of advance scheduling, more often than not assumptions have to be made about ballet stage and orchestra rehearsal requirements. There can and should be a completely integrated programme of opera and ballet, using the resources of a modernized theatre to the greatest advantage, and maximizing box-office revenue by giving the public a wide-ranging bill of fare – all prepared and performed to the highest standards. Nothing less will be acceptable.

An obstacle to the realization of these ideals is the lack of money properly to fund the operation to its full capacity and to enable advantage to be taken of the new facilities by generating more performances than hitherto and hence greater revenue when the House reopens. The ingredients for success are there, but not totally within the reach of the management. It is ironic and tragic that, after all the difficulties and trauma to which the artists and staff of the Royal Opera House have been subjected, and the raising of hopes and expectations as the Lottery money was announced, this is so.

Incorrect calculations of the cost of running the new Covent Garden are probably one reason, but another must surely be wrong assumptions of the levels of grant that would be awarded. To generate the level of activity to make the enlarged opera house cost-effective requires sums of money which you can for ever dream of but never realize. Whatever money this government was going to allocate to the arts, it was unlikely to be sufficient to make good the ravages of past underfunding and to give arts organizations throughout the country a real degree of financial stability. Furthermore, the attitude of other arts communities towards Covent Garden is relevant. They would have been unwilling to sit quietly if they saw the Royal Opera House's subvention being massively increased at their expense. They are aware of mismanagement and the constant upward movement of seat prices in attempts to meet rising costs and to reduce, if not eliminate, deficits. Such high prices could not be maintained, but their reduction without any other changes would require an unachievable amount of public money. Reduction of activity seemed the only way out, in the hope that better solutions would be found in future years, after a leaner than hoped-for beginning.

Let us hope that such better solutions do not remain wishful thinking. What is immediately important, however, is that the House will reopen in December 1999, on time and on budget, according to all reports. For artists and staff to return to work in a restored and enlarged theatre is both a thrill and a challenge, to which all will rise.

A new music director, Antonio Pappano, has been appointed to succeed Bernard Haitink in 2002. He will be responsible for the Royal Opera and the orchestra, working closely with the director of the Royal Ballet and Michael Kaiser. This is good news, but in my judgement there is a still a gap in the artistic hierarchy, with no overall artistic director in place to ensure the close and complementary planning of opera and ballet performances and to oversee the multitude of activities which must take place if the spaces about to be available in the enlarged theatre are to be used fully and imaginatively to the benefit of the public and of the Royal Opera House itself.

The House must change its image and make itself a place where people want to go for leisure and refreshment. It should present itself no longer as just an opera house but as a theatre complex where all sorts of entertainment go on. Of course opera and ballet will occupy pride of place, and the intention must remain the presentation of these to the highest standards. But there is so much else which can be accommodated in the studio theatre, the studios (when not required for rehearsal) and all the foyer spaces, as well as the auditorium itself from time to time.

This is not a matter of planning a handful of lunchtime recitals as an add-on to the opera and ballet programme. What is required is a structured programme for the whole year, devised under the direction of a single overall artistic director working in collaboration with the music director and the Royal Ballet director, and maximizing the use of spaces and time.

Of course the reopening of Covent Garden will be welcomed and applauded by the regular opera- and ballet-goers, but there is a real danger – even every possibility – that the image of the House will remain much as it has been in recent years, with some seat prices reduced but everything else the same as before, only in a modernized theatre.

It is this modernized theatre, with all its up-to-date facilities, which provides the management with a serious opportunity to shed the past and to go into the next century offering the world not just high-quality opera and ballet, but a mass of other entertainment too. If people can come and choose what they want to see or hear, it may even be that those who shy away from opera and ballet find themselves drawn in and becoming aficionados.

As the opening approaches, shortage of funding bedevils Covent Garden and leaves part of the first year unfilled by its own companies. Short-termism was perhaps unavoidable, but to plug this gap the management has invited the impresarios Victor and Lilan Hochauser to present a thirteen-week season of their own devising. The Hochausers have an admirable record of presenting British and foreign companies in London and elsewhere, but as a solution to the problem this is harking back two or three decades to when the Met in New York was rented to

Sol Hurok for a similar period and for the same purpose. The Hochausers' season has no connection to the Royal Opera House itself and to its overall planning, even if the Royal Ballet companies are part of the programme.

This could have been a golden opportunity to do something different and to show the public how changed the Royal Opera House is to be – that it has learned its lessons, that it recognizes the changing world around it, and that it is determined to win back its status as a great opera house, but also to offer much else besides, as a place of wide and diverse entertainment.

None of this will come for nothing, of course, but the possible range and nature of what could be presented there must surely bring a good chance of additional public funding and sponsorship.

The potential for the future is huge. It will take courage and imagination to fulfil it. The means successfully to do so can be found. Covent Garden's nineteenth-century cloak will then be cast aside and new standards for the use of a great theatre will be set, for the world to admire and perhaps even copy.

The extent to which Covent Garden can or wishes to fulfil these ideals remains to be seen. There may still linger the concept of a bastion of opera and ballet, which will admit little else. I hope not. The importance of education and its integration within rehearsal and performance planning seems to be well in place. Access, which interestingly enough was a point of discussion and policy within a year or two of Covent Garden's reopening in the 1940s, is another matter. There is extra capacity in the modernized theatre, but this is less than a hundred places. The announced increase in Arts Council funding will make only a marginal difference to the balancing of budgets in relation to expected box-office income and the ability to make significant reductions in seat prices. Even so, it is encouraging to discover that most prices are to be lower and that weekend performances will be at reduced prices. What is also important is how prices are scaled and distributed. In my view, all seats in the amphitheatre should be priced as modestly as possible. This, however, is not sufficient in itself to win wide public support, because there are those who, for one reason or another, do not wish to sit upstairs, and look instead for affordable seats in the stalls circle. These must be provided.

What has become a mystique around buying Covent Garden tickets must be removed. My fear is that too many layers of privilege will continue. In a recent statement the Royal Opera House announced that an allocation of 20 per cent of tickets throughout the House would be available to the public. This is hardly what the public want to hear; their expectation as tax-payers is that the majority, if not all, of the seats are available to them on application. Over-subscription causes disappointment, but is more understandable if the public is assured of what is available to them. Real openness and candour on this issue are essential, not only for the sake of opera and ballet lovers who long to see Covent Garden as a place for them, but also to secure public funding.

The future is not yet sure – but it can be, if government confidence is restored and if the public is able to see that the Royal Opera House is a place for them, whatever their tastes and aspirations.

Bibliography

Sir Thomas Beecham, *A Mingled Chime* (1945)

Alexander Bland, *The Royal Ballet: The First Fifty Years* (1981)

Clive Boursnell and Colin Thubron, *The Royal Opera House, Covent Garden* (1982)

Richard Buckle, *Buckle at the Ballet* (1980)

Tyrone Guthrie, *A Life in the Theatre*

Montague Haltrecht, *The Quiet Showman: David Webster and the Royal Opera House* (1973)

Peter Heyworth, *Otto Klemperer, Vol. 2*

Spike Hughes, *Glyndebourne* (1965)

Julie Kavanagh, *Secret Muses: The Life of Frederick Ashton* (1996)

John Percival, *Nureyev* (1975)

Kathrine Sorley Walker, *Ninette de Valois* (1987)

David Wooldridge, *A Conductor's World* (1970)

25 Years of Opera and Ballet at the Royal Opera House: exhibition catalogue, Royal Opera House and the Victoria & Albert Museum, 1971

Annual Reports of the Royal Opera House, 1946–97

Index